HERALDS AND ANGELS

HERALDS AND ANGELS

The House of Fairfax 1841–1990

GAVIN SOUTER

MELBOURNE UNIVERSITY PRESS
1991

First published 1991
Printed in Australia by
Brown Prior Anderson Pty Ltd, Burwood, Victoria, for
Melbourne University Press, Carlton, Victoria 3053
U.S.A. and Canada: International Specialized Book Services, Inc.,
5602 N.E. Hassalo Street, Portland, Oregon 97213-3640

National Library of Australia Cataloguing-in-Publication entry

Souter, Gavin, 1929– .
Heralds and angels: the house of Fairfax 1841–1990.

Bibliography.
Includes index.
ISBN 0 522 84449 9.

1. Fairfax, Warwick, 1960– . 2. Fairfax family. 3. John Fairfax & Sons—History. 4. John Fairfax & Sons—Reorganization. 5. Newspaper publishing—Australia—History. 6. Consolidation and merger of corporations—Australia. 7. Corporate reorganizations—Australia. I. Title.

338.76107994

Preface

This book was commissioned by John Fairfax Ltd to commemorate 150 years of the Fairfax family proprietorship. Although the proprietorship failed narrowly to reach that sesquicentenary, going into receivership on 10 December 1990, it had nevertheless lasted a remarkable 149 years, 10 months and 2 days. During that time five generations of the family have watched over and helped to build an organization which within the Australian community has been loved, feared, despised, but always, I believe, respected.

The proprietorship began when John Fairfax, in partnership with a friend, purchased the ten-year-old *Sydney Herald*. The paper was then renamed the *Sydney Morning Herald*, a masthead destined to be the mainstay of what eventually became the world's oldest continuously owned newspaper proprietorship. It also became the linchpin of Fairfax family life.

Each generation of our family developed the company cautiously and conservatively, recognizing the honour of being charged with such a great responsibility. Sanctimonious as this sounds, we have, with the occasional blemish, devoted our lives to a cause and a course embarked upon by John Fairfax in 1841.

For its centenary in 1941, John Fairfax & Sons Pty Ltd—a private company wholly owned by members of the Fairfax family—published *The Story of John Fairfax*, by one of the founder's great-grandsons, John F. Fairfax. 'Sometimes we have failed', wrote J. F. Fairfax about the first four generations, 'and sometimes we have succeeded. If there have been weak links in the chain, the chain is multiple linked—and the chain has held'.

As the present book was being prepared for publication that chain of family continuity, greatly weakened as it had been by recent events, finally broke apart.

For commemoration of the expected sesquicentenary on 8 February 1991, the board of John Fairfax Ltd had decided in September 1987 to commission a book by Gavin Souter updating his earlier history of the company—*Company of Heralds*, which was published for the 150th anniversary of the *Sydney Morning Herald* in 1981. The board agreed that Mr Souter should have access to all the company's documents, including board minutes, as had been the case with *Company of Heralds*.

In September 1987 John Fairfax Ltd was a thriving public company controlled by the Fairfax family. It was also under siege from a takeover bid by one of the founder's great-great-grandsons, Warwick Fairfax. Within a matter of weeks Warwick succeeded in privatizing the company, though at great cost and with borrowed funds. My cousin James Fairfax who had been chairman of the board since 1977, and myself (deputy chairman since 1985), my father Sir Vincent, and the two other directors, Sir David Griffin and Sir Eric Neal, all resigned in favour of a new board on 7 December 1987.

Warwick Fairfax had been told about the commissioning of the book. Regrettably he declined to have any communication with the author, but the management of the company fully observed the spirit and letter of the author's agreement, allowing him the kind of access which the public company had assigned.

As a result we now have this unique record of a period of cataclysmic change, not only for the Fairfax group but for the entire Australian media. What was intended to be merely an update of the company's history turned out to be the story of a disastrous takeover, and the end of a commercial dynasty.

Mr Souter's manuscript has been read and commented upon by myself and several others from both the public and privatised companies. But the final decision on content and interpretation has been the author's alone.

Finally, a word about the company's remaining core assets. The perennial success of the *Sydney Morning Herald* led eventually to development of the *Australian Financial Review* and acquisition of the *Age*. Whatever may lie ahead for the Fairfax group, one trusts that those proud mastheads will continue to flourish.

John B. Fairfax

Contents

Illustrations

PLATES

TEXT ILLUSTRATIONS

Acknowledgements and thanks are due to the photographic staffs of John Fairfax Group Pty Ltd and David Syme & Co Ltd; Geoff Pryor, *Canberra Times*, for the cartoon 'Young Genghis Fairfax' (facing p. 305); Ward O'Neill, for drawings of Fairwater (p. 26) and Ghiberti's angels (p. 243); Patrick Cook, for cartoons on pages 226 and 248; *Australian Business*, for the photograph of Laurie Connell and Warwick Fairfax facing page 208; and the Los Angeles Public Library for the angel on page 329.

Foreword

It is a kind of poetic justice, though much to be deplored in the circumstances, that the house of Fairfax should have crowned 150 years of worthwhile endeavour by itself becoming intensely newsworthy. Suddenly the hunter of news became prey to its own profession, pursued by journalists, photographers, cartoonists and television cameramen. The headlines were insistent, and almost invariably grim: '$1bn private bid for Fairfax', 'Fairfax empire split up', 'Fairfax totters under back-breaking debt' and, finally, 'Banks end the Fairfax era'.

The first of those headlines appeared on 1 September 1987, the day after 26-year-old Warwick Fairfax had announced a bid to privatize John Fairfax Ltd, the corporate descendant of a proprietorship founded by his great-great-grandfather. From then on, almost everything that could go wrong for Warwick Fairfax did go wrong. His takeover was not quite the biggest in Australian history, but it may well have been the unluckiest and the least adroit.

Warwick's plan assumed that other branches of the controlling Fairfax family would not have to be bought out, but would remain as minority shareholders, and that his takeover vehicle, Tryart Pty Ltd, would be able to repay its bank funding by selling off some of the captured assets. Both assumptions were false.

The world stock market crashed just at the wrong time for Warwick. He persisted nevertheless, and gained control of the company at enormous cost in bank debt. Although Tryart engineered the sale of some Fairfax assets, the proceeds were not nearly sufficient to reduce its debt to a serviceable level. The new proprietor fell out with his original advisers and had to enlist new ones.

His privatized company, John Fairfax Group Pty Ltd, borrowed more hundreds of millions from another bank. It became embroiled in an extraordinary court case, and in 1988 it refinanced with long-term bank debt and American junk bonds. Then the economy faltered, the interest burden weighed too heavily, the company restructured itself, tried in vain to do so again, and then went into receivership.

With all this going on during the last three years, the relatively tractable subject-matter of my book took on an entirely different aspect. As originally proposed for the sesquicentenary of the Fairfax proprietorship in 1991, the book was to have recorded the activities of John Fairfax Ltd and its subsidiaries since the publication of *Company of Heralds* in 1981. Then the bombshell exploded.

In addition to dealing with events at a comfortable remove —for example, Fairfax's unsuccessful bid for the Herald and Weekly Times, its purchase of a television station in Melbourne, the subsequent sale of its television network, and the death of Sir Warwick Fairfax—the book now had to keep up with a desperate struggle for corporate survival which was taking new twists and turns every day.

This was a bit like writing a history of World War II in 1944, but at least I could parley with both sides. Although Warwick Fairfax and his mother, Lady Fairfax, declined to speak, the proprietor did not impede the co-operation which I continued to receive from Fairfax directors and management, and I thank him for that. I also thank the board of John Fairfax Ltd, for initiating this book, and of John Fairfax Group Pty Ltd, for allowing it to continue.

My closest colleague has been the Fairfax archivist, Eileen Dwyer, who helped with research and word-processed the manuscript. She has my gratitude.

Thanks are due to many others, for various forms of help: from John Fairfax Ltd, James Fairfax, John B. Fairfax, R. P. Falkingham, T. H. Farrell, D. N. Bowman, G. J. Gardiner, M. V. Suich, F. R. Brenchley, John Richardson, Ron Ford, John Benaud, Barry Moore, Ian Cumming and Terry Waterer; from Tryart Pty Ltd, Martin Dougherty and W. B. Reuter; from John Fairfax Group Pty Ltd, P. F. S. King, C. J. Anderson, B. N. Kelman, R. A. Johnston, Michael Smith, Bill Beerworth, Jerry Austin, Max Pride, Frank McMahon, Peter Gaunt, John Newnham, Max Garden, Adrian Deamer, Alan Bailey, Stephen Bradshaw, Dorothy Ball and Penny Seeger; from David Syme & Co Ltd, G. J. Taylor, W. G. Bland and Creighton Burns; Ranald Macdonald; the former director of Melbourne University Press, Peter Ryan; from Citibank, Gerry van der Merwe, and Mary Reemst; from ANZ, John McConnell and John Conn; in Los Angeles, John Barber, William E. Simon, Michael Milken, Peter Ackerman, Bruce Raben, James Zimmerman, Karen Shishino, Ted McAniff, Jay Herron and Maxwell McCrohon; from Macquarie Bank, Mark Johnson and David Poole; from Australian Associated Press, Lee Casey; from Baring Brothers Burrows and Partners, Mark Burrows; Neil McPhee, QC; from Mallesons Stephen Jaques, Rod Halstead and Libby Slater; from Touche Ross, Gavan Smith;

Caroline Simpson, Annette Dupree, Annalise Thomas, Hanne Van de Wiel, Alan Anderson, Cedric Symonds and Father Emmet Costello; V. J. Carroll, John Alexander, Andrew Clark, Bob Johnson, Peter Robinson, Alan Kohler, Glenda Korporaal, Alan Deans, John Hurst, Robert Whitehead, Trevor Sykes, Catherine Armitage, David Marr, Brian Toohey, Valerie Lawson, Robert Haupt, Marian Wilkinson, Colleen Ryan, David Dale, Franca Bopf, Peter Allen, Tony Stephens, Neil Mercer, Dennis Muller, Bob Bottom, George Masterman, QC, Ronald McKie, and the late Peter Hastings. I also thank Margaret Jones, the Fairfax reference and pictorial libraries, the Fairfax photographic department, Gretel Blackburn and Ngaire Souter.

I hope that *Heralds and Angels* will not be confused with *Company of Heralds*. It is a new book about a different subject, and overlaps the content of its predecessor only in Chapter Two.

Although I did not set out purposely to defend the public company, or to censure the young proprietor, in fact I have done both. Readers may, of course, form their own conclusions, but mine are roughly as follows.

The privatization of John Fairfax Ltd was an unnecessary disaster. It was unnecessary because the reasons which Warwick Fairfax adduced for undertaking it did not exist. The public company was not being mismanaged, and it could not have been taken over by anyone outside the Fairfax family so long as that family retained its majority shareholding. There was every indication that the family would have stayed together but for Warwick's intervention.

His intervention was disastrous in many ways, but perhaps the worst disaster is still to come. Although the takeover did not diminish the company's cash flow, it did weaken the competitive positions of the *Sydney Morning Herald*, the *Age*, and the *Australian Financial Review*. It also raised the prospect that one or more of Australia's three best newspapers might be sold, leading perhaps to further undesirable consolidation of ownership.

It is possible, of course, that these papers would continue as usual under new ownership but alternatively—and many would say, more likely—they might find their wings clipped by a proprietorship careless of the standards formerly observed by the Fairfax companies, public and private. That would be the worst consequence of Warwick Fairfax's impetuosity, for heralds need wings no less than angels do.

Gavin Souter

Simplified Fairfax Family Tree

- John Fairfax (1805–1877)
  - James Reading Fairfax (1834–1919)
    - James Oswald Fairfax (1863–1928)
      - Warwick Oswald Fairfax (1901–1987)
        - James Oswald Fairfax (1933–)
        - Warwick Geoffrey Oswald Fairfax (1960–)
    - John Hubert Fraser Fairfax (1872–1950)
      - Vincent Charles Fairfax (1909–)
        - John Brehmer Fairfax (1942–)

1
Icebergs

Gone were the days when Sir Warwick Fairfax could count on reaching his mother's age of ninety-three. That confident assumption, shared by others in the family, derived from Sir Warwick's strong sense of heredity; but now it looked as though heredity was letting him down. As his eighty-fifth birthday approached, in December 1986, the doyen of the world's oldest publishing family was gravely ill at Fairwater, the harbourside mansion at 560 New South Head Road, Double Bay, where he had been born. In all probability his life would soon be ending there as well.

Although weakened by a stroke, and beset by the recurrence of an earlier cancer, Sir Warwick was not paralysed nor yet totally confined to his four-poster bed. Some days he would sit in his upstairs bedroom talking with Father Emmet Costello, a Jesuit who enjoyed matching theology with his ecumenical Anglican friend. Sir Warwick would also scan the pages of the *Sydney Morning Herald*, a newspaper synonymous with the Fairfax name for five generations. He received certain visitors from John Fairfax Ltd, the publishing company of which he was a director and former chairman, and he was well aware of an upheaval then taking place in the media industry—the biggest newspaper takeover Australia had ever known.

John Fairfax Ltd, the public company which had evolved from a private one founded by Sir Warwick's great-grandfather, was still controlled by descendants of that first John Fairfax. It was the oldest and most profitable newspaper group in Australia, earning its most recent annual net profit of $74 114 000 before tax mainly from fifty-three newspapers and seventy-nine magazines (notably the *Sydney Morning Herald*, the Melbourne *Age* and the *Australian Financial Review*), television stations ATN7 in Sydney and BTQ in Brisbane, and the nationwide Macquarie radio network. In this fiercely competitive field, the company had two major rivals: Rupert Murdoch, the former Australian turned global entrepreneur and American citizen; and the Herald and Weekly Times Ltd, a Victorian company with interlocking interests in other states.

Murdoch's News Ltd, a wholly owned subsidiary of his international News Corporation Ltd, published thirty-five newspapers (notably the national *Australian*, the *Daily Telegraph* and *Daily Mirror* in Sydney, the *News* in Adelaide and the *Daily Sun* in Brisbane) and News Corporation held a 50 per cent interest in Australia's largest commercial airline, Ansett. Another subsidiary of News Corporation owned two television stations, TEN10 in Sydney and ATV10 in Melbourne.

As for the Herald and Weekly Times, it published forty newspapers (notably the afternoon *Herald* and morning *Sun News-Pictorial* in Melbourne) and owned two television stations, HSV7 in Melbourne and ADS7 in Adelaide. HWT was also a major shareholder in Queensland Press Ltd (publisher of the *Courier Mail* and *Sunday Mail* in Brisbane), Advertiser Newspapers Ltd (the Adelaide *Advertiser*) and Davies Brothers Ltd (Hobart *Mercury*). These three allies reciprocated by holding shares in HWT or some of its affiliated companies, a useful defence against takeover raids. The chief architect of HWT had been Rupert Murdoch's father, the late Sir Keith Murdoch; but Murdoch the younger had been kept very much at arm's length by his father's successors since the 1950s. In recent times this conservative company had not been performing as well as it might, to say the least, and of all media groups it was the one most tempting to predators. Its shares were held here, there and everywhere, without any strong proprietorial component, and its management was noted more for caution than initiative. One takeover bid, by Rupert Murdoch in 1979, had been foiled when John Fairfax and Queensland Press defensively increased their holdings in the company. Another bid had been made unsuccessfully in 1981 by the West Australian entrepreneur Robert Holmes à Court, and the tracks of his nominee companies were still sometimes to be found on the HWT share register.

During 1986 HWT considered various possibilities of voluntarily merging with someone else, but refrained from taking that step. News Ltd discussed a joint venture in which some of its publications would move to HWT. Holmes à Court, who was then reputedly the country's richest man, and bold enough to have launched an unsuccessful takeover bid for the Broken Hill Proprietary Co. Ltd., suggested a joint venture in Western Australia, where his weekly *Western Mail* was faring badly against HWT's *West Australian*. Finally the Sydney publisher Kerry Packer tried to accomplish what would have been virtually a reverse takeover of HWT. In return for cash, a substantial shareholding and the deputy chairmanship, he proposed to merge all his magazines (notably the *Bulletin*, *Women's Weekly* and *Australian Business*) and electronic assets with the

Melbourne group. From Packer's point of view this was a sensible alternative to making a full bid for the company and its cross-shareholding affiliates. After some hesitation, HWT's board decided against taking such a formidable bird into its nest, and Packer reluctantly sold what shares he had bought in the company.

He sold them to Ronald Brierley, whose Industrial Equity Ltd was thought by some to be contemplating a full bid for HWT. But the next bid of that kind, which was soon to disturb even Sir Warwick Fairfax at Fairwater, came from another quarter. Early in November 1986 HWT's chief executive officer, John D'Arcy, received a telephone call from Rupert Murdoch, who was then visiting Australia. Murdoch expressed interest in making a bid for the company, and said that he did not expect to encounter any trouble with either the Trade Practices Commission or the Foreign Investment Review Board. He flew back to his holiday home at Aspen, Colorado, but returned to Australia on 2 December. Next morning he presented the HWT board with a $1.8 billion bid for all the company's issued capital, offering $12 cash per share or alternatively News Corporation scrip. The offer was undeniably attractive, placing a premium of 50 per cent on a market share price already inflated by rumours that someone, probably Holmes à Court, was about to make a bid. HWT's board advised its shareholders to accept.

Success for Murdoch would strengthen his Australian position enormously, and weaken John Fairfax accordingly. News Ltd's share of the total metropolitan newspaper circulation was 37.8 per cent, compared with HWT's 33.2 per cent and Fairfax's 24.2 per cent. If News acquired HWT and effected certain necessary rationalizations, its share would probably rise to 56 per cent. Unless the Trade Practices Commission decreed otherwise, a combined News/HWT group would then have the capacity to dominate advertising rates throughout Australia by means of network advertising. Murdoch also stood to gain a larger holding in AAP Information Services, a communications network owned principally by HWT (40 per cent), Fairfax (40 per cent) and News (15 per cent).

On the other hand, if Fairfax were to counter the Murdoch bid, it would stand to gain positive advantages at the same time as it thwarted its chief competitor. By acquiring the *Courier Mail*, for example, it would extend to Brisbane its already strong east coast presence in Sydney and Melbourne. It might also win control of Australian Newsprint Mills Holdings Ltd, manufacturer of most of the newsprint used in Australia, which was then owned equally by Fairfax and HWT.

Another feasible prize was HWT's Melbourne television station, although expansion in that medium was now complicated by the federal government's announced intention to change the rules governing ownership of commercial television. Originally the government had intended to restructure only the broadcasting system, as a remedy for certain problems to do with satellite programme services. But the debate eventually grew to include the print media as well.

The new system—which still had to be formalized by parliament, but was to be effective from November 1986—would replace the 20-year-old two-television stations rule with a high degree of deregulation. Any company would be able to own any number of stations, providing access to no more than 75 per cent of the national audience (this was in fact reduced to 60 per cent in the enabling legislation), but the new freedom would be counterbalanced to some extent by a cross-media restriction propounded by the Treasurer, Paul Keating. A new television station could not be acquired in a city where the buyer already owned a newspaper, or vice versa. If this banning of cross-ownership between print and electronic media were to become law, and John Fairfax Ltd had already acquired HSV7, the company would either have to sell its new acquisition or dispose of the Melbourne *Age*. As Paul Keating put it, the big media groups would have to choose between being Princes of Print or Queens of the Screen.

Unlike Fairfax and HWT, Murdoch had been privately briefed by Keating on the coming media changes, and he had later told the Treasurer that if it came to a choice he would prefer to be in newspapers rather than the less profitable medium of television. Keating regarded the break-up of HWT as inevitable, and rightly or wrongly he later took credit for having put that group into what merchant bankers light-heartedly call 'play'.

Sir Warwick was not too ill to perceive the risks and opportunities for John Fairfax Ltd in this deadly 'game'. Indeed the worry of it seemed to be worsening his condition. He lost more weight and gave up venturing downstairs with the help of his butler, Welton, or his chauffeur, Harry Fogarty. Those who went up to see the gaunt old man, for business or personal reasons, were left in little doubt that he was dying.

Only once before, in John Fairfax's lifetime, had a Christmas season confronted this family with circumstances of comparable gravity. On Boxing Day in 1863 John's eldest son and partner, Charles Fairfax, was thrown from a horse and killed. 'Boast not thyself of tomorrow', read a plaque erected to his memory in Sydney's main Congregational church, 'for thou knowest not what a day may bring forth'. Three generations later that dire warning was even more apt. Tomorrow reeked of uncertainty. The balance of media power was about to change with the dismemberment of HWT, and would probably change even further as existing media groups tried to reach the new television limit before their rivals.

Perhaps HWT was not the only company at risk. Someone had

been buying Fairfax shares with enough determination to cause their price to double in the last few weeks, and who could be sure that this was merely a tribute to the company's growing profitability? There was also the question of Fairfax family unity. Death was about to visit one of the family's three shareholding blocs, which between them controlled nearly half the issued capital. And although the family shareholders had hitherto shown a united front, keeping the company impregnable, who could say what a day might bring forth?

Family unity was much in the mind of Mary Fairfax, Sir Warwick's third wife, when in early December she ordered the printing of 2000 Christmas cards for Fairwater. Lady Fairfax's cards always carried a selection of quotations from her reading during the year, and for 1986 she grouped some of these under the heading of 'Families'. First came a passage from *Hold the Dream*, a recent novel by Barbara Taylor Bradford about a dynastic business empire, the assets of which included a fictional *Yorkshire Morning Gazette*:

> Their grandmother's strictest rule, drilled into them continually, was to always check with at least one member of the family in any emergency before acting, to resist talking to strangers, to be supportive of each other and most importantly to close ranks to protect the family . . . How ungrateful and even unconscionable we would be if we were indifferent to our inheritances, turned away from them. It would be negating our forebears' superhuman efforts.

Then came two authentic dynasties, the Smorgons of Melbourne and the Guggenheims of New York.

> The evolution of [Smorgon Consolidated Industries] into Australia's largest private company', said a recent report in the *Sydney Morning Herald*, has been based on a few simple rules, with the overriding principle being to keep the family involved and united. The current board has 17 members, each able to veto a majority decision—and each a member of the family'.

From a *New York Times* obituary, Lady Fairfax had also culled Meyer Guggenheim's advice to his seven sons:

> 'My sons, you are like seven sticks. Each singly can very easily be broken. But together you can resist whatever forces may be brought to bear against you. It is my resolution to see you so united as to ensure your invincibility'.

There was no mistaking the message being sent that Christmas from Fairwater to other branches of the family in the eastern suburbs of Sydney—for example, to the house next door, Elaine, which was the home of Sir Vincent Fairfax, an elderly cousin and fellow director of Sir Warwick, and his wife Nancy; Sir Vincent's elder son, John Brehmer Fairfax, who was deputy chairman of John Fairfax Ltd, and his wife Libby, in Lang Rd, Centennial Park; Caroline Simpson, Sir Warwick's daughter by his first marriage, and her husband Philip, in Fairfax Road, Bellevue Hill; Annalise Thomas, Sir Warwick's daughter by his second marriage, and her husband David, in Edward St, Woollahra; and James Oswald Fairfax, Sir Warwick's unmarried son by his first marriage, and the company's present chairman, in Lindsay Ave, Darling Point.

The message was clearly an appeal for solidarity, but how would it be received by those for whom it was particularly intended? The fact of the matter was that the family's united front already had one or two gaps in it. As will be explained more fully in later chapters, solidarity had on occasion been honoured in the breach rather than the observance, and these breaches had left a residue of resentment and suspicion.

Sir Warwick and Lady Fairfax, his wife of the last twenty-seven years, felt that he had been prevented by others, inside and outside the family, from playing as significant a part in the company's affairs as was his due. He had been a director of the public company and its private predecessor for nearly sixty years, and chairman for 46 of those years. He had also wanted to be chief executive for a time; yet when he eventually came to hold that kind of position during the 1970s, it happened under such ambiguous and finally acrimonious circumstances that he felt himself cheated. When he lost his quasi-executive role in 1976, he also lost the chairmanship to his first-born son. This was not readily forgiven. James and his sister Caroline kept their distance from Fairwater for the next four years. The gate between Fairwater and Elaine opened even less frequently than in the past, and chance encounters on Seven Shillings Beach, the narrow strip of sand behind both houses, were occasions for deftly administered snubs.

On the other side of this estrangement, Sir Warwick's fellow directors at Broadway had no doubts about the wisdom of separating family from management, or of transferring the chairmanship from a septuagenarian to his 43-year-old son. They held firmly to a long established principle of strong professional management under the overall authority of the board, and believed that their actions had been in the best interests of the company. James and his father became reconciled in 1980, but before long another contentious matter arose.

In 1984 the group general manager, G. J. Gardiner, went to the board with a proposal to raise capital for further commercial expansion by issuing participating irredeemable preference shares (PIPS). As will be explained more fully in a later chapter, this was a plan designed to raise capital without requiring family shareholders to make any further investment in order to preserve their controlling influence. Because PIPS shareholders would have no voting rights, the family need not increase its holdings to preserve the voting status quo. There was even substantial gain in store for the family, because shareholders not wishing to buy PIPS could sell their rights to do so.

Three of the four family directors (James Fairfax; his second cousin, John Fairfax; and his first cousin once removed, Sir Vincent Fairfax) and the board's two non-family members (Sir David Griffin and Arthur Lissenden) agreed with Gardiner that PIPS was the best solution to a difficult problem. Only Sir Warwick disagreed. He feared that new legislation might one day give PIPS shareholders the right to vote, and thus weaken the family's hold on the company. He questioned the general manager's motives for bringing the proposal forward, and took quite seriously an unlikely rumour, brought back from New York by a barrister of his acquaintance, that Gardiner was acting in league with Robert Holmes à Court to dilute family control. James Fairfax laughed this off when his father relayed it to him; but the incident nevertheless cast a shadow over Sir Warwick's previously good relations with the young general manager.

Greg Gardiner, although only forty-three at the time of the HWT takeover bid, had been group general manager for six years. Cheerfully athletic in appearance, he had an impressive background of hard work and rapid progress in several industries. After gaining the Leaving Certificate at Randwick High School, he had become a trainee at Unilever, while at the same time, as an evening student, taking an economics degree at Sydney University. From Unilever's advertising agency, Lintas, he moved to two other agencies, NAS and J. Walter Thompson; then to the newsprint company Bowater Corporation of Australia, as personal assistant to the chairman, Arthur Lissenden; and from there to one of Sydney's two largest merchant banks, Development Finance Corporation. At DFC in 1974 he put together Australia's largest takeover to that time, the capture of Porter, Galbraith and Hanson by Felt and Textiles Ltd. On Lissenden's recommendation he came to John Fairfax Limited in 1975 as administration manager working closely with the general manager.

Sir Warwick and Lady Fairfax continued to oppose the PIPS issue, making their objections known in many quarters, not least the stockbroking community. The Sydney Stock Exchange Committee demanded certain unacceptable alterations before listing the issue, and reluctantly John Fairfax Ltd withdrew it. This time the boot was on the other foot, and Sir Warwick's fellow directors felt the kind of chagrin, even outrage, which he himself had felt upon losing the chairmanship. With the worsening of Sir Warwick's illness, bygones became bygones—or rather, bygones were not permitted to impair business and social propriety. Yet both sides remained suspicious of each other.

Knowing that he had only a little while to live, Sir Warwick knew also that something of great significance to the company's future was likely to occur soon after his death, and that it would probably be set in motion by his second son, who was then in the United States completing a master's degree at Harvard University's Graduate School of Business Administration.

Warwick Geoffrey Oswald Fairfax, twenty-six years of age, was the only issue of Sir Warwick's third marriage, though in 1969 the Fairfaxes had adopted two English babies, Charles and Anna. Lean of stature and rather long in the face, young Warwick bore sufficient resemblance to his father for the old man, with his strong sense of heredity, to have seen in him—as one member of the family, Annalise Thomas, put it—'his own immortality'. According to later testimony, the possibility of young Warwick mounting a takeover of John Fairfax Ltd in order to privatize the company had been under consideration at Fairwater since 1984. Sir Warwick and Lady Fairfax discussed it openly, and sometimes while their son was present, with such family advisers as Carnegie Fieldhouse and Martin Dougherty—the former a solicitor, and the latter a public relations consultant who had earlier organized publicity against the PIPS proposal. During the Harvard summer vacation in mid-1986, the two Warwicks spent a good deal of time together, talking about the young man's future.

Although no definite plan of action was decided, there can be no doubt that by the end of the year Sir Warwick knew that his son, after completing his Harvard course, would probably try to privatize the company. That would mean a return to the proprietorship which had preceded the formation of the public company in 1956. Other members of the family would continue to hold shares, but W. G. O. Fairfax would be the proprietor.

Sir Warwick's fellow directors knew nothing of this. Their only concern about Fairwater was that during the previous year Lady Fairfax had joined the board of Industrial Equity Ltd, Ronald Brierley's company which was thought to be on the prowl for media assets. 'As you may have seen', wrote Lady Fairfax to her stepson James, 'Ron Brierley offered me a seat on his board. It is my little indulgence as my business outlet. I told him he has no chance of getting one Fairfax share from me, ever'. In replying, the chairman wished his stepmother every success, but went on to mention a radio interview during which an IEL director had said that Lady Fairfax 'brings a wealth of business experience . . . in managing the Fairfax family fortune'.

'There is a clear implication', wrote James Fairfax, 'that a family company exists comprising the major family holdings of which you are a director. This sort of thing can only cause apprehensiveness among members of the family, which I am sure is not your intention'.

Another family director, John Fairfax, went further in a confidential memorandum, saying that Lady Fairfax's appointment could be seen as 'injudicious, dangerous and ambitious':

> It is injudicious for a wife of a director of a family-controlled John Fairfax Limited to accept a directorship of a company like IEL which is highly skilled in corporate raiding, to whom Fairfax could be seen as a potential situation stock. It is dangerous because of a potential conflict of interest . . . It cannot be regarded as a 'little indulgence.' IEL is large and successful and must see some advantage in the appointment. Fairfax mathematically is safe from takeover offers but any degree of split in the family could cause disaster and the regulations of the Security Industry could be adjusted to make . . . family control vulnerable to a challenge.
>
> It is ambitious because she is an ambitious person. Some possible objective could be: (a) Increased power to influence Fairfax policy by her association with IEL's expertise. (b) Appointment to Fairfax board . . . (c) Reinstatement of [Sir] Warwick as chairman. (d) Establish Warwick Junior as Chief Executive of Fairfax. Maybe and even (e) The advancement of a group who need media power in Australia.

The object of this suspicion, a vivacious dark-haired woman, considerably younger than her husband, was one of the best known social figures in Australia. Mary Fairfax was famous for her parties and receptions at Fairwater, her effervescent manner, and her work for the arts and charity. Some idea of this work could be gained from her entry in *Who's Who*: founder of the Opera Foundation and Australian Opera Auditions, founder and president of Friends of the Ballet, honorary Consul of Monaco, past president of the Smith Family Summer Committee, member of the board of trustees of the Art Gallery of New South Wales, and honorary positions with the Elizabethan Theatre Trust and the Australian Red Cross. Her recreations were listed as 'working, the arts, writing, poetry, sculpture, fashion, entertaining, reading, swimming, walking, travel'.

Lady Fairfax was justly proud of having been a successful business woman early in life. She had come to Australia from Poland with her parents, Kevin and Anna Wein, during the 1920s, and her father had soon prospered in the retail clothing business. After completing her education at the Presbyterian Ladies College, Croydon, and the University of Sydney, she too went into the clothing business, running several shops with a member of her family and later with her first husband, a prominent Sydney solicitor. Now, in her sixties, Lady Fairfax could also pride herself on being one of the few

Australian women with a seat on the board of a major company. This could indeed have produced a conflict of interest if IEL had moved against the HWT, for such a bid would almost certainly have provoked defensive or competitive action by John Fairfax Ltd. As it happened, however, the attack was made by Murdoch.

The bid was not unexpected. At a Fairfax board meeting on 20 November 1986 Gardiner had told directors that his contacts led him to believe that something was afoot. If someone made a bid for HWT, he said, John Fairfax Ltd would have to consider making a counter-bid in excess of $1.2 billion. There would be enormous complexities, and the board would need to see the environment as it existed when the first bid was made.

John Fairfax, who was acting as chairman in the absence of James Fairfax overseas, said the environment would obviously be very different from that in which the company had gone to the defence of HWT in 1979. Sir Eric Neal asked whether other competitors were likely to be interested in the same components of the HWT group as Fairfax might be. Gardiner replied that if Holmes à Court was a bidder he would want everything. Murdoch would have Trade Practice problems, but his main interest would be in Melbourne, and that was why Fairfax 'would have to have a go'.

James Fairfax, who had been in China and Japan for the past four weeks, heard of Murdoch's $1.8 billion bid from the *Sydney Morning Herald*'s Tokyo correspondent, who contacted him at Narita airport on his way back to Sydney on Wednesday evening, 3 December. Uncertain of his father's attitude towards the bid, he arranged as soon as possible for Gardiner to visit Fairwater. This visit took place on the Friday, and Gardiner later reported to the chairman that although Lady Fairfax thought there were better ways of spending money than countering a bid for HWT, Sir Warwick believed that Murdoch should be opposed.

James Fairfax, then fifty-three years old, had been chairman for more than nine years. Educated at Geelong Grammar School and Balliol, he had been a director since the age of 24. In spite of his long service on the board, and large shareholding in the company, some had formerly been inclined to wonder whether his heart was really in the business. His chief personal interest was art collecting—initially Australian art of all periods, but from the mid-1960s with an increasing emphasis on European art of the seventeenth and eighteenth centuries. He was a member of the council of the Australian National Gallery in Canberra, and of the International Council of the Museum of Modern Art in New York, and was also a member of the board of management at Royal Alexandra Hospital for Children. Unassuming as he was in manner, it would not have been surprising if one day he had shrugged off the cares of directorship.

With his accession to the chairmanship, however, James Fairfax surprised the rest of the board with his businesslike but consensual conduct of meetings, and with his personal firmness on particular issues. He applied himself assiduously, though at a certain remove, to the affairs of the company; displayed a clear understanding of his own and the general manager's respective roles; and established good relations with the company's executives and editors. His sometimes languid manner concealed a keen sense of humour and much enthusiasm for matters far removed from the company's headquarters at Broadway, near the centre of Sydney. Nothing pleased him more than a journey with friends to some distant part of the world, and there were few countries he had not visited. There was no waning of his commitment to the company; but so accustomed had he become to the board–management dichotomy, and such was his confidence in the management, that he felt well able to absent himself from time to time.

On Friday, the day Gardiner went to Fairwater, James Fairfax drove to Retford Park, his 300-acre estate near Bowral in the verdant southern highlands of New South Wales. That evening one of the three Rolls-Royces at Fairwater brought an unexpected visitor down the long tree-lined drive to James's resplendent home, a two-storey century-old mansion with cast iron verandas and a pink and white portico tower. The visitor was Lady Fairfax's adopted son, Charles, delivering a letter from her to the chairman. James was astounded to read that on the previous evening Rupert Murdoch had called at Fairwater while on his way to the Vaucluse home of his partner in Ansett Airlines, Sir Peter Abeles.

The purpose of Murdoch's visit had been to tell Lady Fairfax, whom he had met previously in New York, that if James Fairfax communicated with him personally and in private, 'as chairman to chairman', it would be possible for John Fairfax Ltd to acquire HSV-7 in News Ltd's eventual sale of unwanted HWT assets. 'It seems to me', she wrote, 'that Rupert wanted on a long-term basis to find a way for both your organisations to live together amicably. As a token of good faith he suggested you might care to work together to stop the proposed cross-ownership law so disadvantageous to both'.

Lady Fairfax felt that she had acted in good faith by relaying this offer to the chairman. He, on the other hand, felt that she had been decidedly indiscreet in receiving such a visitor at such a time. As the board had not decided on its own course of action, it certainly did not want to make any deals with Murdoch yet. What if it decided to talk to HWT, or to some new bidder for the company, such as Holmes à Court? John Fairfax Ltd could then be seriously disadvantaged if it became known that a senior member of the family had been talking confidentially to Murdoch.

On Saturday morning James telephoned his stepmother to

remonstrate with her and ask whether his father knew about Murdoch's visit. When she replied that he did not, the chairman insisted that she tell Sir Warwick immediately. Twenty minutes later Lady Fairfax rang back, saying tearfully that she may have been wrong, but had meant well. She then put Sir Warwick on. He thanked his son for calling, and agreed with what he had said to Lady Fairfax.

On Monday 8 December James received a longer letter from his stepmother, written after Gardiner's discussion with Sir Warwick and herself on the Friday, but presumably before the letter about Murdoch's visit. In this she expressed deep concern about the possible effect of increased debt, should the company decide to borrow for a counter-bid, on the family's dividend income. That income was expected soon to be substantially increased by the removal of double taxation of dividends (dividend imputation), but what if the dividend rate had to be lowered?

> Most of us have been so looking forward to those imputed dividends which should reap us a bonanza in about six months' time and treble our income. With such debts, should we risk our whole lifestyle and that of our dependants on the assurances of any chief executive, no matter how talented?

Would it not be wiser, she asked, to form a takeover consortium in which Fairfax took no more than two-fifths of the risk? James visited Fairwater the following day and discussed the HWT situation for more than an hour. To his relief he found that both his father and Lady Fairfax were now firmly of the view that Murdoch's bid should be resisted.

But how? The matter was first discussed by Fairfax directors on11 December, at a meeting in Melbourne; and on the previous day it had also come before the board of David Syme & Co Ltd, a wholly owned Fairfax subsidiary whose main publication was the Melbourne *Age*. James Fairfax chaired the Syme meeting, which was also attended by two other directors from Sydney, John Fairfax and Greg Gardiner. According to the minutes, the managing director of David Syme, G. J. Taylor, said that Syme personnel believed that John Fairfax Ltd should react to the Murdoch bid.

> This did not necessarily mean overbidding Mr Murdoch. But he did not believe John Fairfax could sit back for the next three months and allow a Murdoch bid—or any other bid—to succeed. It would not be wise for John Fairfax Ltd to remain mute . . .
>
> Mr Gardiner said he had no doubt that a higher bid could be mounted on the basis of the value of the individual properties. The problem was the bottom line. The current offer represented 55 times last year's profit.
>
> The Murdoch bid could be looked at as a takeover bid, but it was

> really a matter of raising capital and strengthening the News balance sheet. Mr Murdoch had a problem with his balance sheet and the one way to correct it was to issue additional capital. Mr Murdoch had the choice of issuing the additional capital to the market or of using the mechanism of a takeover of the HWT [with scrip in News Corporation Ltd as an alternative to cash].
>
> It was a brilliant bid, so there needed to be a brilliant response to counter it. Perhaps the best outcome would be a successful Holmes à Court bid as that would preserve the current position of three major media companies in Australia.
>
> Mr Gardiner said that whoever over-bid Mr Murdoch would be in for a lot of financial pain. John Fairfax Ltd could bid and then find itself in a worse position than it would be in if it did nothing.

Gardiner had already held two telephone conversations with Robert Holmes à Court since the Murdoch announcement, and Holmes à Court phoned him again on 11 December. These were exploratory calls, long calls punctuated by Holmes à Court's celebrated five-minute silences, a technique which Gardiner well knew was designed to trick unwary competitors into saying more than they intended. The chess player, as Holmes à Court was sometimes called, struck Gardiner as being more like a fencer. 'He would spend hours on the phone', Gardiner later recalled,

> to a point where you would say, 'I'm sorry, I've got to go. I can't waste this time.' He likes talking in the hope that you will say something that will lead him off on a particular angle. It's like fencing, an intellectual thing all the time. It sounds very intelligent and impressive, but when you analyse it there is nothing in there. It is just a series of words. And you keep saying to yourself, What is this about?

At the Fairfax meeting in Melbourne on 11 December, no decision was taken about the matter uppermost in directors' minds. But the probable options were canvassed. Gardiner was convinced that Holmes à Court would soon bid against Murdoch, and that, he said, was when the crunch would come for Fairfax. The company would then have to decide whether to go in hard against HWT, or to go in parallel with Holmes à Court by bidding for HWT's affiliate, Queensland Press. The latter course would put great financial pressure on Murdoch by forcing him to bid for the interlocking company as well as for HWT. Although the Fairfax directors were philosophically averse to the first option, carrying as it would unwanted connotations of monopoly, they acknowledged that commercial pragmatism might require them to choose it. The second option, on the other hand, could have the preferable effect of leaving the print media in three main hands: Fairfax, Murdoch and Holmes à Court.

During the next few days Gardiner received four more telephone calls from Holmes à Court. The fencer was still deciding which way to go. On 12 December Industrial Equity sold its 12 per cent holding in HWT to News Ltd, and Murdoch, rejoicing in that gain, flew back to Aspen for a white Christmas. Gardiner spent much time conferring with the board's legal adviser, Rod Halstead of Mallesons Stephen Jaques, and with Tony Berg of the Macquarie Bank.

On 17 December John Fairfax had lunch at La Colonna restaurant with his cousin Warwick, who had returned from Harvard for Christmas. These two had not seen much of each other in the past, for there was a gap of eighteen years between them, and for the last seven years Warwick had been living in England, where he had taken a degree at Oxford, and the United States, where before going to Harvard he had worked for three years at the Chase Manhattan Corporation in New York. Unlike Warwick, whose newspaper experience was confined to a brief period in the marketing department of the *Los Angeles Times*, or James, who had trained as a journalist on the *Glasgow Herald*, John had followed the example of his father, Sir Vincent, by working as a cadet reporter on the *Sydney Morning Herald* and then gaining practical experience in other departments of the company.

On one occasion, while working in the *Herald*'s Canberra bureau, John was suspended without pay for a week because of a mistake he had made in a court report. He was treated like any other member of the staff, and this enhanced his reputation for being down to earth and unpretentious. After working in the London office and the circulation and advertising departments, he became successively personal assistant to the general manager; manager of Federal Capital Press of Australia Pty Ltd, which published the *Canberra Times*; and in 1979 a director of John Fairfax Ltd and chairman of the company's magazine subsidiary, Sungravure Pty Ltd.

The lunch at La Colonna left John Fairfax feeling, as he recorded in a file note, 'that the environment was right for the three arms of the Fairfax family to co-operate in a better way than had been the case in the past 50 years or so'. Warwick said he was looking forward to returning to Australia during the following year, and would like to find some role for himself in the company's marketing area. 'I discussed the possibility of him becoming a director in the event of his father's death', wrote John,

> and he said this was not necessarily important to him, particularly if it was going to interfere with the executive type role that he wanted to play in the company . . . He said that although he had not mentioned it to his mother or father he thought that when he returned to Sydney he might take an apartment on the north shore rather than the eastern suburbs. He was conscious of wanting to be independent of his parents . . .

During this conversation John Fairfax told his cousin about a form of equity raising which the Macquarie Bank had suggested as one of the means by which John Fairfax Ltd could reduce its borrowings after a successful bid for the entire HWT group. This 'Koitaki-type issue', based upon a form of equity raising previously employed by the entrepreneurial financial services group of that name, involved the issue of redeemable preference shares, convertible into shares of Advertiser Newspapers Ltd, which would by then have become a Fairfax subsidiary. With a first conversion date of perhaps five years ahead, such an issue would have the advantage of raising immediate funds for Fairfax without diluting either the interests of the Fairfax family or the company's stake in Advertiser. Warwick appeared to regard this as an acceptable means of raising money, preferable to other methods which had been proposed in the past. But he said that he would be concerned about any dilution of the family holding, as 'there were no doubt predators such as Holmes à Court waiting to pounce'.

John Fairfax thought that his cousin had 'benefited tremendously from his period in the US and particularly from his Harvard course'.

> While he is intelligent, [he wrote,] he is still relatively young and inexperienced. At James's suggestion I invited him to attend the next critical board meeting as an observer. He was sufficiently humble to say that if this suited the directors then by all means he would be happy to attend. He did not wish to impose himself on the board.

This meeting was held on 23 December in the board room at Broadway, a wood-panelled sanctum on the fourteenth floor, heavy with portraits of four Fairfax generations. Although only an observer, young Warwick was also a necessary link with Fairwater, for his father's alternate director—an old family friend, the Melbourne businessman Sir Rupert Clarke—had not been able to attend. The directors had before them a strategy paper prepared by Macquarie Bank on the basis that Fairfax had the following order of priorities: preventing News acquiring HWT; Fairfax acquiring Queensland Press; and Fairfax having a preference, if a choice had to be made, for print media over electronic media.

The first option was for Fairfax to make an all-cash bid of approximately $20 per share ($4 above the current market price) for Queensland Press, costing $890 million, while at the same time Holmes à Court would be bidding for HWT. Queensland Press held 25.53 per cent of HWT shares, and was itself owned by HWT to the extent of 43.58 per cent. Murdoch's bid for HWT contained a condition that the company should not sell any of its shares in Queensland Press or Advertiser Newspapers. This would act as a strong deterrent against the HWT board accepting any bid for Queensland Press, as such acceptance in breach of Murdoch's condition might deprive HWT shareholders of his bid for their company. If a Fairfax bid for Queensland Press was to succeed, Holmes à Court's bid for HWT, if and when he made it, should expressly allow the sale of Queensland Press shares.

The Macquarie paper suggested that, if necessary, Fairfax could encourage Holmes à Court to follow through with his bid for HWT by offering him Sydney's ATN7 as the keystone for a television network including HWT's Adelaide and Melbourne stations. 'It is recognised', the paper stated, 'that the major weakness of this strategy is that Holmes à Court is not a reliable partner and may not decide to bid or may withdraw, and that he is susceptible to being suborned by News'. In that kind of event Fairfax's second option would be to bid directly for HWT, offering up to $15 per share, which, if fully accepted, would cost $2.25 billion.

This would give Fairfax not only 100 per cent of HWT but also control of Queensland Press and Advertiser Newspapers. The bid could be funded by short-term debt, and the debt could be reduced in three ways: by selling David Syme to Queensland Press and Advertiser (both of which Fairfax would then control through HWT), payment being made with cash received by those companies for their cross-holdings in HWT; by selling off certain HWT assets, including the Melbourne *Herald* and the *Sun News-Pictorial*; and by the Koitaki-type issue. At the end of the day, as merchant bankers say, Fairfax would probably be left with a cash surplus of $100 million.

At the end of this particular day, 23 December, the Fairfax directors authorized Gardiner to put in a bid either for Queensland Press Ltd or HWT. Although they favoured the first alternative, they left the choice and timing to the general manager, who was to advise directors of his intention as soon as possible in advance. Finance was no obstacle. Gardiner simply made two telephone calls—one to the National Australia Bank, and another to Westpac. Both banks thought well enough of Fairfax to approve loans of up to $1.5 billion each. The National agreed within two days, and Westpac within a week.

On the evening of 23 December Lady Fairfax held a birthday party for her husband. John and Libby Fairfax were already on their way to Adelaide for Christmas, but all other branches of the extended family were present at Fairwater. Sir Warwick himself was too weak to come down, but the guests, accompanied by an accordionist playing carols, went upstairs to his bedroom. During the evening James Fairfax talked to his stepmother about the day's eventful board meeting, mentioning the possibility that the company might have to sell ATN7. As chairman of Amalgamated Television Services Pty Ltd, he said, he would be sorry to see that happen.

Next morning Holmes à Court announced a counter-bid of $13 cash a share, with a scrip alternative, for all shares in HWT, an offer valuing the company at $1.98 billion. This was $50 million more than his unsuccessful bid for BHP several months before, and thus was the highest takeover bid in Australia's corporate history. The bid, made through J. N. Taylor Holdings Ltd, a subsidiary of Holmes à Court's Bell Group Ltd, was subject to two conditions: one, that there should be no material changes to the HWT business or assets (including the sale of shares in any associated company); and the other, that the offeror should become entitled to not less than 90 per cent of all HWT shares before the offer closed. There was no telling whether this bid was serious or whether, as someone in the Murdoch camp remarked, Holmes à Court was merely booking a seat at the card table. Many regarded his minimum acceptance condition as ample evidence of insincerity, for Murdoch already held more than 10 per cent. Holmes à Court rejected this argument, saying that once he gained more than 50 per cent he would drop that condition.

On Christmas Eve, Lady Fairfax wrote a long letter to James, continuing their discussion at the birthday party:

> I cannot tell you what it means to me that you have included me as well as Warwick in your thinking and decisions about the company. By way of a reference, may I include a track record. My latest contribution to Industrial Equity and Brierley Investments has not been discussed by the board, so I feel I can tell you confidentially my lateral thinking contribution to the above companies, as an example of the way my brain ticks. You have probably seen in the financial press loud complaints by Ron Brierley that capital gains tax adversely affects IEL shareholders and has prevented the merger of BIL and IEL despite the best legal and banking advice. I was unwilling to accept this as a finite conclusion . . . I contacted one of my own advisers, reputedly the best of his kind for individually solving these kinds of problems, and asked him if he had any solution, which he had and it looks as though the matter will be resolved favourably . . .
>
> IEL have the best lawyers and bankers world-wide and managers of great experience and expertise, as, no doubt, has John Fairfax. Yet if I can be of the above use to IEL, where a very small proportion of my own money is involved, how much more so are my desires to assist in achieving the best possible situation with the least possible risk and yet still beat Murdoch for our family and John Fairfax Limited. Our family has so much money at stake. Our family has so much more to lose than the best bankers or the best managers, who will survive regardless.
>
> I did not sleep at all last night when you told me how sad you would be if Channel 7, your baby, was sold. In view of the proposed new legislation, our family are being advised to sell a Sydney television station where we are protected by the grandfather clause. There are probably alternatives. Perhaps our family can save this baby if it does not increase the family risk . . . Should we succeed [in

> the HWT contest], I would so much like for the family to keep Channel 7 in Melbourne as its ultimate value with Channel 7 in Sydney would be so much greater . . .

Between Christmas and New Year Sir Warwick wrote to James Fairfax requesting that his legal adviser, Carnegie Fieldhouse, be permitted to replace Sir Rupert Clarke as his alternate director. 'Should I die', he wrote, 'I also request that, at the appropriate time, you and the Board agree that Carney Fieldhouse be appointed director to represent my family interest pending your brother's agreement to become a director'. Sir Warwick's death seemed close indeed, and his friend Father Costello, a history teacher at Riverview College, began visiting him almost daily, even though there was no longer any chance of real conversation.

Lady Fairfax also wrote to the chairman on 31 December saying that she had heard Murdoch was back in Sydney.

> He has told his executives that he will 'knock Holmes à Court out of the fight' . . . Our strategy seems, in part, to hinge upon coming to an acceptable agreement with Holmes à Court. Most major company chairmen I know distrust Holmes à Court. They say Holmes à Court even if he seems totally legally tied up before any transaction, usually finds legal loopholes to others' disadvantage. Finally, they say that dealings with him are a nightmare and a destroyer of tranquillity . . . Our family might have more peace of mind if you, the Board and Greg were in the position of control, as the owner of HWT. Then, being in a stronger position as owner of the total, at your choice, selling portions to whoever you all wished, than being a supplicant of anyone. I am confident that with your known reputation for careful and fair assessment of any views expressed to you, that your judgment, as always, will be excellent. I wish you good luck in the fight. The family could not have a greater champion.

On New Year's Day the HWT board announced that Holmes à Court had increased his offer of $13 per share by 50 cents, and on 2 January it switched its recommendation from Murdoch to Holmes à Court 'in the absence of a more attractive offer'. That day the Fairfax board approved a decision by Gardiner to bid $20 a share for Queensland Press. Gardiner immediately telephoned Holmes à Court and—after much hesitation on the latter's part, real or feigned—persuaded him to drop the condition preventing HWT from selling its shares in Queensland Press.

On the day the Fairfax bid was announced—Sunday 4 January—James Fairfax left Sydney on a long-arranged journey to Antarctica. He had offered to cancel the trip, but Gardiner said there was no need to do that.

Accompanied by Lady (Dorothy) Edwards and another Sydney friend, Richard Walker, James flew by way of Tahiti and Easter

Island to Santiago, Chile, where the party was joined by a friend from New York, Douglas Drehmann. From Santiago they flew to Puerto Williams, the world's southernmost town on a Chilean island south of Tierra del Fuego. On 11 January they boarded the *Society Explorer*, a luxurious expedition ship whose reinforced hull and radar allowed it to cruise in waters which even the *Titanic* would have avoided.

With 100 passengers on board, the air-conditioned *Society Explorer* crossed Drake Passage on an 11-day round trip to Graham Land, the northernmost part of the Antarctic continent. The first iceberg was sighted two days out, and soon there were many more, some of them up to 100 metres across. The passengers' log for that day recorded sightings of Minke whales and Chinstrap penguins.

Back in Australia, the takeover was becoming more and more complex. During the first week of January Holmes à Court announced that he would sell his 24 per cent holding in Queensland Press to Fairfax, and argued that Murdoch's American citizenship, acquired sixteen months earlier for reasons not unconnected with business, would constrain him under provisions of the Broadcasting and Television Act from buying more than 15 per cent of HWT. News Ltd, whose holding was then 12 per cent, promptly registered a revised Part A statement (the statement given to a target company, outlining necessary information, before a takeover offer is made) concerning the matter of citizenship. This included a restructuring of News Ltd's share capital designed to ensure that its bid would not give rise to any problems under the Act.

After some deft work with companies called Votraint No 275 Pty Ltd and Travinto Nominees (ACT) Pty Ltd, News Ltd felt able to put forward the remarkable proposition that it was controlled neither by News Corporation nor by Rupert Murdoch. Accordingly, it went on, any risk of revocation or non-renewal of television licences, should News Ltd gain full control of HWT, had been reduced if not eliminated. The Australian Broadcasting Tribunal was still pondering this *tour de force* of corporate juggling, and on Friday 9 January Holmes à Court applied successfully to the Victorian Supreme Court for an interim injunction restraining News Ltd from lifting its HWT holding above 15 per cent.On the same day Greg Gardiner caught an afternoon plane to join his family at a holiday unit on Queensland's Gold Coast. At Coolangatta airport he received a message from Fairfax's chief editorial executive, M. V. Suich, that Murdoch accompanied by the managing director of News Ltd, Ken Cowley, had been seen at 2.15 p.m. entering the Queensland Press building in Brisbane.

This was completely unexpected, for it had been assumed that when Murdoch had left Australia two days earlier he was bound for New York. In fact he had gone to New Zealand, visited Lake Tapoe and then chartered an aircraft to take him directly to Brisbane. With only 30 minutes warning by telephone, he walked into the Queensland Press board room, where a meeting of Melbourne and Brisbane directors was in progress, and made two announcements. He increased his cash offer for HWT to $15 per share ($1.50 more than Holmes à Court's revised offer, valuing the company at $2.3 billion), and offered $23 per share for Queensland Press ($3 more than the Fairfax offer, valuing the company at $1.02 billion). He said the offers would lapse unless accepted by 5 p.m., then left the board room to wait in an adjoining office.

As soon as Gardiner reached his holiday unit, at 3.20 p.m., he embarked upon nine hours of virtually continuous telephone calls to Brisbane, Sydney and Melbourne. First he telephoned the chairman and chief executive of Queensland Press, Keith McDonald, who was known as a strong supporter of News Ltd's bid for HWT. He warned McDonald that the Queensland Press directors would be running a very serious legal risk if they accepted Murdoch's offer without at least conferring with John Fairfax Ltd, which was prepared, he said, to consider increasing its offer significantly. He rang back an hour later to repeat his warning in a form of words which he felt confident would deter the Queensland board from making a hasty decision. It did have that effect. The chairman of HWT, John Dahlsen, delivered a speech which lasted long past Murdoch's deadline, and the meeting ended without any decision.

Murdoch returned to New York, frustrated by his failure in Brisbane and beginning to see merit in reaching some sort of accommodation with Holmes à Court before Fairfax became a third bidder for HWT itself. In all the phone calls between Holmes à Court and Gardiner, Holmes à Court had never concealed his opportunistic nature. 'Look Greg', he would say, 'I assure you I am serious about going ahead, but I've got a pain threshold and I have to look to my own interests. If the deal gets good enough I'd have to sell to Murdoch'.

Gardiner understood that, and passed his awareness on to the board. Consequently he was not entirely surprised, though disappointed, when one of Holmes à Court's lieutenants, Bert Reuter, telephoned him on Sunday night, 11 January, to say that Murdoch had been in touch with Holmes à Court and a deal had been struck between the two.

Wednesday 14 January was one of the summer's hottest days in Sydney. Father Costello thought of foregoing his usual drive from Riverview to Fairwater, but after lunch he decided to go. 'Thank God you're here', said Welton, the butler, at the front door. 'The doctor has just been. I don't think Sir Warwick has long to live'. Caroline Simpson had also been to see her father earlier that afternoon, and had found him 'struggling to go and unable to speak'.

In the upstairs room, where Lady Fairfax and a nurse were standing by, Father Costello took Sir Warwick's hand and said: 'Dear Warwick, have no worries. Just give yourself over to Christ with boundless optimism'. He and Lady Fairfax recited the Lord's Prayer, then left the room. As they were going downstairs, the nurse called after them that Sir Warwick was dead. The time was 2.25 p.m.

Caroline Simpson booked a telephone call to her brother, which reached the *Society Explorer*, by way of a satellite over the south Atlantic, at 1.30 a.m. Antarctic time. James Fairfax spent the next two hours making and receiving more phone calls. One of these came from Gardiner, who apologized for ringing at such an inconvenient hour. 'That's all right', replied the chairman. 'I'm in my pyjamas and dressing gown up on the bridge, and I can see icebergs.'

'There are a few icebergs back here too', said Gardiner. After offering his condolences, he told the chairman that Holmes à Court seemed about to strike a deal with Murdoch, and that John Fairfax Ltd had raised its bid for Queensland Press to $24. The latter was conditional upon the Queensland Press board accepting Holmes à Court's offer for HWT, an offer now likely to be withdrawn for pragmatic reasons.

Later the same day in Antarctica, James Fairfax and his companions made their first landings in rubber Zodiac launches—first at Paulet Island, a breeding ground for Adelie penguins, and some hours later at the Argentine Esperanza base in Hope Bay on the continental mainland.

Two days later James Fairfax received a cable from Gardiner informing him that on the night of Thursday 15 January (Australian time) Holmes à Court, in Perth, had accepted an invitation from Murdoch, in New York, to sell his shares in HWT and Queensland Press. If Murdoch's bid for HWT succeeded, he would repay Holmes à Court's favour by letting him buy HSV7 for $260 million and the *West Australian* for $200 million.

> Queensland board also accepted Murdoch offer [said the cable]. Murdoch thus has approx 44 per cent of HWT and in unbeatable position. JFL . . . not able to mount a practical and effective full bid for HWT. We have announced today our withdrawal from proceeding with Qld Press bid. Sorry unable to deliver success.

Gardiner had tried to telephone McDonald in the Queensland Press board room, but no one there would accept his call. The withdrawal of Holmes à Court left only one bid for HWT—Murdoch's $15 per share or scrip, which by then carried the HWT board's recommendation.

Murdoch's horoscope for the day, as published in his own *New York Post*, was sent to Broadway by the *Australian Financial Review*'s New York correspondent, Anne Summers. It said: 'Quite recently you have been cautioned not to take on any further financial commitments. And just how precarious the situation has become will be painfully apparent soon'. It was true that Murdoch's outlay would be about $1.5 billion more than he had originally offered, a most unwelcome addition in the short term to his already daringly high level of borrowing. On the other hand, he would be selling off some of the booty for more than $1.2 billion; the assets retained by him would make his group the world's largest publisher of English-language newspaper titles; and the scrip offer would help his balance sheet.

Soon afterwards, the legal avenue first exploited by Holmes à Court gave John Fairfax an opportunity for another throw, this time against Murdoch's bid for HWT. Although the Federal government had announced that it had no objection to Murdoch's bid under its foreign investment policy, on 20 January the Federal Court confirmed the authority of the Television and Broadcasting Act to prevent foreign ownership or control of electronic media licences. Next day Fairfax took action in the Victorian Supreme Court to prevent HWT registering purchases of its shares by News Ltd; it also announced its intention of making a takeover offer for all HWT shares at the price of $16 per share, which would value the company at $2.5 billion.

'We have come late to this auction', wrote Gardiner to John Dahlsen,

> because our initial preferred course was to see the Herald and Weekly Times remain an independent entity as this company demonstrated in the most practical way in 1979 and 1982. That is no longer possible, but the divestments that Fairfax proposes will maintain at the very minimum three major publishing companies in the field, with room for more to emerge.

He also telephoned James Fairfax, who by that time was nearing the end of the cruise at Punta Arenas, Chile.

Not only had the company come to this auction late, it had come *too* late. On 19 January Advertiser Newspapers decided to sell its 11 per cent of HWT to Murdoch, and—courts permitting—this would give him a controlling interest. As the Fairfax bid was conditional on 50.1 per cent acceptance, it could succeed only if the legal process stopped Murdoch's bid on grounds of citizenship and television licences. He had no intention of letting that happen. On 22 January the HWT board announced that it would not recommend the Fairfax bid; on 2 February the Australian Broadcasting Tribunal began an inquiry into the News Ltd bid; and on 5 February HWT called tenders for its television stations and other assets.

In the first few weeks of 1987 ownership of Australia's television networks changed out of all recognition, and in such a way as to rid

Murdoch of any impediment to his takeover bid. Murdoch sold his Channel 10s in Sydney and Melbourne to the Lismore-based Northern Star Holdings Ltd; Kerry Packer sold his Channel 9s in Sydney and Melbourne to the West Australian entrepreneur Alan Bond; and HWT (which by then was virtually Murdoch) sold its Channel 7 in Adelaide to yet another West Australian, Kerry Stokes, and the Melbourne channel not to Holmes à Court, despite Murdoch's earlier undertaking, but to a higher bidder—John Fairfax Ltd.

Holmes à Court had been gazumped, but Murdoch was later reported to have made amends by letting him reduce his payment for the *West Australian* by however many millions the top offer for HSV7 exceeded the previously agreed price of $260 million. Gardiner, determined to win HSV7, approached the auction with an offer to HWT of $1 million more than the highest bid by anyone else. This secured the channel for John Fairfax Ltd, at a price of $320 million. Thus Holmes à Court presumably bought the *West Australian* for only $140 million.

Although HSV7 was already a working partner with Fairfax's ATN7 (Sydney) and BTQ7 (Brisbane) in the Seven network, it had been the network's weak link, lacking initiative and, as Gardiner put it, 'always crying poor mouth and being the poor cousin'. Here was a chance to gain full working control of the network. If the new media ownership legislation created an insurmountable obstacle, Fairfax could always sell HSV7, or sell all three stations. But if the Bill failed to pass through parliament (and there was still some possibility of that) Fairfax alone would have television, radio and newspapers in Sydney and Melbourne. It was a gamble, but one that Gardiner thought worth while.

As a consequence of Fairfax's continuing legal action, News Ltd also agreed to let it have Murdoch's *Northern Daily Leader* in Tamworth (price $5 million) and fifteen other country newspapers owned by HWT in New South Wales ($40 million). While selling these and other assets, News Ltd kept for itself the *Herald* and *Sun News-Pictorial* in Melbourne, control of Queensland Press, Advertiser Newspapers and Davies Brothers, a large suburban newspaper network in Melbourne, and a half share of Australian Newsprint Mills. Allowing for the proceeds of asset stripping, the cross-shareholdings between HWT and Queensland Press, and the sale of News Ltd's own television stations in Melbourne and Sydney, the total cash outlay for News Ltd was no more than $400 million.

At the next Fairfax board meeting, on 19 February, Gardiner warned the directors to expect strong competition from a greatly strengthened Murdoch group. 'Mr Gardiner said the additional market now being offered by News Ltd Australia-wide could on one interpretation virtually render as irrelevant the *Sun-Herald* and the *Sun*. He believed News Ltd would mount a massive campaign to convince advertisers, and the campaign, he believed, would have considerable substance.' Sir Vincent Fairfax said he found it difficult to accept the HSV7 purchase as worth while. The chairman did not agree, saying that HSV7 had dragged the Seven Network down for years, and that now Fairfax would be able to get a good network going. He also commended the general manager for the effort he had put into the takeover. There would always be differing views, he said, but he agreed completely with Mr Gardiner on the tactics which had been adopted.

Like a requiem bringing repose after weeks of corporate turmoil, Sir Warwick Fairfax's funeral service was held at St Andrew's Cathedral on Friday 30 January. His life, for which the funeral service was a thanksgiving, had been accorded many tributes during the last few days. One of the most eloquent, and unashamedly old-fashioned, came in a letter to James Fairfax from his old headmaster at Geelong Grammar School, Sir James Darling:

> When I think of him I am reminded of those great noblemen in the Trollope political novels, the old Duke of Omnium and Plantagenet Palliser, who while inheriting great wealth were always conscious of the responsibility that went with it, whether they liked it or not; and the same, I am sure, is what supports you. There was once a time when great businesses could be conducted at least with a certain amount of dignity, even grace, but things are different today and it must be hard to maintain your own standards in the face of all these bandits by whom you are surrounded . . . Your father was a difficult man to know well, perhaps because he had not enough amiable vices, and seemed more aloof than he would have wished to be; but he had integrity and honour and brains and courage and you will miss his wisdom and experience in the present crisis.

'My dominating reaction to his death', wrote Sir Vincent Fairfax to James,

> is the realisation of his impact on what we have referred to as 'the *Herald*'. You rightly have acknowledged him as the greatest since John. How do we replace him? Is it different now it is 'the company'?
>
> I suppose part of my fear that 'lights' might go out lies in the greatness of Warwick to which you have referred. Can we maintain and expand the greatness in a much more complex world?
>
> I have always felt most thankful that you have carried your responsibilities so well and have been sound in your judgment. I have tried to support you within my capacity and am proud of you.
>
> Another comfort is that you and John make a favourable assessment of Warwick [Jr] . . .

The funeral was organized by Lady Fairfax, Caroline Simpson and Annalise Thomas. Lady Fairfax surprised her two stepdaughters by some of the suggestions she made for the service: participation by a Buddhist monk as witness of Sir Warwick's ecumenical approach to religion, and a song from *The Mikado*, Yum Yum's dignified and beautiful 'The sun, whose rays are all ablaze, with ever living glory'. As it turned out, however, the final arrangements were traditionally Anglican, with only a hint of Gilbert and Sullivan in the tune of 'Onward Christian Soldiers', composed—as Canon J. E. Whild of St Mark's, Darling Point, reminded Lady Fairfax—by Sir Arthur Sullivan.

The Cathedral was crowded with family, friends, colleagues, employees and official guests: Sir Warwick's first two wives, Mrs M. E. (Betty) Fairfax and Mrs Hanne Van de Wiel; his two sons, two daughters, two adopted children and virtually all members of the extended family; Sir Rupert and Lady Clarke, Sir Frank and Lady Renouf, Carnegie Fieldhouse and Martin Dougherty and their wives; Dr Roger Dunlop, who had attended Sir Warwick in his last weeks; two former Prime Ministers, Sir William McMahon and the Hon. E. G. Whitlam; the Governor, Chief Justice, Premier and Leader of the Opposition in New South Wales, and the Lord Mayor of Sydney. James Fairfax escorted Lady Fairfax to and from her seat, between himself and young Warwick. James also read the first lesson, from Isaiah 40:

> All flesh is grass, and all the goodliness thereof is as the flower of the field.The grass withereth, the flower fadeth: because the spirit of the Lord bloweth upon it: surely the people is grass . . .

Then came a more hopeful lesson from John I, read by Warwick Fairfax, himself an evangelical Christian. Whether by intention or otherwise, this recalled the traditional Fairfax motto which appeared on the order of service: *Lucem fer fax*, a Latin pun on the family name, meaning 'O torch, bear light!'

> And the light shineth in darkness; and the darkness comprehendeth it not. There was a man sent from God, whose name was John.The same came for a witness, to bear witness of the Light, that all men through him might believe . . .

The eulogy was read by a former Governor of New South Wales, Sir Roden Cutler. 'The *Sydney Morning Herald* was Warwick Fairfax's life', he said,

> and he had very definite views on the way in which it should be conducted . . . He wrote during the years of the Depression that 'a newspaper must have soul as well as brain, brawn as well as mechanism . . . There must be a policy applied with patient care, of unremitting service to the public.' Again in 1940 he reminded the paper's reporting staff by memo that 'throughout its history the *Herald* has been no respecter of persons, bodies, institutions or

governments, except in so far as it considered they were following the public interest. It should be borne in mind, of course, that the news is expected to be complete and is not expected to be moulded in conformity with the known editorial policy of the *Herald*, political or otherwise.' This clarity of mind, integrity and determined character marked all that Warwick Fairfax said and did . . .

Next in the order of service was a reading by Annalise Thomas from the manuscript of her father's last book, a work of theological speculation entitled *Purpose*. 'I prefer an incomprehensible God to a meaningless world', Sir Warwick had written.

> The only other course I have is to relapse into my own ego which would be hell. Not, of course, completely incomprehensible since the key to it is love. But God's love does not exclude suffering inflicted by the evil of other men or by natural causes or death. It does not exclude the spiritual and emotional suffering which is the consequence of our falling away from the will of God. And it does not exclude death, which comes to the young, the innocent and to all, which cannot be in God's judgment the evil it appears to us.

From the Cathedral Sir Warwick's funeral procession wound its way out of the central city, with all traffic lights turned to green, along New South Head Road and through Double Bay, where Sir Warwick's Phantom V Rolls-Royce—driven by his chauffeur and carrying Lady Fairfax, James, Warwick, Charles and Anna—halted for half a minute outside Fairwater. Then on it went through Rose

Bay to South Head Cemetery where, after a burial service, the coffin was lowered into its grave beside a tall granite cross.

This family burial ground affords a glimpse of the ocean, that stretch of it just south of the Heads upon which, in the year 1838, one might easily have seen the sails of a ship bringing John and Sarah Fairfax and their four children from England to Sydney. John and Sarah were not themselves buried at South Head, but eleven of their descendants were. On the base of the granite cross, where Sir Warwick's name was soon to be chiselled, were the names of Sir James Reading Fairfax, his wife Lucy, Sir James Oswald Fairfax, his wife Mabel, Geoffrey Evan Fairfax, his sister Mary Elizabeth Fairfax, Dr Edward Wilfred Fairfax, his wife Mary Marguerite, John Hubert Fairfax, and his wife Ruth. Our narrative will now turn back briefly to some of those earlier flowers of the field.

2
Heralds

I

The Fairfaxes came to Australia from Warwickshire, a county long regarded as the heart of England, not only because of its geographical position, but also for such evocative connotations as Shakespeare, Lady Godiva, Kenilworth Castle, Rugby School and the Forest of Arden. The heart of Warwickshire itself is Warwick, and it was in this quintessentially English town beside the River Avon that John Fairfax began his life on 24 October 1805. His family name was of Anglo-Saxon origin, meaning 'fair hair,' and so too was the name of his birthplace, which meant 'dairy farm beside a weir'.

If there were Fairfaxes on that ancient farm, nothing about them has survived. John Fairfax's earliest known ancestor, a miller named Robert Fairfax, was buried in 1545 at Barford, a village four miles down the Avon from Warwick. More than a century later, a Barford household of the same name became one of the wonders of England. 'There are now four generations of Fairfaxes in Barford', wrote the rector of St Peter's, Barford, in 1647,

> and three of them double, viz., Samuel Fairfax as aforesaid; Mr John and Elizabeth, his father and mother; Mr John and Eleanor, his grandfather and grandmother; Mr Richard and Alice, his great-grandfather and great-grandmother. Not one of these three pairs hath been twice married and each of them is an honour to marriage. They all dwell together in one house and eat together at one table. The like hereunto is hardly, if at all, to be found.

Twelve years later this remarkable household was celebrated in the Latin and English verse of Edward Leigh's *England Described*:

> Fairfax the fourth is born! A gallant boy;
> Father's, grandfather's great-grandfather's joy.
> Under one roof these dwell with their three wives,
> And at one table eat what Heaven gives.

Kindred though they were, these worthy Fairfaxes were not in the direct line of descent from the first Robert of the sixteenth century to the John of this narrative. They bear useful witness, however, to the traditions of stability and godliness inherited by John Fairfax and transmitted by him to succeeding generations. From Robert Fairfax the line of descent proceeded through two Johns to a third, who in the first half of the eighteenth century was Mayor of Warwick. The Mayor had two children—an elder son, who inherited and squandered his estate, and a younger son, William Fairfax.

William was apprenticed to a flax-dresser, and little else is known about him. His own son, another William Fairfax, worked in the building and furnishing trades at Warwick and married a woman of firm Dissenting religious conviction, Elizabeth Jesson. Elizabeth induced her husband to follow her example by leaving the Established Church of England and joining the Independent Chapel. She was also to exercise a strong religious influence upon their two children—another William Fairfax, who went into his father's trades, and more particularly the younger son, John.

Dissenters of various sects had separated themselves from the Established Church principally because they wanted chapels free from State interference, and because, within their chapels, they wanted congregations untrammelled by ecclesiastical hierarchy. Their rejection of control was a spiritual expression of economic free enterprise, holding to what one theologian termed the Three Protestant Onlies: 'The word of God only, the work of the Holy Spirit only, and the sacrifice of Christ only'. Such independence was likely to bring rewards in this world as well as the next. It was therefore not surprising that the Independent Chapel, or Congregational Church as it became known, consisted in the main of respectable people of the middle class.

John Fairfax grew up in Warwick, going to school there until the age of twelve, when he was apprenticed to a local bookseller, librarian and printer. In his early twenties he worked in London as a typesetter. Returning to Warwickshire in 1827 he started his own business as a printer and stationer—not at Warwick but at Leamington Priors, a newly popular spa resort only two miles away—and married the daughter of another Dissenting Warwick family, Sarah Reading. Leamington had everything to attract the patronage of fashionable society except a newspaper to bruit the excellence of its mineral springs and hospitality. John Fairfax tried to remedy that by establishing the *Leamington Spa Sketch Book*. While promising to advance the interest of the town, he also said that his work would be 'strictly independent; and though he will endeavour to obtain the good will of all, he will not sacrifice the public good by overlooking public nuisances or official negligence'.

Although the threepenny weekly *Sketch Book* was 'a faithful and Fair fact recorder', as one contributor observed, it recorded little more than the comings and goings of nobility and gentry. After four months it was succeeded by a more thoroughgoing newspaper, the weekly *Leamington Spa Courier*, a sevenpenny broadsheet of four pages printed by James Sharp and John Fairfax. But although the *Courier* has continued to the present day, Fairfax's name disappeared from its imprint in December 1828.

For the next seven years he carried on business in Leamington as a printer, bookseller and stationer. He became a deacon of the Independent Chapel, and was one of the principal founders of a new chapel—a building 'neat, substantial and convenient', as one Dissenting clergyman declared, avoiding 'the extremes of a bald and naked meanness on the one hand and a gaudy and superfluous elegance on the other', and according well with 'the dignified simplicity of that system of ecclesiastical policy' which was to be maintained there.

In 1835 John Fairfax returned to journalism as co-proprietor of the *Leamington Chronicle*. Again the partnership was short-lived, but this time it was the other partner's name which disappeared, leaving Fairfax the sole owner in June 1836. Unlike the *Courier*, which was addressing itself to a Tory readership, the *Chronicle* gave free play to principles which, although not Whiggish in a party sense, were 'decidedly liberal'. Reform was the order of the day, and under Fairfax's proprietorship the *Chronicle* wanted to see the principles of the 1832 Reform Act worked out in every department of the State—financial, civil, military and ecclesiastical.

In his early thirties, by which time he was the father of three children, John Fairfax—according to the later recollection of a contemporary at Leamington—was

> firmly knit and upright, with a head of hair in which no trace appeared to denote advancing age . . . brave of heart, of sound and robust intelligence, transparently honest, and unswerving in obedience to a high moral principle that placed him at a disadvantage among the pettier struggles in the midst of which his local lot was cast.

A fellow Dissenter, the Reverend Joseph Beasley, remembered him many years later as being 'pre-eminently the accomplished man of business and the faithful servant of Christ', a combination far from rare in the denomination to which Beasley and Fairfax belonged.

> I remember well the lively interest with which he was wont to quote a saying which he heard from the lips of the Rev. J. A. James to a busy and successful tradesman, 'It is well, Sir, to be busy for both worlds' . . . He believed that any young man may succeed if he chooses. 'Let him,' he would say, 'be humble and learn, let him be willing to work and wait, let him show himself a man of integrity, let him be a true follower of Christ and God will not suffer his life to be a failure.

This confidence was sorely tested during John Fairfax's proprietorship of the *Chronicle* by some protracted and costly libel litigation. His God did not suffer him to fail in court, but the cost of having to defend himself successfully, not once but twice, proved to be financially crippling.

So ended his life in England. Emigration was a natural enough response to such an unexpected turn of events. But why did Fairfax choose as his destination a remote colony to which Britain was still transporting convicts? In the absence of any recorded explanation, the most plausible reason is that one of his nephews, Alfred Fairfax, had travelled to New South Wales the year before, and was still living there.

The party bound for Sydney consisted of John and Sarah Fairfax, who were then aged thirty-three and thirty, Sarah being seven months pregnant; their children, Charles John, aged nine, Emily, six, and James Reading, three; John's widowed mother, Mrs Elizabeth Fairfax; and Sarah's brother, James Reading. They travelled as unassisted steerage passengers on board the barque *Lady Fitzherbert*, which sailed from Gravesend on 17 May. Somewhere between Tenerife and Cape Town, Sarah Fairfax gave birth to a son, Richard. The *Lady Fitzherbert* had a reasonably good passage, and on the morning of 25 September she came within sight of South Head.

Later in life John Fairfax told his children that at this penultimate moment of the voyage, as he looked at the high cliffs of Sydney, his courage temporarily failed him and he broke down under the thought of bringing his family to a land so strange and seemingly with so little promise. This was the only time he had ever given way to despondency, he said, and he quickly overcame the feeling by his trust in God.

Busy for both worlds, he had entered a lottery for the ship's date of arrival and it was his ticket that won the steerage passengers' £5 prize. Added to the only other money in his possession, this windfall brought his total capital to £10.

The colony to which Fairfax came in 1838 was observing its fiftieth anniversary. No longer the rude and brutal settlement of earlier years, though chained convicts could still be seen in its streets, Sydney nowadays surprised the visitor with its size, neatness and industrious activity. It had five main newspapers, the most successful of which was a seven-year-old Tory tri-weekly called the *Sydney Herald*. John Fairfax moved his family into a house in Gloucester Street, conveniently close to that part of the town where most printing offices were located, and found his first employment as a typesetter for the *Commercial Journal and Advertiser*.

The early months of the Fairfaxes' new life were blighted by the death of their baby, but in February 1839 John improved the family's situation by becoming librarian at the Australian Subscription

Library, a job which enabled him to meet many of Sydney's leading citizens, and which also left him sufficient time to undertake other work.

Within two years of his arrival, Fairfax had made a place for himself in the printing and Congregational communities of Sydney. Once again his thoughts turned to newspaper proprietorship—this time to the colony's only daily paper, the *Sydney Herald*. The *Herald* had taken its name, meaning 'messenger', from the *Glasgow Herald*, for which one of its co-founders had formerly worked. It was thriving commercially, and the ultra-Tory editorial policy of its founders—Alfred Ward Stephens, Frederick Michael Stokes and William McGarvie—had recently become slightly less reactionary. The *Herald*'s two mottoes, taken from Pope's imitations of Horace, were 'In moderation placing all my glory, While Tories call me Whig—and Whigs a Tory', and 'Sworn to no Master, of no Sect am I'. Although these had often been ignored by the paper, they chimed well with some of the non-party sentiments which Fairfax had espoused in the *Leamington Chronicle*.

On 8 February 1841 the last remaining founder of the *Herald*, Frederick Stokes, sold out to the paper's parliamentary and court reporter, 27-year-old Charles Kemp, and John Fairfax. The purchase price was the considerable sum of £10 000, but Stokes facilitated the transaction by extending long-term credit. The partners were also helped to meet their first payment by such businessmen and Congregational deacons as David Jones, a Welsh merchant who had been in Sydney for five years, Joseph Thompson, a stock and share broker, and Ambrose Foss, an auctioneer.

Kemp, who had come to Australia with his parents at the age of twelve, was a man of shrewd business acumen and High Anglican faith. Clearly his ecclesiastical principles would have been an embarrassment to Fairfax in his own church. Yet the two men were good friends as well as fellow heralds, and for six years they lived in adjoining houses. Kemp controlled the editorial side of the business, and Fairfax looked after the printing side.

With the closing of the rival *Australian* in 1848, the *Sydney Morning Herald* (as it had been renamed in 1842) became the colony's oldest newspaper. It was only seventeen years of age, but some deemed the paper old beyond its years. John Fairfax's Leamington liberalism had undergone a sea change; whether because of middle age or antipodean conditions, his outlook had hardened into something more like Toryism than the moderation of Pope's motto, which incidentally had been dropped from the *Herald*'s masthead in 1847.

At about this time, after the *Herald* had been deprecating 'the tyranny of mobs' (by which it meant democracy), the satirical journal *Heads of the People* referred to 'Dear lachrymose old Granny' who failed to see that 'a mob-cap is a cap of liberty'. This was the first known use of the nickname to which critics of the *Herald* resorted with increasing frequency during the 1850s, and which readers eventually adopted as an affectionate, if sometimes exasperated, form of address.

Under Kemp and Fairfax, Granny Herald set her face against certain inevitable changes for what seemed to her, and to most of her readers, good and sufficient reason. To liberals and radicals she seemed to display the fussiness and selfishness that sometimes accompany old age. But to those of her own persuasion (and there were many of them) her staunch upholding of Protestant Christianity, British monarchy, the rule of law, middle-class values, private property and free enterprise capitalism seemed rather to provide the comforting reassurance of a wise old grandmother. By the time she turned twenty-one, in 1852, Granny Herald had a healthy circulation of 4000.

Kemp and Fairfax had by then, in Kemp's words, 'amassed a comfortable fortune'. For some time Kemp had been intending to withdraw from the partnership and devote himself to other business activities and politics. On 30 September 1853 he sold his interest in the *Herald* to John Fairfax for £17 500. Fairfax took his son Charles into partnership, and during the following year appointed the *Herald*'s first official editor—a Congregational minister, the Reverend John West.

In 1858 the main part of the family moved from Macquarie Street to Ginahgulla, a large two-storeyed Gothic Revival house of brick and stone which John Fairfax built on the beautiful and sparsely settled eminence of Bellevue Hill, overlooking the harbour. Set upon several acres of cleared land, Ginahgulla had its own dairy and a dining room spacious enough to seat thirty people for meals and two hundred at a musicale or chapel service.For some years, in partial emulation of the long-lived Fairfaxes of Barford, this large household included two grandmothers—the widowed mothers of John and Sarah.

When entertaining at home, the family would sing around the piano (John's favourite party song was the parliamentary-sounding 'Mr Speaker, Tho' 'Tis Late'), and play various parlour games. At such gatherings it was customary for guests to record their personal tastes in what was called a Characteristic Album. John Fairfax's entry made suitably wholesome reading: 'Favourite virtue, Truth; Favourite author, Scott; Favourite hero, Nelson; Favourite air, *Angels Ever Bright and Fair*, Favourite motto, Pray Without Season'.

Religion was second nature to the man. He served for many years as a deacon at the Pitt Street Congregational Church, was superintendent of the Sunday School there until his fiftieth birthday, and in 1875 he laid the foundation stone for a Congregational church in Woollahra.

In 1856 he contested a by-election for one of the Sydney seats in the new Legislative Assembly of New South Wales. He stood as a Liberal (according to some of his opponents, 'Conservative' would have been more accurate), and was defeated by a Catholic candidate, W. B. Dalley. Any sense of political failure which Fairfax may have felt would surely have been assuaged by commercial success. The *Herald*'s circulation of 6600 was half as large again as the combined circulation of all other Sydney newspapers, and in the wider sphere of the British Empire it was third only to those of the *Times* and *Telegraph* in London.

In June 1856 the business moved to a new building—on a triangular site bounded by Pitt, Hunter and O'Connell streets—which was to be its home for the next seventy-three years. On the last day of that year John Fairfax took his second son, James, into partnership with himself and Charles on a 50 per cent—25 per cent—25 per cent basis. Next day the *Herald*'s imprint changed to 'John Fairfax & Sons', and thenceforth the business was a family partnership in that name.

John Fairfax was well served by the second generation. Charles was a particularly strong force in the firm, but his years were numbered. In the seven years of life left to him, during which he was principal lieutenant to his father and mentor to his younger brother, the business continued to expand. In 1860 John Fairfax & Sons freed itself from the last encumbrance of flat-bed printing by the installation of a Richard Hoe rotary press imported from New York. This printed both the *Herald* and the *Sydney Mail*, a threepenny weekly which had been launched that year at Charles Fairfax's instigation. The *Mail*, intended particularly for country readers, was the first of its kind in New South Wales. Its format and content were to change considerably during its long and successful life; but even in its infancy, when it was merely a résumé of the *Herald*, it achieved a circulation of 5000.

Each year it was the family's custom to gather at Ginahgulla on New Year's Day, which happened also to be Charles Fairfax's birthday. The gathering on 1 January 1863 for his thirty-fourth birthday was to have been a particularly festive occasion, for Charles and his family had only recently returned from an 18-month sojourn in England. But the gathering never took place. On Boxing Day Charles visited his cousin and brother-in-law, Alfred Fairfax, at Burwood. After lunch Alfred was called to a nearby suburb on business. When Charles offered to accompany him, Alfred said there were two saddle horses in the stable, and that he should take the bay horse, as the black one might be too much for him. Alfred left first in a dogcart, and looking back he saw Charles following on the black horse. It was already playing up. The horse broke into a gallop, and Charles was thrown on to a heap of blue metal at the side of the road. Later in the afternoon he died at his cousin's home.

This was the first personal tragedy John and Sarah Fairfax had suffered for many years, and they were severely affected by it. Their third son, Edward, joined the family firm and in 1865 he too was admitted to partnership. During the next few years the *Herald* continued to grow while its main competitor—the *Empire*, founded by Henry Parkes and later revived by Samuel Bennett—declined and fell. In 1875 Bennett incorporated the *Empire* in his *Evening News*, leaving the *Herald* in sole occupation of the morning field for a few years.

In 1871 the Fairfaxes' only daughter, Emily Ross, was killed in a coach accident. Eighteen months later came the deaths of two of their oldest friends, Mr and Mrs David Jones, within three weeks of one another. 'They were the first on our arrival to say "Come and take a cup of tea,"' wrote John Fairfax, 'and were always kind and friendly. Now I and dear Mamma stand Nos 1 and 2 in our church roll. Who next?'

Sarah Fairfax died in August 1875, and John was not long in following her. In his seventy-second year he became ill and took to his bed at Ginahgulla. James visited him every day, and read to him from the Bible and the *Herald*. One morning, after reading a Psalm, James opened the *Herald* only to be stopped by his father. 'No thank you, James', he said. 'I have done with that.' He died the following day, 16 June 1877.

Pitt Street Congregational Church was draped in black for its senior deacon's funeral service, and the organist played John Fairfax's favourite air from Handel's oratorio, *Theodora*.

> Angels ever bright and fair,
> Take, O take me to your care.
> Speed to your own courts my flight
> Clad in robes of virgin white.

On the first, worldly stage of that flight the funeral cortege moved slowly up Pitt Street towards the mortuary station at Redfern: first the hearse and three family carriages; then the staff of the *Herald* office, numbering between 300 and 400, all on foot; and finally a line of carriages containing the Lieutenant-Governor, ministers of government and religion, members of parliament, and private citizens. From Redfern the mourners proceeded by train to Rookwood necropolis, and on foot to the family vault where Sarah and other Fairfaxes had already been interred.

John Fairfax's estate was sworn at less than £80 000, which suggests that he had transferred more than a few assets before his death.

The value of the business and its annual profit at this time are not known, but about 70 per cent of Saturday's *Herald* was classified advertising. In 1873, after the collapse of a friend's gold-mining venture, John Fairfax had remarked with satisfaction: 'After all, the *Herald* is the best mine'. James and Edward inherited their father's interest in the business equally, each becoming a half-owner. But although Edward Fairfax spent twenty-four years of his life as a joint proprietor, he always acknowledged his elder brother's seniority.

II

James Reading Fairfax brought a familiar brand of benevolence and authority to the position of senior proprietor, which he occupied for forty-two years. Built even more sturdily than his father, and cutting an almost regal figure with his silvery Edwardian beard and moustache, James was a pillar not only of the Congregational Church, but also of Sydney's commercial, social and artistic life. He was a director of the Bank of New South Wales, the Australian Mutual Provident Society, the Perpetual Trustee Company and Burns Philp & Co Ltd. He served repeatedly as president of the Young Men's Christian Association in Sydney, and was one of the founders of the Boys' Brigade and chairman of the Ragged Schools Committee; he was a connoisseur and patron of art, particularly of drawing and sculpture, being one of the founders and an early president of the National Art Gallery of New South Wales; he was president of the Royal Sydney Golf Club for fourteen years, and Commodore of the Royal Sydney Yacht Squadron for fifteen years.

In 1884 James and his wife Lucy built a summer residence in the southern highlands—Woodside, at Moss Vale, a red brick villa nearly as large as Ginahgulla. Family and staff moved there by train after Christmas, leaving Ginahgulla closed, with all its furniture swathed in white calico, and stayed there until Easter. An advance party would be sent ahead to prepare Woodside for its summer life by unswathing the furniture and airing the rooms, and likewise to Ginahgulla for the return to Sydney.

These annual migrations were logistical exercises of some complexity, but nothing compared to the family's periodic expeditions abroad. James and Lucy, accompanied at first by all their seven children, made four extended tours—in 1872 for one year, 1881 for two and a half years, 1889 for two and a half years, and 1899 for three years. They visited every continent of the world, every country of Europe, Palestine, Russia, Japan, the United States and parts of South America. During the 1881 expedition, their second and third sons, Geoffrey Evan and James Oswald, entered Balliol College,

Oxford, thus beginning a family tradition which was to continue in later generations. Both rowed for their college, and both later went to the Bar at the Inner Temple.

For this sojourn abroad, James left John Fairfax & Sons in the hands of his brother and a general manager, the first ever appointed by the family from outside its own ranks. Hugh George, appointed in 1878, was a former general manager of the Melbourne *Argus* and the best-known Australian newspaper executive of his day. During his term of office the *Herald* was deprived of its short-lived monopoly in the morning field by the appearance in 1879 of the liberal *Sydney Daily Telegraph*. It was soon rivalling the *Herald*'s circulation, though not its advertising revenue.

The unexpected death of Hugh George in 1886, from a heart attack while visiting Melbourne on business, helped bring to a head certain changes then being contemplated by James Reading Fairfax. Although the proficiency of the late general manager had never been in doubt, the senior proprietor had at times wondered whether perhaps he was *too* proficient for the family's good. 'My impression', wrote James to Edward, who was visiting England at the time of George's death,

> is that it would be better to keep the control in our own hands and that we have no business manager again but let our sons gradually get the reins. There is a risk which I fancy you must see that a General Manager may assume more than the proprietors care for, the policy for the future I would suggest is that we have thoroughly competent heads to each department but that the firm shall be the general manager of the whole.

As Edward Fairfax seemed to be tiring of business life, and finding London more congenial than Sydney, James decided to buy his brother's interest in the business and bring in three of his sons—Charles, Geoff and Jim. Charles had already decided to join the company, and James now asked Geoff and Jim to choose between law and journalism.

What he proposed was that Charles should take charge of the accounting and clerical departments of the firm; Geoff, if he chose journalism, should control the mechanical and technical departments, including telegraphic communication; and Jim should devote all his attention to editorial work, particularly for the *Herald*.

Charles became a partner in 1888. In the following year Edward Fairfax '[freed] himself from the cares of one of the most exacting of public positions' and took his family to England, where he was to spend the remaining sixteen years of his life. At the same time Geoffrey and James, aged twenty-eight and twenty-six respectively, did as their father had wanted and became partners with him and Charles.

Such was the senior proprietor's confidence in his elder sons and staff that in 1889 he and his wife, accompanied by their 31-year-old daughter Mary, embarked upon another long stay in England and Europe. Their fourth son, Harold, was at Balliol, and the other two boys, Hubert and Wilfred, were at Bath College. Settling in London for the winter, James engaged in a busy round of duties and pleasures: attending art exhibitions, purchasing replicas of classical sculpture for the New South Wales Gallery, visiting Edison's rooms in South Kensington for a demonstration of the phonograph, keeping in touch with Fleet Street and Sydney, and laying a foundation stone in Leamington Spa for an addition to the church which his father had helped to found half a century before.

With the coming of spring in 1890 James, Lucy and Mary—accompanied by a courier and a maid—set off for the French Riviera and Italy. James had a good knowledge of Europe, and few of its artistic achievements escaped his appreciative notice. It was his intention to present the New South Wales Gallery with a plaster cast of one of Europe's medieval church doors. In France he inspected the cathedrals at Rouen and Chartres; thence onward by easy stages to Cannes, Nice and Florence. In Florence, at the Church of San Giovanni, he was overwhelmed by the great bronze doors of the Baptistery—especially the northern one, named 'The Gates of Paradise'.

Created over a period of sixteen years in the mid fifteenth century by Lorenzo Ghiberti, this masterpiece consists of ten bas-relief panels portraying separate Old Testament scenes, starting with the Garden of Eden, the Fall and Expulsion, and ending with the Judgment of Solomon. James wrote to his fellow gallery trustees, offering to donate a plaster replica of the door, which was available from a studio in Florence. The trustees cabled their acceptance, and four months later 'The Gates of Paradise' were shipped to Sydney.

This white plaster door, five metres high and three metres wide, was hailed as the most important donation yet made to the Gallery. It was installed in the fine arts room and given a more authentic appearance with bronze paint. But as public taste changed, and the Gallery's collection became larger, 'The Gates of Paradise' were displayed less and less prominently. During the 1970s all ten panels of Ghiberti's extraordinary work—Adam and Eve, Cain and Abel, Noah, Abraham, Moses, Joshua and the rest—were relegated to a storage shed. There they were to languish until providentially, as will be recounted later in this narrative, their day of resurrection would arrive.

In 1891 the senior proprietor rejoined his three eldest sons in Sydney. Charles Fairfax spent nine more years with the firm, then followed his uncle's example by retiring and settling in England. Geoffrey and James remained co-proprietors with Sir James Reading Fairfax (he was knighted in 1898), and it was in this triumvirate that proprietorial authority mainly resided for half a century after John Fairfax's death.

The two brothers married two sisters—Lena and Mabel, daughters of Captain Francis Hixson, R.N., Captain Commanding the New South Wales Naval Brigade, and his wife Sarah, who was the great-granddaughter of a Third Fleet convict and emancipist entrepreneur, Simeon Lord. Their weddings, in 1891 and 1892, took place not at one of the Congregational churches still being attended by Sir James and his daughter Mary, but at St Andrew's Cathedral, for the brothers had transferred their allegiance to the Church of England. To anyone as much a part of the Sydney establishment as they were, religious dissent must have seemed out of tune with social conformity. Geoff and Jim Fairfax belonged inherently to the privileged community of the eastern suburbs. Most of their married lives were to be spent in the two adjoining homes which they purchased below Bellevue Hill, Elaine and Fairwater.

In spite of his former concern that Hugh George might have been taking too much upon himself, Sir James soon acknowledged that the firm could no longer do without a general manager. That position was filled in 1887 by Samuel Cook, a former parliamentary reporter for the *Herald* and editor of a short-lived Fairfax afternoon paper, the *Echo*. In appearance Cook was not unlike either his predecessor or the chief proprietor. Indeed, if there was a peculiarly *Sydney Morning Herald* physiognomy in the late nineteenth century, its purest form was surely represented by the upright, solid and bearded figures of George, Cook and Sir James.

The greatest change under Cook's management was the mechanization of typesetting. Despite the economic and financial depression of the early 1890s, which the company survived without serious disadvantage, Hattersley typesetting and type-replacing machines were introduced in 1895, effecting a reduction of forty-five employees in the composing room at Hunter Street. New rates of pay for mechanical setting were negotiated with the Chapel, and for the first time in the company's history women were employed in the composing room to replace type in the Hattersley magazines. The Fairfax Chapel protested strongly against the employment of female replacers, which its membership regarded as only one step removed from the employment of female compositors at less than the male rate. As it turned out, however, women were not employed as compositors in the Fairfax office until the late twentieth century, and those employed to load the Hattersley machines were made redundant in 1901 by the Monoline, which did away with the need to replace type.

Cook was succeeded in 1907 by William George Conley, who had joined the *Herald* as a 30-year-old reporter in 1898. Sir James was still the senior proprietor, but by this time he was in his mid-seventies and content to leave most of the firm's business to a third generation of heralds, 'Mr J. O.' and 'Mr Geoffrey'.

III

Although two years younger than his brother, and somewhat reserved in contrast to the other's friendly and convivial nature, James Oswald Fairfax was the more forceful of the two. He was said to have mellowed late in life, but in this period before World War I he was distinctly austere. Once, offended by the unexpected sight of an uncouth boxer and his trainer in the *Herald* office, he ordered the sporting staff to cease covering that sport. Mr J. O. had a good head for business, but a poor voice, which he seemed to dread hearing. Perhaps for this reason he spoke in a concise manner which could sometimes be unnerving to others. Mr Geoffrey, on the other hand, was a willing talker who liked engaging staff in mutually enjoyable conversation. He drank freely at lunch and dinner—certainly more than Mr J. O., but not so much that his enjoyment of life was impaired.

During the war, in 1916, the partnership of John Fairfax & Sons had become a limited company, John Fairfax & Sons Ltd, with the three equal partners becoming permanent directors, and two of Sir James's younger sons becoming 'ordinary directors' without shares. These younger members of the third generation were John Hubert Fraser Fairfax, a grazier with properties in New South Wales and Queensland, and Dr Edward Wilfred Fairfax, a medical practitioner who joined the Australian Army Medical Corps and served as senior physician at the 1st Australian General Hospital in France.

There were probably two reasons for this change: conversion to a company would limit liability in the event of business failure, and would facilitate the transfer of interests in the business by means of shares. There was nothing to be lost, either, for companies were not yet taxed in respect of income distributed to shareholders, as they would be later in the century.

The years of peace began sombrely for John Fairfax & Sons Ltd with the death of its senior proprietor, and an annual loss—possibly the first ever sustained by the Fairfaxes in Sydney. Sir James died at Ginahgulla on 28 March 1919, and after a funeral service at the sandstone Congregational Church in Jersey Road, Woollahra, he was buried in the new Fairfax family vault at South Head cemetery. A stained glass window was later erected to his memory in the Jersey

Road church, where he had been a deacon for forty-five years. It showed the Saviour, bearded like Sir James, restoring sight to the blind man Bartimaeus; above, two angels bright and fair; and below, the words 'Who went about doing good'.

Sir James left Ginahgulla to his wife, and after her death, which came six years later, to his only daughter, Mary, who did not marry. His shares in the company he divided between five of his six surviving children. The only one not to benefit from his father's will was Charles in London. After this distribution of shares, the company was still firmly controlled by J. O. and Geoffrey Fairfax, each holding 15 704 shares compared with a combined holding of only 6584 by the three other shareholders: J. H. F. Fairfax, Dr Wilfred Fairfax and Miss Mary Fairfax.

The trading loss for 1918–19 was caused mainly by a sharp rise in the price of newsprint during the war, and the fact that the company waited too long before increasing the *Herald*'s cover charge from 1d to 1½d. There were no more trading losses, even though the price of newsprint continued to rise. From 1920 onwards the company declared a dividend of 10 per cent every year, taking out £38 000 from each year's trading surplus. These dividends, combined with directors' fees and other forms of income, would have placed the two principal proprietors among the highest income earners in Australia.

During Conley's general managership the *Herald* became known as a 'river of gold', brim-full with almost the whole of Sydney's classified advertising, and the company erected a new building for itself on an enlargement of the Hunter Street site. A new triangular building of twelve levels, with presses in an excavated basement and a curved portico of polished Tuscan columns at the front apex, was erected in three stages between 1922 and 1929.

Sir James (J.O. had been knighted in 1926) and 'Lady Jim', as Mabel Fairfax was known to family and friends, were almost as prominent in business and society as the previous Sir James and his wife had been. Like his father, Sir James was a director of the Australian Mutual Provident Society and the Perpetual Trustee Company, and chairman of the Boys' Brigade. He too enjoyed sailing and golf, and he was one of Sydney's early motorists, driving a six horse-power De Dion in 1903. Lady Jim was an excellent golfer (she won the Royal Sydney associates' championship four times), and a devoted gardener at Fairwater and Sospel, their holiday home at Leura, in the Blue Mountains.

In 1927 the board of John Fairfax & Sons Ltd was enlarged from two directors to four. W. G. Conley resigned from the general managership, which remained vacant for the time being, and was appointed to the board, where doubtless he also retained some of the chief executive's function. The company's capital was increased by 1000 £10 shares, and these were issued to Conley on the understanding that he would retain them only so long as he remained a director. The second new director was Sir James's 25-year-old son, the same Warwick Oswald Fairfax with whom this book began. In him we reach a fourth generation, and a thread which will run through our narrative fabric for the next sixty years.

'Fairfax the fourth is born! A gallant boy; Father's, grandfather's, great-grandfather's joy . . .'. The seventeenth-century couplet applied equally well to the Fairfaxes of Australia, for in Warwick Fairfax resided the traditions of father, grandfather and great-grandfather, and the hopes of his own generation. It had been obvious that he would become the dominant Fairfax shareholder, for of the two major shareholders since Sir James Reading Fairfax's death in 1919, Geoffrey Fairfax had no issue, and Sir James Oswald had only the one child. No one had foreseen, however, that Warwick Fairfax would have to assume prime responsibility so early as he did, or that he would have to do it bereft of all his predecessors on the board.

It would soon become tragically clear that the start of Warwick Fairfax's career coincided with the end of an old era. The *Sydney Morning Herald* was approaching its first centenary, and as if to dispose of the old establishment before a new century began, death came successively to Sir James Reading Fairfax, W. G. Conley, and Geoffrey Fairfax.

Warwick Fairfax was the only survivor of that board, and he represented a distinct departure from the family mould. The last three generations of Fairfax men had tended towards middle stature and rather heavy features; Fairfax the fourth was slender and tall (six feet two inches) with the face of a scholar or perhaps a young priest. It was a long, introspective face with wide-set intelligent blue eyes and a large angular nose. He resembled his mother more than his father, and she had resembled her mother, so perhaps there was something of his maternal grandmother's family, the Lords, in his heredity.

As a child and young man he was shy; a slow worker, but a careful and industrious one. His parents were strict with him. They had high expectations and he tried hard to please them. Warwick spent a considerable part of his childhood on nearby Bellevue Hill, where he received his early education at the house of the Stephen family (he shared a tutor with Alastair Stephen, the great-grandson of a former Chief Justice of New South Wales, who later in life would become legal adviser to John Fairfax & Sons), and where he sometimes stayed with his grandparents, who were still living at Ginahgulla with unabated Victorian propriety. Each morning before breakfast the entire Ginahgulla household, including servants, would assemble in the dining room, where Sir James would open Fletcher's *Family Devotion*, containing a short service for every day in the year.

Only after fifteen minutes of psalms, lessons and prayer would breakfast begin.

At the age of eleven Warwick was taken to England by his parents and enrolled for a year at Warden House, a preparatory school in Deal, Kent. In 1915 he started at Geelong Church of England Grammar School, where he spent the next five years, distinguishing himself at classical studies but not at sport. At first he was known as 'Tinny', a nickname based upon the assumption that because he was both rich and shy he was 'a little tin god'.

After passing the Leaving Certificate in 1917, he took it twice more with further subjects in 1918 and 1919, gaining second class honours in Latin and Greek in his final year. His pre-ordained destination was his father's college at Oxford, where he enrolled in 1921.

While at Balliol, Warwick kept in touch with the company through its London office, which had been established in 1923 by a rising young *Herald* journalist sent from Sydney, Rupert Henderson. These two could scarcely have been more different in temperament: one a slightly gauche, dreamy patrician; the other an assertive, earthy little live wire. They found a common interest in politics, however, and whenever Warwick visited London he called on Rupert Henderson in Fleet Street. The association formed in this way was to become steadily more important to both men in the years ahead.

Warwick Fairfax graduated in 1925 with a Second in Philosophy, Politics and Economics. A First may have eluded him, but ever after he was grateful to Balliol for bringing out his aptitude for philosophy. He joined the staff of the *Herald* in September of that year, became a director in 1927, and on 24 March 1928 married Marcie Elizabeth Wilson, the only child of a Sydney barrister. Readers of the social pages were already aware of this match: according to a report of someone else's recent wedding, 'Mr Warwick Fairfax, looking as if he carried the whole weight of England's policy with relation to China on his young shoulders, chaperoned his fiancee, Miss Betty Wilson, a dainty and girlish figure in parchment tucked voile embroidered in tangerine'. The Fairfax wedding took place at St Mark's Church of England, Darling Point, and the *Herald*'s full column report of it was studded with names illustrious in Sydney society. Ten days later the couple sailed for Europe.

Their honeymoon was brought to a sudden end by the news that Sir James had died of a heart attack while playing golf at Royal Sydney. Seven months later Conley died of blood poisoning, a complication following the extraction of an infected tooth, and in April 1930 came the death of Geoffrey Fairfax, whose health had been deteriorating since his wife's death four years earlier. Geoffrey's shares in the company were bequeathed in equal parts to his two younger brothers, J. H. F. Fairfax and Dr Wilfred Fairfax, and to his nephew Warwick.

Dr Fairfax and J. H. F. Fairfax joined the board, and on 30 June 1930 a meeting of shareholders resolved—on the motion of Warwick's mother, seconded by his aunt, Miss Mary Fairfax—that Warwick Fairfax be appointed managing director. After distribution of the shares formerly held by the three deceased directors, the company's 38 998 £10 shares were held exclusively by the Fairfax family.

Warwick Fairfax personally held 35 per cent of the company's shares, and his mother held her 7802 shares (half of Sir James Oswald's holding, the other half having gone to Warwick) in the form of a trust which on her death would go to her son. From Sir James's estate Lady Fairfax also received Fairwater, and she continued to live there until her death in 1965. In 1931 Warwick Fairfax built his own house on Bellevue Hill, not far from Ginahgulla, where Miss Mary Fairfax lived. The new house was named Barford, in memory of the Warwickshire village once renowned for a household of four Fairfax generations.

IV

For much of the half century between the *Herald*'s centenary in 1931 and its sesquicentenary in 1981 the senior representatives of the Fairfax family and management were Warwick Fairfax and Rupert Henderson. It took them seven years to establish their uneasy yet enduring alliance, but once Henderson became general manager there was no holding him. The river of gold gathered one tributary after another until, like the modest Avon and other Warwickshire streams turning into the great River Severn, it became a multi-media confluence in full spate.

The relative status of the general manager and the managing director had been defined grandiloquently in a centennial history, edited by Warwick Fairfax himself:

> There [in the front room on the first floor of the *Herald* building] sits one man, and in his hands are gathered up, taut and responsive to his every touch, the strings that operate every part of the complex whole. A word from him, and action springs that may reach the uttermost ends of the earth. He is the General Manager—the supreme executive authority over every aspect of the paper's activities, literary, mechanical, advertising and all else; and behind him, representing the family that owns the papers, is the Managing Director—ultimate authority for every vital decision on all matters whatsoever affecting the policy, contents and conduct of the *Herald*.

What this meant in the 1930s was that Warwick Fairfax supervised and had ultimate authority, but that, within the ambit of his supervision and authority, the general manager ran the company. Two general managers had to fail before Henderson could gather into his own forceful hands the strings of executive power. Charles Harris gambled and drank too much for the family's liking, and was succeeded, after four years of mediocre performance, by Athol Hugh Stuart.

During his brief but eventful general managership, Stuart collaborated with Sir Keith Murdoch of the Herald and Weekly Times in the formation of an overseas newsgathering consortium (Australian Associated Press), and in establishing a newsprint industry in Tasmania (Australian Newsprint Mills Pty Ltd). As ANM and the non-profitmaking co-operative AAP developed in later years they became virtually equal partnerships owned by their two founders, HWT and Fairfax.

Early in Stuart's general managership the company found itself challenged by the *Australian Women's Weekly*, which had been launched in 1933 by a bold young newcomer to the industry, Frank Packer. The *Herald* responded to this by incorporating a weekly 24-page tabloid women's supplement. From 1936 onwards the paper also faced renewed competition from its old rival, the *Daily Telegraph*, vastly improved under new ownership by Frank Packer's company, Consolidated Press Ltd. In 1937 John Fairfax was converted to a proprietary company, a new corporate form conferring on family companies certain advantages not enjoyed by public companies. For example, John Fairfax & Sons Pty Ltd would not in future be required to publish its balance sheet.

After five years in office, Stuart had become so eccentric, even violent, that in August 1938 he was prevailed upon to resign on grounds of mental instability. The managing director decided upon this course of action in consultation with Henderson, who had been secretary to the general manager for the past three years and now agreed to succeed Stuart.

Rupert Albert Geary Henderson ('Rags', in common parlance) was five years older than the 37-year-old managing director, and far more at home in the workaday world of business and publishing. His family roots in Australia went back even further than those of Warwick Fairfax (he was the great-great-grandson of two Irish convicts transported to Sydney for seven years in 1793), but there had been no silver spoon in his infant mouth. He was the eldest of six sons in a somewhat unhappy inner Sydney home and at the age of thirteen, before completing his last year at primary school, he left home to work, first as a cabin boy on coastal steamers, then as a solicitor's clerk, and in 1915 as a cadet journalist on the *Herald*. After becoming chief political correspondent, and then running the

London office for two years, he had performed well as advertising manager of the *Sydney Mail* and circulation manager of the *Herald*.

As general manager, his first concern was to remedy the company's annual rate of profit, which had fallen each year since 1936. With the managing director's approval, Henderson carried out an extensive reorganization designed to reduce costs and increase revenue. His efforts to this end—involving heavy capital expenditure on new presses which, by an engineering miracle of excavation and underpinning, were installed beneath the existing press room—left John Fairfax & Sons more than adequately prepared to withstand the strains of World War II. Indeed the rate of profit became a wartime embarrassment to the company in its often acrimonious dealings with the Menzies–Fadden government.

Thanks to the new presses and a policy of restricting wartime circulation in order to devote as much of its rationed newsprint as possible to classified advertising, the company's profit after income tax had risen from £89 500 in 1939 to £123 500 in 1940 and £176 500 in 1941. Part of this profit was used by the directors to expand the company's pension scheme. Since 1931 the company had allocated £30 000 to its non-contributory Centenary Fund, from which certain members of the staff received pensions after long service. To mark the centenary of John Fairfax's connection with the *Herald*, commemorated in February 1941, another £35 000 was set aside for the establishment, as soon as possible after the war, of another pension scheme to which both firm and staff would contribute.

Warwick Fairfax was beset by periodic illnesses during the war. These often kept him from the office, but did not prevent him from taking part in the company's most important concerns, notably a hard and ultimately successful struggle against what the newspaper publishers, led principally by Henderson, regarded as excessively strict wartime censorship.

This Fairfax, tall and lean with thick brown hair worn rather longer than was usual at that time, bore no resemblance to his father, grandfather or great-grandfather. His general demeanour was grave and studious. He was interested not only in politics but also in art, philosophy, history, religion and ballet. Writing under the pseudonym of 'Jaques', he sometimes served the *Herald* as art critic. He was quite good at it, but not good enough for a hypercritical Robert Menzies. 'I share your angry pleasure at the spectacle of Warwick Fairfax writing art criticism', wrote Menzies to his friend and correspondent, the artist Sir Lionel Lindsay, 'but you have perhaps failed to give due weight to the profound fact that a man who is writing art criticism cannot at the same time write anything else'.

At other times, however, the managing director wrote on a variety of subjects. During the 1943 election campaign, writing as 'A Political Observer', he contributed several perceptive articles on

Australia's main political leaders. Although the *Herald* did not go as far as urging its readers to vote Labor at this election, its support for certain 'candidates of ability and promise' from both main parties was the least conservative position it had ever adopted in its long commentary on the Australian political process.

Warwick Fairfax was undoubtedly the best journalist his family had ever produced, though one of his cousins—Dr Wilfred's son, John Fitzgerald Fairfax—acquitted himself well as a *Herald* war correspondent in the Pacific. A writing proprietor could be a mixed blessing, however, and in 1944 the managing director went too far for the liking of his general manager.

During November and December—inspired by recent industrial turmoil, not least in the newspaper industry—Fairfax wrote a series of articles under his own name, entitled 'What Is Behind Strikes?' The essential problem, he concluded, was not political but rather moral and ethical. On 27 December he returned to this subject in another article entitled 'Ethics and National Life: the Need for a New Basis'. The Christian message must be given in its original simplicity, he said, purged of all 'theological fugginess' and bearing the stamp of absolute sincerity. No church or sect in its existing form, he went on, provided such a message. Most of them were wealthy, and had interests not completely detached from social, economic and political considerations.

Several days later Henderson addressed a sternly worded memorandum to the managing director. The relationship between these two men was formal (not until late in the war did 'Mr Fairfax' invite 'Mr Henderson' to call him Warwick) yet also intense. It was characterized by seigneurial prerogative on the one hand, and dedicated loyalty on the other; mutual respect for one another's intelligence; admiration on Henderson's part for Fairfax's idealism, a somewhat awed respect by Fairfax for the other's worldly wisdom, and also a certain amount of resentment by Henderson.

'This bloke', Henderson once said of Fairfax, with his usual touch of hyperbole,

> if he once had you down he'd kick your guts out. Your only chance with this bloke was to stand up to him. Stuart once said to me that the Fairfaxes regarded him as a dog. They were very fond of him. They patted him on the head. They threw him an occasional bone. Good doggie!

Henderson had no intention of being treated that way himself, and it is doubtful whether anyone familiar with the kinetic energy of that wiry little figure would have been rash enough to pat him on the head. His facial features were not particularly prepossessing—a straight and narrow nose, a longish chin, and a mouth which, although not exactly crooked, gave the impression of having been injured at some time—yet he used them, as he used his rather harsh voice, to project a personality of unusual magnetism. He spoke theatrically, shouting when sufficiently carried away by emotion, and at other times speaking so softly that people strained to hear. When talking, he was rarely still: his long bony hands were constantly on the move, and his whole body twisted and turned to reinforce his words. It was a performance admittedly, but there was never anything spurious or forced about the way Rupert Henderson confronted the world.

In his memorandum to Fairfax, he said that the 'Ethics and National Life' article had probably damaged the *Herald*'s good will with an important section of its readers. 'As I am no longer in agreement with your views', he wrote, 'have apparently lost your confidence, and am not receiving your co-operation, I desire to tender my resignation, which I now formally do'.

Fairfax declared himself 'astonished and disappointed' by this attitude, but said he intended to pursue the issue of moral and ethical regeneration. Henderson then renewed his attack.

> You appear to have developed an evangelical fervour and a belief that it is your task to bring about a spiritual revival. The subject is dynamite, but surely if it is to be tackled it should be by the 'Herald' and not made a personal crusade . . .
>
> I acknowledge freely and fully the support, understanding and encouragement I have invariably received from you. Even in this conflict I do not question your desire to be fair, impersonal and objective. I feel, however, that obsessed by your enthusiasm you have lost your sense of balance. Your judgment has always been soundest when your interest has been least . . .

By some means not disclosed in correspondence, feelings were assuaged and the crisis was resolved. Henderson did not resign, the *Herald* henceforth had less to do with religion, and the two men resumed their former relationship, or an approximation of it.

One reason for Henderson's opposition to the crusade for spiritual revival—a reason undeclared, but nonetheless relevant—was that Warwick and Betty Fairfax had decided to obtain a divorce. Seven weeks after the publication of 'Ethics and National Life', the *Herald* carried a court report that Warwick Fairfax had been directed to return to his wife within twenty-one days. His failure to comply with this direction led to an uncontested divorce, ending a seventeen-year marriage with the issue of two children, Caroline Elizabeth Oswald Fairfax and Adam James Oswald Fairfax. The son was never to become known by his first name, and later in life he divested himself of it legally.

The arrival of Fairfax the fifth in 1933 had been reported discreetly by a three-line birth notice in the *Herald*, and portentously

Four generations: (above) Sir James Reading Fairfax and Lady (Lucy) Fairfax in the garden at Ginahgulla, 1914, with their grandchildren Margaret, Vincent, Hubert, John (on the ground) and Warwick Oswald Fairfax (far right), recently returned from boarding school in England; (left) Warwick's father, Sir James Oswald Fairfax, and his cousin Sir Vincent Fairfax; (below) Warwick Oswald Fairfax at the age of fifty-one. The portrait on the wall is that of John Fairfax, the first proprietor.

Fairfax the fifth: James Oswald Fairfax, chairman of the company from 1977 to 1987, with his father, Sir Warwick Fairfax, and the Premier of New South Wales, Neville Wran, in 1981. They are standing on Fairfax Lookout, part of a cliff-top walkway in Sydney Harbour National Park which was funded by John Fairfax Ltd during the sesquicentenary of the *Sydney Morning Herald*.

Lady Fairfax at Sir Warwick's funeral, 30 January 1987, with (from left) James, Charles, Anna and Warwick junior

elsewhere in the press. Under the headline 'Australia's Richest Baby Is Born', *Truth* said it was not generally realized

> that the 'Herald' is a kind of religion, fetish, family totem—call it what you will—of the Fairfaxes . . . This latest fifth-generation baby boy makes that fetish safe and makes the control of the paper secure, because the Fairfaxes would consider it a form of sacrilege to retire from or to relinquish the famous organ.

Warwick Fairfax remarried in 1948. His second wife—Mrs Hanne Anderson, Danish by birth—had come to Australia in 1941 as a refugee from Bangkok, where her English husband had worked for the Shell oil company. The Andersons were separated by the war. Twenty-five-year-old Hanne, her infant son Alan and a Siamese amah reached Sydney by ship shortly before Pearl Harbour, and found accommodation in Manly. The husband went to Singapore, and spent the rest of the war in Japanese captivity.

Hanne Anderson was befriended by the Danish Consul-General in Sydney, Erik Fischer, and his wife, who was the ballerina Helene Kirsova. The Fischers entertained frequently at their home in Clifton Gardens, and among the predominantly artistic guests met there by Hanne was Warwick Fairfax. They became friends, decided to marry, but could not do so until each obtained a divorce. The marriage took place at St Paul's Church, Cobbitty, not far from Harrington Park, a 1765-acre property about 35 miles from Sydney which had been purchased by John Fairfax & Sons in 1944 and thereafter was used by the managing director as his country residence. Warwick Fairfax bred poll herefords there, and found the property's early nineteenth-century homestead, shaded by conifers on a hill rising gently out of broad pastures, a congenial place for writing.

The kind of energy which the managing director had previously expended on articles for the *Herald* now went into a new interest, the writing of plays. His first, *A Victorian Marriage*, set in nineteenth-century Sydney, had a favourably reviewed but brief season at St James's Hall in 1951. This was followed by *Vintage for Heroes* (1952), a less successful play comparing Greek and Roman attitudes to the Platonic ideal of 'bridging the gap between earth and heaven by means of the love of beauty'; and finally *The Bishop's Wife* (1956), favourably reviewed, dealing with the subject of divorce. The Bishop's wife was about to leave her husband for an army major, and according to the *Herald*'s review the effects of this crisis on the Bishop's religious faith were examined with 'much baring of the inner soul, rather in the style of *The Cocktail Party*'.

Another of Warwick Fairfax's absorbing interests during the 1950s and early 1960s was the writing of a book on religion and metaphysics, *The Triple Abyss: Towards a Modern Synthesis*, published in 1965 by an English firm, Geoffrey Bles. 'I feel most intensely the truth of this cosmic synthesis', he wrote in the conclusion, 'for reasons scarcely communicable in words. But there are two reasons that apply to anything which we believe: that it makes sense, and that it works'.

By the end of World War II, the proprietorial future of John Fairfax & Sons seemed to lie with three of its sons, or rather cousins: Warwick, of course; Vincent Charles Fairfax, who had replaced his father on the board when J. H. F. Fairfax retired in 1946; and John Fitzgerald Fairfax, who had been a director since 1941, and had taken over his own father's duties when Dr Wilfred Fairfax retired in 1944. The board now consisted only of these three cousins—'the head, the hands and the heart', as the *Herald* librarian and old family retainer, Percy Allen, once described the intellectual Warwick, the practical Vincent and the popular but erratic John. As a team, they were not to be as complementary or harmonious as that description implied.

Vincent, eight years younger than Warwick, was born on his father's cattle property, Marinya, near Toowoomba. He too was an only child, educated at Geelong Grammar and Oxford; but he was made of different, more rural stuff than Warwick. At Geelong he was called 'Beak', in allusion to his sharp but robust facial features. This country cousin was no scholar (the headmaster at Geelong advised him to go to Brasenose College at Oxford, saying that he would probably be unhappy at Balliol); but he had a good head on his shoulders, and after coming down from Brasenose worked as a cadet journalist and advertising manager on the *Herald*. During the war he served in the AIF, ending as a major at Corps headquarters in Borneo.

Although his father's interests were by then more corporate than rural (Hubert Fairfax retained directorships with the Bank of New South Wales and the AMP Society after retiring from the Fairfax board), he still owned two cattle properties near Goondiwindi. During the immediate post-war years, Vincent regularly accompanied his father by train to Goondiwindi and back. Vincent, his wife Nancy and their four children lived at Woollahra, but moved to Elaine after Hubert's death in 1950.

John Fitzgerald Fairfax was different again, though he too had been educated at Geelong and Oxford. His dealings with the staff were less formal than those of Warwick, or even the more gregarious Vincent. One young woman journalist remembered him ever after for stopping her abruptly in the corridor one day and entreating her earnestly: 'Don't ever get a *Sydney Morning Herald* face!' He went canoeing on country rivers, and wrote gracefully about such pleasures in the *Sydney Mail* and later in a book of essays entitled *Run o'Waters*. John Fairfax was also the author of *The Story of John*

Fairfax, a biography of his namesake and great-grandfather which had been published by the company in 1941.

The emergence of a fifth generation in these branches of the family, and the advanced age of three survivors of the third generation, had been exercising the mind of Rupert Henderson. His most immediate concern, shared by the directors, was the possible effect which sudden death and consequent liability for heavy succession duties would have upon the Fairfax family's control of the company. Beyond that, Henderson also believed that family control should be further protected by consolidating ownership of the company's shares in as few hands as possible.

The Company's 38 998 issued £10 shares were all owned by ten members of the family, the principal shareholders being Warwick Fairfax (owning or controlling 21 492 shares), his Uncle Hubert (7124) and Uncle Wilfred (6724). At the end of the war the two uncles were aged 73 and 71, and an aunt, Miss Mary Fairfax, who held 2256 shares, was 85. What if these three were to die soon? Combined State death duty and Federal estate duty varied from 39 per cent on estates of £100 000 to 47 per cent on £700 000. Large sums of money would obviously be required, compelling the sale of holdings outside the family.

This problem was solved in 1945 by subdividing each of the 75 000 £10 ordinary shares of the company's nominal capital into one ordinary share of £1, five A preference shares of £1 each, and four B preference shares of £1 each. Preference shareholders had no votes, so if preference shares ever had to be sold outside the family, voting rights would not go with them. The subdivision was eventually effected with urgency, for Miss Mary Fairfax was failing fast. On 18 May 1945 an extraordinary general meeting of shareholders passed a resolution subdividing the shares. Miss Fairfax died two days later, leaving half her shares to Vincent, and half to John.

There was still the need to consolidate. It is not necessary to explain all the transfers of shares within the family at this time. Suffice to say that, mainly by dint of Henderson's persuasion, the ownership which towards the end of the war had been dispersed within the family (though Warwick Fairfax was already the largest single shareholder) was consolidated during the next few years in the ownership of Warwick and his cousin Vincent. By 1950 Warwick Fairfax owned 16 162 of the 38 998 ordinary (voting) shares, and by virtue of joint ownership and family relationship probably controlled another 11 841 ordinary shares. Vincent Fairfax owned the remaining 10 995 ordinary shares.

One means by which Henderson brought about this consolidation was persuading John Fitzgerald Fairfax to resign as a director and sell all his ordinary shares to the other two cousins. 'Is it abdication?' asked *Smith's Weekly* in July 1946, when a 25-word announcement of the resignation appeared in the *Herald*. 'Fairfaxes have traditionally been a closely-knit family . . . and [John Fairfax's] exit from the proprietary with so great an economy of words betokens, maybe, that the latest antics of Granny are not making for Fairfax unity.'

What it really betokened was firstly a desire on the part of the company for the greater security provided by fewer shareholders, and secondly a certain amount of misgiving, at least on Henderson's part, about what he regarded as eccentricity or unreliability in John Fairfax's behaviour. John held the general manager in great respect, and when Henderson asked him to resign and sell his 4069 ordinary shares for the sake of family consolidation, he did so—transferring 3052 to Warwick and 1017 to Vincent.

The rest of John's life was tragically short. His first marriage ended in divorce; he remarried, and took an interest in a south coast newspaper. His moods became less stable, and for a period he underwent psychiatric treatment. At other times he was the same charming John, still able to enjoy the pleasures of country life at Gocup, his property near Tumut. Then one day in 1951, at Gocup, he took a shotgun and killed himself.

There was still room for more consolidation, but Vincent Fairfax proved more difficult to persuade than John. As a director of the company Vincent found himself precluded from active participation in the *Herald*'s affairs below board level, and when the Bank of New South Wales offered him a seat on its board in 1953 he gladly accepted it. Soon afterwards, to his astonishment, Warwick Fairfax and Henderson asked him to leave the Fairfax board. It was the company's policy that working partners should not hold any other positions which might prejudicially affect the *Herald*'s editorial policy. But Vincent Fairfax did not regard himself as a 'working' partner; indeed that had been why he had welcomed the offer of another directorship. Warwick Fairfax and Henderson were insistent, and he resigned.

They also asked him to pass in his shares, but this he refused to do. Although there was no outward bitterness over the incident, Vincent was greatly hurt by it. He knew very well that his cousin and Henderson had come to the view that it would be safer to run the company through one Fairfax rather than three: John had left in 1946, and now it was Vincent's turn to go. He went; but as will be seen later, by holding on to his shares he kept a foot in the boardroom door.

For the next three years the board consisted only of Warwick Fairfax and Rupert Henderson, the latter having become a director in 1949, when certain structural changes were made to the company. In that year the company issued 5010 A Preference shares to thirty-four people outside the family, mainly senior members of the management and staff. The motive for such an apparent departure from the policy of consolidation was to free the company from the burden of undistributed profits tax by acquiring 'non-private' status. And in fact, it was no real departure from policy, for preference shares carried no voting rights.

At the time of this share issue, Rupert Henderson not only joined the board but also became managing director. Warwick Fairfax took the new title of governing director, and the general managership went to the news editor of the *Herald*, Angus Henry McLachlan.

McLachlan, forty-one years old and unmarried, was fervently devoted to the *Sydney Morning Herald*, to which he had come from the Melbourne *Herald* in 1935. He was a tall, balding man possessed of authority and charm in equal measure. After thirteen years as news editor, during which time he modernized the paper, putting news on its front page instead of classified advertisements in 1944, he could have advanced only to the editorship or the general managership. Although McLachlan had been a good news executive, Warwick Fairfax probably took the view that he was not suitable for the editorship because most of his career had been spent on the news side rather than the policy side of journalism. In any case, a friend of the governing director's from Balliol days, Hugh McClure Smith, had been appointed editor in 1938. McClure Smith held that position until 1952, when he was succeeded by a young Scot from the London *Times*, John Douglas Pringle.

Although McLachlan had no previous business or financial experience, he developed an intuitive rapport with Henderson, who had more than enough experience for both of them. Henderson needed a lieutenant of McLachlan's calibre, as John Fairfax & Sons was about to embark upon an era of unprecedented expansion. Expansion was admittedly overdue, for the company had entered the post-war period with only one masthead to its name—the *Sydney Morning Herald*. The *Sydney Mail* had died of old age in 1938, and two other publications (*Art in Australia* and *Home*) had been suspended for wartime reasons in 1942.

The company's first new steps after the war were somewhat unsteady. In 1948, with newsprint rationing almost ended, it launched *Home*—a sixpenny fortnightly magazine quite different from the pre-war publication of that name—in competition with the longer established *Women's Weekly*. This was not a success. In 1950 it was amalgamated with a Herald and Weekly Times magazine, *Woman's Day*, to form a jointly owned *Woman's Day and Home*, and two years later John Fairfax sold its share of that partnership to HWT.

A more ambitious project, a broadsheet 'quality' newspaper intended as a Sunday edition of the *Sydney Morning Herald*, was launched in 1949. Warwick Fairfax and Rupert Henderson were keenly interested in this venture (the governing director contributed a column entitled 'Casual Converse', on subjects ranging from modern art to Oliver Cromwell), but the man who gave the *Sunday Herald* its distinctive quality, and exercised full control over its birth and early life, was Angus McLachlan. Unfortunately the *Sunday Herald* failed to attract national advertisers away from the more popular *Sunday Telegraph* and *Sunday Sun*, and for the next four years it ran at a heavy loss.

In 1951 the company launched a third enterprise which was to develop steadily into Australia's most successful post-war newspaper. The *Australian Financial Review* began life as a weekly, turned bi-weekly ten years later, and daily in 1963. Under the managing editorship of V. J. Carroll from 1964 onwards the *Review* went from strength to strength in circulation, advertising revenue and rigorous financial, economic and political journalism.

While the *Review* was in its infancy, and the *Sunday Herald* was still struggling to survive, Henderson acted with a boldness which marked John Fairfax & Sons indelibly as an empire-builder. The company did not set out deliberately to build an empire in the same thrusting manner as, say, Sir Keith Murdoch. Yet once there was need for action to protect the 'crown jewels', as Henderson termed the *Herald*, John Fairfax could move as quickly and decisively as any other company.

Such was the company's reaction in August 1953 when its main competitor, Frank Packer, offered to buy all the issued ordinary shares in one of his three Sydney rivals—Associated Newspapers Ltd, publisher of the *Sun*, *Sunday Sun* and several magazines. Packer had idle press capacity, which he wanted to use for the *Sun* as well as his *Telegraphs*. On the other hand, Fairfax's interests were mainly negative: it did not want Consolidated Press to grow stronger, for the *Telegraph* was asserting its circulation supremacy over the *Herald*; and it did not want the Herald and Weekly Times unfurling its colours in New South Wales. The Melbourne group had already made one overture to Associated Newspapers, and seemed anxious to improve on Packer's bid.

Henderson's strong instinct was to beat them both to the prize. With Warwick Fairfax's approval, he persuaded the board of Associated Newspapers to sell all its unissued ordinary shares, thus giving John Fairfax & Sons a 39 per cent holding in the company, which would severely handicap Packer in any direct approach he might make to shareholders. This strategy succeeded in spite of strenuous legal efforts by Packer to thwart it. The immediate effect was that of a merger, but before three more years had passed all Associated Newspapers Ltd's ordinary shares had been acquired by John Fairfax.

The change most urgently needed after the initial share purchase was an amalgamation of the *Sunday Sun* with the failing *Sunday*

Herald. The resulting *Sun-Herald*, a popular tabloid, made its first appearance on 11 October 1953. Two other consequences of the merger were an expansion of Associated's magazine subsidiary, Sungravure Ltd, and the reorganization of one of its main magazines, *Woman*. In 1956 Sungravure purchased HWT's *Woman's Day and Home* and combined it with *Woman* under the title of *Woman's Day*.

The merger with Associated Newspapers was a sharp reminder to John Fairfax & Sons that it already needed more space than its building at Hunter Street could provide. The press capacity required by any newspaper company is governed by the size of its largest issue, and for some time past Saturday's issue of the *Herald*—its rich array of classified advertisements representing the Koh-i-noor of the crown jewels—had been stretching that finite capacity to its limit. For months before the merger the Fairfax board had been aware of the need to find a new site and build larger premises. Now that the opportunity also presented itself for day (*Sun*) as well as night (*Herald*) printing, Henderson pressed ahead quickly to bring the two daily papers, the *Sun-Herald* and the *Financial Review* under one roof. The Hunter Street building was sold to the Bank of New South Wales for £1 500 000; a site about two and a half times larger was purchased on Broadway, outside the central business district; and on 21–22 December 1955 the staff of John Fairfax & Sons moved into a new 14-storey building, where they were later joined by Associated Newspapers.

Yet another consequence which may be said to have followed from the merger was the formation of a consortium in 1954 to apply for one of Sydney's first television broadcasting licences. John Fairfax might well have entered the new industry even if no merger had taken place, for Consolidated Press was an applicant, and that move by a rival would probably have demanded matching. But the merger made participation all the more likely because Associated Newspapers already owned the Sydney radio station 2UE, and was keen to enter television.

The consortium, Amalgamated Television Services Pty Ltd, consisted of several broadcasting and manufacturing companies as well as John Fairfax and Associated Newspapers. Its application was successful, and Channel ATN7 began broadcasting on 2 December 1956. In the years ahead, Fairfax's stake became progressively larger, reaching 94 per cent in 1964.

The more John Fairfax & Sons branched out in the 1950s, the greater became the strain on its sources of capital. At one stage, indeed, the company's liquidity deteriorated to such an extent that its banker of many years standing, the ANZ, declined temporarily to honour any of its cheques. The loophole against undistributed profits tax had been closed by legislative amendment, meaning that in spite of its A Preference share issue Fairfax was again being taxed as a private company. As it therefore had to distribute profits rather than plough them back into the business, perhaps the only remedy for its shortage of capital was to become a public company.

Discussion along these lines had started in 1955 between the board and F. E. Trigg, a senior partner in the accounting firm of Price Waterhouse & Co. Trigg was asked to prepare a scheme for the merger of Fairfax and Associated interests in a new public holding company which would protect Fairfax family control and facilitate the raising of finance.

The new company, John Fairfax Ltd, was incorporated on 9 April, and on 30 April two million of its ordinary shares which had not been taken up by former shareholders in the private company were offered to the public. Their market price gradually declined to 18s 4½d by the end of the year, and did not return to par until the second half of 1957; but from then on it made steady progress, reaching 39 shillings by the end of 1958.

In its new public form, the Fairfax organization consisted of the holding company and various subsidiary companies—notably John Fairfax & Sons Pty Ltd, the operating company which was proprietor and publisher of the *Sydney Morning Herald*, publisher of the *Sun*, proprietor and publisher of the *Australian Financial Review*, and publisher and joint proprietor of the *Sun-Herald*; Associated Newspapers Ltd, proprietor of the *Sun*, owner of Sungravure Pty Ltd, joint proprietor of the *Sun-Herald*, and itself owned to an increasing extent by John Fairfax & Sons Pty Ltd; and Amalgamated Television Services Pty Ltd, owned to an increasing extent by John Fairfax & Sons Pty Ltd.

Warwick Fairfax became chairman of the new company's board, and Henderson its managing director. The only other inaugural director was Vincent Fairfax, whose substantial shareholding clearly entitled him to a seat in the fourteenth floor boardroom. In May 1957 Warwick Fairfax's 24-year-old son James also joined the board. Warwick Fairfax was chairman of directors of the operating company as well as the holding company, and his only fellow director of the former was Henderson who, although he had resigned as managing director of the operating company, would still be the prime driving force of the entire organization. McLachlan was general manager of both the operating and holding companies. In another adjustment to the new public status, John Fairfax & Sons Pty Ltd sold Harrington Park to Warwick Fairfax for £97 937.

During the first few years of the public company's existence, which were also the last few years of Rupert Henderson's reign as chief executive, something happened which had more effect inside John Fairfax Ltd than any of the commercial transactions in that eventful period. The crisis occurred on Friday 13 January 1961, when Warwick Fairfax resigned from the chairmanship and Henderson was elected in his place. But its origin went back to 1957.

Through a mutual friend—the Norwegian Consul-General, Sigurd Klingenberg—Warwick and Hanne Fairfax had become friendly with a Sydney solicitor, Cedric Symonds, and his wife Mary. In December 1957, while Mrs Fairfax was overseas, the Symondses had a dispute at their new harbourside home in Elizabeth Bay; Mrs Symonds left the home and went to stay with her father in Bellevue Hill. In August 1958 Cedric Symonds divorced his wife on grounds of failure to comply with an order for restitution of conjugal rights. Seven months later Mrs Hanne Fairfax obtained a divorce on similar grounds. She had two children: her 18-year-old son by her first marriage, and an 8-year-old daughter, Annalise Maria Oswald Fairfax.

That was not the end of the matter. In February 1959 Cedric Symonds issued a Supreme Court writ against Warwick Fairfax, alleging that he had induced Mrs Symonds to leave her husband, and claiming damages of £100 000. In the nature of legal proceedings, this case was not expected to reach court for some time. Warwick Fairfax and Mary Symonds were married at Barford shortly after midnight on 3–4 July 1959, at which time his second wife's divorce decree became absolute. Next morning they left on an extended honeymoon trip to Europe—by ship, for Warwick Fairfax had forsworn air travel after a frightening flight from Sydney to Melbourne some time in the 1940s.

Mary Fairfax, born in the city of Warsaw on 15 August 1922, was someone markedly different from the four generations of Fairfax women who had preceded her. She and her immigrant parents had settled during the 1920s at Broken Hill, where the father traded as a hawker, and later in Sydney, where he opened dress shops in Oxford and Liverpool streets. With business prospering, the family lived first at Bondi then at Rose Bay, Dover Heights and finally Bellevue Hill. Mary Wein completed her secondary education at Croydon Presbyterian Ladies' College in 1939, then studied Pharmacy at Sydney University. She practised briefly as a pharmacist, but her real bent was for business. In 1947 she went into partnership with her brother, Paul Wein, in successful clothing ventures at Auburn and Marrickville, and eventually took over her father's city shops. According to someone who knew her at that time, she was an astute business woman.

In December 1945 she married Cedric Symonds, who was then completing his articles before being admitted as a solicitor. The wedding took place at the Liberal Jewish Synagogue in Woollahra, Temple Emanuel, and they lived at Bondi and Point Piper before moving into the house at Elizabeth Bay, which was to be Mary Symonds's home for only six months. They had a son, born in 1951.

The new Mrs Fairfax was refreshingly informal and effusive. Not surprisingly, considering her business background, she took a close interest in her new husband's work. In her vivacious company the 58-year-old Warwick Fairfax altered perceptibly. As chairman of a large public company he had many responsibilities. But it was Henderson's firmly held and often repeated view that the proprietor's place was at the top, not in the hurly-burly of day-to-day business. In practice, then, while retaining and fulfilling his responsibilities, Fairfax had become less closely concerned with the practical running of the company since the war, and less closely still since the company had acquired public status. He never lost touch with the highest levels of company business and editorial policy, but none the less devoted himself increasingly to Harrington Park and writing.

Much of this remoteness was to be altered by the new marriage. The chairman gained a new lease of life: he became happier, his health improved, and in due course he began to involve himself more in the daily concerns of the office. Another effect of the marriage was a further loosening of the association between Fairfax and Henderson. Henderson came to resent the new order of things, and Fairfax understandably took exception to that resentment. Their estrangement was not complete, for there was still some degree of respect on both sides; nor did it become apparent immediately, for the newly married Fairfaxes spent ten months overseas.

In line with past family precautions, Warwick Fairfax took steps to minimize the possibility that, in the event of his own death, the costly burden of estate duty might oblige his heirs to sell some of their shares, with consequent weakening of family control. Most of the 53 per cent of John Fairfax Ltd shares held by the Fairfax family was owned by or aligned with the three family directors—Warwick, James and Vincent.

Until 1959 James had owned only 13 496 £1 shares (about 3 per cent of the issued capital), most of which had been transferred to him by his father. In April 1959, however, Warwick Fairfax arranged the transfer of an additional 595 760 £1 shares to his son, who was to pay for them progressively with the dividends which they generated. These shares were originally held jointly by Warwick Fairfax and a trust company called Kinghaven Pty Ltd; as they were paid for, they passed to Kinghaven alone, which eventually meant James Fairfax alone. The voting rights passed to him as he paid for the shares.

By the end of 1960 James had bought 116 960 of the £1 Kinghaven shares. During that year the 4 million £1 shares of John Fairfax Ltd were subdivided into 16 million 5-shilling shares, and there had been a bonus issue of one for four—that is, one new 5-shilling share for every £1 share already held. (The market value of the new

5-shilling shares was about 26 shillings, corresponding roughly to that of the former £1 shares.) Thus the total parcel which by that time James Fairfax owned or could rely on for voting purposes, including purchases he had made on the market, amounted to 2 757 060 5-shilling shares. Vincent Fairfax owned or controlled 2 711 905, and together these two holdings outnumbered Warwick Fairfax's parcel of 4 819 550. Never in the public company's short history or the proprietary company's longer history had there been a formal poll at a shareholders' meeting. But the ratio of shares held by the three major shareholders was certainly something to be kept in mind.

As the time for Cedric Symonds's suit against Warwick Fairfax drew near, late in 1960, it came to the company's knowledge that Symonds was proposing to make allegations and call evidence which might reflect adversely on the chairman and consequently upon the company. By that time Warwick and Mary Fairfax had a son, Warwick Geoffrey Oswald Fairfax, born on 2 December 1960. Symonds had also remarried in October of that year, and Warwick Fairfax was optimistic that at an appropriate time the matter between them could be settled. Henderson conferred with McLachlan, James Fairfax and Vincent Fairfax, and decided with them that until a satisfactory conclusion was reached Warwick Fairfax should cease to be chairman and Henderson should take his place.

When Henderson conveyed this decision to the chairman on 5 January 1961, Fairfax reacted with an angry sense of betrayal. He called James into his office and in the course of a very heated discussion accused his son of betraying him. He also alleged that Henderson was using the situation in order to advance his own position. Such suspicion was only natural, for Fairfax understood from the attitude of his fellow directors that he was to remain out of office permanently.

That impression proved to be mistaken. At Warwick Fairfax's request, Henderson gave a written undertaking that if, after his proposed resignation from the chairmanship, Fairfax in certain circumstances requested Henderson to do so, he (Henderson) would use his influence on the other directors, and if necessary exercise his casting vote as chairman, to ensure Fairfax's reinstatement as chairman. The request would have to be 'timely and appropriate after the withdrawal, settlement or verdict' of the Symonds litigation, and consideration of timeliness and appropriateness would depend upon 'any undue embarrassment which may have been caused to the company as the result of such litigation'. 'If and when you return as chairman', Henderson's letter of undertaking stated, 'it will be necessary to have a clear understanding of your functions, and it may be that the board will decide to define these'.

On 12 January, at his father's request, James Fairfax confirmed in writing a verbal agreement made between the two of them two years earlier concerning the Kinghaven parcel of Fairfax shares: that in the event of his dying without 'surviving legitimate male issue' the Kinghaven shares which had been transferred to him by his father would pass to a trust to be created by him. If the trustees in their discretion so decided, the shares would then go to Warwick Fairfax's son by his present marriage, young Warwick; and if they did not so decide, they would hold the shares on trust and pay the income to James's half-brother during his lifetime. In the latter case, after the half-brother's own death, the trustees could either retain the shares on trust for any male issue of his, or 'sell them to such person or persons connected with John Fairfax Ltd . . . as the trustees may deem fit'.

The day after this letter was written, the board accepted Warwick Fairfax's resignation from the chairmanship, and elected Henderson in his place. The Symonds case was settled out of court on terms not disclosed. On 9 March Henderson told his fellow directors, firstly, that the matter prompting Fairfax's resignation had been disposed of satisfactorily and, secondly, that he had reminded Fairfax that if re-elected he would have to accept the fact that his powers as chairman came only from the board of directors. Henderson then resigned from his four-week-long chairmanship, and Warwick Fairfax—chastised, but as future events would show, not chastened—was unanimously re-elected.

During the latter years of Henderson's term as chief executive, he extended the bounds of empire in television and radio as well as the printed word. In 1957, for example, John Fairfax Ltd contributed to the initial capital of a consortium applying for one of two television licences in Brisbane. As with ATN in Sydney, Fairfax later came to control this Brisbane station, QTQ.

In 1958 a situation arose which seemed similar to that of Associated Newspapers five years earlier. One of Fairfax's two remaining rivals in Sydney, Truth and Sportsman Ltd, was up for sale. Its two principal assets, the evening *Daily Mirror* and the weekly scandal-sheet, *Truth*, had both fallen behind their competitors in circulation, and the company's proprietor, Ezra Norton, was anxious to retire. Norton first negotiated inconclusively with the Herald and Weekly Times, then went to John Fairfax.

What followed was not Henderson's, nor indeed John Fairfax's, finest hour. A direct purchase would obviously expose the company to accusations of monopoly, and in any case the *Mirror* and *Truth* (or rather the *Sunday Mirror*, as Norton had recently renamed it) were not exactly its kind of papers. The solution, decided Henderson, was to give the *Mirror* the appearance of independence by disguising to some extent the actual involvement of John Fairfax Ltd in the purchase of Norton's company. The purchase was made by a shelf company, O'Connell Pty Ltd, and for the next nineteen months the *Mirrors* were run by remote control from Broadway, with an appearance of independence that deceived hardly anyone. To cap it all, the two papers were losing money.

For these and other reasons, Henderson reacted favourably to a bid in 1960 for the purchase of Mirror Newspapers Ltd, as Truth and Sportsman had been renamed. The bidder was Keith Rupert Murdoch, the 29-year-old son of Sir Keith Murdoch. On Sir Keith's death eight years before, Rupert Murdoch had inherited his controlling interest in News Ltd, Adelaide, certain non-newspaper assets (his father had not been a large shareholder in HWT, and had given that company an option over his interests in the *Courier-Mail*), and all his father's ambition and daring.

With ability and flair, Murdoch the Younger quickly extended News Ltd's interests from Adelaide to Perth. In February 1960 he also purchased Cumberland Newspapers Pty Ltd, a chain of twenty-four free suburban newspapers in Sydney. Soon afterwards, Fairfax and Consolidated Press joined forces to oppose him with a fifty-fifty venture, Suburban Publications Pty Ltd; but now, with Mirror Newspapers, Murdoch would have a firmer foothold in Sydney. John Fairfax's capital gain from the sale was about £500 000, but the advantage to Murdoch was relatively much greater. After the final details had been settled, he danced a little jig on the parquet tiles of the executive floor at Broadway.

Rupert Murdoch had good reason to rejoice, for the *Mirror* deal was a vital stepping stone in his career. It gave him a substantial Sydney base from which to expand; he was able to use Mirror Newspapers plant in Sydney, Melbourne and Brisbane to print the *Australian*, a national newspaper which he launched in 1964; and he used some of that company's assets to finance his eventual expansion overseas. When Murdoch's competition later became more intense, particularly with his purchase of the *Daily* and *Sunday Telegraphs* from Packer in 1972, Warwick Fairfax would say to Henderson with perfect justification: 'Well, it's all your fault, you brought him into Sydney'.

Three other deals made by Henderson during the 1960s were more advantageous to the company. In 1961 John Fairfax Ltd acquired a 45 per cent interest (later increased to 100 per cent) in Newcastle Newspapers Pty Ltd, publisher of the *Newcastle Morning Herald* and *Newcastle Sun*. Three years later it acquired Federal Capital Press of Australia Pty Ltd, publisher of the *Canberra Times* and part owner of the Canberra television station CTC. Also in 1964 John Fairfax Ltd purchased the Australian assets of the British radio and television group, Associated Television Corporation Ltd (ATV), issuing 2 200 000 new shares from its own nominal capital to help finance the purchase.

This was the last major deal of Henderson's managing directorship. At the time it seemed a frighteningly expensive gain, snatched at the last minute from Sir Frank Packer's grasp; but in due course it proved to be the crowning success of Henderson's spectacular career. ATV held interlocking interests in a number of Australian radio stations and television companies. After some restructuring, John Fairfax Ltd floated those interests as a public company, Macquarie Broadcasting Holdings Ltd, which controlled six major radio stations including 2GB in Sydney. Its own shareholding started at 25 per cent, but in 1978 Macquarie became a wholly owned Fairfax subsidiary.

Henderson was sixty-eight years old when the ATV deal was concluded. Although he had been talking lately about the possibility of retirement, he was nonetheless taken aback by the alacrity with which the chairman suggested that he step down at the end of the year. The fact of the matter, he told McLachlan, was that he was being sacked. There was some of Henderson's habitual exaggeration in the remark, but there was also some truth in it.

Henderson retired on 31 December 1964, and McLachlan became the company's seventh non-family chief executive. Henderson had been chief executive for twenty-six years—two years longer than the original John Fairfax's chief proprietorship—and even at the end of his sixties he still had a long and prosperous business career ahead of him. He remained a director of John Fairfax Ltd for another fourteen years, and chairman of Amalgamated Television Services for ten more years. During that time he also flourished as a newspaper proprietor in his own right. Having built an empire for the Fairfax family, he proceeded to expand a modest but substantial chain of country newspapers which somehow, in all those years of empire-building, he had found the time and energy to create for himself.

Under the terms of appointment upon which he had insisted, the new managing director was to be responsible only to his fellow directors. The chairman would have no executive authority, and if there was any disagreement between him and the managing director—an event considered all too likely by McLachlan—the board would decide. But even so, McLachlan had serious misgivings about his chances of working harmoniously with the chairman.

Angus McLachlan had not made the transition from journalism to business with anything like the same gusto as his predecessor. For Henderson, good journalist though he had been, the change had meant liberation; for McLachlan it was more like captivity. Gone was the zest with which he had once viewed the ever-changing kaleidoscope of each day's news. In its place there was a less congenial concern with pounds, shillings and pence—or, as Australia adopted decimal currency in 1966, with dollars and cents. McLachlan had no innate feeling for big business, and lacking that, he lacked also the kind of daring and ruthlessness which distinguished Henderson, Packer and the two Murdochs. This made him more anxious to consolidate what had already been achieved than to expand in the Henderson manner.

Despite his caution, however, McLachlan could appreciate the stern necessity of beating rivals to a kill. One quarry which the company could not afford to ignore, even in its then state of repletion, was David Syme & Co Ltd, publisher of the 110-year-old *Age* in Melbourne. There was a natural affinity of tradition, readership, editorial content and advertising volume between Fairfax and Syme, but there was a significant difference in ownership. Whereas control of John Fairfax Ltd was still vested in the shareholdings of only three Fairfaxes, control of David Syme was shared by many members of the Syme family.

Such fragmentation was made to order for a takeover bid—or, rather, it was soon to become so. Sixty per cent of the company's ordinary shares were still under a legal embargo imposed by the late David Syme's will in 1908. Syme had left his estate in trust during the lifetime of his five sons, with a proviso that upon the death of the last surviving son the trust estate would be divided equally among surviving grandchildren. In anticipation of that event the *Age* itself was transferred in 1948 from the Trust to the newly incorporated David Syme & Co Ltd. The Trust lasted longer than expected; but by 1965 the sole surviving son, Oswald Syme, was eighty-seven years old, and there were eighteen surviving grandchildren. Before much longer death would terminate the Syme Trust and the family shareholding, scattered to the wind, would be up for grabs.

Late in 1964 or early 1965 the chairman of David Syme & Co Ltd—Colonel E. H. B. Neill, whose wife was Oswald Syme's daughter—revealed to Warwick Fairfax that some of the Syme beneficiaries were anxious to sell their shares. All these grandchildren were potentially rich, but in the meantime some of them were quite hard pressed financially. Could John Fairfax propose any way, asked Colonel Neill, for the beneficiaries to obtain cash before the Trust ended?

The matter assumed greater urgency when it became known that Colonel Neill had also been in touch with the Herald and Weekly Times, which already owned nearly 10 per cent of the Syme shares. Out of several confidential discussions—in which the main participants were Warwick Fairfax, Rupert Henderson, R. P. Falkingham, the treasurer or chief financial executive of John Fairfax Ltd, Colonel Neill, and C. R. (Ranald) Macdonald, a young grandson of Oswald Syme who had recently been appointed managing director of David Syme—emerged a plan of deferred sale. The potential beneficiaries of the Syme Trust would sell an agreed proportion of their Syme shares to John Fairfax Ltd, with the price being paid immediately but the shares being transferred only at the conclusion of the Trust, which was to say upon Oswald Syme's death.

By this means the Syme beneficiaries and John Fairfax Ltd eventually achieved their separate but complementary objectives. McLachlan defined the Fairfax objectives as 'to preserve the independence of the *Age* and to prevent its falling into the hands of other newspapers, particularly the Melbourne *Herald*'. The beneficiaries' objectives were to obtain cash, to preserve the independence of the *Age* and to preserve their own managerial control.

It was more easily said than done, of course, but on 13 December 1966 Oswald Syme and Warwick Fairfax were able to announce the formation of a shareholding partnership between John Fairfax Ltd and the Syme beneficiaries. Although it was highly probable that Fairfax would eventually become the majority shareholder in both the partnership and David Syme & Co Ltd, the partnership deed required its signatories

> to maintain the independence of the company, to sustain and foster the traditions of the late David Syme . . . and in particular to maintain the influence of the Syme family in the affairs of the company as publisher of the *Age* [and] to maintain the *Age* as an independent newspaper of high quality and responsibility . . .

Formal provisions were made to give the Syme partners, so long as they held at least 10 per cent of the shares, the same number of directors on the David Syme board as John Fairfax Ltd would have. And in the event of disagreement, the Syme minority would have power of veto.

The deal was not completed any too soon, for Oswald Syme died in October 1967. By that time the partnership held 67.1 per cent of David Syme's ordinary shares (Fairfax, 45.4 per cent; Syme Partners, 21.7 per cent). In 1972 the Fairfax holding rose to more than 50 per cent, making David Syme a subsidiary, albeit a privileged one, of John Fairfax Ltd.

The last subsidiary acquired by John Fairfax Ltd during McLachlan's managing directorship, in 1969, was South Coast Times Pty Ltd, publisher of the 114-year-old *Illawarra Mercury*, a daily newspaper printed in Wollongong and circulated widely on the south coast of New South Wales. South Coast Times Pty Ltd was controlled by none other than Rupert Henderson. The price was a generous $2 400 000. It was payable over ten years, however, and because the *Mercury* prospered more than had been expected, its profits easily provided the cash required to meet the instalments.

In 1967 the newly knighted Sir Warwick Fairfax and Lady Fairfax had departed for London, by ship as usual, intending to be away for seven months. As it turned out, the trip lasted twenty months, for while they were abroad Lady Fairfax suffered a miscarriage requiring prolonged medical attention and convalescence. They set up a home in London with their son Warwick, and, after the miscarriage, established the residential qualification necessary to adopt two English babies, Anna Bella and Charles Thomas.

From this sojourn comes a vignette of the 6-year-old Warwick Geoffrey Oswald Fairfax, recounted by the Duchess of Bedford in her autobiography, published several years later. The Bedfords had one day entertained the Fairfaxes, including young Warwick, at Woburn Abbey. Next morning the Duchess was surprised to be told by the watchman that Master Warwick Fairfax was in the West Hall.

> 'You must be wrong', she said. 'He was here yesterday'. 'Yes, I know', replied the watchman. 'But he is here again today.'

The child had come to have another look at the Duke's model trains. 'My mother and father have gone out this morning', he told the Duchess.

> They left early, so I told Nanny to go and do an errand. While she was doing it I ordered the Rolls, and told the chauffeur to go to Woburn Abbey. I have told him to go to the village, have his lunch and be back here at 5 o'clock.

Distant though Sir Warwick was from Sydney, he kept in touch with his fellow directors either through McLachlan, who was taking the chair at board meetings, or by direct correspondence. He read the *Herald* and *Sun* regularly, and when he addressed a long critique of both papers to the managing director in July 1968 it was circulated to all directors and made the subject of a special board meeting. Thus, when Sir Warwick returned to Sydney in December of that year, McLachlan had good reason to suspect that his own authority as chief executive might soon be challenged. The Fairfaxes took up residence at Fairwater, which had been vacant since the death of 'Lady Jim' in 1965.

McLachlan's foreboding about his relationship with the chairman was confirmed by a telephone call from Harrington Park on 6 January 1969. Sir Warwick was ringing to complain about a *Herald* editorial on the monarchy and republicanism, which had displayed rather more interest in the latter than might have been expected. He had been so angry when he read it, he told McLachlan, that he waited two days in order to calm down. His first reaction had been that the editor should be sacked, but now he thought it would be sufficient to publish a recantation, no matter how embarrassing that might be for John Pringle, who had returned to the editorship in 1965 after a distinguished career in Fleet Street.

McLachlan agreed that the leader might have been misunderstood by readers, but said it had to be remembered that views about the monarchy and the Commonwealth were changing, and it would be well for the *Herald* to think and talk about this. In response Sir Warwick remarked coldly that five generations of Fairfaxes had supported Britain and he was not going to see that changed. At his insistence another leader, unequivocally pro-monarchy, was published to make amends.

Several days later the managing director suffered a severe coronary occlusion, from which he took months to recover. Once the probable duration of McLachlan's absence from the office became known, the chairman presented his fellow directors with a draft resolution entrusting himself with full executive and administrative powers. No resolution was passed, but the feeling of the meeting was that the chairman should carry on informally without any delegation of power from the board. For the rest of the year the treasurer controlled financial affairs; the editorial manager, L. L. Leck, ran the newspapers; and the chairman increasingly asserted his amorphous but formidable authority.

By December, McLachlan had come to accept medical advice that he should not return to the managing directorship. McLachlan, Henderson and Vincent Fairfax, unwilling to let Sir Warwick formally assume executive control at the age of 68, favoured the treasurer, R. P. Falkingham, as the next managing director. Sir Warwick, on the other hand, argued that he should himself be appointed executive chairman, without a managing director.

James Fairfax cleared the way towards a compromise. Although originally opposed to Falkingham's appointment as managing director, he now proposed that Falkingham be made general manager, that McLachlan remain on the board, and that Sir Warwick be formally granted the executive powers which he was already exercising *de facto*. This was done under article 91 of the company's articles of association:

> The directors may delegate any of their powers to committees consisting of such member or members of their body as they think fit; and a committee so formed shall in the exercise of the powers so delegated conform to any regulations that may be imposed on it by the directors.

At a board meeting on 23 December 1969 Sir Warwick was constituted a 'Committee of One', endowed by the directors with 'all the administrative and management powers exercisable by them under the Articles of Association'. The position of managing director ceased to exist, and Falkingham—a tubby, gravel-voiced former banker—became the general manager, responsible for day-to-day management and administration subject to the control and direction of the chairman.

This board meeting marked the beginning of something which Sir

Warwick had coveted for most of his life. He had presided over the company, private and public, for forty years—first as managing director, then as governing director and finally as chairman—but only in the last few months had he tasted the kind of practical power which had formerly been the prerogative of such chief executives as Conley, Stuart, Henderson and McLachlan. The taste had been delicious. Now his fellow directors were granting him the formal powers which they had withheld eleven months previously. They had denied him the title of chief executive, but a rose by any other name, even 'Committee of One', would smell as sweet.

The Committee of One lasted for seven years—seven years of steady growth, of consolidation rather than omnivorous acquisition. In 1970, on Falkingham's recommendation, John Fairfax Ltd bought 25 per cent of the issued capital in The Land Newspaper Ltd, publisher of the weekly rural newspaper the *Land*, and that interest was later increased to 100 per cent. In 1971 the company also launched a new paper, the *National Times*. This was intended by its chief begetter, the managing editor of the *Australian Financial Review*, V. J. Carroll, to be a national weekend newspaper with heavier analytical content than that provided by existing Sunday or Saturday papers, and with a substantial business content to attract executive readers and national advertising. After a hard struggle for survival in its early months, the *National Times* found its stride, and a growing readership, during the approach to the 1972 election and the succeeding Whitlam years.

The chairman kept a careful eye on the *Herald*'s editorial page, and it did not take him long to cross swords with Pringle over an Easter Saturday editorial which approached that season in a humanist rather than religious way. Pringle had already given notice of his intention to resign in eight months time, but now it was agreed that he should go immediately.

During Sir Warwick's executive chairmanship, the company obtained a grant of arms from Garter King-of-Arms in London. Its central symbol, derived from Sir Warwick's personal Arms, was a winged torch, denoting a herald bearing news. The Latin motto from the same source—meaning 'O Torch, bear light!'—now seemed particularly appropriate to the flickering condition of the company's Sydney heralds.

In the first half of the 1970s the *Herald* itself was the only consistent profit-maker of the five. Some lost consistently, while others moved disconcertingly in and out of profit. The problem was not so much editorial content as a failure by the company to adjust advertising rates, and the impact of electronic media on newspaper reading. Even the *Herald*'s circulation was falling, but it was only thanks to the company's original torch-bearer that the five papers remained collectively in profit. If Garter King-of-Arms had known that the five-paper profit before tax dwindled from $4 million in 1970 to about $1 million in 1976, he might well have concluded that there was more than a hint of supplication in the words, 'O Torch, bear light!'

Throughout the Committee of One period, there was considerable ambiguity about executive power. On one hand, the chairman who could send an editor packing believed with good reason that he was the company's chief executive; yet, on the other hand, Falkingham performed most of the functions expected of a chief executive, and was regarded as such by all directors except Sir Warwick. As time went by, Sir Warwick's four fellow directors became increasingly dissatisfied with the Committee of One.

There were several ingredients in their dissatisfaction. First, they resented the fact that the chairman often gave directions to senior executives without consulting the general manager beforehand, and sometimes without informing him afterwards. Secondly, Lady Fairfax was making her presence felt in the office, and offering articles for publication in the *Herald*. One of these, published in 1974, was a tribute to the Lord Chancellor of the United Kingdom:

> At dinner I sat next to Lord Hailsham [she wrote]. Never in my life have I met a man of such quality. Never in my life have I met such a lover of life, such a believer in Faith.
>
> This classical scholar with total unselfconsciousness brought us back to Troy. With fire and passion, in the Greek, flowed the famous poem with fervour and love so great that those of us who did not understand a word of the language were transported to this time, to this place, to this history, by a personality strong enough to keep alight a sacred fire.

Mary Fairfax was by then one of Australia's most prominent social figures, and she entertained with a panache that sometimes took other members of the family aback. As founder and director of the Australian Opera Auditions, for example, she celebrated the opening of Sydney's Opera House in 1973 by holding a ball for a thousand people at Fairwater. A searchlight showed the way in from New South Head Road, and one of the more famous guests, Mrs Imelda Marcos, was welcomed by a Scottish pipe band playing 'Ho ro, my nut-brown maiden'.

Thirdly, the other directors became increasingly irritated by Sir Warwick's manner at board meetings. To them he seemed intolerant of criticism and inclined to curtail discussion of matters which they felt should be fully aired at board level. And finally, in this catalogue of dissatisfaction, the other directors were concerned that Sir Warwick was taking outside legal and financial advice on company matters.

In May 1975 he called a meeting with James, John and Vincent

Fairfax to consider restructuring the company. Basically this proposal reflected a concern about the effect of inflation and a lower Fairfax dividend rate upon the family's income. Some of the remedies suggested by Sir Warwick's advisers were for the company's television interests to be floated as a separate publicly listed company, by which means John Fairfax Ltd would be freed from restrictions of the Broadcasting and Television Act, and for the Fairfax family to privatize the residual company. A privatized John Fairfax Ltd could therefore be moved offshore, where the family shareholders would be protected from tax and death duties.

Sir Warwick's relatives showed little enthusiasm for this. 'There do not appear to be any advantages in reverting to private company status', wrote John Fairfax in a file note,

> except the possible avoidance of high tax rates by establishing a company in say Singapore . . . The public and the Government are likely to be most suspicious, and the move will attract a great deal of attention and much adverse criticism . . . Is it good for an old-established Australian company to by-pass the traditional methods of financing to use 'overseas channels'?

After Sir Warwick's advisers had modified the scheme somewhat, it was placed before the board in October. There were still to be two companies, one foreign-based. There was also to be a substantial return of capital to John Fairfax Ltd shareholders, with the payout being replaced by the issue of debentures. The company's own financial adviser, Trigg, condemned the proposal not only on financial grounds, but because in his view it would damage the company's reputation. It was not proceeded with, but its mere submission had the effect of putting the majority of directors on their guard about the company's future.

Some idea of the intensity of feeling during the Committee of One period may be gained from a confidential memorandum sent to his father, the recently knighted Sir Vincent, by John Brehmer Fairfax, while he was personal assistant to the general manager:

> I suggest that the situation regarding authority at top level that exists in the company at the moment is almost unique . . . The chairman uses his power and authority by interference when he wants to, but lets the general manager be responsible for the day-to-day running, the performance etc. He is likely to belittle the general manager to the extent that Mr Falkingham is frequently isolated and humiliated. There is no doubt in my mind that he is an extremely competent general manager—given half the chance to be that . . . I am afraid the chairman commands little respect throughout the building, yet he is being allowed to act in a dictatorial, irrelevant and time-consuming manner . . .
>
> If the baddies are winning and eating away at the foundations of an empire, it must be irresponsible for the goodies to sit alongside and

cheer. The ball is in the goodies' court. In a few years' time it may not be, nor ever be again.

The matter of the chairmanship became urgent in July 1976, when Sir Warwick tabled a proposal to increase the general manager's salary, with the implication that his own salary should also be revised accordingly. The board approved Falkingham's increase, but postponed the other matter for further consideration. As if to spur them on, the chairman of Federal Capital Press, R. V. Cater, complained to Henderson—still vitally involved with the company despite his eighty years—that during a visit to Canberra Sir Warwick had undermined Cater's authority by talking to the editor of the *Canberra Times* without Cater's knowledge.

On 18 August James and Sir Vincent Fairfax conferred with Henderson in his city office. They (and also McLachlan, who was in hospital again after another heart attack) felt that to increase the chairman's salary would confirm his claim to be the chief executive, and would probably be construed as signifying approval, which was not their intention at all.

In Sir Vincent's view, the time had come for a new generation of the Fairfax family to assume the chairman's responsibility. Sir Warwick, although well preserved both physically and mentally, was seventy-four years old. James Fairfax, aged forty-three, had been performing well as chairman of Amalgamated Television Services Pty Ltd since 1974, but had not been made deputy chairman of John Fairfax Ltd. It seemed to Sir Vincent that James should have been given that post and should now succeed his father. James himself, although having previously defended Sir Warwick, agreed at this meeting that his father should be removed from the chairmanship.

Although John Fairfax Ltd had been a public company for the last twenty years, the Fairfax family still owned 48 per cent of its shares. Sir Warwick and Lady Fairfax controlled 12 per cent, Sir Vincent and his family 14 per cent, and James Fairfax 18 per cent. As James had not married, and seemed unlikely to do so, the Kinghaven parcel would almost certainly—in accordance with the 1961 arrangement—pass eventually to his half-brother, Warwick, who was then a 15-year-old schoolboy at Cranbrook School, across the road from Fairwater. But so long as James lived, the dividend income and voting rights were his. Clearly any decision made by James and Sir Vincent on the present issue would prevail. They decided that Henderson should see the chairman immediately and tell him that the board had decided to terminate his executive authority and wanted him to resign from the chairmanship in favour of James.

'This is not on merit', said Sir Warwick, when Henderson broke the news to him in the chairman's office at Broadway. Henderson then said: 'It is an insult to me to suggest that it is not on merit'. To which Sir Warwick replied, 'All right, it's an insult'.

Their raised voices could be heard in the next room by James Fairfax. Sir Warwick later summoned his son into the room for an hour of what James later recalled as 'torrid dialogue' and what Sir Warwick described as having been 'stiff and cold'.

It was not hard to understand Sir Warwick's feelings, or the family estrangement produced by this climactic event. Sir Warwick saw himself as having been betrayed by his fellow directors after almost seven years as the Committee of One—a period which he believed had been the most fruitful and significant part of his long chief proprietorship and chairmanship. Twenty years previously he had owned or controlled 74 per cent of the private company's shares. In the meantime, he had transferred such a proportion of his shares in the public company to James that his own son and his cousin could out-vote him. And now they wanted him to go—not only from the Committee of One, which would have been hard enough for his pride to endure, but from the chairmanship as well. As one of his friends was to tell Henderson a few days later, Sir Warwick was like a wounded tiger. At the next annual meeting, in October, Sir Warwick announced his intention to resign as chairman on 1 March 1977.

V

The first board meeting under James Fairfax's chairmanship, on 17 March, showed just how deep the feelings were on both sides. The issues canvassed are now somewhat obscure but, according to the minutes, Henderson accused Sir Warwick of having engaged in discussions with the managing director of David Syme, Ranald Macdonald, concerning a possible takeover of John Fairfax Ltd.

> Sir Warwick said that was vague. If Mr Henderson could not be more specific he did not have a charge. Mr Henderson said he had had confirmation from a number of people, among them Sir Philip Jones [chairman of the Herald and Weekly Times], Mr James Wolfensohn [an international financier], Lord Barnetson [the chairman of Reuters], Rupert Murdoch and Sir Warwick's own solicitor. There had been certain activities detrimental to the company. The arrangement made and undertakings given were subject to some conditions. Sir Warwick must honour them. Failure to do so would inevitably influence the board in its consideration of two important matters:
>
> 1. The recommendation to shareholders of payment of a retirement allowance to Sir Warwick as retiring chairman.
> 2. Sir Warwick's continuation in office as a member of the present board.

Mr Henderson said his advice to the other directors would be to refuse to pay a retiring allowance or retain a seat on the board unless the board received firm assurances.

Sir Warwick said no one else had been asked to give assurances.

Mr Henderson said no one else had been in such a privileged position.

Sir Warwick said he was not privileged. Even the meanest cleaner is given a week's notice. He was not given even a day.

Vague though Henderson's charges were, and vaguer still the record of them in the board's minutes, there can be no doubt that Sir Warwick was indeed considering some sort of action to gain control of the company. In later years Ranald Macdonald recalled that, while he and his family were holidaying at Fairwater in January 1977, Sir Warwick discussed the issue of control with him—not privatization, but the regaining of control by Sir Warwick's own branch of the family, including both his sons. 'Sir Warwick felt that he had been wronged', said Macdonald. 'He thought he should still be running what he saw as his birthright, and therefore he wanted to buy it back.'

Whatever the plan may have been, it did not go ahead. An uneasy truce was declared. Sir Warwick resigned from the Syme board, but remained a director of John Fairfax Ltd—albeit a very critical one. In June he sent a 21-page criticism of the new chairman and the general manager to all his fellow directors. 'The split in the Fairfax proprietary', he wrote,

> produced by the action of the directors on August 18, has presented a bonus to all our enemies. They now see this great company, with all its traditions, in the hands of a General Manager who has never been a newspaper man and with a chairman who in 20 years has never made a strong personal impact in the newspaper world . . .

In reply, James Fairfax defended the management and said that he himself possessed the full confidence of all directors bar one. The chairman no longer held any delegated power, and Falkingham was indisputably the chief executive. During the next few months two outside directors of wide experience accepted invitations to join the board. They were Arthur Lissenden and Sir David Griffin, a former Lord Mayor of Sydney and chairman of the mining company Nabalco Pty Ltd. Rupert Henderson retired as a director in 1978, and in 1979 John B. Fairfax, who had spent the last three years as manager of Federal Capital Press in Canberra, became the seventh member of the board.

With the possible exception of the mid-1950s, the second half of the 1970s brought changes of greater significance to John Fairfax Ltd than any other comparable period in its history up to that time. In those few years the company consolidated its holdings by regaining full ownership of the magazine-producing Sungravure Pty Ltd, 50 per cent of which had been sold to International Publishing Corporation Ltd in 1969; and by purchasing what shares it did not already own in Macquarie Broadcasting Holdings and Newcastle Newspapers. But two more events overshadowed all others. One involved the greatest innovation in printing technology since the fifteenth century; the other, sudden and totally unexpected, was the biggest and most controversial deal the company had yet made.

The chief executive during this transitional and hazardous period was the first since Harris, at the end of the 1920s, who had never been a journalist. This was not the disadvantage it might have been earlier, for in place of a predominantly newspaper-publishing company there was now a media investment empire which also drew profits and losses from television, radio and even such non-media investments as travel agencies. What the chief executive needed in such circumstances was not a bias towards newspapers but rather the ability to manage all facets of a greatly diversified business.

Falkingham possessed that ability. There was a dogged, orderly quality about him which may have been inherited from his father, a stonemason from Leeds who had emigrated to Western Australia, set himself up as a builder and become Mayor of Busselton. The son, for all his pin-striped propriety, would also have seemed at home in builder's overalls. Rather surprisingly, Falkingham was never invited by the directors to join them at lunch during board meetings, which he attended as chief executive. He therefore took perverse pleasure in setting up a general manager's dining room across the corridor from the directors' dining room. When everyone came downstairs from the board room, the directors turned left and the general manager, alone or with guests of his own, turned right.

Although autocratic by nature and much influenced by Henderson's style of management, Falkingham was nevertheless humanitarian. In the tradition of his lifelong Methodism he brought to the general managership a genuine concern for social welfare. The Fairfax family, with its own not dissimilar Congregational background, had always taken a paternalistic interest in the staff, and that concern did not diminish as the family company became larger and more impersonal.

Among several measures, Falkingham brought about an increase in the company's contribution to its Retirement Fund, and—to mark the centenary of John Fairfax's death in 1977—the establishment of a new Long Service Retirement Fund without employee contribution. The latter was designed for purposes of corporate defence as well as the encouragement of staff loyalty. Indeed all Fairfax retirement and superannuation funds were required by their trust deeds to invest their assets in John Fairfax shares. Between them these funds held about 10 per cent of the company's issued capital—a reassuring back-up to the Fairfax family's shareholding, as family members were inclined to remind themselves whenever the risk of a takeover attempt (barely conceivable though that was) came to mind.

Tackling the problem of the five Sydney newspapers, which had sustained collective losses of $3 000 000 in 1976–77 and $2 200 000 in 1977–78, Falkingham persuaded the board to adopt more realistic rates and prices. The five papers moved collectively back into profit in each of the next two years, and the group profit, although not as high as it would have been with better results from the Sydney papers, showed an upward trend. In the last three years of the 1970s—during which time the company made two bonus issues of one for four and paid annual dividends of 21, 20 and 17.5 per cent—the group profits before tax were $15 532 000, $17 243 000 and $20 050 000.

Although politically as conservative as any of his predecessors, Falkingham subscribed to a concept of editorial diversity which had then emerged within the Fairfax group. By dint of heresy and persuasion, such editors as Vic Carroll, Max Walsh and Fred Brenchley of the *Australian Financial Review* and Max Suich of the *National Times* had won the sort of autonomy that would have seemed out of the question only a few years before. Whereas it had once seemed natural for all Fairfax publications to sail under the winged torch of editorial conformity, now the board found virtue in separate sailing orders. Editors and senior journalists who had formerly come under deep proprietorial suspicion for daring to diverge from corporate orthodoxy (on the subject of Vietnam, for example) found themselves not merely tolerated but consulted and heeded by management and board.

In spite of the healthier financial state of the Sydney papers, the declining circulation of the *Sydney Morning Herald* prompted the board in 1977 to appoint the executive editor of Sydney publications—D. N. Bowman, a former managing editor of the *Canberra Times*—as editor-in-chief of the *Herald* with full responsibility for all editorial content. This meant control of news as well as leaders and features, which previously had always come under divided control by a news editor as well as the editor.

The *Herald*'s circulation had declined steadily from 295 000 at the end of Pringle's second editorship to 269 000 late in 1976, whereas the *Daily Telegraph*'s circulation had risen during the same period of seven years, under Rupert Murdoch's ownership, from 319 000 to 333 000. There was a marked improvement in the appearance and content of the *Herald* under Bowman's direction, and better promotion; yet the paper's circulation hardly budged.

While Bowman and others struggled at this Sisyphean task, a newly appointed assistant general manager, T. H. Farrell, was directing a different sort of effort towards the implementation of new printing technology—the use of photo-composing in place of hot metal, and electronic input by means of computerized visual display terminals (VDTs). This was as much a revolution for journalism and printing as the jet engine had been for aviation, and it came at a most opportune time. By reducing the labour content of production it offered newspapers an opportunity to break out of the double bind of falling revenues and rising costs, and no publisher in the world was more painfully aware of that bind than John Fairfax Ltd.

All journalists would eventually be doing without typewriters and copy paper. Their stories would be written and sub-edited on the keyboards of VDT computer screens, then prepared for printing not by linotype operators and compositors of the Gutenburg era, but by white-coated photo-compositors pasting columns of photographed 'cold type' on to page boards from which direct printing plates would be made. The revolution had started gradually in the 1960s. It gathered momentum at Broadway in the late 1970s, but by 1980 the Dutch firm chosen by Farrell and others to preside over progressive introduction of the new technology—Arsycom—still had a long way to go. About 20 per cent of all production at Broadway was then by cold type, but only a small proportion of that photo-typesetting was yet being keyboarded on VDTs.

The climax of Falkingham's eventful general managership remains to be told. On the morning of Tuesday 20 November 1979 he received a telephone call from an informant telling him that Rupert Murdoch was about to announce a takeover bid for slightly more than 50 per cent of shares in the Herald and Weekly Times. Falkingham immediately telephoned the chief executive of that company, Keith (later Sir Keith) Macpherson, and said: 'This is going to shock you if you haven't already heard it'.

'I have heard', replied Macpherson. 'Rupert Murdoch and Ken May [Sir Kenneth May, managing director of News Ltd] have just left.'

Before ringing off, Falkingham assured Macpherson that Fairfax would do anything it could to help the Melbourne Herald group maintain its independence. He then called in the chief financial executive, G. J. Gardiner, and after discussion with the chairman they decided to start buying HWT shares.

On Tuesday and Wednesday Gardiner stood in the market buying small parcels of HWT shares, and was making ready to take the price initiative. On Wednesday morning Sir Warwick, who was in London, rang Falkingham to warn him that if Murdoch succeeded he would 'make a fortune and use that fortune to starve [John

Fairfax] to death'. At a board meeting that afternoon the other directors decided that—in spite of the enormous sum of money which would be involved, and difficulties which might arise from Fairfax's majority shareholding in HWT's Melbourne competitor, David Syme, and HWT's 14.1 per cent holding in Syme—the company should acquire a large enough percentage of HWT shares to thwart Murdoch's bid.

If Murdoch succeeded, they reasoned, News Ltd would be Australia's largest media organization, leaving John Fairfax much the smaller of only two major newspaper owners in the country. HWT ranked thirty-sixth on the list of Australia's 100 biggest companies, with market capital (number of issued shares multiplied by market price) of $175 million. News Ltd was fifty-third ($124 million) and John Fairfax was eighty-third ($77 million).

The Fairfax board felt it was undesirable in the public interest that one company should control as many Australian newspapers as Murdoch would if his bid succeeded; undesirable from the *Age*'s point of view that such a ruthless and efficient proprietor as Murdoch should become its competitor; and undesirable from Fairfax's point of view that its main competitor should become so much stronger. A victorious Murdoch could use his profits to damage Fairfax, and with HWT's power on the board of Australian Newsprint Mills he would also be in a position to deny increases in the price of newsprint in order to reduce his own costs.

The board resolved to buy up to 15 per cent of HWT's shares. Any more than that would involve unacceptable difficulties under the Broadcasting and Television Act, but a parcel within that limit, combined with the friendly holdings of Queensland Press and Advertiser Newspapers, would probably be sufficient to deny Murdoch control.

Gardiner had raised short-term finance of $80 million—considerably more than would be required for the purpose, as it turned out—and on Thursday morning the company's brokers began buying in earnest. As it happened, Murdoch's pitch had already been queered by a direction from the Trade Practices Commission to stop buying HWT shares at noon on Thursday, and to refrain from further purchases for thirty days while the Commission considered the implications of his bid. Before noon, Murdoch sold his HWT shareholding and renounced the takeover bid.

John Fairfax's eventual holding in HWT was 14.9 per cent, which amounted to an investment of $52 300 000. If sold on a normal market, these shares would have returned only about $32 million. The company had paid a premium of about $20 million over the market price to get them, and had also bought trouble with the Broadcasting and Television Act. The purchase constituted a prescribed interest under that Act, obliging Fairfax to sell its interests in the Canberra and Brisbane television stations, CTC and QTQ.

At board and senior management levels, however, there were few misgivings about either the sudden doubling of the company's annual interest burden from $5 224 000 to $10 083 000, the disposal of two profitable television stations, or the stern disapproval of the share purchase expressed in Melbourne by some of the Syme partners, particularly Ranald Macdonald, and a speedily organized Friends of the Age.

At Broadway the Melbourne investment was regarded as a necessary defensive action ('scotching the snake' was how one director described it) and also a good long-term investment even at the premium price. As a precaution, however, Fairfax came to an agreement with Queensland Press Ltd that if either company should decide to sell its holding in HWT it would give the other company first opportunity to buy.

As John Fairfax Ltd prepared to commemorate the 150th anniversary of the *Sydney Morning Herald*, it underwent a process of managerial renewal somewhat reminiscent of the proprietorial changes which had preceded a similar commemoration half a century earlier. Shortly before the *Herald*'s centenary in 1931, following the deaths of his father and uncle, Warwick Fairfax had been appointed managing director of John Fairfax & Sons Ltd. And now, with the retirement of Falkingham on the eve of the sesquicentenary, a new management team took office.

Among the company's various commemorative undertakings for the sesquicentenary on 18 April 1981 was the construction of Fairfax Lookout on North Head, one of the two headlands at the entrance to Sydney Harbour. At the opening ceremony Sir Warwick and James Fairfax, who had recently broken the ice of four years estrangement, could clearly see the cliffs of South Head which had caused their ancestor to quail momentarily when he caught sight of them from the deck of the *Lady Fitzherbert*. The Fairfaxes had come a long way in five generations, but Fairfax the Fourth and Fifth, standing together that day, could hardly have foreseen what fate had in store for their family and its company in a few years time.

3
Changes

I

It came as no surprise to the other directors when Sir Warwick Fairfax, still nursing his wounds, disagreed with them on the matter of managerial succession. They were well accustomed to his minority opinions, always tenaciously held, and the appointment of Falkingham's successor had been bound to aggravate a sense of grievance in one who had himself been deprived of executive power only three years before. Furthermore, Falkingham's recommendation on this matter represented such a break with past Fairfax practice that Sir Warwick had been bound to oppose it. The real surprise was that his fellow directors, no less conservative than he, accepted the general manager's advice so readily. They perceived a need for change, and acted accordingly.

Falkingham had been an efficient general manager—a lesser Henderson, not without vision, but cautious rather than venturesome. Under his stewardship the company prospered, but did not grow. He protected editorial integrity, yet in terms of circulation the *Herald* was still becalmed. The *Sun* was falling further behind the *Mirror*, Sungravure's magazines were floundering, and Macquarie Broadcasting was in trouble. And its strategic shareholding in HWT, purchased at takeover prices, was now showing a substantial loss.

Perhaps only in circumstances such as these would the board have endorsed, indeed welcomed, Falkingham's recommendation that he be succeeded by two young men of acknowledged ability but relatively short experience—Gregory John Gardiner, the 36-year-old chief financial executive who had borne the brunt of the HWT rescue operation; and Maxwell Victor Suich, forty-one, a former editor of the *National Times*. At a meeting of directors in February 1980 Falkingham proposed that Gardiner be appointed general manager responsible for the administration and conduct of John Fairfax Ltd and all its subsidiary operations, except editorial administration of the group's five Sydney newspapers, for which Suich, as chief editorial executive, would be responsible.

As mentioned already, Gardiner had been introduced to the company by Arthur Lissenden four years earlier after a brief but impressive career in advertising, newsprint and merchant banking. He kept a low profile at Broadway, but some guessed that this affable, shrewd young man with good connections in the financial community was being groomed by Falkingham. 'He has not quite enough maturity and experience', wrote Falkingham in his recommendation to the board. 'However, he is more mature and experienced than many of his age and I have made great efforts to educate and train him.'

Suich had also been groomed. Born in Sydney and educated at Canterbury Boys' High School, he served as a cadet journalist on the *Sydney Morning Herald* during the late 1950s. For the next few years he worked on other Australian papers and as a freelance foreign correspondent, coming to Falkingham's attention during the early 1970s while he was the *Financial Review*'s correspondent in Tokyo. The general manager thought him 'a lively, vibrant sort of person' worth keeping in mind for editorial responsibility. Returning to Sydney, Suich fitted naturally into the informal, hard-minded coterie of the *Review*, where he was for a short time associate editor, and its offshoot the *National Times*, which he edited with prodigious energy from 1973 to 1978. Falkingham then sent him successively to the *Sun-Herald* as managing editor for nine months, and Macquarie Broadcasting as executive director of its premier station, 2GB.

Stocky, gregarious and bluntly spoken, with balding red hair, Suich reminded some of his older colleagues of a grown-up Ginger Meggs. That image was belied, however, by the scepticism and serious purpose always discernible beneath Suich's semi-larrikin surface. His surname, pronounced 'Such', was thought to be of Croatian origin; but his father, an Anzac who lost one of his legs at Gallipoli, had at least two generations of English ancestry behind him.

In spite of their respective strengths, Suich and Gardiner were too great a departure from Fairfax orthodoxy for Sir Warwick's liking. 'This matter is so important', he wrote to his fellow directors on 21 February, 'that I feel I have to place my opinions on record'.

> This is not because I have any doubt of the integrity or the ability of Gardiner, particularly after hearing Mr Lissenden's knowledge of him. Nor would his age necessarily rule him out.
>
> But the fact is he has been less than five years with the company, during which time his duties have been concerned only with the financial and business sides of our operations.
>
> If he becomes general manager, he will be called upon to make decisions at short notice, day or night, involving vital and complex issues of our operations, including news, advertising, plans to meet action by competitors, industrial disputes and so forth.

The Fairfax building at the corner of Hunter, Pitt and O'Connell streets, as depicted in the *Sydney Morning Herald*'s centenary supplement, 1931

In 1955 John Fairfax & Sons moved into the Herald-Sun building at Broadway.

Fairfax management 1938–80
(left) R. A. G. Henderson, general manager 1938–49 and managing director 1949–64
(below left) A. H. McLachlan, general manager 1949–65 and managing director 1965–69
(below) R. P. Falkingham, general manager 1970–80

> It could be said that many of the issues would be taken with the advice of his colleague in the second position, who would be a newspaper man . . .
>
> Now it would be a different matter if you had as his colleague an experienced man with complete understanding of the traditions of the Fairfaxes and of *The Sydney Morning Herald* and who had been present when such emergencies were being dealt with in the past.
>
> But, under the proposed structure, you haven't, have you?
>
> We now come to Suich . . . There is no doubt that he is a first-class journalist and that his career has been successful . . . He was one of a group of eight or ten very able people on the *Financial Review* and the *National Times* brought in through the ability of Carroll. All of them have contributed greatly to the success of these two papers; most of them have caused us embarrassment at times; some of them, including Suich himself, have deeply shocked us and done us harm with important sections of readers . . .
>
> Had this been due just to the exuberance of youth, it would not have been so difficult to deal with. But it was not. It was due to a different point of view, held sincerely but obstinately, no contrition seemed to be felt and discipline was accepted with a very bad grace and, indeed, sometimes completely defied. This was partly because of a firm conviction, very often held nowadays, in the rights of editors and executives controlling newspapers to determine their own policy. I do not know what the evidence is that Suich has abandoned this . . .
>
> The suggestion now is that Suich would have complete control over all newspaper activities, including the *Herald*.
>
> It could be argued that this risk should be taken if you have a sound and experienced executive above him accustomed to dealing with these issues in the light of the Fairfax traditions.
>
> But, under the proposed structure, you haven't, have you?
>
> Although I would disagree, it might be argued that the appointment of either Gardiner or Suich would be an acceptable risk. The appointment of both of them is a totally unacceptable one which the board, in the interests of the shareholders and the community, most definitely should not take.

The other directors had already made up their minds, and at the next board meeting—Sir Warwick raising no further objection—Gardiner and Suich were appointed.

Sir Warwick took the rebuff stoically. Although continuing to dissent from time to time, he went along quietly, even constructively, with other changes soon to be approved by the board. He also resumed normal social relations with his son. Lady Fairfax may well have played a part in this reconciliation, for during the previous year she had written amicably to her stepson, putting forward Ranald Macdonald, the managing director of David Syme & Co Ltd, as a possible candidate to succeed Falkingham, and complimenting James Fairfax on his conduct of the chairmanship.

'I should like to think of you as chairman of John Fairfax International', she wrote,

> using the widely different family talents, so that your company is the top communication group in every respect. I do not see your Company as an orange, about the possession of whose segments the family wastes energy. I see, as the years go on, your Chairmanship creating a vast orange grove, giving yourself and the Fairfax family increasing status, increasing power, increasing ability for the public good and increasing financial strength.

In their new executive capacities, Gardiner and Suich would of course be subject to control and direction by the board, and by board resolution the chief editorial executive was to be responsible 'in consultation with the general manager'. Both would attend board meetings, and in the event of disagreement between themselves they could take the matter there. Never having met before, they approached each other cautiously—in Suich's words, 'sniffing around each other like a couple of cattle dogs'. Each must have passed inspection, for in the seven years their duumvirate was to last they worked together without friction.

Although Gardiner could not assume office until October, when Falkingham was to retire and take a seat on the board left vacant by Angus McLachlan's retirement, Suich moved into his new office on the editorial floor in July 1980. His first priority was the departure of the *Sydney Morning Herald*'s editor-in-chief, David Bowman, a fundamental step, in his view, for which he had obtained a warrant from Falkingham, Gardiner and the chairman before accepting the new job. Suich was convinced that Bowman had failed, and in any case the two of them shared a mutual antipathy going back to the time when Bowman, as the company's executive editor, had held some executive responsibility for Suich's *National Times*.

Bowman and his principal lieutenant until shortly before Suich's arrival—the news editor for the last seven years, Alan Dobbyn—had striven to improve the *Herald*. But in the previous 12 months its circulation had fallen from 265 377 to 258 175. The momentum of decline was increasing, Suich told the September board, and he proposed replacing Bowman with either V. J. Carroll, the former managing editor of the *Financial Review*, who had recently returned from an extended period of leave after four difficult years as chief executive of the ailing Sungravure magazine subsidiary, or M. S. Walsh, the present managing editor of the *Review*. Although acknowledging Walsh's ability, the directors preferred Carroll. Walsh's brilliance would tend to make the *Herald* his paper, said James Fairfax, and the *Herald* had never been anyone's paper, not even the Fairfaxes'. Sir Warwick said that Walsh would be difficult and challenging as a personality; on the other hand, Carroll had been tired and dispirited when he left Sungravure, and it would be difficult for him to recapture the zest required for the new position.

Suich said he had no qualms about recommending Carroll on the score of energy, but stamina was a question mark. The *Herald* would benefit greatly from his extraordinary skills as a team leader until one of the paper's younger men had developed sufficiently to succeed him. It was agreed that Carroll should become editor-in-chief, but that Bowman should not be informed of this until after the approaching federal election, which was then only four weeks away. (Max Walsh remained with the *Financial Review* for six more months, then resigned to join the Packer organization as a political commentator on television. Although succeeding in that medium, he also became from 1984 onwards a contributing columnist in the *Sydney Morning Herald*.)

In a final conversation with Bowman on 20 October, two days after the election, Suich criticized various aspects of the *Herald* including its editorial administration, news coverage, layout, Saturday magazine and business pages. He made unfavourable comparisons with the *Age*, whose circulation seemed likely soon to surpass that of the *Herald*, and concluded by saying that it would be in Bowman's best interests, and those of the *Herald*, for him to step down and take a year's leave on full pay. 'You have had long hours', he said, 'production problems and much pressure in this job; you need to relax away from deadlines, read and think. You seem to me to be in a somewhat similar situation to that which I was in when I left the *National Times* after editing the paper for five years'.

In a note to directors, Suich reported that Bowman had taken the news in 'a very correct and courteous fashion' and that 'as far as such an unpleasant matter can be done it was done well, particularly by him'.

Bowman wrote to each of the directors, defending his conduct of the paper and asking to be heard by the board. 'Charges of this nature are easy to level', he wrote,

> but that does not mean they have substance. So far as they do, I have always recognised and acknowledged the paper's weaknesses and worked to cure them. I believe that I should have received the help of the board and the Chief Editorial Executive in overcoming them . . . I could understand, certainly, though I should greatly regret, if the Chief Editorial Executive wanted his own man in my post, and would not have been surprised if that had been broached with me. What I do not accept is that I should have been summarily despatched on the grounds of inadequacy and incompetence. I consider this to be a trumped up case. I have been dismissed from my post wrongly, for reasons that constitute a grave and unjustified slur on my professional capacity and judgment.

Bowman was not invited to address the board, though directors expressed their appreciation of his loyalty and diligence on both the *Herald* and the *Canberra Times*. He declined the offer of 12 months leave, and retired immediately.

This was the first of many changes to the *Herald*'s editorial structure. Carroll, then in his fifty-seventh year, assumed the title of editor and was joined in January 1981 by Christopher John Anderson, 36-year-old editor of the *Sun-Herald*, who now became the *Herald*'s deputy editor. Uncertain about his future working relationship with Carroll, Anderson insisted upon retaining his editorship of the *Sun-Herald* as well as the new position. After three months, however, he severed his connection with the Sunday paper and was succeeded there by Peter Allen.

Alan Dobbyn, who later managed the company's London office for several years, had been succeeded as news editor by Peter Bowers, formerly the *Herald*'s political correspondent in Canberra. Bowers, declining to serve under Anderson with his own role as news editor circumscribed, returned to Canberra as national columnist.

Vic Carroll was a Queenslander who, after war service in New Guinea and Borneo, started his journalistic career as financial editor of the *Courier-Mail* in Brisbane. The Fairfax executive who hired him to become financial editor of the *Sun-Herald* thought him 'rather a reserved type who could be very determined and possibly even stubborn'. That was putting it mildly. He was very much a shirt-sleeves editor. When the pace quickened in the news room each evening, he was usually to be found at the back bench reading copy as it reached his basket. Although inclined to be aloof on first acquaintance, he soon became animated in conversation with reporters about their stories. He would suggest ways of making a good story better, watch its placement in the paper and often take a hand in devising the headline for it. Although seldom writing for the paper himself, Carroll had a keen sense of style and a loathing of inaccuracy and what he termed 'PR bullshit'.

The deputy editor, quietly spoken and coolly self-assertive, made up for any energy which the editor might have lacked. He was to be Carroll's legs, as Suich put it; but in fact he was considerably more than that. Chris Anderson was born into an English market-gardening family living at Theydon Bois, near Epping Forest just outside London. The Andersons emigrated to Australia in 1947, when he was three, and settled at Thirlmere, an antipodean version of Theydon Bois on the southern side of Sydney, where they took up poultry and fruit farming. Chris was very much the youngest child, for his brother and sister—twins—were already twenty-one years old when the family emigrated. He went to nearby Picton High School and, by grace of a Commonwealth scholarship, to Sydney

University, where he graduated Bachelor of Economics with honours in Government.

Abandoning earlier thoughts of an academic career, he served part of a cadetship on the *Daily Mirror*, worked for two years as a journalist on the *Herald* and then for three years as Canberra correspondent of the *Sun-Herald*, becoming editor of that paper in 1979. Although not part of the *Financial Review/National Times* brotherhood, Anderson had impressed Suich when they worked together on the *Sun-Herald*. He was a tireless organizer, constantly generating story ideas and encouraging more relaxed styles of writing and presentation.

Adept at expanding the boundaries of what was publishable, Anderson would nevertheless listen carefully to words of caution from his colleagues. The only time he went too far on the *Sun-Herald* was in publishing a front-page lead under the headline 'Not the Mafia..?' The story was based upon part of an anonymous document which the *Sun-Herald* reported that it had obtained from a Labor member of the New South Wales parliament, Michael Maher, MLA. It had come to Maher from the Commissioner for Community Relations and former Labor MP for Riverina, Al Grassby.

Apparently written by two detectives, the document made new allegations about the disappearance of the anti-drugs campaigner Donald Mackay in Griffith. This was a subject likely to interest any editor. But certain parts of the document, not referred to in the *Sun-Herald* story, were in fact so scurrilous as to put the authenticity of the whole under grave suspicion: they accused Mackay's widow, her son and the family's solicitor of having conspired to murder him. On the other hand, however, the *Sun-Herald* had good reason to believe—erroneously, as it turned out—that Maher was going to read the document in parliament, so making all of it available for publication. The author of the *Sun-Herald* story, Tony Stephens, allowed the Homicide Squad to take a copy of the document for examination, and in a break-out to his story the crime investigator Bob Bottom was quoted as saying that the document might be 'an attempt to whitewash any involvement by the Italian Mafia minority that indisputably operates in Griffith'. In retrospect, Anderson's decision to publish was seen by all, including himself, to have been a mistake. But it was hardly the kind of mistake for which a competitive editor could fairly be blamed.

Carroll and Anderson quickly made their mark, indeed many marks, on the *Herald*. The appearance of the paper was improved with wider news columns (the number of columns per page was reduced from nine to eight), a cleaner and slightly larger masthead, and more innovative layout. The business pages were made more accessible for non-expert readers under the temporary editorship of Ian Hicks, a versatile editorial executive who, although by no means a financial expert, turned his hand to that as ably as he had to the *Herald*'s coverage of its own sesquicentenary.

On the back page of the news section appeared a new daily column which soon became a proving ground for more permissive editorial standards. 'Stay In Touch' was intended by Carroll to be a news and consumer service column dealing with everything from gold prices to movie openings and best vegetable buys. But the inaugural editor, David Dale, brazenly interpreted his brief as 'an excuse to make disgraceful puns, annoy politicians, miss the point of movies and plays, and repeat barely plausible tales of human and animal excess'.

The column became a batch of pungent, ribald items appearing under such deceptively strait-laced rubrics as 'Great Moments In Bureaucracy', 'What They Did In Canberra' and 'Is This A Record?' and decorated with ingenious cartoons by Matthew Martin and 'Colquhoun' (Chris Hemming). It was never boring, and its *succès de scandale* signalled more clearly than anything else in the paper that the *Herald* was courting new and younger readers. To everyone's surprise the column under Dale's editorship provoked only three libel writs, none of which succeeded. The Premier, Neville Wran, issued a writ over two songs about himself which were submitted in one of Dale's popular reader-participation competitions, but he did not proceed with it. Another writ concerned the application of the word 'asshole' to one of Sydney's more notorious tax consultants. Anderson asked Dale how it was to be spelt, and raised no objection when told that the American spelling would be used. The *Herald*'s defamation lawyer ruled that no matter how it was spelt the word would be fair comment and therefore defensible at law.

In its quest for new readers the *Herald* adopted a more magazine-like tone and provided more space for the lifestyle consumerism ('Your Guide To . . .') which Suich had pioneered on the *National Times*. Eric Beecher, editor of the *Age*'s weekend magazine, was brought to Sydney to launch four daily magazine sections in 1982—'The Guide' (television and radio programmes), 'Good Living' (restaurants, wines), 'Life and Home' (later renamed 'Style') and 'Metro' (theatre guide). A fifth section, 'Money', completed the weekday series in 1984.

Although only thirty years old, Beecher was already a veteran journalist, having started a national cricket magazine as long ago as 1968 in association with another 17-year-old tyro. His rise on the *Herald* was meteoric. After successfully launching the magazine sections, he was appointed assistant editor. By that time Carroll had become editor-in-chief, and Anderson editor. In February 1984 Carroll stepped down for reasons of health and took up a corporate executive appointment reporting to the general manager. Anderson became the editor-in-chief, and Beecher the editor.

Never had the editorial staff been so young. Senior journalists like H. G. Kippax (associate editor), Peter Hastings (foreign editor), Alan Peterson (news editor) and Margaret Jones (literary editor) seemed veritable Methuselahs among the new recruits from university and school. As Suich proudly informed the board, all editors of the new magazine sections were under the age of thirty.

The courting of new readers involved some risk of losing old ones. This worried the directors, whose average age was more than twice that of the editors of 'Good Living' and 'Stay In Touch', and well out of the 20- to 45-year-old age group at which Carroll, Anderson and Beecher were aiming the *Herald*. At the board meeting in June 1982 all directors present expressed concern about the paper. According to the minutes,

> Sir Vincent said he was concerned that the *Sydney Morning Herald* was not appealing to the people it used to appeal to. He noticed this particularly with people from interstate and from other countries. They all referred to the *Australian* and not now to the *Herald*. They could not identify with the *Herald* as they did with the *Australian*. He was worried whether we had become a little cynical in tone and whether this did not reflect in the paper . . .
>
> Sir David Griffin said he thought along the same lines as Sir Vincent regarding the *Herald*. The front page had improved. However, he was concerned to know who the *Herald* readers were. Yesterday the Falklands victory was announced. This was a tremendous event for him and for *Herald* readers. The front page of the *Australian* with the heading '15 000 Captured' was excellent. Then look at the heading on the front page of the *Herald* which read 'War Over, Talks Begin Again'.
>
> Mr John Fairfax said he wished to endorse what Sir Vincent and Sir David had said. He had tried to put in the report of his overseas trip that he could not find overseas a quality paper trying to emulate the magazine approach of the *Herald*. He thought some emphasis had gone out of the news. One of Mr Carroll's aims was to attract some younger readers to the *Herald*. We must recognise this. However, there ought to be a balance. We had to be careful to look after our old loyal readers while getting new younger ones. It was an area in which all the Board were concerned. They received a lot of comments and feedback daily . . .
>
> Mr Lissenden said he thought people liked to be told the facts clearly and bluntly. An example was the unprovoked aggression in the Falklands. The *Herald* should have said so bluntly.

In reply, Suich said that the *Herald* was going through a period of evolution more rapidly than he would have preferred because it had been neglected for so long. He did not think there was any lowering in the quality or tone of the paper or that the magazine approach was unique. The *Age* and the *New York Times* were going even further in that direction. On the Falklands war, Carroll had made a very careful decision not to appear to be completely in the British camp. Readers' letters showed no distaste for the *Herald*'s coverage. There were two intertwining strands in the *Herald*: Carroll was the intellectual, and the much younger Anderson was trying to put more appeal and a youthful approach into the paper.

At the next board meeting, Suich said he had recently looked back to compare the current *Herald* with that of two years ago, before Carroll took over.

> The paper was [now] vastly better, much cleaner looking and its political and economic coverage much improved. But there were also things specifically aimed at [the 20-to 45-year-old] market and the board had noted how the reporting of social issues, attitudes towards sex, alcohol and drugs, had changed and become more frank. This was a deliberate approach and he thought quite successful.
>
> However, he had made a point of talking to Mr Carroll and some of our marketing department to see whether there was any weight of market discontent with the changes. It seemed fair to say that the paper's reputation and market acceptance was greater if anything than two years ago and that the only major impact on circulation in that period had been a noticeable trend of growth in the first 18 months, a slight decline when the price was increased in October and quite a sharp decline after the recent price increase. Price sensitivity did seem to be the market problem.
>
> Mr. J.B. Fairfax said he thought the *Herald* was a very improved paper. However, recently the Dale column talked about orgasms. There were a number of words and expressions that the *Sydney Morning Herald* should not use and that was one.

In this time of rapidly changing standards it was not surprising that the board, on Sir Warwick's urging, gave some consideration to the company's editorial philosophy. Although editorial policy was not normally discussed at board meetings, Sir David Griffin had taken exception to a *Herald* leader in July 1983, written by Ross Gittins, which seemed to Sir David to be advocating the introduction of death duty. Sir David said he did not think many *Herald* readers wanted probate reintroduced, and he asked whether Suich and Carroll had received guidance that this was to be the paper's point of view.

Suich replied that, to be fair, Gittins had merely been discussing the subject. Carroll was seeking to develop a style of editorial which was more an essay than a statement of opinion.

Editorial 'guidance' no longer operated as it had in earlier decades. The board still set principles, but within those parameters it expected editors to set their own policy. Suich saw his editorial role as that of a quarter-back directing the attacking play and liaising between largely autonomous editors and the directors. On the *Herald* Suich, Carroll and Anderson used to meet James Fairfax once a week in Carroll's office to discuss editorial matters. This was the chairman's way of keeping in touch with policy. Sometimes he would question the paper's position—as, for example, when, being urged by members of the Australian Jewish community to make the *Herald* more sympathetic to Israel, he sought reassurance about Carroll's even-handed approach on the Middle East. But there was no question of 'guidance' being given.

James did, however, respond to his fellow directors' occasional qualms about policy by inviting them to two working dinners at his Darling Point home, in January and March 1984, specifically to discuss editorial principles. Sir Warwick Fairfax drew up an agenda for the first dinner, and as a result of that discussion he was asked to draft a set of principles. The resulting memorandum, entitled 'The *Sydney Morning Herald*: Traditions and Policies', was adopted at the second dinner.

> As the chairman remarked [said the memorandum], this should not be treated as Holy Writ . . .The principles of the *Herald* have been re-interpreted in my time and, indeed, by me; and no doubt they will be in the future. But if changes go beyond certain limits, it will cease to represent the Fairfax tradition or *Herald* policy.
>
> My aim is to set down, first, what these principles are and, secondly, the reasons for them and how they may be applied.
>
> I began reading the *Herald* in 1914 on returning from school in England and, apart from other reasons, the war made it impossible not to do so. Before that, there was life with my father and Uncle Geoffrey and with my grandfather, Sir James Reading Fairfax, who I saw a good deal of and who lived until I was 18. He was already seven years old when John Fairfax took over the *Herald*. In fact, my whole life has been involved with the *Herald*.
>
> Here are some of the principles.
>
> 1. Belief in the Christian faith from a Protestant but not a sectarian viewpoint and in the fellowship of all Christians. Sympathy with those of other religions and belief that those with no religion are still under the care of God.
>
> 2. Loyalty to the Sovereign and support of the British monarchy as an institution.
>
> 3. Belief that newspapers, no matter who owns them or controls them, exist as a service to the public. A newspaper should therefore inform the public as accurately and impartially as possible.
>
> 4. The service a newspaper offers is not only to record the facts but to provide a commentary on them. Since this commentary is intended to influence the actions of those who read or hear of it, it should have no other aim but the welfare of the community . . .

From this overture and the discussion of it by directors there emerged a statement of fundamental principles. It was certainly not Holy Writ, but rather a convenient summary of principles which the *Sydney Morning Herald* had espoused consistently in the past, and which the present proprietorship regarded as still being essential elements of its editorial policy. Some editors, conscious of the autonomy which they and their colleagues had already won from the board, made light of this declaration. But Max Suich, iconoclast though he was, took the statement at face value and thereafter made a point of conveying the essence of it in writing to newly appointed editors.

> In the editorial opinion columns [he wrote to a new editor of the *Sun-Herald*, Peter Smark], the company's papers will support the maintenance of a free enterprise capitalist economic system, a parliamentary democracy and a system of morals based on the teachings of the Christian church. The rule of law and observance of Constitutional processes are to be supported in all cases.
>
> In this context there are four issues on which the Fairfax papers have a firm policy:
>
> (a) Atheism: While recognising the widespread nature of this view in the community and the undoubted need to report such views, no Fairfax paper in its editorial <u>opinion</u> should support this view.
>
> (b) Republicanism: The Fairfax papers support the monarchical system and while not denying republicanism its supporters, no Fairfax paper should support a republic for Australia.
>
> (c) Liberal democracy—the Fairfax papers are committed to supporting the present democratic system of government in Australia, the continuation of the universal franchise and the rule of law.
>
> (d) Economic theory: All the Fairfax papers will obviously discuss Socialist and Marxist policies and their support in the community but the papers in the group are committed to supporting a free enterprise system and the right to private property. Within this area two sensitive issues are resumption by governments of private property and taxation policy—not only personal and company taxation but capital gains, gift and death duties and taxes . . .
>
> If the above sounds like the support of motherhood you are right. But the policies themselves, while rarely challenged in Australia, are central to the stability of our democracy and, if challenged, need strong support. Occasionally, when the going gets rough, this provides a highly desirable framework within which to work.

By 1985 the *Herald* had become not only a better but also a larger and more varied paper. In October 1984 it responded to the fragmentation of display advertising, caused by the exodus of city retailers to the suburbs, with a weekly regional supplement, The Northern Herald. This was followed eight months later by The Eastern Herald. Another addition in October 1984 was Good Weekend, the first attempt by an Australian newspaper at the kind of high-gloss colour magazine pioneered in London during the 1960s by the *Sunday Times* and the *Observer*.

Good Weekend was born out of the need to find room for more

advertising in Saturday's *Herald*. Restricted by a press capacity that was inadequate for its potential size on Friday nights, the paper could no longer handle the full volume of advertising at its disposal. The general manager Broadway, Fred Brenchley, wanted to make more capacity available for advertising at this crucial stage of the week by pre-printing the Saturday features, arts and books section, Good Weekend. When Suich objected to the Thursday deadline which this would impose on features, they began thinking instead about a separate colour magazine printed away from Broadway, and abridgement of the magazine pages in the main paper as a means of releasing more press capacity on Friday nights.

The *Herald*'s manager, Peter Gaunt, said a new display advertising market was waiting to be tapped by a high-gloss, up-market magazine, and indeed it was. Good Weekend eventually became the company's fourth largest profit earner—after the *Herald*, *Age* and *Financial Review*. Its first advertising manager, recruited from Australian Consolidated Press, was Tony Whiting.

The first editor was Valerie Lawson, a New Zealander who had joined the *Financial Review* under Max Walsh's editorship to write about the advertising industry, and later married Vic Carroll. After moving to the *Herald* in 1981, and transforming its Saturday magazine pages, she left Broadway to become associate editor of the *Bulletin*. Five months later she accepted an invitation back to Broadway to launch the colour magazine.

She did this successfully, avoiding Fleet Street clichés and commissioning solid, readable features. The first cover story was 'The Life and Times of Lionel Murphy'. Good Weekend was printed by Eastern Suburbs Newspapers, in which John Fairfax Ltd had an interest, and in 1985 Macquarie Publications Pty Ltd at Dubbo (another company partly owned by Fairfax) began printing additional copies for inclusion with the *Age*.

One might have expected these improvements to turn the *Herald*'s circulation around. But their only discernible effect was a slowing down of the paper's earlier decline. In four years since the change of executives the *Herald*'s circulation had fallen from 259 803 to 254 356. Nor was the *Herald* the only broadsheet to disappoint its producers in this way. The *Age*, in spite of its good showing early in the period, fell from 244 238 to 236 229, and the *Australian* from a mere 126 484 to 124 109. The *Herald*'s circulation would start to rise again in the near future; but for the time being there was only one consolation to be drawn from an otherwise disheartening outcome. While the number of *Herald* readers over the age of fifty fell by 3.5 per cent, those in every age group between eighteen and forty-nine showed small percentage increases. Such were the meagre rewards of four years hard work with the printed word in the age of television.

II

Although the directors had not said so in as many words, Greg Gardiner took up the general managership believing that they wanted more growth and a different, less formal atmosphere than had prevailed under his predecessors. One of the first things he did was suggest to James Fairfax that the directors' lift—one of six in the front foyer, beneath Salvatore Zofrea's vivid sesquicentennial mural—should be unlocked and made available for general use. This improved the service, and signalled a willingness by the new managers to unlock other parts of the company as well. Even the boardroom was opened for occasional staff meetings. The practice of offering discounts to advertisers, frowned upon in Falkingham's time although competitors like Murdoch would discount at the drop of a hat, became respectable under Gardiner and the chief advertising manager, Malcolm Stening. Promotional expenditure, once deemed a useless extravagance, now came to be regarded as money well spent. From a modest promotional outlay of $2 million in 1980, the annual figure rose quickly to $8 million, and later to as much as $14 million. Why not blow one's own trumpet? Reflecting this new mood, the company's annual report became more informative and more self-confident, replete with photographs of executives and staff as well as directors.

Gardiner's successor as chief financial executive was Ron Cotton, a former general manager and controller of Ampol Ltd who moved to Broadway early in 1981. The two did not form as close a working relationship as that which had existed between Falkingham and Gardiner, and after five years Cotton resigned. Others on the fourteenth floor were the assistant general manager, Tom Farrell, then approaching the end of his career and still deeply involved with intractable problems of technological change; the chief accountant, Barry Moore; the new company secretary, George Foster; and the administration manager, Philip Allen, a newly arrived commercial solicitor who had worked with Gardiner in his merchant bank days.

Just as Max Suich had a first priority in the *Herald*, so Gardiner was obliged early in his new job to address the far more serious plight of Sungravure Pty Ltd. Sungravure was the wholly owned subsidiary which had been acquired along with Associated Newspapers during the 1950s. It employed five hundred people and published such magazines as *Woman's Day*, *People With Pix*, *Cosmopolitan*, *Dolly* and *Electronics Australia*. It was also losing money hand over fist—$300 000 in 1978, $500 000 in 1979, $5 000 000 in 1980, and an estimated $3 700 000 in 1980–81.

Vic Carroll, Sungravure's chief executive from 1975 to 1979, and his successor in that position, F. R. Brenchley, both saw the root of the company's trouble as being the outdated printing method used in its factory at Rosebery. Rotogravure printing, originally the most suitable method available, had been surpassed by improved methods of offset printing—particularly for relatively small print runs like those of *Woman's Day* and *People With Pix*. It produced excellent colour, but needed large runs to justify the high cost of making gravure cylinders. Consolidated Press still used gravure to print *Australian Women's Weekly*, the market leader, whose circulation (821 000) was nearly twice that of *Woman's Day*, and so did some publishers in the large population markets of North America and Europe. *Woman's Day*, once second only to *Women's Weekly*, had been overtaken in the late 1970s by Rupert Murdoch's *New Idea*, which was printed on web offset presses. Web offset presses were smaller and more efficient than gravure. They were specially designed to produce the standard A4 page size favoured by popular women's magazines, whereas Australian gravure factories mainly produced 'picture book' size.

Gardiner, in his capacity as a director of Sungravure, had already reached the same conclusion as Carroll and Brenchley. When he first saw the press room at Rosebery it reminded him of something noisy and dirty left over from the industrial revolution. Its finished products were inferior, and he could not help concluding that the staff, constantly comparing *Woman's Day* unfavourably with *New Idea*, had developed a defeatist attitude. It was a case, he felt, of the tune being called by the factory rather than by the magazines and their readers' expectations.

So what was to be done? Gardiner saw no reason why Sungravure should continue to be printer as well as publisher. Indeed he saw many reasons, industrial as well as commercial, why it should cease printing altogether and contract that phase of its operation to offset printeries. Some of the company's smaller magazines were already being printed that way in Japan and by Macquarie Publications in Dubbo.

The chairman of Sungravure, John B. Fairfax, agreed with Gardiner. But Falkingham, while still general manager, had been adamantly opposed to the idea. His Methodist conscience seemed to baulk at the large-scale retrenchment which would follow any decision to close the plant. Arguing that Fairfax should keep its gravure facility, if only for the sake of run-of-press colour pre-prints, he advocated palliative measures to upgrade Rosebery until a new factory could be built.

The matter came to a head early in 1981 when Kerry Packer of Consolidated Press offered $3 million for *Woman's Day*, which he intended turning into a monthly publication. If *Woman's Day* was sold, Sungravure would no longer need its factory. The other magazines collectively made a profit of about $400 000 a year, and could be printed elsewhere. At the Fairfax board meeting in February, Gardiner said that he felt very diffident about raising such a matter, for to some extent it was an admission of defeat. Did the board want him to look further into the proposal? If *Woman's Day* was to be sold, the most logical purchaser would be the Herald and Weekly Times. But the price offered by Packer was 'brilliant'.

Falkingham, who was by then a director, said the price was 'derisory' and the 'idea of dismissing 500 people [was] repugnant to the whole philosophy of the company'.

> Mr Falkingham said there were very strong and compelling reasons for not disposing of any publication to a competitor, particularly to one whose avowed objectives included the destruction of this organisation and of the family which owned it. If the proposal were adopted it would undoubtedly redound to our greater detriment and the benefits of monopoly would be shared by both of our competitors.

John B. Fairfax reluctantly but firmly supported selling the *Woman's Day* title and disposing of the factory. Sir Warwick Fairfax also thought it best to sell and close. Year after year, he said, the board had been trying to solve the problem of Sungravure's profitability. The problem now was that the women's magazine market was saturated and that an enormous amount of money was being spent to keep its fortunes afloat. The field was no longer profitable, and Packer himself had undoubtedly lost a great deal of money in it. James Fairfax said he favoured an approach to the Herald and Weekly Times without any initiatives that would require disclosure of the approach from Packer. This was agreed to by the board.

When the board met again in March, there was another proposal to be considered. John Sands Pty Ltd—the wholly owned subsidiary of Textron, an American multi-national group—had shown interest in a joint venture merging the best of Sungravure's plant with its own offset plant at Artarmon. The new company would produce all Sungravure magazines and pre-prints. Sands had a very efficient Toshiba press, and was already printing such magazines as *Family Circle, Time, Reader's Digest* and *Newsweek*.

The board also had before it a report by Gardiner on the future of Sungravure, canvassing three options: (1) continue to publish *Woman's Day* from Rosebery, (2) sell *Woman's Day* and close the Rosebery plant, and (3) retain *Woman's Day* and close Rosebery. The Herald and Weekly Times had not been interested in *Woman's Day*, but Packer was still keen and there were some intimations from Consolidated Press that he might improve upon his original offer. After hearing a further report from Brenchley, the board adopted

Gardiner's third option and instructed him to pursue the joint company proposal with John Sands. Falkingham argued for improvements at Rosebery without going to Artarmon, but from his point of view the Sands alternative would at least require less retrenchment than a closure resulting from the sale of *Woman's Day*.

Nothing came of it. Textron agreed in principle to the joint company, but requirements by the Foreign Investment Review Board eventually brought negotiations to a standstill. When the Fairfax board met on 18 June Gardiner said there was less than a fifty-fifty chance of concluding any deal with John Sands. To make matters worse, the Rosebery plant was now under industrial siege. Sungravure's printers had been on strike since 2 June for higher pay and three weeks pay rather than two weeks in the event of redundancy. This started as a normal enough dispute, but its mood was soon exacerbated by the knowledge—obtained from board papers which had somehow found their way to the union Chapel at Rosebery—that closure was one of the options being considered by Fairfax.

The strike became unusually bitter. Axes were used by strikers to cut the main water pipe into the building. Rubble was dumped in order to hamper access to the building, and this provided ammunition for damage to windows and cars. Women crossing the picket line were hit with stones, and some of the strikers were arrested. As Fred Brenchley was seeing someone into a taxi, a full beer can whistled past his head and broke one of the taxi's windows.

So far during the strike *Woman's Day* had been printed on time by non-union labour, but two issues of *People With Pix* had been farmed out to Wilke and Co Ltd, a Melbourne offset printery owned by the Herald and Weekly Times. Gardiner warned the Chapel at Broadway, which was not yet involved in the strike, that Fairfax could not sustain the Rosebery plant if *Woman's Day* had to go off the market. By the time the board met in June the union leadership seemed anxious to settle, although the rank and file were pressing for an extension of hostilities. In negotiation with management the unions had agreed to certain concessions in work practice, and had also arrived at a mutually acceptable basis for severance pay in the event of closure at Rosebery.

Although no decision was reached by the board on 18 June, and Falkingham departed the next day for a holiday in Canada and England feeling that Rosebery was safe for the present, time was in fact about to run out. The dispute continued, and during the last week of June there were also disruptions to production at Broadway, Newcastle and Wollongong in support of the Sungravure strikers. Brenchley arranged for *Woman's Day* to be published at the Wilke plant, and on 29 June Gardiner recommended to a board meeting convened at 8.30 a.m. that the plant be closed immediately. In the absence of James Fairfax, who was in France, John Fairfax acted as chairman. Sir Vincent Fairfax and Falkingham were also overseas.

The acting chairman told the meeting that Gardiner had telephoned Falkingham at Banff in the Canadian Rockies to obtain an expression of his views, and had found him still strongly opposed to closure. (According to Falkingham's later recollection, Gardiner told him that he would not take any action on Sungravure without getting in touch with him again. To this, Falkingham said: 'If you're going to close, I'll come back'.) John Fairfax had later telephoned Falkingham in Montreal, and he now tendered a report of that conversation, the intensity of which astounded the other directors.

Accusing Gardiner of pushing the matter through during his absence, Falkingham described the recommendation as a 'fraud'. 'You're a funny old board', he said, 'if you decide to do a thing like this with three directors absent'. If the recommendation was endorsed, he would resign from the board and ask that his reasons for doing so be made public. Even if it did not go through he would no longer be able to work in harmony with Gardiner or represent him on the boards of any subsidiary or associated companies. 'The whole thing is a racket that has been put to you while I am away. It is outrageous.'

Sir Warwick Fairfax said he was profoundly shocked by some of Falkingham's statements, but none the less felt complete confidence in the general manager and his recommendation. Gardiner said he had been greatly disturbed by Falkingham's comments. He had never felt that their relations had been on anything but a basis of complete trust. There was no doubt, he said, that Falkingham had an overwhelming interest in preserving the jobs of Sungravure employees.

After having heard from Gardiner in Banff, Falkingham had posted a long handwritten memorandum to his secretary in Sydney for typing and circulating to the directors. In it he reiterated his arguments for keeping the plant going, and suggested engaging a major overseas rotogravure printer to report on the possibilities of improving quality and/or reducing costs by further capital expenditure. He warned against transferring Fairfax's pre-printing and magazine printing to the Herald and Weekly Times, referring to that group as 'incompetent, antagonistic . . . and always impossible to work with', and stressed the obligation to survive. That obligation, he wrote, was owed to the

> shareholders (our papers will be greatly disadvantaged if Sungravure does not survive), to the community (diversity of information: contemplate the further charges of 'concentration of control of the media' that would arise if we closed our plant and had its products printed by Melbourne Herald) and to our employees (500, I think, most with families and many who have worked nowhere else).

This memorandum arrived during the meeting, was read by the four directors present, but did not dissuade them from accepting Gardiner's recommendation.

The factory closed that day, and was sold in the following year for more than $2 500 000. Three hundred and seventy-five production workers were retrenched. They were offered a severance package based on three weeks pay for every year of service (this was the agreed rate for technologically induced retrenchment rather than a lower rate prescribed for economically induced retrenchment) and accepted it unanimously on 1 July.

The Gordian knot had been cut, and Sungravure changed its name—first to Magazine Promotions Australia Pty Ltd, and five years later to Fairfax Magazines Pty Ltd. Most of the magazines were printed by Wilke until 1984, when the job was divided between Eastern Suburbs Newspapers and Macquarie Publications, both of which owned offset presses. For the time being, pre-prints were handled by a Wilke subsidiary in Melbourne.

In May 1982 Fred Brenchley left Magazine Promotions to take up a new executive position at Broadway. He was replaced by Peter Gaunt, and when Gaunt resigned to work for Reader's Digest in 1983 the general managership went to the company's business manager, John Hemming. In 1984 the company made a profit for the first time in five years; in 1985 its contribution to group profit after tax was $2 006 000; and in 1987, $3 664 000.

Production costs were reduced, even though the price of paper increased; and the advertising manager, Sandra Yates, proved to be an exceptionally good marketer. Basically, the growth in profit came from improved sales by the magazines. *Woman's Day* did not catch up with *New Idea*, which had gained relatively more when *Women's Weekly* went monthly in 1982; but by 1987 its circulation had risen to 704 900, compared with *New Idea*'s 942 765. *People With Pix*, which had never been effectively promoted in the past, turned into what Hemming called a 'cash cow'. From a circulation of less than 100 000 in 1981, it rose to 230 601 in 1986, thereby overtaking its competitor, HWT's *Australasian Post*.

There was one less happy sequel to the successful closure of Rosebery. Falkingham's fellow directors were not prepared to overlook his outburst from Montreal. Although they respected his intellect and past service to the company, some of them thought that he had failed to make the necessary transition from chief executive to membership of the board. Falkingham denied this, and was gratified by Gardiner's acknowledgement on one occasion that he was 'bending over backwards' to avoid any such failing.

Some directors also surmised that in his conversation with John Fairfax he may have been employing the kind of theatrical hyperbole used so effectively by Rupert Henderson, and had simply overdone it. Others suspected that he may have been in bad health at the time, and although Falkingham made no such excuse there may indeed have been something in that.

The fact remained that he had declared himself unable to work in harmony with the present chief executive, and willing to resign from the board. He came to the board on 23 July with a letter of resignation in his pocket, but sensing the mood of the meeting he quickly decided not to resign under pressure. All seven directors were present. The only other person in attendance was the general manager, and he kept the minutes instead of the company secretary. Falkingham spoke first, commenting in detail on the minutes of the previous meeting and criticizing the report of his remarks from Montreal:

> Mr John Fairfax clearly believes he had my authority to report in such manner to the board and his sincerity must be unquestioned. I, with equal clarity, am certain that I had no such understanding. Perhaps the vagaries of international telephones were at fault. The voice of Mr Fairfax was muffled and crossed with an angry French voice, and we were at one stage cut off. I, of course, do not accuse Mr Fairfax of being untruthful, but neither do I expect to be the subject of such an accusation.
>
> I believed we were conducting a private conversation such as directors of companies have, and must have, about their companies' affairs. In such circumstances confidentiality is assured unless both agree otherwise. If I had known I was to be reported I would have summarised my memorandum which was then in limbo; and if I had sent a message to the board in the terms reported I would never have agreed to it being relayed to, or in the presence of, executives.
>
> There are words and phrases in the report which I did not employ but I don't want to get into a discussion about the content. Certainly I was aggrieved at the direction events had taken . . . I now share the responsibility for a board decision from which I dissented and in relation to which I had no opportunity for debate. What I have said in this context applies regardless of who may be the dissident minority and I do not, of course, claim special privilege for me. Indeed, as I have many times told Mr Gardiner, I don't want to be cast in the role of the old nark who thinks he is still the general manager.

At one point in Falkingham's address, Sir Warwick could not conceal his amusement. 'Sir Warwick, please don't snigger while I am talking', said Falkingham, only to be reprimanded by James Fairfax for not directing his remarks to the chair.

John Fairfax spoke next, saying that he had made clear at the outset of the conversation that it was to be relayed to the board. He had taken extensive notes, and had no doubt as to the accuracy of his report.

During the ensuing discussion it became clear that Falkingham had no supporters. Sir David Griffin said that Falkingham had fired a broadside; Sir Vincent said that whenever a director mistrusted a chief executive there had to be either a new chief executive or a new director; and Sir Warwick asked whether Falkingham still intended to resign. The chairman then put a leading question to Gardiner: Did he feel that he could work with Falkingham in future? The general manager replied that in view of the criticisms and accusations, and the strength with which they had been made, he could see that there would be some real difficulties in his future relationship with Falkingham. While he had had a particularly close and strong relationship with him in the past, and had enormous respect for him, there were subjects on which Falkingham and he were diametrically opposed.

Arthur Lissenden said he had been involved in a number of palace revolutions, and felt that in this case the use of a committee should be considered. The chairman said a committee would create more problems than it solved. This was a full board matter.

Falkingham cited his own former relationship with Rupert Henderson. Henderson had been an unrelenting critic of his, yet they still maintained an excellent relationship. He was sorry if directors had taken offence at his conversation. It had not been intended. Was there anything more for him to say?

The chairman said it was difficult to square Falkingham's claim of 'no offence' with the statements as reported by John Fairfax. Rupert Henderson was no paragon at presenting views, and the chairman did not think his methods in that regard should be emulated. It was Falkingham, not Henderson; and Gardiner was not Falkingham. The comparison was not valid.

Sir Vincent said he had very real doubts about former chief executives joining the boards of companies from which they had recently retired. It was generally not successful. Some adopted too soft a line, some too strong a line. In his opinion Falkingham fell into the latter category. He was far too black and white, and seemed not to recognize the necessary shades of grey. He chimed in too quickly before other directors with comments which were too absolute, thus restricting discussion that would otherwise have flowed more freely.

The meeting ended inconclusively, with the chairman remarking that the situation required further thought by all. Six days later James Fairfax went to see Falkingham on what, he told him, was the most difficult assignment he had ever had in his life. The directors, he said, were unanimously of the opinion that for the good of the company Falkingham should leave the board. If he did not do so voluntarily, they would call a general meeting of shareholders, under a rarely invoked section of the Companies Act, for the specific purpose of removing him.

Falkingham denied that his resignation would be in the company's best interest, but he said he would think about it. He went to see McLachlan, and then Henderson, who offered to sound out the other directors. Sir Vincent told Henderson he would be agreeable to Falkingham remaining on the board, but James said that Sir Warwick would never agree. Bowing to the inevitable, Henderson advised Falkingham to attend no more board meetings and resign after the next annual meeting on 28 October.

Falkingham took that advice. He attended the annual meeting, and resigned three days later. At his own request there were no eulogies or expressions of regret by the company about this unusual resignation—the first since Vincent Fairfax's in 1953—or indeed about Falkingham's departure from all other Fairfax directorships. His resignation from the main board was accorded only two sentences in the *Herald*'s finance pages, and that was the way he wanted it.

Gardiner said he was 'deeply and sincerely sorry' to see him go and when Falkingham replied that he found this hard to believe he repeated it. In a warmly couched letter, James Fairfax acknowledged the great value of his twenty-four years of service to the company and thanked him for the mutual trust and confidence which had always existed between them. Two years later Falkingham became chairman of a company half owned by a friend of his in advertising, Neville Jeffress, and that remained his only business interest.

III

The new executive position to which Fred Brenchley moved from Magazine Promotions—general manager Broadway—entailed a priority no less urgent for him than the *Herald* had been for Suich, or Rosebery for Gardiner. Brenchley's most pressing concern was Broadway's long overdue typesetting revolution, but before we come to that the nature of his new position needs to be explained. In February 1982 Gardiner convinced the board that an enterprise as large as John Fairfax Ltd, with turnover of $400 million and no fewer than thirteen discrete divisions, required a rather different management structure. The position of general manager Broadway was created to relieve Gardiner of day-to-day pressure from the Broadway newspaper operations, and allow him to discharge adequately the functions implicit in his new title, group general manager. Although ultimately still responsible for the commercial side of Broadway, he would now have more time to plan and direct the growth of the group as a whole.

The general manager Broadway would be responsible to the group general manager for all the production, marketing and personnel functions of the Broadway complex, just as the general managers of Amalgamated Television Services and Macquarie Broadcasting, for example, were responsible to him for their divisions. The general manager Broadway would also liaise with Max Suich, just as Suich already did with Gardiner. Suich's continued attendance at board meetings and his direct access to the chairman would proclaim his relative seniority to the general manager Broadway. But Brenchley's office near that of the general manager on the fourteenth floor, and eventually his attendance at board meetings whenever matters under his responsibility were discussed, left no one in doubt that he was running Broadway. As Suich put it, he was responsible for the words and Brenchley for the music.

One part of the Broadway orchestra—a new system of computerized typesetting which the company expected would eventually usher its five Sydney newspapers into the cost-efficient era of cold type—was distinctly out of tune. It had been like that for some years when Brenchley moved to Sungravure in 1980, and on his return to Broadway he was dismayed to notice little if any improvement. Yet this was a technological revolution that simply had to succeed if the company was to remain competitive. Not only was cold type (photographic images on paper rather than raised lead letters) far more economical than typesetting with hot metal, but hot-metal machinery was fast disappearing from the industry.

With hot metal, everything had to be keyboarded twice—first by the journalist on a typewriter, and then, after sub-editing, by the typesetter on a linotype machine. Metal type and the curved metal plates used to print pages were heavy and cumbersome. They had to be melted down for re-use. The system was five hundred years old, and looked it.

With cold type, the journalist alone entered editorial copy on the screen of a VDT. Once in the system's memory bank, it could be called up for sub-editing on another screen and coded for automatic photo-composing—the production of printed letters on photographic paper, cut and pasted on to a page-sized board by the photo-compositor. The board would then be photographed to make a light plastic plate which could be wrapped around the press drum in place of the old curved metal forme. This 'direct printing' eliminated the costly stereo stage of metal plate-making. For classified advertising, the typesetting revolution promised similar advantages. Advertisements would be keyboarded by telephonists on VDTs, automatically sorted into classifications and alphabetical order, and typeset into full pages without further human intervention.

Such promises proved harder to keep than anyone expected. Part of the trouble was that in the mid-1970s, when Fairfax crossed the typesetting Rubicon, the means of setting type electronically were more advanced than the computers which were needed to assemble information for setting. Furthermore, the company's requirements were unusual. It needed a system for three daily papers and two weeklies, and the volume of classified advertising in the *Sydney Morning Herald* was among the largest in the world. Saturday's *Herald* was then carrying up to 120 pages of small, single-column advertisements making extensive use of logotypes.

The output device, chosen in 1974, was the best of its kind at that time—a Digiset, made in Germany by the Siemens group, and capable, among other functions, of composing full-sized newspaper pages. Siemens could not provide the computer system needed to supply the Digisets with information for typesetting, but it recommended two computer software firms. As with the output device, this fateful choice was made primarily by the executive manager, Tom Farrell, the chief production manager, R. W. Weston, and the research and development manager, George Finn. They chose one of the firms recommended by Siemens—Arsycom, a Dutch company whose name was an acronym for 'Architecture of Systems with Computers'. Arsycom was new to this field, but then the field itself was new. The company had a reputation for skill in linking large numbers of computers and VDTs, and had recently received orders for typesetting systems from two Dutch newspapers, whose requirements were considerably less complex than those of the *Herald*.

In July 1975 Farrell wrote to Falkingham from Amsterdam saying:

> We have reached agreement [with Arsycom] on a scheme for the phased introduction into our Broadway plant of computers and other equipment which will effect the greatest change in production methods in the *Herald* since the introduction of the linotype. By December 1976 we will have the capacity to produce full pages of classified ads with logos inserted automatically at the rate of a page every one and a half minutes right up to the limit of our capacity to keyboard the ads into the system and our capacity to make the plates at the process engraving end. All sorting and classifying of the ads will be done automatically.

A contract was signed in October and Arsycom began work on a system which was to consist of seven PDP-11 computers with a joint data base for classified ads and editorial, 200 Australian-made VDTs, six Harris 2200 display ad terminals and two Digiset typesetters. It was to cost 4 666 000 guilders (at that time the equivalent of about $A1 555 000), and was to be operational by November 1976.

These estimates were woefully over-confident. Arsycom had underestimated both the number of computers it would need and the volume of traffic flowing between the computers. Time and again the target date had to be revised, and new agreements written.

The cost rose into the millions, not only because of unexpected technical difficulties but also because of improvement in the Dutch guilder's rate of exchange with the Australian dollar.

In August 1977 the authoritative computer journal *Seybold Report* sounded an ominous note of caution about the project. 'Rather than start with a 'system' and then select the appropriate output typesetters', it reported,

> Sydney apparently selected the output devices before addressing the problem of how they would be integrated and into what kind of a system. (A course of action we generally would not recommend!) . . . We find ourselves wondering whether the Sydney System, intended to be Arsycom's *pièce de résistance*, will in fact materialise as planned . . . It strikes us, frankly, that the editing capabilities of the present system are limited . . . Nor do we think that the daisy-chain interface would be viable in an intensely editorial environment . . . We presume that the Fairfax group and Arsycom have thought through all of the implications of the requirement to process such a tremendous volume of classified ads and that this most important portion of the system will do what it is supposed to do.

By 1979 when editorial production began, Fairfax's own system engineers were confirming Seybold's doubts. 'The system will not handle the work load for both editorial and classified advertising', said one report. 'The full [seven-computer] system working at full capacity will only handle one-twentieth of the work load specified in the contract for the full system. With the current hardware it is impossible in the near future (two years), to produce a system that will handle the work load.'

In May 1979 Farrell complained to Arsycom in the strongest possible terms about its preference for solving Broadway's problems in Amsterdam rather than on the spot. 'We have seen deadlines come and go', he wrote,

> many promises and hopes unfulfilled; and I cannot tolerate the situation any longer . . . I insist that you send to Sydney at the very earliest opportunity a team of Arsycom people who can solve all the outstanding problems in our system, and I insist that they stay until the job is finished and running to our satisfaction.

Five months later he sent a telex to Amsterdam saying that despite some progress there were still not enough Arsycom personnel in Sydney to handle 'hour by hour and day by day problems.' 'Your delay in delivering a viable system', he wrote, 'continues to hamper every aspect of our business operations and is costing us heavily in lost custom, while assisting the opposition'.

Because the system's work load could not be handled through the joint data base, classified and editorial had to be separated in 1980. This created more difficulties, for there was no longer any security of dual file. Under the split configuration, if material was lost from one data base there was no copy of it. The classified system began making up 'Positions Vacant' advertisements in single columns during 1980, but full pages were still more than it could handle. The editorial system, at its best, was adequate; at its worst, it was a nightmare. The system was introduced gradually, straining editorial patience more and more as it spread. There were few occasions when it seriously interfered with edition times, but the tension of unexpected 'crashes' and repeated loss of stories began to affect morale and health to an extent beyond the compensation of special VDT allowances paid to journalists.

In September 1980, within a few weeks of his retirement as general manager, Falkingham instructed Farrell to obtain another progress report from Arsycom, 'who have cost us several million dollars in lost potential savings'. 'It seems to me', he wrote with his usual cogency,

> that although there have been frequent references to minor advances and fine tunings we are not in a significantly better position than we were 15 months ago when I expressed enough concern about the outlook to say I thought we should cancel the Arsycom deal and start again . . .
>
> Far from solving our production problems the incursion into the new technology so far has intensified them because, in anticipation of the system working, we allowed our hot metal staffs to run down (particularly by ceasing to bring in the great numbers of apprentices we used to employ) and although we might yet emerge in an atmosphere of triumph we appear at the moment to be on the brink of becoming a laughing stock amongst our production and journalistic employees and in the eyes of other newspaper companies.

By that time Max Suich had been in his new position for two months. Suich was not mechanically minded (in Farrell's judgement, he 'didn't know the difference between a typewriter and a telephone'); but he knew a production problem when he encountered one, and it did not take him long to decide that something drastic had to be done about Arsycom.

His closest ally in this crisis was a relatively junior executive in the composing department—the assistant composing manager, Terry Waterer. A man of limited education, but well endowed with practical experience and determination, Waterer knew better than most people how serious the Arsycom situation was. The chief production manager, Weston, instructed him to keep his worries to himself. Torn between loyalty to his superior and loyalty to the company, Waterer began suffering from tension headaches. At one stage he went into retreat for religious solace. 'I was scared of what was happening', he later recalled, 'and what the company didn't know'.

Finally he went to see the chief editorial executive, and in Suich's words 'blew the whistle on what was actually going on in Arsycom in detail'. 'The system was not only sending us broke', said Suich, 'but was destroying our morale. People were being torn apart in this company between the reality and the illusion of Arsycom'. Suich and Waterer formed a close, confidential relationship. 'I used to tell Max everything that went on', recalled Waterer. 'He'd call me up and say: "Terry, Bob Weston says this, what do you think?" And I used to say, "Well, that can't happen because of such and such." No doubt Max used to tell Greg Gardiner, and so the coup began.'

At board level, concern was still tempered with hope. In October 1980 the managing Director of Arsycom, D. A. Schwarz, attended a meeting of the board. Welcoming him, the chairman said:

> We made plans for a phased changeover to the new technology. Unfortunately there have been delays and postponements and this has thrown our planning into some confusion. There has been a considerable cost to us in terms of lost opportunity for gaining revenue. For example, we believe we could greatly expand our classified advertising business if we now had a reliable system producing made-up pages of advertisements at a suitable speed . . .We appreciate the progress that has been made and the contribution of your system to our present production, but we had expected, and had planned for, much more.

Schwarz admitted that for various reasons delay had been greater than might reasonably have been anticipated. His company 'felt very bad about it', and had contributed $2 million of its own money to the project. He went on to promise completion of the system in three phases: reliable page makeup within four weeks; upgraded hardware, expanded memory facility and increased safety margins by the end of March 1981; and improved editorial and advertising response times for a completed system by October 1981.

Tom Farrell, the assistant general manager who had carried main responsibility for the project from its inception, told the directors that Arsycom's system was being asked to do too much at the present time. On the basis of volumes five years ago, he said, the system should be operating with a 25 to 30 per cent safety margin. None of that margin was now left. Sir Warwick said that if Fairfax was asking too much, then perhaps it too should take some of the responsibility for delay. Farrell said he thought so, because of Arsycom's own financial involvement; that company would have been bankrupt, he said, but for Schwarz's contribution from his personal fortune. Max Suich was less sympathetic. If the system was not performing satisfactorily by next March, he said, the company would know that it was in serious trouble.

None of Schwarz's objectives was achieved. In May 1981 Fairfax entered into a five-year agreement transferring Arsycom's responsibility to its Australian representative, Harri van den Berg, who thus became the principal contractor. His company, Beta Typesetting Systems Pty Ltd, undertook to develop an enhanced system in three phases: rejoining the two data bases, installing a new network to increase the speed and volume of communications between computers, and increasing the computer power. All this was to be done by the end of the year.

Instead, things went from bad to worse. The data bases were rejoined in August, but after a fortnight of crashes they had to be split again. A second attempt at Phase I also failed, and the split system continued to produce lost time, corruptions and scattered text during October and November. Journalists stopped work in protest. The *Financial Review* avoided losing whole pages only by filling in with pictures and house ads. A third attempt was made in February 1982, and for a while it seemed that the joined system was at last working satisfactorily. New dates were set for completion of Phase II, but in June the new network was eight months behind schedule.

By then—and, as some thought, not before time—Suich had given up illusion and faced reality. He persuaded Gardiner that the company should be looking for a new system altogether, and that Fred Brenchley was the person to handle this crucial change. Brenchley had no electronic experience; but at Rosebery, particularly during the strike, he had amply demonstrated his ability to get things done.

Educated like Suich and Gardiner at a Sydney high school (Cleveland Street), Brenchley was forty years old, bearded, bespectacled and outgoing. He had joined the *Financial Review* in 1970, been Canberra correspondent for the *National Times*, and edited the *Financial Review* from 1978 until his move to Sungravure in 1980.

When Brenchley took up his new appointment in May 1982, he quickly learnt the worst about Arsycom's many failings on both the editorial and advertising fronts. The *Herald*'s chief classified manager, John Newnham, and the classified manager, Max Garden, urged him to solve their problems by installing the kind of system which was operating successfully at the *Age*. Arsycom's response time could be as long as 25 seconds. 'Journalists have to put up with this', said Newnham, 'but our customers won't'. Furthermore, Arsycom was not helping the classified telephonists to become sales advisers as well as copytakers. 'The *Age* reports great success with the sale of highlight lines on classifieds', said Newnham. 'Our system has no facility to sell highlight lines. The *Age* and the *Telegraph* can quote exact costs to classified customers by the push of a button. We have to guess.'

Above all, Newnham argued against replacement of the editorial system alone. 'Don't bail editorial out and leave us with the *Titanic*', he said. 'It has the potential to send us broke.' That possibility was receding, however, for Suich and Brenchley were already committed to getting everybody off the *Titanic*. On 11 June Suich put it to Gardiner that the company should decide in principle to replace Arsycom-Beta with a new production system.

'If, in the meantime', he wrote,

> between decision in principle and the finalisation of specifications for a new system a final success is achieved by Arsycom-Beta, well and good. But in the likely event that this will not occur I propose that we build into the 1982/83 budget the necessary funding to investigate and place an order for an alternative system . . .I think we must face the fact that our only alternative to the above is to be plagued by production crises and financial uncertainties for another two years at least—a scenario which would be tragic for this company.

To drive the point home, Brenchley and Waterer arranged to load the system with every possible demand that could be made upon it. The result was predictably, though only temporarily, disastrous.

On Brenchley's recommendation, Gardiner obtained quick board approval on 17 June to move away from Arsycom-Beta. Farrell was overseas, but Gardiner, in answer to a question from one of the directors, said he thought the assistant general manager was aware of the views which he was expressing.

The search for a new system was entrusted mainly to Frank McMahon, the company's data processing manager, Terry Waterer, who had recently succeeded Weston as chief production manager, and Graham Stevenson, the editorial technology manager. After a detailed study of requirements they invited proposals from five leading suppliers of composition systems. Four responded, but only two of those met the fundamental criterion of providing off-the-shelf systems proven by use. One was Atex Inc, whose system, manufactured in Bedford, Massachusetts, was already operating at the Melbourne *Age, Boston Globe, Richmond Times* and *USA Today*. The other was Systems Integrators Inc. (SII), in Sacramento, California, whose system could be seen working at the *Washington Post, Houston Chronicle* and *Los Angeles Times*.

McMahon, Waterer and Stevenson—accompanied by the research and development manager, George Finn, the editorial systems manager, John Waugh, and the systems development supervisor, Terry Gallagher—were sent by Brenchley to the United States in October to visit and inspect the suppliers and their customers. On their return, they at first favoured Atex as being a proven system and therefore the safer choice. But it was not the better system. The state of the art was undoubtedly SII, and during long and earnest debate the selection team swung round to unanimous support for that system. Not only was it better able to meet the functional requirements of editorial, advertising and production departments, they reported, but its potential for the future was greater, should the need arise to increase the number of system users, or should new functions become available.

If a new system was to be introduced in place of Arsycom, it would have to be done quickly, for the company's redundancy agreement with the Printing and Kindred Industries Union ran only until December 1984. And if that agreement had to be renegotiated, the PKIU would undoubtedly try to strike an even harder bargain than the terms already agreed upon for redundancy caused by technological change. For many printers who would not be staying on with the new technology, the prospect of redundancy was financially attractive and its recurring postponement a cause of annoyance.

On 9 December the board considered a recommendation from Brenchley for the introduction of the SII system at a cost of $15 million. Gardiner said the cost was large, but something had to be done to break out of the present situation. The new system would make the company hum instead of limping from crisis to crisis. Arthur Lissenden asked whether the company had any financial redress against Arsycom, on which it had spent $7 million, and Tom Farrell said not as far as he was aware. This was Farrell's last board appearance as assistant general manager, for he retired later that month.

Approving the purchase of a new system at a price not to exceed $15 million, the board authorized management to negotiate with both SII and Atex for the best price and installation schedules. In March 1983 a contract was signed for an SII System/55 comprising two configurations, one each for editorial and classified advertising, both interfacing with Coyote VDTs manufactured by SII, and both using Tandem Non-Stop II computers. The installation schedule was as tight as anyone could wish, and it went like clockwork.

As if to remove any last trace of doubt about the wisdom of this change, Arsycom put on its worst ever performance. During April the system went down 191 times for a total of 2777 minutes—an average of six 'downs', resulting in 92 minutes of lost production, every day. It failed on three consecutive Friday nights, each time threatening but not quite preventing publication of the largest *Herald* of the week.

The SII editorial system was delivered in August, and in November the *National Times* became the first Broadway paper to be written, sub-edited and set entirely by that means. The *Sun*, *Sun-Herald* and *Financial Review* followed at monthly intervals, and on Sunday night, 25 March 1984, the *Herald*'s printers rattled their galleys (tin type-trays) against steel trolleys and benchtops—not in farewell to a retiring brother or welcome to an apprentice coming out of his time, which were the usual reasons for a 'galley rattle', but in farewell to lead type. Monday's *Herald* was printed with hot metal, and Tuesday's was entirely cold type.

When direct printing with plastic plates was introduced a few days later, the last vestige of lead disappeared from Broadway. Out of approximately 1400 production positions in the newspaper plant, 364 were made redundant by the new technology. Two hundred and eighty-six printers terminated voluntarily; thirty transferred to publishing, press room and other departments; and the rest were accounted for by natural attrition.

There was no redundancy in the editorial department. On the contrary, journalists assumed a larger part in production, for the new technology enabled them to take over the typesetters' function as well as their own. In the *Herald* of 27 March a front-page story welcomed the Coyote terminals whose pervasive, quiet clicking had transformed the work practices of reporters and sub-editors and would soon make possible substantial increases in the company's editorial budget.

> Typewriters lie abandoned in dusty corners of the newsroom. Only a handful of journalists still use them for personal notes and rough drafts. The newsroom is coming to terms with a machine that contains the entire Macquarie dictionary to check spelling and the whole *New York Times* and wire services each day . . .The *Herald* is nearly paperless from the time a journalist types a story [on screen] until it hits the street.

Arsycom was used to a decreasing extent until May 1984, when the new advertising system came into operation and SII took over completely, with 650 Coyotes.

On 30 June Fairfax terminated the Beta Typesetting Systems agreement, which was due to run until May 1986, on grounds that Beta had failed to perform in accordance with it. Beta took legal action, claiming $355 378 as fees for the unexpired part of the agreement, plus damages. Fairfax issued a counter-claim for damages, but eventually both actions lapsed without reaching court.

So ended this painful and costly episode. Fairfax had embraced the new technology with great expectations, but too impetuously. Expecting more than the technology of the time could deliver, the company then waited far too long before acknowledging that a mistake had been made. At least, however, a useful lesson in caution had been learnt. During the next few years Brenchley was to recommend huge expenditure on new equipment for the plant at Broadway, and his golden rule on such occasions was always never to buy anything unless it could first be seen working successfully somewhere else.

The Broadway plant had changed very little since its construction during the 1950s, and had not been adequately maintained. By the time computerized typesetting and direct printing were introduced in 1984 the press room was equipped with one line (22 units) of approximately 40-year-old Hoe presses, one line (22 units) of 30-year-old Crabtree presses, and two lines (40 units) of 9- to 20-year-old Goss presses. The company also had in storage two Goss Mark II high-speed presses which it had purchased from the *Chicago Tribune* in 1982.

Something had to be done about this plant. Ideally the company could have invested in a 'green field' site re-equipped with new offset presses. This option would have cost at least $300 million. It was considered, but thought to be too costly. Instead Brenchley recommended to the board that the company upgrade its plant by installing some of the Chicago units and putting letterpress colour on them. This was a compromise designed to secure production until the next century without need of vast capital expenditure.

All in all, counting the SII system, John Fairfax was to spend some $80 million on upgrading the Broadway plant during the 1980s. In the second half of that decade the press room was equipped with Japanese TKS four-colour satellite units and the existing Goss colour decks were altered to run four-colour across the web. The publishing room was equipped with Swiss Ferag equipment for inserting advertising sheets and brochures into the printed papers.

The TKS colour units and decks came in response to a difficult management brief: 'How can Broadway maintain its colour and quality edge over an aggressive competitor and at the same time minimise expenditure on new plant until a decision is made on the long-term production requirements in the Sydney newspaper market?' Not surprisingly, given that warning about expenditure, the result was less than ideal. Previously Broadway had been able to print only single colours on newsprint as it was running through the press. Brenchley wanted process colour in the *Sun* and the *Herald*. The TKS four-colour units and the colour decks made this possible, but in the view of many at Broadway the resultant letterpress quality fell far short of what could have been achieved with new offset presses such as those used by the *Newcastle Herald* and *Illawarra Mercury*.

On the other hand, all the technical and industrial advice available to Brenchley was against combining offset with letterpress. Offset printing would have required its own award, with higher rates of pay than for letterpress, and this would almost certainly have created industrial tension. The upgrading was far from perfect, but there were reasons for the lack of perfection.

4
Capital

I

Each passing decade seemed to bring its own particular crisis for the Fairfax family. It will be recalled that after three generations of family unity the first tremor of dissension made itself felt during the 1940s when John Fitzgerald Fairfax was squeezed off the board and talked into selling his shares to Warwick and Vincent. In the 1950s Vincent Fairfax came under similar pressure from his fellow directors, Warwick Fairfax and Rupert Henderson. He resigned from the board of the private company, but prudently held on to all his shares and joined the board of the public company when that came into existence three years later. Warwick's turn came in the 1960s: denied support by the rest of the board, including his son James, he was obliged to stand down from the chairmanship until the danger of some potentially embarrassing litigation had passed. Warwick Fairfax considered himself to have been betrayed—not only in that brief crisis, but again during the 1970s, when he was made to resign from the chairmanship in favour of James.

What next? Although the pre-eminent crisis of the 1980s still lay concealed ahead, beyond imagining, a tremor of considerable magnitude did run through the House of Fairfax more or less on schedule in 1984, shaking the foundations of family unity just as roughly as anything that had gone before. It concerned a proposal by Gardiner to raise capital for the first time in twenty years. In order to understand why all but one of the directors thought this was necessary, and why Sir Warwick thought it not only unnecessary but also dangerous, we must first look at the substantially higher level of corporate growth achieved by the new management team since 1981. This will involve one or two digressions, but in due course we shall return to the delicate subject of capital.

In 1981 Gardiner and Cotton commenced a review of the company and its balance sheet to determine strategies for improving profitability by turning loss-making operations into profit, or selling them; acquiring another television station and more radio stations, newspapers and magazines; reducing corporate borrowings and lengthening their terms; strengthening the balance sheet and the company's performance ratios; and developing an adequate capital base, commensurate with the growth of the company's assets and business, to support a strong level of corporate growth. During the next three years, in spite of business recession in 1982–83, a number of objectives were achieved. All of these strengthened the company; but some of them, requiring heavy investment, ran counter to the aim of reducing corporate borrowing.

The first major achievement was selling back to the Herald and Weekly Times group most of the 14.9 per cent of HWT shares which Fairfax had bought for $52.3 million in 1979 to keep its Melbourne ally out of Murdoch's clutches. This parcel, purchased at takeover prices with borrowed funds, had lost value alarmingly. It was therefore with great relief that in July 1982, after another takeover bid for HWT (by Robert Holmes à Court) had loomed and passed away, Gardiner persuaded Queensland Press Ltd to buy 12 per cent for $43 million, leaving Fairfax with only 2.9 per cent of HWT. The transaction raised Queensland Press's holding to 26.9 per cent.

Normally, by reason of an amendment to the Companies Act, this would have required Queensland Press to make a full bid for HWT. As it happened, however, the company enjoyed an immunity provided by its agreement with John Fairfax, entered into before the Act had been amended, that in the event of one company deciding to sell its HWT shares it would give the other first option to buy. One of Holmes à Court's associated companies mounted a legal challenge to the sale, but nothing came of it. Soon afterwards Fairfax also sold its remaining 2.9 per cent to Queensland Press. This effectively ended the option agreement between Fairfax and Queensland Press, but in Gardiner's view that no longer mattered, for HWT then seemed safe from Murdoch's unwanted attention.

As a corollary of these share sales—which obliged Queensland Press to reduce its television holdings in compliance with the Broadcasting and Television Act—Fairfax paid Queensland Press $5.1 million for a 19.9 per cent interest in Brisbane TV, the operator of station BTQ7. Thus, at the price of $14 a share, Fairfax went part of the way towards acquiring a companion station for its wholly owned ATN7 in Sydney.

Its reason for not going any further immediately was Gardiner's concern, shared by the board, to bring the company's borrowings back to a more conservative level. Gardiner intended to acquire a further 3 per cent of Brisbane TV each six months, as provided for in the Broadcasting and Television Act, once the Australian Broadcasting Tribunal had approved the initial purchase. The tribunal took almost a year to do that, and before Fairfax made any further purchase the highly profitable Brisbane TV came under takeover pressure. The predator was Television Wollongong Transmissions Ltd, a company whose major shareholder, Bruce Gordon, was an Australian citizen living in New York, a man well known to Gardiner and the general manager of ATN, Ted Thomas. At its meeting in September 1983 the Fairfax board authorized Gardiner to bid against TWT for full acquisition of Brisbane TV, offering up to $19 per share.

That proved a long way short of the mark. Bruce Gordon, a former Australian representative for Paramount Pictures and later president of Paramount Television International, was on his yacht at Rhode Island watching another predator's boat, *Australia II*, win the America's Cup. One of his guests on board was Ted Thomas. They picked each other's brains about BTQ, and at every opportunity Thomas telephoned Gardiner in Sydney. TWT lifted the bidding above $20, and it also began to look as if Holmes à Court might join the hunt. He was already bidding against Fairfax in another contest, concerning David Syme & Co Ltd, which will be recounted later.

The December meeting of the board authorized Gardiner to offer up to $26 per share, which would value BTQ at $43 million. Gardiner looked back wistfully at the $14 he had paid for such shares only seventeen months before, but told the directors they could afford to offer as much as $37.22 a share before the return would become negative on a profit basis. The Brisbane station's annual profit was now three times higher than when Fairfax had first bought in ($7 million before tax) and television stations generally were escalating in price.

The price which finally persuaded TWT to sell its holding just before Christmas, for a capital gain of $5 million, was $27.50. The full cost to Fairfax was $45.3 million, roughly twice as much as the $23.1 million which would have been required at $14 per share. Gardiner justified this seeming exorbitance, saying that he felt more comfortable paying $27.50 a share than he had when paying $14 a share in 1982. The $14 was more expensive in terms of profit than $27.50 was in 1983, for in 1982 no one would have anticipated that BTQ was on the verge of earning such high profits. It continued to prosper, contributing about $3 million to group profit in each of the next three years; but the price of that welcome cash flow was to be found in the company's level of outside borrowing, which rose from $81.7 million in 1983 to $105.2 million in 1984.

Other factors were also at work in determining this level of debt. The company had of course recouped $43 million by its sale of HWT shares. But against this, in addition to the outlay for BTQ, it was in the process of raising its ownership of David Syme from 57.46 per cent to 100 per cent. And here we come to a second digression. The partnership between John Fairfax and shareholding members of the Syme family had not been without tension since its formation in 1966, and more particularly since Fairfax lifted its shareholding above 50 per cent in 1972, making David Syme one of its subsidiaries. The *Age* had been preserved, in the full spirit of the Syme–Fairfax Partnership Deed, as an independent paper of high quality and responsibility. The Deed also provided safeguards for both Syme and Fairfax sides of the partnership. The six-member board consisted of three Melbourne directors and three Sydney directors, with no provision in the articles of association for a casting vote by the chairman. Thus, in the event of a 3–3 deadlock, the matter would lapse for want of a majority. This effectively gave both sides a right of veto. It was sometimes said that the Syme Partners had the right to appoint the company's chief executive. More correctly, neither side had the power to foist an unwelcome chief executive on the other. At the time the partnership was formed, the managing director had been Ranald Macdonald—whose mother, Nancy Neill, was one of David Syme's grandchildren—and he continued to hold that position.

Macdonald and his fellow Melbourne directors felt that he also should have been chairman of the board. But because the Fairfax directors maintained that the chairman and the chief executive should not be the same person, there was no permanent chairman. The Fairfax directors [from 1981 onwards: James Fairfax, John Fairfax and Gardiner] agreed that the chairman ought to be from Melbourne and, while the stalemate over Macdonald continued, a 'meeting chairmanship' rotated between the three Syme directors.

For all their usefulness, these safeguards did not preclude sharp differences of opinion around the board table, usually concerning commercial decisions by the managing director. Macdonald had presided over major achievements by his company—notably the move to a new building in Spencer Street, installation of offset presses, the use of colour before other newspapers, and improved marketing. He was energetic and exuberant, a man of high ideals and great personal charm; but in the opinion of the directors from Sydney he was also what Gardiner once called 'a moonbeam in a jar', liable to lead the company along hazardous paths.

One such path led to Computicket Australia Pty Ltd, the booking agency in which—on Macdonald's recommendation, and with reluctant approval by the Fairfax directors—David Syme had invested $250 000 in 1977. To Macdonald's disappointment, John Fairfax Ltd did not follow Syme's example. The agency later collapsed and in 1981 its prime mover, the theatrical entrepreneur Harry M. Miller, was found guilty of fraudulent misappropriation and sentenced to three years in gaol. The financial loss to David Syme was relatively small, and some of Macdonald's Melbourne colleagues later acknowledged that they too might have been taken in by Computicket. The Fairfax directors were less sympathetic.

1981 was a particularly bad year for Syme–Fairfax harmony. In

February Macdonald appeared before an Inquiry into the Ownership and Control of Newspapers In Victoria—the only inquiry of its kind ever held in Australia—conducted by a retired Supreme Court judge, the Hon. J. G. Norris, QC. The Norris Inquiry had been commissioned by the Hamer Government as a result of sustained protest by Friends of the Age and others, amongst whom Ranald Macdonald had been foremost, at Fairfax's acquisition of its 14.9 per cent holding in HWT. Macdonald was in no way inhibited by Syme's partnership with Fairfax. In his view the 14.9 per cent compromised Fairfax's 57.46 per cent holding in Syme, threatening the presentation of diverse opinion in the Melbourne press, allowing domination of that market and consequently reducing newspaper competition. He asked Fairfax to sell its Melbourne Herald shares, and made appropriate representations to the Trade Practices Commission, in each case to no avail.

Appearing as a witness before the Norris Inquiry for several days—not on behalf of David Syme, but in a personal capacity, briefing his own counsel—Macdonald returned to the attack. In his evidence-in-chief he said that Fairfax's decision to buy the 14.9 per cent had been made without consideration for the *Age* or David Syme, and that it had been damaging for the company, the paper and the public.

> I know that the board of Fairfax and the board of the Herald, and our board, made reassuring public noises [he said]. But to really understand it further one ought to recognise that The Herald has 14.1 per cent in The Age and the lever to the partnership that was set up between the Syme shareholders and Fairfax as a company was that The Herald was in competition to Fairfax in Melbourne. The basis of the partnership, therefore, was that we would have to work together or else the Melbourne Herald, being the major outside shareholder—having the ability at an annual meeting to dominate or at least not just dominate, but pass resolutions, which could only be voted on by the remaining shareholders under the terms of the partnership—meant that it gave a potential lever which I am in no way suggesting would be used by the current leadership of Fairfax, nor by members of the family that I know, but it was, as I have said before, a Sword of Damocles, and still is . . .

Macdonald had opposed concentration of media ownership often enough in the past, but on this occasion it was a case of one partner criticizing another. The directors of John Fairfax Ltd, confident of their own propriety in having gone to the Melbourne Herald's defence, had much to say about him at their February board meeting. Arthur Lissenden thought Macdonald could not possibly stay as managing director. Gardiner said that Macdonald, through his evidence, was doing the press collectively an enormous disservice, the repercussions of which would be felt for years. Although it was possible for Fairfax's own counsel to give him an uncomfortable time on cross-examination, he did not think it would be wise at this juncture to have a public fight. James Fairfax also counselled patience. Macdonald's evidence did not differ much from what he had said publicly eighteen months before, and on that occasion the Fairfax board had decided there was nothing to be gained by taking action against him.

Gardiner and Tom Farrell later gave extensive evidence at the Norris Inquiry, but refrained from picking up any of the more provocative gauntlets thrown down by Macdonald. So far as the HWT purchase was concerned, Gardiner made no apology for having further complicated the cross-holdings in Melbourne.

> I think primarily there was this respect for The Herald and Weekly Times group and the feeling that the maintenance of the independence of that group would be in the interests of Victoria and Australia. There were other commercial interests from our own point of view . . . the question of the joint [Fairfax/HWT] ownership of Australian Newsprint Mills, the question of AAP and to some extent the question of the two Channel 7 stations, the 7 Station in Sydney and the 7 Station in Melbourne. After considering all of these matters the board took a decision to acquire that 14.9 per cent interest.

In his 1981 report Norris made various recommendations, including the establishment of a Press Amalgamations Authority, to prevent any further concentration of ownership which might diminish the variety of information, ideas and opinion in Victorian newspapers. Those in the industry who regarded such government regulation as a threat to press freedom need not have worried, for the Victorian Government ignored the Norris Report.

Another subject of concern at the February meeting of the Fairfax board was David Syme's participation in a joint venture with Henry Jones IXL Ltd and CRA Ltd to purchase 61.2 per cent of Rediffusion Television Ltd (RTV), a company holding one of the two television licences in Hong Kong. RTV had already lost more than its capital. Its station, running a poor second in the ratings, broadcast in English and Chinese. Almost all the drama programmes shown on the Chinese language channel had to be produced locally, with very limited prospect of international re-sale. Syme's initial investment was $A2 million, but after deferred purchase of the property from which RTV operated, its full outlay was expected to be twice that amount.

Falkingham, who was still a director of both Fairfax and Syme, placed on record his determined opposition to the proposal, which seemed to him 'another Computicket'. James Fairfax said that he and Gardiner did not share Falkingham's view, and it should be remembered that the Fairfax representatives on the Syme board had voted to approve the proposal.

That did not mean they liked the sound of it; rather it meant that, because of the partnership deed, they felt obliged to let Macdonald have his way. In Gardiner's mind there was also some thought of allowing Macdonald to face the consequences of his own decisions.

To Macdonald, it must also be said, the venture seemed a sensible path into the electronic media. Because of the tracing provisions of the Broadcasting and Television Act, Fairfax's electronic interests, combined with its holdings in Syme and HWT, prevented Syme from moving into Australian television, or even into Australian radio beyond a 15 per cent interest which it already had in one FM station. So why not try Hong Kong? During the next two years that path led deeper into loss. Macdonald, ever-confident, reminded Fairfax of its own record of persevering with loss-makers until they emerged from the red. In 1982 the Australian consortium bought out the 38.8 per cent of RTV owned by Rediffusion (Hong Kong) Ltd and on-sold 50 per cent of the entire share capital to a Hong Kong partner—the Chiu family, whose business interests included banking, hotels, cinemas and film production. It was hoped that the Chius would provide local management expertise and a background in the entertainment industry as well as increasing the station's capital base. The restructured company was named Asian Television Ltd; the head of the Chiu family, Deacon Chiu, was appointed chairman; and Macdonald was deputy chairman. Syme's further injection of capital at this stage was $A7.5 million.

Nothing improved. At the Fairfax board meeting in April 1983, Gardiner warned directors that Asian Television would run out of its current level of cash some time in June. The Chius were expecting all shareholders to contribute additional funds. In one move by Syme, he said, all the profit worked for by the Fairfax group could disappear. He had warned Macdonald that Syme was facing a major write-off, but Macdonald had not been able to see that. According to the minutes, Gardiner said that

> Whilst the three Fairfax directors on the Syme board had endorsed the proposal to invest in Hong Kong television they in fact had considerable reservations. They were all against the recommendation but Mr Macdonald persisted. There was the thought at the back of the Fairfax directors' minds that Mr Macdonald might act as he did in the Norris inquiry. They had ultimately agreed because the Fairfax/Syme agreement was non-commercial . . .
>
> Mr Gardiner said he had innumerable discussions with Mr Macdonald and had tried to get close to him. However, the attempts had fallen on stony ground . . .
>
> Mr Lissenden said . . . we needed to be thinking of who would be

> capable of performing as a chief executive [of David Syme] should the board be faced with a major decision of this nature.
>
> Mr Gardiner said that was a good point and he had been thinking about it.
>
> Sir David Griffin said the board had reached the point where it was the responsibility of the directors to be thinking of what they should do if there was a strategy out of the partnership.

A solution to most of these problems presented itself two months later. A mutual acquaintance of Gardiner and Macdonald, the merchant banker David Block, told Gardiner that Macdonald 'wanted to see him about the shares'. Somewhat taken aback, Gardiner said that Fairfax had no intention of selling its controlling interest in David Syme.

'I'm sorry I didn't make that clearer', replied Block. 'What Ranald means is for Fairfax to buy his shares and all the other Syme family shares.'

Gardiner immediately contacted Macdonald, who said he had come to the conclusion that his future no longer lay with David Syme. He wanted to pursue some other career, and asked if Fairfax would be interested in buying his and the rest of the family's shares, amounting to 15.31 per cent of Syme's issued capital. Whether or not the trouble in Hong Kong was a factor in his decision, there were undoubtedly other factors as well. He later acknowledged having become increasingly aware of conflict at board level ('The idea of the partnership was that you wouldn't vote three-three, yet we frequently seemed to have to go to a vote'), and some of the larger shareholders in the family had been asking how they could get out.

'The family gradually reduced', Macdonald told a radio reporter in Melbourne.

> After all, [there were] a hundred-odd members of the family, and they sold some of their shares and they had to be picked up. Only a few of us could [buy them]. Then it reached the stage in the last six months or year that the prices went incredibly high and therefore that trickle became a torrent. I had to determine whether all the shares should end up with me in huge financial commitments and I should be the only person holding the side together . . . and commit myself for the next ten or 20 years. I really did think that was wrong. I think 19 years running a paper is wrong anyway. It's too long.

When Gardiner reported Macdonald's overture to the Fairfax board in June, Sir Warwick added the news that he had been approached by a former Lord Mayor of Melbourne, R. J. Walker, asking whether Fairfax would be interested in selling its Syme shares to a group of Melbourne businessmen for $17 million. The directors at first wondered whether the two matters might be connected, but further inquiries by Gardiner showed that Macdonald was not associated with Walker's group, and that he wanted the purchase to proceed as expeditiously as possible. Nothing further was heard from Walker.

Although the 'natural' price of Syme shares was generally put at about $2, shares had recently changed hands for as much as $2.90, probably because of certain spectacular developments in Reuters which, as will be explained later, were soon to benefit Australian media companies. Gardiner advised the Fairfax board to be more generous than it needed to be under a pricing formula contained in the partnership agreement, and suggested an offer which Macdonald, who was himself the largest family shareholder, could put confidently to the rest of the family—$3.80. The Fairfax directors authorized him to put that to the Symes and authorized him also to consider making a takeover bid at the same price for all other shares in the company. There was risk, of course, that a full takeover bid would again cause the kind of public concern which had led to the Norris Inquiry. But as Gardiner reminded the board, the Syme–Fairfax partnership deed provided some defence against criticism. Under that agreement, Syme shareholders wishing to sell were obliged to offer their shares to Fairfax, and Fairfax was obliged to buy them. At this board meeting, in August, the directors also agreed to invest a further $700 000 in Asia Television to keep it operating until Syme and the other two Australian partners could extricate themselves from a situation which Gardiner, who had become a director of that company, described as 'absolutely appalling'.

At a meeting on 14 September the great majority of the Syme family shareholders, owning 13.54 per cent out of the family's 15.31 per cent, accepted the offer of $3.80. Fairfax, with its stake in David Syme thus enlarged to 71 per cent, announced the next day that it would proceed to bid at the same price for full ownership. While the Fairfax directors were meeting that day, news reached them that the Victorian Premier, John Cain, had issued a statement saying he was 'sufficiently Victorian and sufficiently parochial to not want to see the *Age* controlled from Sydney', and would be exploring means to block a Fairfax takeover. The directors guessed that he was taking a leaf out of Hamer's book to protect himself politically. They hoped there would be no resurrection of the Norris Report, and neither there was. With Ranald Macdonald remaining *hors de combat*, Cain did not deem it necessary to persevere with the issue.

Apart from the few shares still owned by some family members, 14.1 per cent of Syme was held by HWT and about 15 per cent by others outside the family. With HWT's parcel, which at first Gardiner was reasonably confident of acquiring, Fairfax would need only an additional 4 per cent to achieve 90 per cent of the share capital. Ninety per cent was one of the two pre-requisites for compulsory acquisition of remaining shares, and, with most of the Symes squared away, the company did not anticipate difficulty in complying with the second condition, which was to acquire 75 per cent of the company's individual shareholdings.

In October, however, only a few days before HWT's board was due to consider the Fairfax offer, Holmes à Court's Bell Group offered $5 a share for the HWT holding. This placed considerable strain on the already rather tense alliance between HWT and Fairfax. HWT had its shareholders' interests to protect, but Fairfax, while invoking the loyalty which it expected from an ally, felt that to match Bell's offer would be unfair to the Syme vendors. After some hard words between Gardiner and HWT's chairman and chief executive, Sir Keith Macpherson, and a strongly worded letter from James Fairfax to Macpherson, Sir Keith wrote to James on 17 November:

> . . . I must say that in recent times there appears to have developed a rather cavalier attitude on the part of Fairfax that we must at all times accept their point of view—almost as if we owe it to your company.
>
> I am just as aware as you are that Holmes à Court's offer is purely disruptive, but I make the point that it is I who have to answer to our shareholders, not you.
>
> You say there is clearly no legal barrier to our accepting the lower offer and that may be true in the strict sense. However, the offer has obviously been made to embarrass us and create discussion, and could lead to investigation and maybe action by the NCSC, and possibly litigation induced by Bell . . .
>
> You say you are unaware of a single occasion on which you have let us down. I agree with that, but must say that the same applies on our side.
>
> What does upset me is the suggestion that we must automatically accept the Fairfax viewpoint . . .
>
> Finally, I have to say James, we are not convinced that we should accept your offer for the Syme shares. I would hope that you will be prepared to talk about it.

In reply, James Fairfax denied the development of any cavalier attitude on Fairfax's part. 'Our view', he wrote, 'is that even the potentially harshest critics of your acceptance at the lower price would acknowledge publicly that you have every right to do so and that commercial logic would be with you if you did . . .'

In the absence of a matching offer from Fairfax, HWT decided to keep its Syme shares as a strategic investment. It did agree, however, to the reciprocal selling of two smaller cross-holdings. Fairfax sold its remaining 2.9 per cent of HWT's share capital to Queensland Press, and HWT sold to a Fairfax retirement fund its own holding of

1.72 per cent in John Fairfax Ltd. 'With the cross-holdings split away', remarked the Fairfax minutes with evident satisfaction, 'the two companies would be as separate as they could be. The only overlaps left would be down the line i.e. ANM, AAP and the Seven Network'.

And, of course, David Syme. So far as that was concerned, HWT's attitude left Fairfax owning 83.7 per cent of a publicly listed company with outside shareholders, one of whom might at any time decide to deal with Holmes à Court. But at least Fairfax could now release itself from an uncomfortable partnership. At the annual general meeting of David Syme on 18 October 1983, James Fairfax read into the minutes an undertaking of respect for the independence of the *Age*.

> The resignation of Mr Ranald Macdonald [he said], effectively the last of the Syme family associated at management level with David Syme & Co. Ltd, must be viewed with some sadness. To say that it follows a trend in which, world wide, the strong link between founding family and great newspaper is disappearing does nothing, I am sure, to alleviate the feelings which Mr Macdonald and the Syme family must have today . . .
>
> It is the intention of John Fairfax & Sons Ltd to strengthen and extend the high level of communications service which David Syme & Co Ltd provided to the Victorian community. In particular the independent character and editorial attitude of the *Age* will continue to be encouraged. The company will continue to operate as an independent entity and it is our aim to have a majority of Victorian residents on the board.

The 17-year-old Syme–Fairfax agreement ceased on 14 March 1984, and from that date the new managing director was 49-year-old G. J. Taylor, a former editor-in-chief of the *Age* who had later shown great administrative ability as group operations manager. There would be no 'Melbourne for Melburnians' outcry about this appointment, for although Tasmanian by birth Greg Taylor had spent almost all of his career on the *Age* and was held in high regard by the staff.

With the partnership gone, the way was clear for a permanent chairman. John B. Fairfax sounded James out about his own chances of being appointed to that post. These two second cousins, then aged forty-one and fifty respectively, had never enjoyed a close or easy relationship. Their personalities and interests were different. They had adjoining offices at Broadway, with a connecting door; but in the course of nine years, by John's count, James had come through that door only three times. John put this down to his cousin's natural reserve, and to a certain protectiveness about the chairmanship.

Although James kept his distance, he acknowledged John's right to some form of titular recognition. In 1981, at a rare lunch together,

James said he thought that at an appropriate time John should assume a new post of deputy chairman of John Fairfax Ltd. He himself would probably relinquish the chairmanship in his early sixties, said James, leaving the way open for his cousin. According to John's record of this conversation, James remarked that some time in the future they would both be 'faced with the entry of young Warwick into the organisation'. James's stepbrother, then aged eighteen, was still at Oxford, but would soon be going to work for a merchant bank in the United States. His mother would probably seek an early seat on the board for Warwick, said James, and the general manager would need to have a large say in his involvement with the company when the time came.

As for the Syme chairmanship, John was to be disappointed. Sir Warwick suggested to James that he, James, should become chairman of David Syme as well as the parent company. Gardiner agreed, and James adopted that course. The deputy chairman was W. G. Bland, a new director and former general manager of David Syme.

In April 1984 Sir Keith Macpherson surprised Gardiner with a letter saying that HWT 'really should dispose of' its Syme shares. The two chief executives had been arguing by telephone quite recently about another cause of friction between their companies—Salmat Pty Ltd, a Sydney letterbox distribution company, in which Gardiner and Brenchley had been trying to arrange a joint Fairfax-HWT investment. Brenchley had talked down the asking price for 49 per cent of Salmat, from $5 million to $4 million, and was still trying to lower it further and lift the stake to 50 per cent. Although the deal seemed to be going ahead, there was disagreement between HWT and Fairfax as to how they should divide the 49 or 50 per cent. Fairfax wanted a 50/50 split, but HWT wanted 67 per cent for itself. In February, without warning, HWT went to Salmat with an offer of $5 million for 49 per cent. Naturally Salmat accepted.

Sir Keith telephoned Gardiner to say that he had deferred making a public announcement in the hope that Fairfax would participate on the basis of two-thirds for HWT and one-third for Fairfax. At the next board meeting Gardiner said that HWT's treatment of Fairfax as a partner was beyond his comprehension.

> Sir Keith had said he thought Fairfax would have acted in the same way if they had not [the minutes stated]. Mr Gardiner said he had replied that Fairfax would never have acted in such a way to a partner. [HWT] had paid $1.5 million more than need have been paid. Even if they were to reduce the price to us and were prepared to offer a 50 per cent interest, we would still not be prepared as a matter of principle to participate.

And now Sir Keith was talking about selling the Syme shares! Some of the Fairfax directors speculated that he may have been trying to make amends, if not for Salmat then perhaps for past failure by the HWT group's television station in Adelaide to meet its share of the Seven Network's payment for access to a communications satellite. As it happened, however, no amends were made. Months went by with virtually no increase in Fairfax's percentage of Syme. On 28 March 1985 Fairfax made a second offer of $6 per share. Before the end of stock exchange trading that day, competitive bidding by Bell had driven the price of Syme shares to $9.30.

Next day HWT offered its 14.1 per cent holding at arm's length on the open market at $10.20 per share. Brokers for Fairfax and Bell shouted 'Buy' simultaneously, and in the uproar there was confusion as to who had shouted first, and how many shares had been bought. Bell took out a writ claiming to have bought all of HWT's 1 693 600 Syme shares and seeking performance of the contract. It also obtained injunctions from the Victorian Supreme Court restraining HWT from selling the shares, Fairfax from seeking to buy them, and the Melbourne Stock Exchange from proceeding with an inquiry into the purported transactions.

The court handed the matter back to the Stock Exchange, which ruled on 22 April that HWT had sold one million of its Syme shares and the purchaser had been John Fairfax. Although this lifted its holding to 92 per cent, Fairfax still lacked the 75 per cent of Syme's 375 individual shareholders which it also needed before being able to gather the remaining shares by compulsory acquisition. It bought the balance of HWT's parcel at the same price, lifting its holding to 97.7 per cent; but 101 shareholders, including twenty-eight members of the Syme family, were still holding on to their shares. Fairfax needed seventeen of those holdings.

On 17 May, like a villain appearing in the last act of a Victorian melodrama, Holmes à Court foreshadowed a formal bid of $12 for all Syme shares, including those held by Fairfax. That was enough to send the market price over $14. Holmes à Court did not serve a Part A statement initiating his bid until the last day of Fairfax's takeover offer, 28 June, and in the meantime acceptances had been trickling in to Fairfax. It was touch and go, but on 1 July 1985 Fairfax was able to despatch its notice of compulsory acquisition to the remaining shareholders. Eight days later David Syme & Co Ltd was removed from the Stock Exchange list.

Holmes à Court accepted defeat with an ironic repudiation of spoiling tactics. 'Although I am advised legally that we are able to defeat your compulsory acquisition . . . by resorting to various artificial devices', he wrote to Gardiner,

> it seems to me that we would, in that event, be 'spoilers.' As you know our offer to you and other shareholders at $12 per share was genuine and unconditional, I think it has now run its course. I

propose to not proceed with our offer and sell our shareholding to you.

'He is a cheeky devil', wrote Gardiner in a note to directors, 'attempting to snatch the best from the jaws of defeat'.

And so David Syme became a fully-owned and very profitable subsidiary of John Fairfax Ltd. Its future profitability was indeed far greater than anyone could have predicted. The Hong Kong venture ended dismally, with the Chius buying out their Australian partners at a price which left David Syme with a net loss of more than $5 million. That was soon forgotten, however, as the company's annual profits continued to rise at an extraordinary rate. Thanks to the closing down of some loss-makers, the efficient introduction of computerized typesetting, but most of all a boom in classified advertising which enabled the Saturday *Age* to become larger than the *Sydney Morning Herald*, David Syme's pre-tax profit rose from $3.7 million in 1982–83 to $8.9 million in 1983–84 and $30.42 million in 1984–85.

II

The beginning of David Syme's prodigious upturn was already apparent in June 1984 when Gardiner presented the board with budget figures for the next financial year. There were other favourable signs as well. The Broadway papers would now have all the benefits of new technology, Brisbane TV would contribute a full year's profit for the first time, Magazine Promotions was going from strength to strength, ratings for four of the seven Macquarie radio stations were projected to be in first position during the coming year, and the Canberra, Newcastle and Wollongong newspapers had collectively become even more profitable than the *Age*, being exceeded only by the *Sydney Morning Herald*.

John Fairfax had now entered a new era, Gardiner told the board, and was a different kind of company from the one it had been only two or three years before. The projected profit was almost $80 million, compared with $52 million in the year just ending, and that projection was based on more conservatively expressed profit figures than those for probably any other company in Australia. The budgeted turnover was $690 million compared with $581 million for the current year and, at the present rate of growth, turnover would probably pass the billion mark in two or three years time. Three years earlier, said Gardiner, John Fairfax had ranked one-hundredth in the list of Australia's largest companies. Now it had moved to 47, only six places behind HWT, which no doubt was 'helping to contribute to that company's paranoia'.

During the previous financial year, John Fairfax Ltd had changed banks, appointing Westpac Banking Corporation and National Australia Bank as its trading banks in place of the Australia and New Zealand Banking Group. The association with ANZ—going back to one of its ancestors, the Union Bank, in the last century—had worn rather thin of late. Long past, but not yet forgotten, was the acutely embarrassing liquidity crisis, when the ANZ had for a time refused to honour Fairfax cheques. What rankled with the company now was the bank's lack of flexibility despite frequent requests for an increase in overdrafts and other facilities. As the Fairfax group already had an easier relationship with Westpac and NAB through some of its subsidiaries, the board decided to give them all its corporate business, amounting to more than $600 million a year.

In addition to profits generated by normal business growth, Fairfax, along with other shareholders in Australian Associated Press Pty Ltd, received a lavish windfall in June 1984 from the public floating of Reuters Ltd, in which AAP was a 13.89 per cent shareholder. AAP's holding in Reuters was valued in the company's accounts at only $141 187—the actual cost of buying the shares in 1947. But although AAP had always been a non-profit co-operative, it stood to gain enormous financial benefit from the transformation of Reuters Ltd, which had become highly profitable in the expanding electronic information field, into Reuters Holdings Plc, with a market capitalization of nearly $A1000 million.

The British shareholders in Reuters, most of whom were straitened by Fleet Street's hard times, wanted urgently to claim some of the new wealth blooming on video screens served by Reuters financial and economic services around the world. The major partners in AAP—Fairfax, 48 per cent, and HWT, 44 per cent (Rupert Murdoch's News Ltd was represented only by the Adelaide *News*, with 5.6 per cent)—were at first reluctant to see the old Reuters club dissolved. They had considerable influence there, and the Reuters boardroom provided them with a valuable listening post in Fleet Street.

Although at first not fully believing in the promised windfall, they recognized the strength of the British shareholders' wish to go public. The decision had to be unanimous, and the main Australian negotiators—Max Suich and the executive director of HWT, Lyle Turnbull—were able to secure certain safeguards and concessions in return for AAP's agreement.

Existing shareholders in Reuters Ltd agreed to the sale of 44 per cent of the new company outside the present ownership. They would control 56 per cent of votes in Reuters Holdings by owning 100 million non-marketable A shares carrying four votes each. A second class of capital—320 million B shares, carrying only one vote each—would be issued to the A shareholders in proportion to the size of their shareholdings, and would be sold by them. As well as controlling a majority of votes, the existing owners would be entitled to appoint a majority of the new company's directors. Furthermore the Reuters board of trustees, of which Angus McLachlan was chairman at the time of the float, would have a 'golden share', enabling it to veto any board resolution deemed not to be in accordance with the original Reuters Trust.

AAP Pty Ltd received 13.89 per cent of the issue. Foreseeing the need to channel proceeds from the sale of B shares to AAP's shareholders, and recognizing that AAP had also become a profit-making company through its own expansion into electronic services, the general manager, Lee Casey, proposed a restructuring of the organization. In 1983 AAP Pty Ltd became a holding company for the Reuters shares, and was joined by a profit and loss operating company, AAP Information Services Pty Ltd.

This provided an opportunity for News Ltd to acquire a more realistic shareholding in AAP. Murdoch was already a major shareholder in Reuters through his English papers, and News Ltd had become AAP's largest subscriber apart from the two founding partners. Deciding that Murdoch's group would be better in than out, Fairfax and HWT settled on a division of shares giving each of them 42.8 per cent in AAP and 39.9 per cent in AAPIS, and Murdoch 12 per cent and 15 per cent. The major partners had three directors each, and News Ltd had one. It might have seemed that News Ltd would have a swinging vote, but in reality Fairfax and HWT continued to observe a long-standing agreement, known to News Ltd, that they would not vote against one another on the AAP board.

AAP's sale of Reuters B shares in 1984, and three more transactions of the same kind in 1986, returned no less than $295 million, of which Fairfax received $124 million. As Gardiner informed the board in his 1984–85 budget submission, Fairfax's first instalment of $15 million from the Reuters float would reduce the company's debt burden sufficiently to cut its interest bill by 15 per cent in the coming year. Yet in spite of that good fortune, and sharply rising profitability, the group's cumulative borrowing was expected to reach $104 million in the coming year, together with leasing obligations of about $40 million. 'Despite our strengths, and being an excellent generator of cash', Gardiner reported,

> our borrowings are still increasing and the gearing ratios [between shareholders' funds and outside borrowing] remain reasonable only due to asset revaluations. This is because the company has received no external cash into the business from shareholders for the inordinately long period of twenty years. There would be few companies of comparable growth and size in the country who could make that claim.

And so we return to the subject of capital, a subject of increasing significance to management, board and family since Gardiner first broached it in 1982. The last capital raising had been in 1964, when the company issued 2 200 000 ordinary shares to finance the purchase of ATV's radio and television interests in Australia. Since then family members had shown reluctance to make further heavy investment in the company, which they would all need to do in the event of a capital raising if the family was to preserve its percentage of ownership. During the early 1980s that percentage varied between 47 and 49 per cent. The company's retirement funds owned another 10 per cent, and the remaining 40 per cent was held by outsiders. When Gardiner suggested the raising of $10 million ordinary (which was to say, voting) capital and $20 million preference (non-voting) capital in 1982, John B. Fairfax said he agreed with the need for capital raising but, as a member of the family, he felt that it was like taking bad medicine. The sooner it was over the better, and then the company could get on to other things.

Other things took priority, as it happened, and no medicine was taken that year. In 1983 Gardiner again suggested a one-for-ten issue of ordinary shares to raise $10 million. The family gathered at James Fairfax's Darling Point home to discuss the matter but, as Sir Warwick was found to have serious reservations, the board later postponed consideration for another year. At the June 1984 board meeting, in conjunction with his budget submission, Gardiner presented a discussion paper making the case for raising capital and outlining alternative ways of doing so:

> Why do we need to consider a capital raising? This is the crucial question. True, it can be said that the company has performed well and is now in its strongest position ever. This raises the question, 'Why can't it continue to carry on without a capital raising?' The answer is 'It can'—but the issue is deeper than such a simple question . . .The crux of the matter is not one of finding the money but rather one of strengthening the equity base of the company and its gearing in order to ensure that there is no impediment to it being able to respond in the best possible financial, economic and profitable manner to any opportunity for growth and development which may arise or be planned . . .
>
> One can also argue that in view of the dramatic improvement in profitability, our share price growth [from $1.75 in 1981 to $6.04 in 1984] and the nature of the capital market this year, now is a most appropriate and prudent time to review the whole issue of capital raising.

The type of share issue favoured by Gardiner, to which the board now turned its mainly favourable attention, was an unconventional one known as 'participating irredeemable preference shares' (PIPS). A submission prepared by Gardiner and Ron Cotton in July proposed a two-for-one issue of 6 per cent PIPS, to raise $96 million. The main advantage of this scheme, said Gardiner, was that it would raise equity without any need for existing shareholders to subscribe new funds if they did not wish to do so, for it would not dilute current voting rights and control. PIPS would be similar to non-voting ordinary shares, yet attractive to new shareholders because of their relatively high yield after tax. And because PIPS were non-voting, the Fairfaxes could sell their own rights to the issue, at considerable gain, without loss of control.

The scheme found favour with all directors except Sir Warwick Fairfax. Before the next board meeting on 16 August, he circulated a memorandum of dissent fortified with legal opinion. In essence, he asserted that no convincing case had been made for the raising of capital; that PIPS would entail financial disadvantages for ordinary shareholders because existing profitability would have to be more widely shared; and that a PIPS issue would open the way to loss of control by the Fairfaxes.

Among the alleged disadvantages was a claim that PIPS, being irredeemable, would render impossible the kind of privatization which Kerry Packer had brought about at Consolidated Press in 1983. 'Privatisation has been discussed as a possible if remote aim', wrote Sir Warwick,

> designed to place Fairfax control beyond the possibility of attack and return to the Fairfaxes the full advantages of profits and capital gain which they enjoyed before the company became public in 1956. There are no adequate reasons for making this aim, which has been achieved by other companies, impossible.

As for dilution of control, Sir Warwick cited the opinion of A. B. Shand, QC, that it was impossible to say no occasion would arise when PIPS shareholders could exercise a vote. Stock exchanges were already concerned about the alleged unfairness of non-voting shares, and who could be sure that amending legislation would not be introduced one day? 'The effect of the issue of PIPS shares', Shand advised,

> is to introduce into the structure of the company 20 million 'wild cards', which will have the effect of reducing the Fairfax family shareholding overall to a little under 36 per cent of the issued capital of the company, on the assumption that each family member disposes of his rights to such shares. Whilst the present constitution of the board ensures that the family controls decisions made of any important kind, there is no necessary assurance that this situation will last indefinitely . . .The well known example of the successful bid by Mr Holmes à Court [for Associated Communications Corporation] in London comes to mind, where he used massive acquisition of non-voting shares eventually to gain total control.

In a long reply to this memorandum, also circulated before the next board meeting, Gardiner contradicted Sir Warwick point by point. PIPS would not disadvantage ordinary shareholders, for rather than selling off a share of the existing cake it involved the baking of a cake bigger than the mere addition of the extra capital ingredient raised by PIPS. It would not dilute family control, for even in the unlikely event of enfranchising legislation there would be ample time for the family and the Fairfax retirement funds to raise their combined holding (43 per cent of a PIPS-enlarged company) well above 50 per cent.

Nor would PIPS make privatization impossible. The method to achieve complete acquisition might change, for example to a scheme of arrangement; but total acquisition would still be entirely possible. 'My understanding', wrote Gardiner, 'and I think that of the board at large, was that there was relatively little if any interest by the family in making such a move to privatisation'.

As for the reference to Holmes à Court's capture of Lord Grade's ACC two years earlier, Gardiner referred the directors to a memorandum from the Fairfax solicitors, Stephen Jaques, examining that coup in some detail. ACC had only 150 000 voting ordinary shares, held almost entirely by Lord Grade and other members of the board, and 50 million 'A' non-voting ordinary shares. Holmes à Court first acquired a holding of 30 per cent of the non-voting shares, which he later increased to 51 per cent. For reasons hard to comprehend, Lord Grade then offered him a seat on the board and 3 per cent of the voting shares.

Although still without significant voting power, Holmes à Court was soon elevated to a position of virtual control by the sudden resignation of Lord Grade, who also sold 27 per cent of the voting shares to Holmes à Court's Bell Group. This really had nothing to do with the PIPS argument. It was simply an example of one man's apparent charm and another man's folly.

At the August board meeting James Fairfax proposed a resolution authorizing the group general manager to proceed with the PIPS raising, and was supported by all other directors except his father. Sir Warwick asked that his dissent be recorded, but said he would agree to have his rights to the issue underwritten with those of the other major shareholders.

When they met again on 6 September, Sir Warwick's opposition had hardened to the extent that he was no longer willing to participate in the family underwriting. This gave cause for alarm, as any breaking of ranks by the family could be expected to affect the market price. Seldom had the board experienced such a sharp, albeit one-sided division of opinion, and seldom had Sir Warwick, then in his eighty-third year, been so fighting fit. He began by saying that he was obliged to take note of the opinions of directors of his own investment companies, Rockwood Pastoral Co Pty Ltd and Tailer Investments Pty Ltd. Among those directors were the Melbourne baronet, Sir Rupert Clarke, who was a vice-chairman of the National Australia Bank and godfather to young Warwick; Max Sandow, a former New South Wales Manager of the ANZ group; and John Fletcher, a former president of the Rural Bank.

> If they said the issue was a bad idea, it was not for the group general manager to say that was a wrong opinion [said Sir Warwick].
>
> The chairman said a lack of respect had been shown to Mr Gardiner.
>
> Sir Warwick said that was not the case. Mr Gardiner had said it was a personal reflection on him but he disagreed with that. Mr Gardiner had said he was entitled to full acquiescence and had felt aggrieved because of the opinions of Mr John Fletcher, Mr Max Sandow and Sir Rupert Clarke. These were all men of some eminence. Mr Gardiner thought these people were all wrong.
>
> Sir Warwick said he was sorry but he thought Mr Gardiner was wrong. He could not fault the opinions of his advisers and he was just as convinced that he was right as Mr Gardiner was convinced he was wrong. He rejected the opinion that it was wrong to disagree with Mr Gardiner . . .
>
> The group general manager might have brilliant ideas but he had not revealed them. It was about time the board heard what would be done with the money. He stood right behind his memorandum. He believed what he had said was right and true and did not regret saying it, and he had the same rights as the group general manger. If he could not persuade the board, they and their children and the ordinary shareholders would suffer.

Sir Vincent said he hoped Sir Warwick would not make his decision public. He had been encouraged by the fact that Sir Warwick would be participating. But now Sir Warwick had changed his mind. A dissenting director would be in an extreme position, said Sir Vincent, if he did anything to frustrate the will of the board.

Sir Warwick replied that he would not be accused of breach of faith. He had done what he had done on legal advice and was doing something he thought was in the interests of all.

John B. Fairfax said Sir Warwick was an honourable person, and a person with a great deal of integrity. He just could not believe that Sir Warwick was doing this to the board. Finally the chairman said that, having listened to the opinions expressed, it was not his intention to attack anyone around the table. He had not disregarded Sir Warwick and his advisers. However, he thought what was proposed was the right thing and he was determined that it should go through.

Soon after this board meeting Sir Warwick heard from a reliable informant who had met the managing director of News Ltd, Ken Cowley, at a football match. Remarking that Murdoch would be keen to buy some of the PIPS, Cowley went on to say that if the Fairfaxes proceeded with this equity raising they would be taken over within two years.

Naturally enough Sir Warwick and Lady Fairfax continued to oppose PIPS, both directly and through the medium of public relations consultant Martin Dougherty. The extent to which their opposition affected the final outcome is hard to assess, but quite possibly they tipped the scales against PIPS in circumstances both frustrating and embarrassing for the company.

Two meetings between the Sydney Stock Exchange's listing manager and Fairfax's underwriters, Dominguez Barry Samuel Montagu, encountered some difficulties, but none regarded by the Fairfax board as insurmountable. Exchange committee members were supplied with details of the securities, which Fairfax proposed to call A shares, and on 11 September the listing manager informed Dominguez that the shares would have to be called 'cumulative participating preference shares'. This was acceptable to Fairfax, and that afternoon the issue was announced.

In making the announcement, the company was under the impression that because the issue had been approved by the full Stock Exchange Committee there would be no further difficulty about listing. On the contrary, however, the Listing Committee of the Stock Exchange had more conditions to make. While these were being negotiated—a process which obliged Fairfax to postpone its annual general meeting for a month—the board was disconcerted by two surprisingly well-informed press reports about the family's disagreement over PIPS—one written by the editor-in-chief of Kerry Packer's *Bulletin*, Trevor Kennedy, and the other by the finance editor of the Melbourne *Herald*, Barrie Dunstan. Kennedy quoted from Gardiner's budget submission to the board and a recent letter from Dominguez to Gardiner, while Dunstan claimed to have read 'several dissenting opinions' circulated to the board by 'the group opposing the planned issue'.

At about the same time the *Australian* reported that 'elements of the Fairfax family' were believed to be 'considering privatising the John Fairfax press group along the successful lines pursued by Mr Kerry Packer'. This was certainly true of Mary Fairfax, for she had raised the subject only a few weeks earlier in a letter to her stepson James. 'Packer has privatised with a loan from a Swiss bank', she wrote. 'We can too, without a penny more from any of us, just a willingness to put all our shares together which is what you wanted before—and that is true safety for all the family with all our shares pro rata in proportion to what they are now.'

'I was never in favour of privatisation', replied James Fairfax, 'and am still not. Indeed Greg Gardiner took the board through it and there was no enthusiasm for it at all'.

Early in October Lady Fairfax invited the Vincent and John B. Fairfaxes to a dinner at Fairwater. Among the guests were Lord Grade, chief witness for the prosecution in the case against non-voting shares, and John Barber, a young American working in the Sydney office of the investment bank Morgan Stanley, who had become friendly with Sir Warwick and Lady Fairfax. 'After we had been there for about twenty minutes', wrote John Fairfax in a file note,

> Sir Warwick and Lord Grade appeared. They had been having discussions in the study. The dinner was pleasant enough. However, towards the end Lew Grade asked my father across the table what he thought of the capital raising venture, to which my father replied that he did not have a particular view. Discussion ensued where Warwick said very little, but Grade said we had to be very careful of Holmes à Court—that that was one of the three or four mistakes he had made in his life, in accepting Holmes à Court's charm and persuasiveness. The same thing could happen to Fairfax with the preference share issue . . .
>
> Later Warwick said something in whispers to John Barber. Shortly after that Barber said he thought the capital raising venture was not a good one if you did not know how you were going to spend the money. It would be better to have specific objects in mind or alternatively to raise the money by using debt . . .
>
> There is no doubt this dinner was a contrived affair to emphasise Warwick's opposition to the capital raising scheme. It is extraordinary that a social occasion should be used with two outside people to demonstrate the differences of opinion.

There was really no need for contrived persuasion, if such it had been, for by then the Stock Exchange, out of professed concern for shareholders' rights, was insisting upon changes which the Fairfax board felt unable to make. On 17 October the chairman of the Exchange, J. K. Bain, wrote to Gardiner setting three conditions to be met before the Exchange would agree to list the cumulative participating preference shares: first, a limit of 40 per cent on the number of preference shares to be issued as a percentage of ordinary shares (Fairfax had originally proposed 75 per cent); second, provision of a mechanism to ensure that if a takeover offer was made for ordinary shares a comparable offer would be made for preference shares; and third, that holders of participating preference shares should become entitled to a vote in the event of any person acquiring more than 50 per cent of the total issued capital, both ordinary and preference shares.

Here were Sir Warwick's worst fears being made palpable. The board unanimously resolved to reject the first and third conditions. In his reply to Bain, Gardiner wrote:

> The directors of John Fairfax Ltd noted with considerable concern the damaging effect which your handling of this matter has had and is having on the company, the interest of its shareholders, its underwriters and advisers. They further ask that you speak with your Committee to seek that the original assent to the issue by the Exchange be honoured.

Unfortunately there were two points of view about that 'original assent'. Fairfax had taken as assent the Exchange's stipulation about naming the shares. 'We cannot understand', wrote Gardiner in an earlier letter to Bain,

> why we were told so definitely and without any qualification at all that the shares must be called 'cumulative participating preference shares' if Committee members, having examined the form of security, had any doubt about the suitability of listing . . . Based upon this authoritative advice in writing from the Exchange (which we had no reason at all to doubt) we announced the issue . . .

Bain, on the other hand, denied that naming amounted to assent. 'The Committee does not acknowledge', he wrote to Gardiner on 23 October,

> that at any stage it approved official quotation of the shares . . . The fact is that [John Fairfax Ltd] and its advisers chose to announce the issue before the question of official quotation was settled and in advance of the full details of the issue being made available to the Stock Exchange. This was despite several warnings to the underwriters that there were strong feelings within the Exchanges that these shares did not have adequate voting rights particularly in the case of a takeover . . . I see little point in the company continuing to run the argument that official quotation should be approved at this stage simply on the basis that the company and its advisers may have formed the incorrect impression early in proceedings that official quotation would be granted.

And that was that. On 26 October Fairfax announced 'with regret and disappointment' that it was obliged to withdraw the issue by reason of the Stock Exchange's refusal to list it. Although one of the directors, Sir David Griffin, was all for going to court, the board confined its outrage to some carefully chosen words in the public announcement:

> Whilst compromises were made by the company and the Exchange in the discussions since the company was first informed that the Exchange had changed its attitude and that the advice previously furnished by the Exchange could no longer be relied on, the company continued to request that the Exchange honour its original attitude to the shares. It is now clear that there is no possibility of this . . . In the current environment of deregulation which has been particularly welcomed abroad by foreign investors, the Exchange Committee's

decision to veto such an innovative proposal will be met with disappointment both in Australia and overseas.

Inside the boardroom, disappointment was compounded with strong suspicion that there had been a breach of confidentiality. While the outcome of negotiations with the Stock Exchange had still been in the balance, John B. Fairfax had referred cautiously to his own suspicions in a private conversation with Sir Warwick. Saying that he expected the leaking of documents to the *Bulletin* and Melbourne *Herald* to be mentioned at the next board meeting, when he would be acting as chairman during James's absence overseas, John asked if Sir Warwick, as a former chairman, had any advice to give him. Sir Warwick said there was no point in pursuing leaks because there was no evidence as to where the respective publications had obtained their information.

John went on to say he had received a number of reports that Sir Warwick and Lady Fairfax had been talking to people in such a way as to show their opposition to PIPS and to denigrate the current management. Sir Warwick said this was an insinuation which could not be substantiated, indeed it was 'like the worst times in Russia where widespread accusations were made without substance'. John replied that he did not wish to be specific, and that the matter was better left for the chairman to deal with when he returned. But it did concern him that these things were being said publicly. They had the effect of showing a lack of confidence in the group general manager and a public split within the family.

Sir Warwick said that if John wanted examples of leakage and lack of confidence, how was it that three days before the capital-raising announcement Sir Warwick had been invited by Rupert Murdoch, via Sir Peter Abeles, to sell his own shares and retain the *Sydney Morning Herald*? John had no answer to that enigmatic question, and Sir Warwick did not elaborate on it, then or later.

James Fairfax returned to find the confidentiality matter unresolved. Three days before the November board meeting, Sir Vincent Fairfax sent him the following note:

Dear James,
Here are some weekend thoughts for you to consider.
It is a difficult course for you to determine when there is a mixture of elements:—
The family solidarity has been threatened.
The company appears wobbly in policy.
The normal board room privacy is a joke.
This all because of Warwick's disregard for realistic corporate behaviour and loyalty.
All the best
Vincent

After much consideration, James decided that a full post-mortem would only worsen matters. But at the meeting he told his fellow directors that since they were all under suspicion, and as he might be questioned about leaks at the annual general meeting, he would ask them to assure him that they totally accepted the principle of board confidentiality and would do everything in their power to ensure that it was preserved in future. Sir Vincent, John Fairfax and Sir David Griffin voiced their assurances and, according to the minutes, 'Sir Warwick Fairfax also indicated his assent'.

As had happened when Sir Warwick was made to stand down from the chairmanship in 1961, his thoughts now turned again to the Kinghaven parcel of Fairfax shares and the arrangement for its transfer to his second son, Warwick G. O. Fairfax, on James Fairfax's death. In 1961, it will be remembered, Sir Warwick had asked James to confirm in writing that in the event of his dying without surviving legitimate male issue the Kinghaven shares which had been transferred to him by his father would pass to a trust, to be created by James, with Warwick junior as primary beneficiary. In accordance with that undertaking Kinghaven had become owned in 1973 by Serpentine Pty Ltd, the trustee of what was known as the Sir Lorimer Dods Settlement.

As a result of inquiries made by his lawyers, Sir Warwick became aware that the Dods Settlement was a discretionary trust. In other words, on James's death the Kinghaven shares would pass to Warwick junior, if he survived James, not automatically but at the discretion of trustees. At Sir Warwick's request a new arrangement was made in 1985 whereby a non-discretionary trust, the Guilford Bell Trust, assumed responsibility for the Kinghaven shares. (Bell, a distinguished Melbourne architect, like the paediatrician Dods, was a long-time friend of James.) Under the Guilford Bell Trust, James was still entitled to the income and voting rights of the Kinghaven shares, but on his death the shares would pass unequivocally to Warwick junior. In 1986 James also added a codicil to his will bequeathing to Warwick junior the voting rights, though not the capital, of all his personal shares in addition to the Kinghaven parcel. Thus was the line of inheritance placed beyond all possible doubt.

At Broadway the urge to raise more share capital had not quite abated. In August 1985, more in hope than with confidence, the company tried another version of PIPS on the Stock Exchange Committee. Again Sir Warwick dug his heels in, this time with the support of advice from the merchant bank, Lloyds International Ltd. The advice from Lloyds was that a PIPS equity raising could pose some long-term risk to the family's control; that a capital issue should only be made to fund a major and identified project; and that, as an alternative to equity raising, the company could borrow

$100 million, either domestically or in the Euromarkets, without significantly impairing its credit rating.

This second PIPS proposal was rejected for the same kind of reason as the first, and this time Gardiner conceded defeat. He had been greatly preoccupied by capital raising since 1981, he told the board in August. Despite the overwhelming need to be properly capitalized, he thought the time had now come when he really had to get off that subject and back to his principal role as chief executive. Forgoing a capital issue would have a significant effect, he said, on the way John Fairfax Ltd could look at expansion in future. It would have to trim its sails and concentrate on reducing borrowings rather than expanding.

As we shall see, however, the company's sails would not be trimmed as much as Gardiner in his despondency was predicting. Despite its two failures with PIPS, Fairfax had already been finding the means to take advantage of opportunities as they presented themselves, and it would continue to do that. Far from reducing its borrowings, the company would almost double them in two years—from $105 million in 1984 to $201 million in 1986.

III

One of the most fruitful opportunities grasped by the Fairfax group during the 1980s was the launching of Australia's first weekly business magazine. In April 1981 the popular 'Business Review' section of the *National Times*, begun during the previous year in response to Kerry Packer's fortnightly *Australian Business*, was hived off as a separate magazine. Published in Melbourne as a joint venture by the *Australian Financial Review* and the *Age*, and edited by Robert Gottliebsen, a former assistant editor of the *Financial Review*, *Business Review Weekly* started with a smaller circulation (25 000) than *Australian Business* (32 000). After being redesigned and renamed *BRW* at the end of its first year, it overtook *Australian Business* in 1983 and maintained the lead even when *Australian Business* became a weekly two years later. In March 1987 their respective circulations were 59 700 and 53 500. Around this thriving masthead assembled a group of predominantly business or financial publications which by the second half of the decade was one of the fastest growing areas in John Fairfax Ltd.

BRW Publications was a Melbourne-based partnership between John Fairfax and David Syme, with a board consisting of Max Suich, Fred Brenchley and the new managing director of David Syme, Greg Taylor. Its first venture after *BRW* was *Personal Investment*, a magazine for individual investors, established in August 1983 on the bare framework of the *Australian Stock Exchange Journal*, purchased from the Stock Exchange for $300 000. In the space of two years its circulation reached 48 000. *Today's Computers,* launched in 1984, did not prosper and after two years it was merged into *BRW*. In 1985, prompted by deregulation of Australia's financial markets and the arrival of sixteen foreign banks, BRW Publications launched a monthly magazine aimed at banking and finance markets in Australia, Asia and the Pacific. This was *Triple A,* named after the top credit rating, and edited by Edna Carew, a former *Financial Review* journalist and author. The managing editor was Stuart Simson who had concurrently become editor of *BRW* upon Gottliebsen's appointment as managing editor, BRW Publications. In 1987 *Triple A* incorporated *Asiabanking,* which had been acquired by Fairfax. Other additions to the BRW group, in 1986, were *Rydges* and *Australian Property News,* acquired along with other Rydges publications for $5 million.

Three other joint ventures with Syme during the 1980s were Fairfax Syme & Weldon Associates, Electronic Publishing and a joint enterprise with Time Inc. In 1981 a consortium of Fairfax, Syme and Kevin Weldon & Associates Pty Ltd began a ten-volume publishing venture as part of Australia's Bicentennial commemoration. *Australians: A Historical Library,* the largest project of its kind ever undertaken in Australia, combined the efforts of more than four hundred writers, researchers and academics. It was completed in 1988, and proved to be one of the lasting monuments left by the Bicentenary.

In September 1985 Electronic Publishing launched through Telecom's Viatel network a financial information and investment service known as Money Watch. By 1987 this very successful service was providing real-time market prices from domestic stock and futures exchanges, with changes in prices being updated automatically on screen.

In 1986 the BRW group went into partnership with Time Inc to publish *Time* in Australia and New Zealand. This arose from BRW's concern at the growing strength of Consolidated Press in the business advertising field, a strength about to be augmented by the incorporation of a *Newsweek* section in the *Bulletin*. Suich tried to talk the *Washington Post* organization (owner of *Newsweek*) into launching an Australian edition of the magazine in partnership with Fairfax, but was unsuccessful. *Newsweek* went into the *Bulletin,* which picked up about 70 per cent of *Newsweek*'s buyers in Australia, thus lifting its own circulation from 94 500 to 125 000.

Turning to *Newsweek*'s global competitor, *Time,* Suich approached Marshall Loeb, the head of magazine development at Time Inc. From this and subsequent negotiations by Brenchley in New York and Australia emerged agreement for Fairfax to buy 50 per cent of Time Inc's South Pacific operation for $A6.25 million.

The BRW group would provide Australian editorial content for an Australian edition, to be known as *Time Australia*, and would manage the New Zealand edition as a scaled-down version of the United States edition.

In sixty years of existence, Time Inc had never before been involved in joint publishing. It was something of a cultural shock for both sides. Brenchley and the Fairfax solicitor Rod Halstead spent several days in a New York conference room negotiating with a team of Time lawyers about price, intellectual property, trademarks and other topics. An agreement was signed in February 1986, and the first issue of *Time Australia* appeared on 21 July.

The editor was Jefferson Penberthy, a former editor of *BRW* and managing editor of the *National Times*, and the senior writer was Tony Maiden, formerly managing editor of the *Financial Review*. It was not their intention to imitate *Time*'s idiosyncratic style, but rather to find a style which was complementary. They seemed to succeed, for there were few brickbats and more than a few bouquets from New York. The Australian circulation rose from 100 000 in 1985 to 107 000 in 1987, and advertising revenues on both sides of the Tasman were satisfactory.

By this time John Fairfax Ltd had also taken its first commercial step into the British market, where the company's founder and namesake had been declared bankrupt more than a century and a half before. It did this by acquiring Britain's oldest magazine, the political and literary weekly *Spectator*. Although the *Spectator*'s circulation had declined from 53 000 to 19 000 since World War II, its quality had been greatly improved in recent years. It was still unabashedly conservative, but was read by people of all shades of opinion in politics, industry, civil service and media.

In 1984 the editor of the *Age*, Creighton Burns, heard from a friend of his—a minor shareholder in The Spectator (1828) Ltd, named after the year of the magazine's foundation—that the *Spectator* was for sale. Burns rang Suich, telling him that the magazine's major shareholder, an English entrepreneur named Algie Cluff, was in Sydney at that time in connection with one of his oil exploration companies. Suich and Brenchley had a drink with Cluff in his hotel room, expressed interest in the magazine, and discovered that he had already received offers—including one, as they found out later, from Kerry Packer. Cluff was leaving Australia the next day, and in the Qantas lounge just before departure he and Brenchley signed an agreement.

The deal was concluded in January 1985, with Cluff selling his 88 per cent holding for £Stg740 000 and the other shareholders selling for a further £Stg75 000. As the *Spectator* had been something of a hobby for Algie Cluff, he made a condition of sale that he should remain chairman of the board. The editor, Charles Moore, and the publisher, James Knox—both young and very able—also chose to stay with the magazine. Suich and Brenchley worked with them on content, design and promotion. The size was changed to A4 on semi-gloss paper, the cover was given better colour, and the *Spectator* launched its first advertising campaign. Subscriptions were handled by an agency partly owned by Datamail, a Melbourne computerized direct mailing house in which Fairfax had recently acquired a 50 per cent interest for $3.75 million. By the end of 1985 the *Spectator*'s circulation had risen to 23 000, and by 1988 it was 35 000 including airmail sales of about 1100 in Australia.

For a few heady weeks towards the end of 1985 it seemed that the modest *Spectator* venture might soon be followed by something much more adventurous—the purchase of a $60 million holding in Fleet Street's *Daily Telegraph* and *Sunday Telegraph*. Gardiner and Suich had earlier approached the chairman of the Telegraph Company, Lord Hartwell, and now, while they were both in London, he asked to see them. At that time Fleet Street was feeling the pinch of declining revenue and rising costs, although help was on the way from new technology. The annual turnover of all Fleet Street publishers was about £Stg1000 million, but the combined profit for all except Rupert Murdoch was a mere £Stg1 million. The *Financial Times* was making £Stg8 million a year, so presumably the other publishers between them were losing £Stg7 million.

The *Daily Telegraph* had a circulation of 1 200 000, a turnover of £Stg120 million, and a current annual loss of £Stg5 million which the company hoped was only temporary. In the course of a recent capital raising for the purchase of new presses, Lord Hartwell's family, which owned 58 per cent of the company, had entered into an agreement with a Canadian entrepreneur, Conrad Black, who owned 14 per cent. As this agreement prevented the family from taking up more shares, and gave Black the right to match any offer made by a third party for the family's shares, it seemed likely that Black would eventually gain control.

Nevertheless Lord Hartwell proposed that Fairfax should buy the *Sunday Telegraph* and its colour magazine. Gardiner demurred, but said Fairfax might be interested in the total company if means could be found to accomplish that. Later one of Lord Hartwell's sons, Nicholas Berry, asked whether Fairfax would take an equity position in the company with a view to managing it and if possible purchasing the Berry family's shares at some time in the future. Back in Sydney Rod Halstead thought at first there was at least a fifty-fifty chance of finding a way around the agreement with Black, and Gardiner told the board that in the event of borrowing $60 million to invest in the London *Telegraph* 'the interest charge against Fairfax profit would be about $9 million a year, which was affordable'. So much for trimming sails! The board authorized investigation of the possibility, but at its next meeting, on 12 December, Gardiner reported failure to find a clear legal and commercial way through the complexities created by the Black agreement. Soon afterwards the Berrys sold Black enough of their shares to give him a controlling interest in the company.

Also during 1985 Fairfax offered $US4 million for a 60 per cent interest in the Hong Kong news magazine, *Asiaweek*, only to be outbid by Time Inc. The company also made its first direct investment in New Zealand, a 50 per cent interest in Fourth Estate Holdings Ltd, publisher of a weekly business paper called *National Business Review*. Fairfax's first contact with this company came about informally through Brenchley's successor as editor of the *Financial Review*, and later its editor-in-chief, P. P. McGuinness. Paddy McGuinness had encountered *NBR* journalists while covering the 1984 New Zealand election, and on his return to Sydney he mentioned their paper to the management. Brenchley, who later went to New Zealand looking for possible acquisitions, was favourably impressed by Fourth Estate, and a price of $A656 000 was eventually negotiated by V. J. Carroll.

The second 50 per cent was purchased for $A4.4 million in December 1986, and in 1987 *NBR* became first a bi-weekly and then a daily. For the first four days of the week the paper was reminiscent of the *Financial Review*; but Friday's edition, consisting of 100 pages packed with colour advertising, was more like *Business Review Weekly*. Between 1985 and 1987, circulation rose from 12 000 a week to 12 000 a day from Monday to Thursdays and 19 000 on Fridays. Although losing money in spite of handsome profit on Fridays, *NBR*'s course seemed set to emulate that of the *Financial Review* by sooner or later moving into net profit. In 1986 Fourth Estate launched a New Zealand edition of *Personal Investment* (relaunched as *New Zealand Personal Investor* after incorporating a competitor) and entered the Money Show business, just as BRW Publications had done in Australia.

Although Fairfax had been disappointed in its hope of investing $60 million in the London *Telegraph*, it spent almost that much on three other opportunities which came its way in 1985. First, it terminated a long-standing but somewhat incongruous partnership with Consolidated Press by buying out Kerry Packer's 50 per cent interest in Suburban Publications Pty Ltd. This company ran a chain of suburban newspapers in Sydney, most of which were wholly owned by the partnership, though some were owned 50 per cent by groups such as the Hannan family in the eastern suburbs and the Engisch family in the Bankstown area. Most of these papers were printed on the only significant offset press in Sydney, a Goss Metro at Bankstown, owned by the partnership.

In 1983 Fairfax and Consolidated rationalized the printing and ownership of their chain by forming another company akin to Suburban Publications, called Suburban Community Newspapers Pty Ltd. Both were owned fifty-fifty by Fairfax and Packer. The new company took all the wholly owned papers, while the old one kept those which were partly owned and also the offset press at Bankstown, valued at $4.9 million.

Two years later—perhaps partly because of a badly deteriorating relationship between Fairfax and Consolidated, to be dealt with in the next chapter—Packer invoked a so-called Savoy Clause in the original company's articles of association. Both companies had such a clause, permitting either side of the ownership to make an offer for the other half on an accept-or-match basis. In April 1985, when Packer offered Fairfax $17.5 million for its 50 per cent of Suburban Publications, Fairfax was bound either to accept, or else to buy Packer's half at the same price. It chose to buy.

There soon arose an acrimonious difference of opinion as to what exactly Fairfax had bought. In February 1985 the board of Suburban Community Newspapers had resolved to transfer ownership of the Goss Metro press from Suburban Publications to itself. Although no reciprocal motion was ever passed by the board of Suburban Publications, whose membership was identical with that of Suburban Community Newspapers, Consolidated Press was under the impression that ownership of the press had in fact moved from the company which it had sold to the one in which it still owned a half interest. Fairfax, on the other hand, insisted that the press belonged to Suburban Publications.

Consolidated Press called in the Fraud Squad and instituted proceedings against Fairfax in the Equity Division of the Supreme Court. Before the dispute came to court, however, it was effectively settled by the sale to Fairfax of Packer's 50 per cent in Suburban Community Newspapers (later renamed Fairfax Community Newspapers Pty Ltd) at an agreed price of $20 million. This left Fairfax fully owning an additional thirteen newspapers, making it the largest of Sydney's three suburban proprietorships—the other two being News Ltd and the Herald and Weekly Times, to the latter of which Packer had recently sold all his regional and suburban papers other than the suburban ones previously owned in partnership with Fairfax. There was some speculation by financial journalists that Packer might be cashing up for a major media acquisition, perhaps even a move against Fairfax; but nothing of this kind eventuated.

Fairfax's third major investment that year was made to raise its holding in Rural Press Ltd from 25.7 per cent to 45 per cent. Rural Press, the public non-listed company formerly known as Land Newspapers Ltd, had developed into a very profitable group publishing the *Land, Queensland Country Life, Grain Farmer, Gympie*

Times and other rural papers in New South Wales and Queensland. In April 1985 the company issued shares to fund its acquisition of the South Australian *Stock Journal*. This provided Fairfax with the opportunity to acquire another 20 per cent of the company, for an outlay of $18 million, making it by far the largest shareholder.

In 1984 Fairfax added to its already substantial list of regional mastheads by purchasing two companies owned by Rupert Henderson—Daniel Bros & Co Pty Ltd and Yass Newspapers Pty Ltd, publishers of newspapers in the Yass, Goulburn and Berrima districts of New South Wales. Henderson was then in his eighty-ninth year, virtually blind, but still a formidable negotiator. Like Sir Warwick Fairfax and Angus McLachlan, he still kept an office at the company's downtown building in Hunter Street. On one occasion at about this time he was greeted in the lift by Mary Fairfax. He apologized for not having recognized her and later took pleasure in recounting her reply. 'Don't worry', said Lady Fairfax to the old man with whom she shared a strong mutual antipathy. 'You may be blind, but you still get things done, which is more than I can say for the management at Broadway these days.'

In the selling of his country newspapers, Henderson suspended negotiations just when Fairfax thought the deal was about to be clinched for $863 000, then resumed negotiations and finally sold for $1 080 000. This was his last newspaper deal, although in the following year a company formerly owned by him, but transferred to members of his immediate family as part of Henderson's long-held policy of divestment, sold its 50 per cent interest in Riverina and Northwest Victoria TV Ltd for $17 million. Rupert Henderson died on 9 September 1986. The personal fortune which he left behind him, both by divestment and to a much smaller extent by probate, amounted to at least $35 million. The bulk of this fortune was left upon trust to his wife, who survived him by only eight weeks; thereafter to his only surviving child, a married daughter, as life tenant; and upon her death to her only child, another daughter.

In October 1984 Fairfax purchased 50 per cent of Longbeach Publications Pty Ltd, publisher of two free weekly papers on the Gold Coast—the *Hinterlander* and the *Tweed Leader*. Two residual shareholders later sold out to Stereo FM Brisbane Ltd, a company in which Fairfax already had a minority holding. Longbeach was losing about $100 000 a year in an unequal struggle against Murdoch's daily tabloid, the *Gold Coast Bulletin*. Fairfax's strategy—directed by Vic Carroll, who had negotiated the purchase, and was now one of the two Fairfax representatives on the Longbeach board—was to combine the *Hinterlander* and *Tweed Leader* into one new paper which would use BTQ in Brisbane to attract advertising. Carroll had seen this work well in Newcastle, but events would show that the *Bulletin* was a very formidable opponent. It was the largest tabloid in Australia, running to as many as 400 revenue-packed pages on Saturdays.

Among the deals made by Fairfax during the first half of the 1980s some were concerned with its own properties. In 1982 the company sold its 22-year-old Blackwattle Bay newsprint store to the Fish Marketing Authority for $4 million, from which the capital gain was $1.6 million. This store had been built beside an inlet of the harbour not far from Broadway in case it ever became necessary to deliver newsprint by barge. In fact, however, delivery was always made by lorry from the wharves or, after Australian Newsprint Mills went into production at Albury in 1981, from the railhead. To replace Blackwattle Bay, the company entered into a 50-year lease with the State Rail Authority for a newsprint terminal and loading facility at Rozelle. Such was the company's appetite for paper that every second day a 15-car train from Albury arrived at Rozelle.

Also in 1982 Fairfax exercised an option to buy the Herald-Sun building at Broadway, which it had been leasing from the AMP Society for the previous twenty-five years. This advantageous option was a legacy from Rupert Henderson, who had negotiated the lease. The company could have entered into another lease in 1982, but was not sure how much longer it would be advisable to remain at Broadway. The *Sun*, as we shall see in the next chapter, was steadily losing ground against the *Mirror*. Sooner or later it might have to be closed, and in that unhappy event Fairfax might decide to move further out of the city, perhaps to a site which had already been investigated at Lidcombe. If the company was then in a position to sell its building, the capital gain would be enormous. An independent valuation had shown the property, for all its ugliness, to be worth between $18 and $25 million. Yet thanks to Rupert Henderson the purchase price, which Fairfax now proceeded to pay, was a mere $1 700 000.

5
Losing Battles

I

One of the most controversial exposés ever published in the *National Times* was its valediction upon the late, but only just late, Sir Robert Askin. The Honorable Sir Robert Askin had been Premier of New South Wales from 1965 to 1975—longer than anyone before him except Sir Henry Parkes, whose five separate terms in the previous century amounted to eleven years. Askin died on a Wednesday, 9 September 1981, and his funeral was announced for the following Monday. On Saturday the *National Times* went to press for Sunday publication with the front page headline, 'Askin: Friend To Organised Crime'.

Rarely if ever had there been a more wilful infringement of the maxim against speaking evil of the dead. On the day before Sir Robert's State funeral, the *National Times* told its readers:

> Sir Robert Askin was an underestimated man. The mark he left on this country was considerable—and has never publicly been discussed.
>
> While Sir Robert Askin was in power, organised crime became institutionalised on a large scale in New South Wales for the first time. Sydney became, and has remained, the crime capital of Australia.
>
> Askin was central to this. His links with three major crime figures, Perc Galea, close friend Joe Taylor and another, allowed the transformation of Sydney's baccarat clubs into fully-fledged casinos.
>
> Askin's links with corrupt police allowed those casinos and SP betting to flourish. The corrupt police included commissioners Allan and Hanson.
>
> According to a reliable source very high in the old Galea empire, Askin and Hanson were paid approximately $100 000 each in bribes a year from the end of the Sydney gang wars in 1967-68 until Askin's retirement. The source is impeccable. This information has not been available for the *National Times* to use until Askin's death . . .
>
> Only now that Askin is dead can the recent history of NSW be explored publicly. It is not a time for holding back, despite the distress these revelations may cause Askin's colleagues and family.

Such are the laws of defamation in this country, that only a royal commission or parliamentary debate could fully protect public discussion about the Askin years while the man lived. Recent commissions into organised crime have never dealt publicly with Askin's role . . .

On the day of the funeral James Fairfax sent a curt memorandum to Max Suich asking to be informed of the circumstances in which the article came to be published. 'I do not of course suggest that any material should be suppressed', he wrote,

but in my view the article should have been held over at least until the following issue and certainly not published the day before the funeral. I think this has damaged the *National Times*—many people will regard the timing as being in very poor taste, a view which I share. One final point—I am usually consulted when the *National Times* proposes to publish highly contentious matter and I think I should have been in this case.

The circumstances were these. The author of the report, David Hickie, had for some time been a close observer and to some extent a confidant of the Galea organization which, until Perc Galea's death in 1977, had been one of the most important sections of organized crime in Sydney. In the course of assembling material from which he was later to write a book about the Galea organization, Hickie obtained very convincing evidence that the organization had made regular payments to Askin and many senior police. By 1981, when David Marr succeeded Evan Whitton as editor of the *National Times*, Askin was known to be seriously ill. With that in mind, Marr—a young lawyer-journalist who had written a widely acclaimed biography of Sir Garfield Barwick—asked Hickie to broaden by further investigation the material which he had already assembled on the Askin years.

'These investigations', wrote Suich in his reply to the chairman,

crossed the track of other investigations by the Commonwealth police, the taxation department and certain politicians, including Mr John Hatton [an Independent MLA] and Mr John Dowd [a Liberal MLA who later became Leader of the Opposition]. It became clear that while the facts had never been published they were well known to a wide range of members of the community, particularly within the political world . . . It was at one time hoped that the paper could bring its inquiries to fruition and publish while [Askin] was alive. This failed because Sir Robert's illness overtook the inquiries.

Marr was all for publishing immediately. Suich, in his capacity as chief editorial executive, would have preferred more documentation; but as a former editor of the *National Times* himself, he recalled earlier occasions when it had been necessary to judge whether a story contained enough on-the-record material to justify unsourced assertions which the paper believed were true. One case concerned a series of articles in 1976 about conditions in New South Wales prisons. From small beginnings, this snowballed into a royal commission.

'It was for these reasons', Suich told the chairman, 'that I was reluctant to impede the honest objectives of the *National Times* editor in wanting to publish'. He accepted the chairman's view that he had erred in the timing of publication, and apologized for not having consulted him on the matter.

At the next board meeting, on 17 September, Sir Warwick Fairfax said he was glad that Suich had acknowledged his error of judgement. It was sixteen years since Askin had come to power, he said, and the fact that the *National Times* had waited until his death before publishing an article of this type brought discredit to the whole Fairfax organization. As discussion went on, however, the directors' main criticism turned from lapse of taste to lack of diligence in getting on to the story earlier. Out of this came another snowball effect. The Askin story, although generally acknowledged as accurate, could not be taken much further, for the trail had gone cold. What could and would be taken further, at the board's direction, was the general investigation of organized crime by the *National Times* and other Fairfax publications. Sir Warwick Fairfax and Sir David Griffin were particularly strong in their support of this unprecedented resolution.

'It should be understood', wrote Suich in a memorandum to Marr and his deputy editor, Brian Toohey,

> that the board, while embarrassed by the nature and timing of the [Askin] story, is unanimous in the view that the investigation of such stories is an important part of the work of all the Fairfax papers . . . No further story relating to Sir Robert Askin is to be published unless you have persuasive and hard on-the-record evidence. This is not to say that you can't use anonymous sources where you are satisfied of their honesty and accuracy, but the reputation of the *National Times* must not be prejudiced by serious charges being made by simple assertion. The *National Times* is to put the maximum available resources into following up the story and publishing the facts not only about Sir Robert Askin but the corruption of other politicians and police—particularly those still living and working in Sydney.

This was rather like urging a bloodhound to improve its scent. During the paper's first ten years it had led the pack at Broadway, far outstripping the *Herald, Sun* and *Sun-Herald* at investigative journalism. Henceforth it was to set an even faster pace, sniffing busily for fresh spoor and baying with renewed zeal after more formidable quarry.

It was hard going, with no guarantee of a trophy at the end of the hunt. There might be a kill—imprisonment for a corrupt minister of the crown, a Senate inquiry into the conduct of a judge—or there might be nothing more than carefully lawyered innuendo leaving an impression of guilt, perhaps well deserved but not proven. Certainly the kills served a high purpose. So too did some of the misses, by raising public awareness and intimidating scoundrels. But a miss being as good as a mile, the *National Times* ran serious risks in this line of work. On one occasion the Federal Treasurer, Paul Keating, after finding himself the unwilling subject of a detailed but inconclusive article in the *National Times*, said with characteristically vivid imagery: 'It's a jungle out there. And I'm a tiger. Where do you shoot a tiger? Between the eyes, that's where. Well they missed, they only wounded me'.

Apart from the fury of wounded tigers, the *National Times* also risked being regarded as a self-appointed Nemesis, obsessed with wrongdoing and retribution. Such a perception could blind readers to the rest of the paper, and was unlikely to do much for circulation and advertising revenue. Although its circulation had risen from 35 000 in 1971 to 104 000 in 1981, the paper had consistently lost money at an average rate of about $500 000 a year. Willing though the board was to persevere until the *National Times* broke into profit, its patience was to be sorely tried over the next few years.

At Marr's urging, the *National Times* ran one more front-page article about Askin. Suich initially agreed to let it run in the next issue; then, after Marr had promised the article during a television interview, he changed his mind about the timing of it. Late the following week Marr rang Suich at a Blue Mountains holiday resort to press the case again. After a certain amount of sparring about the content, Suich said reluctantly: 'OK, it's on your own head'. The story, written by David Hickie and Marian Wilkinson, asserted that Sir Robert, in the last few months of his premiership, had been paid $55 000 by a group of Sydney bookmakers to ensure that bookmakers' turnover tax was not increased. As it happened, the tax *was* increased after Sir Robert's retirement, but that was by the way.

During the next week Marr and other Fairfax editors dined at the Lodge in Canberra with the Prime Minister, Malcolm Fraser. The Prime Minister criticized the *National Times* for running the Askin stories, but changed his attitude when the others present supported Marr with their own testimony about the growth of organized crime in New South Wales.

Suich seemed pleased with the second story; but from that time onwards Marr felt that his relations with the chief editorial executive were deteriorating. Part of the trouble may have been the younger man's lack of experience for the post to which Suich had promoted him. It was also Marr's lot to have to contend with two rises in cover price and the separation of *Business Review*, factors bound to affect circulation, which fell abruptly to 93 000. Suich would like to have devoted more of his own time to the paper with which he had been so closely associated in the past, but he was too busy with other matters. Vic Carroll sat with Marr for the first month, imparting various knacks of the editor's trade. After that Marr was on his own, though increasingly subject to Suich's vehement criticism and at times his uncontrolled anger. 'You couldn't win this man's approval', he recalled later. 'The best was in the worst crises. When things went really bad Max actually sat down and thought about things, and then he was perceptive, helpful and strong.'

The final crisis came in February 1982, over a front-page story by Brian Toohey entitled 'Tax Heist: How hardened criminals and lawyers are combining to cost all Australian taxpayers millions'. This was based on material placed before the Costigan Royal Commission into the Painters and Dockers Union, concerning tax avoidance schemes. One of the lawyers mentioned prominently in the story—L. J. Priestley, QC, who was later appointed to the Supreme Court—took strong exception to it. Through his solicitors Priestley claimed that the material published about him carried the imputation that he had acted in some way improperly, that he was involved in some kind of combination with 'hardened criminals' in order to cheat and defraud Australian taxpayers, and that he had a substantial financial interest in the matter. According to the letter of complaint, he had merely answered certain specific questions of law in relation to a proposed transaction, for which his total fees had been $200.

Marr was attending the Adelaide Festival when this complaint was made. Called back to Sydney by Suich, he acknowledged that the front-page heading was at fault, but maintained with Toohey that the article itself was a fair and accurate account of evidence given in public hearings. Marr then flew back to Adelaide. The next issue of the paper carried the letter of complaint and an apology for any unintended misunderstanding which may have been created by the combination of heading and text.

When Marr returned to Sydney Suich informed him that his handling of the matter raised serious doubts in his own mind about whether Marr had the judgement required to continue editing the paper. Suich had also become uneasy about what he perceived as Marr's inclination to take his own legal advice.

Deciding to quit the editor's chair, Marr took six months leave, then returned to the staff as a writer with salary level preserved. He covered the Royal Commission on Australian Security and Intelligence; wrote a book about one of the subjects of that inquiry, the Ivanov–Combe affair; and in 1985 resigned in order to write a biography of Patrick White.

The change in editorship went smoothly, for although a collective letter to Suich from the staff had expressed regret at Marr's departure, his successor, Brian Toohey, had worked harmoniously with Marr as deputy editor and was well respected on the paper. If one had tried to invent an appropriate editor for the *National Times* in its time of sharpened vigilance, the result could hardly have improved upon Toohey—a short, round bulldog figure with highly developed suspicion, great staying power, and the ability to keep a seemingly endless supply of leaked documents coming his way. He looked more the part than elegant David Marr, and was better equipped to deal with the chief editorial executive. When Suich snapped at him over the phone, 'No, it's not logical', Toohey asked: 'How do you mean 'not logical'? Do you mean Cartesian or Aristotelian? I'll come down and explain if you like'.

After graduating in economics at the University of Queensland, Toohey had worked as a research officer for the Australian Labor Party in Brisbane, and later in Canberra as an aide to the Minister for Defence, Lance Barnard. In 1973 he joined the *Australian Financial Review*, working in Canberra and later in Washington. His interests, as reflected by the *National Times*, ranged from defence and security matters to Sir Peter Abeles and Det-Sgt Roger Rogerson, but this brief account of his editorship must of necessity be selective.

Probably the most effective story of the period was 'Why Jackson Resigned: Eight questions that led to a political crisis'. Written by Marian Wilkinson in October 1983, it recounted a series of questions she had put to the New South Wales Minister for Corrective Services, Rex Jackson—questions pointing so directly to Jackson's having misled parliament that he resigned his portfolio the same day. Based upon Federal Police transcripts of bugged telephone conversations, Wilkinson's questions referred to discussions between the Minister and a Sydney businessman, Keith Harris, about the early release of three prisoners from Broken Hill gaol and arrangements for the payment of money. In an accompanying caricature, the *National Times* artist Jenny Coopes prophetically showed Jackson wearing a broad arrow tie. He was later found guilty of conspiracy and sentenced to nine and a half years imprisonment.

Electronic surveillance also formed the basis of another important, though rather cryptic, Wilkinson story in the following month. Wilkinson, a 29-year-old Queenslander, had joined the paper in 1978 during Whitton's editorship, replacing Andrew Clark, who had pioneered the paper's reporting of organized crime in collaboration with the freelance investigator Bob Bottom. According to Bottom, Wilkinson quickly 'got to know the Sydney scene better than anyone before or after her'. Bottom had in his possession extensive transcripts of many telephone conversations recorded secretly by the New South Wales Police Department's Bureau of Criminal Intelligence. They were dynamite. Wilkinson, through her own police contacts, had seen some of the material, and together with Bottom she began assembling a story to be published under a joint byline. Bottom ran hot and cold about it, finally drawing back on the eve of publication, presumably because his source was still hesitant about lifting the lid of such a Pandora's box. Toohey said it was too late to pull the story out, so it ran with only Wilkinson's byline and a quintessentially *National Times* headline, 'Big Shots Bugged'.

Readers had to take Wilkinson's word for it that the Shots were Big, for they were identified merely as a solicitor called 'Mr Fix-it', a senior New South Wales public servant, a former New South Wales magistrate, a former New South Wales police officer, a judge and a Liberal Party politician. What they were talking about was not clear either, for Wilkinson used cautious paraphrase rather than extensive quotation. To those in the know, however, Pandora's box was open. Bottom, having withdrawn from the *National Times* after a row with Toohey over the timing of Wilkinson's article, and expecting police to raid his home in search of tapes, judged it expedient to leave Sydney. He took all his material to Melbourne, made contact with a journalist friend on the *Age*, Lindsay Murdoch, and went to see Robert Haupt, who was acting as editor in the absence overseas of Creighton Burns. Haupt agreed that Bottom should collaborate with Murdoch and another *Age* investigative reporter, David Wilson, on a more thorough treatment of the tapes. Feeling that it might be hard for Melburnians to appreciate some of the nuances, Haupt suggested to the editor of the *Sydney Morning Herald*, Chris Anderson, that a contact of Bottom's on the *Sydney Morning Herald*, Neil Mercer, should also participate with a view to simultaneous publication in the two papers. Mercer worked for several days with the team in Melbourne, putting together a story for use in the *Herald*.

The *Age* prepared a three-part series entitled 'Network of Influence'. Part One, which was to be published on 2 February 1984 under the front-page headline 'Secret Tapes of Judge', concentrated on conversations between a senior judge and a well known Sydney solicitor. The judge, unidentified for the time being, was no less a figure than Mr Justice Lionel Murphy of the High Court; the solicitor was Morgan Ryan. The *Age* Tapes, as they became known, led inexorably to a political-judicial crisis which was to be terminated only by the judge's illness and death in 1986.

As the *Age* made ready to publish, there was distinctly less enthusiasm about the story at Broadway. The news editor, Denis Muller, first heard about it at 5 p.m. on 1 February, when Chris Anderson—acting editor-in-chief during Carroll's absence, and soon to succeed him in that post—sought Muller's advice. Anderson had no detailed knowledge of what was on the tapes, nor indeed much idea of where the tapes had come from, other than that they had been made illegally by certain members of the New South

Wales police force and that somehow Bob Bottom had got hold of them.

Muller asked whether it was known for certain that the tapes had not been doctored. Anderson thought the *Age* had done some tests, but said Muller should ask Mercer for details. Carroll had been kept informed of progress, he said, and had produced a fall-back formula in case it should be decided not to run Mercer's story. In essence, the fall-back would raise three questions: Why had New South Wales police been making secret tapes illegally? How could it have happened? What would the consequences be? The contents of the tapes were to be skirted around.

Muller found Mercer sitting in the police rounds room. 'The radio was blaring', recalled Muller later,

> and the atmosphere was pretty tense. He had his story written, and passed it over to me. It was broadly similar to the one which was to appear in the *Age* next morning. I gave him Carroll's alternative prescription. Mercer rejected it outright. He said we should either run with the real story or leave it alone. I agreed with him.

As for verification, Mercer said that one of David Syme's subsidiary companies specializing in electronics had carried out tests which satisfied the *Age*. The testing of the 'judge's' voice had admittedly been inconclusive, though certain characteristics made it likely that the voice was indeed Murphy's. Asked how Bottom had obtained the tapes, Mercer replied that Bottom was very cagey about that, but it seemed they had come from police contacts. 'Mercer was absolutely convinced that the tapes were genuine', said Muller, 'and argued passionately for running his story. The trouble was we had nothing first-hand to base our decision on. We were entirely in the hands of the *Age* and Bob Bottom'. Muller's scepticism was reinforced by the fact that Bottom had recently been criticized—unfairly, as would later become apparent—by a commission inquiring into certain allegations which he had made against a magistrate.

At 8.30 p.m. Muller was joined in his office by Anderson, the acting editor Beecher, Mercer and one of the company's lawyers, Graham Bates. 'Who gave you this stuff?' asked Bates, throwing back his head in mock disbelief when Muller mentioned Bottom's name. Beecher and Mercer were in favour of running it; Bates and Muller were against. Finally, at about 9 p.m., Anderson decided to publish nothing about the tapes that night. He may well have reached this decision earlier, for he knew that Suich and Carroll had serious reservations about the story. According to Suich's recollection, he and Carroll over-ruled Anderson, who had originally intended publishing simultaneously with the *Age*.

Suich was totally opposed to publication because the *Herald* knew nothing about the source of the story—a story making grave allegations about prominent people in Sydney. 'I could not defend that to the board', he said later. 'We had a board instruction to find out about organized crime, and here we would have been taking someone else's story.'

In the wake of the *Age*'s disclosures, with the *Herald* deemed by many to have burked the matter, Suich rang Bottom asking him to help in a catching-up operation. Bottom agreed, and on 18 February the *Herald* published a comprehensive report—'Phone Taps in Search of Mr Big', by Neil Mercer and Graham Williams, and 'Ample Scope for Prosecutions', by Malcolm Brown. No longer was the *Age* alone, and no longer was there any chance that the *Age* Tapes would be ignored. Nettled by the failure to use his earlier story, Mercer had passed it on to the *National Times*, where it was incorporated in a report by Marian Wilkinson and himself ('Phone Taps: the Net Widens') one week ahead of the *Herald*'s catch-up story. Anderson reproached him for this, but also confided to Mercer that he would not have blamed him if he had gone out and got drunk for a week.

To remedy the shortcomings exposed by this episode, Anderson appointed Muller an assistant editor with particular responsibility for running a crime unit. In the months ahead, this unit—consisting mainly of Andrew Keenan as principal reporter, and Bottom as consultant and contributing writer—was to produce some outstanding stories, notably ones concerned with Det-Sgt Rogerson, Triad activity in Australia, and police bungling of the investigation into Donald Mackay's disappearance.

One of many sequels flowing from the *Age* Tapes in 1984 was a story which brought the *National Times* into conflict with federal parliament. The story, by Wendy Bacon, made use of evidence given in camera to a Senate Select Committee on the Conduct of a Judge—the judge being Mr Justice Murphy. In closed session the New South Wales Chief Stipendiary Magistrate, C. R. Briese, had alleged that a district court judge, who claimed to be acting at the instigation of a senior government minister, had discussed with him whether it might be possible to influence another magistrate in his hearing of charges against the solicitor Morgan Ryan concerning an alleged immigration racket.

In an explanatory note for the Fairfax board, Max Suich wrote:

> Brian Toohey made the judgment, which I have since endorsed, that this material, while secret to the Committee, should be published. Given the debate over the administration of justice in New South Wales and the debate over the behaviour of Murphy, this material was highly pertinent to the public debate and it seemed highly possible that the material would not come out unless we published it.

The article, published in July, and two other references to the secret material in subsequent issues, were referred by vote of the Senate to the Privileges Committee of that chamber. Suich, Toohey and Bacon were called before the Privileges Committee, but made no apologies. They pleaded public interest and argued that publication, although in conflict with the Senate's Standing Orders, neither impeded the Select Committee nor incommoded its witnesses.

In October the Privileges Committee reported unanimously that the publication of in camera evidence had been a serious contempt, for which Toohey, Bacon and John Fairfax & Sons Ltd were culpable. Here was an opportunity for the Senate to test its previously asserted, though never exercised, power to impose fines. But instead the Privileges Committee recommended in May 1985 'that the Senate not proceed to the imposition of a penalty at this time, but if the same or a similar offence be committed by any of the media for which John Fairfax & Sons Ltd is responsible . . . the Senate should impose an appropriate penalty for the present offence'. This was in effect a good behaviour bond for the duration of the current parliament, with warning of a fine as high as $100 000.

Editorials in the *Herald* and *Financial Review* protested at such a use of parliamentary privilege. 'Whether the *National Times* acted rightly or wrongly is only one issue', said the *Review*.

> Much more important is the attempt by the Senate Committee on Privileges to exercise pre-censorship over media which had nothing whatsoever to do with the alleged offence, and to do so by pretending to possess a power the very existence of which is extremely doubtful. If it does exist, it should be held in reserve for serious offences, and not used as a threat for purposes of censorship. In the meantime, this newspaper can certainly not consider itself bound in advance to some ill-defined bond of 'good behaviour'.

As it happened, however, none of the Fairfax papers trailed its coat; the Senate dealt inconclusively with the Privileges Committee's report; and when parliament was dissolved two years later the Senate's power to fine was still untested.

As Suich wrote in a board report at the time, the Senate was not the only quarter in which the company had made itself unpopular. 'I link these matters together', he wrote,

> because I think they all touch on the reputation of the company and its papers and its legal position. Because of these events we are coming under considerable scrutiny and Fairfax as a company is getting a good deal more attention than we are accustomed to. I would prefer it to be otherwise but I think it is inevitable because we are touching some very tender nerves.

This was certainly a time of great sensitivity, for simultaneously with the Senate case John Fairfax Limited was also embroiled on two other fronts—with the New South Wales Government, and with Kerry Packer. Relations with the Labor Government had been deteriorating during the past three years. In October 1982, over a very long lunch with Suich, the Premier, Neville Wran, accused the Fairfax newspapers of running unwarranted attacks on his Government. According to a file note by Suich, the occasion was fairly cheerful and friendly; but the Premier did avail himself of the opportunity to issue what Suich took to be a number of threats, some clear and some implied. 'He made a number of references to the contributions to Fairfax classified and display advertising revenues by State Government advertising', wrote Suich. 'I took this as a threat to cut back these revenues.'

Far from there being any let-up after this cheerful lunch, the Fairfax papers went on to take a closer interest in the Premier, his ministers and friends. In 1983 Evan Whitton, the former *National Times* editor turned chief reporter for the *Herald*, covered a two-month-long Royal Commission of Inquiry into Certain Committal Proceedings against K. E. Humphreys—an inquiry sometimes mistakenly, but not inaptly, described as the Wran Royal Commission. The committal proceedings in question had dealt with certain charges against Humphreys, a former chairman of the Australian Rugby Football League, concerning the misappropriation of funds belonging to Balmain Rugby League Club.

Originally Vic Carroll had asked Whitton to supplement the *Herald*'s news coverage of this inquiry, at which Wran was expected to give evidence, by writing a fortnightly analysis of it. At Anderson's urging, however, Whitton wrote on a daily basis, modelling his commentaries on the discursive and often irreverent parliamentary sketches in the London *Times* and *Guardian*. He did not exactly tell the Commissioner (who was the Chief Justice of New South Wales, Sir Laurence Street) what to find, but now and then he dropped some broad hints.

What the Commissioner found in his report was that the chief stipendiary magistrate, Murray Farquhar, had influenced the outcome of the committal proceedings against Humphreys, but that in doing so he had not been acting at the direction or request of the Premier and Minister for Police, Neville Wran.

Also during this period the *National Times* published a long piece about the Premier's friend Sir Peter Abeles ('Sir Peter Abeles and TNT's Brush with the Mafia'), and also several articles mentioned previously—'Why Jackson Resigned', 'Big Shots Bugged' and 'Phone Taps: the Net Widens', all by Marian Wilkinson. Even more resented, however, was the *Sydney Morning Herald* of 29 February 1984. At about 10 a.m. that day the group general manager received a phone call from the Federal Treasurer, Paul Keating, saying he was absolutely shocked by the first three pages of the paper.

The first two pages were devoted largely to an attack by the Leader of the National Party, Ian Sinclair, on the findings of a special commission of inquiry conducted by Mr Justice Cross of the Supreme Court into certain allegations made by Sinclair about abuses in the New South Wales justice system. Across the top of the front page was a line of photographs under the heading: 'Sinclair's views of the bookie, businessman, lawyer, judge and Premier'. The bookmaker was Bill Waterhouse, said by Sinclair to have had 'long friendship with Labor politicians'; the solicitor was Morgan Ryan; and the Premier was described in a caption as having once 'pencilled for Waterhouse'. On Page Two an edited text of Sinclair's statement in the House of Representatives was published across seven columns under the headline, 'Ian Sinclair: How could Cross get it so wrong?' On Page Three there was a more compressed report of the Premier's reply to an accusation, made five days earlier by the Deputy Leader of the Opposition, Rosemary Foot, that the Government had shown 'deliberate and systematic favouritism' towards Warren Anderson, a property developer who, according to Mrs Foot, enjoyed intimacy with the right wing of the Labor Party at all levels.

Although there were reasons of news judgement and page layout for the placing of these stories, an impression was none the less conveyed that Sinclair's statement was more important than Wran's. It was therefore hardly surprising that the Premier felt himself to have been treated unfairly.

The Treasurer told Gardiner he was ringing not as a federal politician but in relation to State politics. If Fairfax did not get Wran removed, he said according to Gardiner's file note, it must understand that Wran would go for it with a vengeance, and Federal Labour would put its back into his efforts to crush the company.

Later that day Gardiner received a similar but angrier call from the Premier. The *Herald*, he said, had reached its pinnacle as an organ of the Liberal Party. He was not being paranoid, but had simply had a bellyfull of having his head hit every time he raised it. He was sick and tired of being portrayed as a crook. He had had a gutful of it. Although he was not a great believer in conspiracy theories, it was patently obvious that there was a conspiracy with the *Age*, the *Herald* and the *National Times* all involved. Fairfax was going to pay the price for this. All of its interests at some time wanted something from the Government.He could assure Gardiner that he did not forget easily and that he would devote a lifetime to bring Fairfax and the *Herald* down.

The intensity of the Premier's feeling was more easily appreciated when it became known a few days later that preparations were being made by him for an early election. During the short campaign for that election in March, the *Herald*'s editorials were as strongly critical of Wran's Government as the Premier would have expected. But this was not to say that the *Herald* was 'an organ of the Liberal Party'. Although such a jibe might have seemed apt enough in the past, when the *Herald*'s electoral policies had been almost exclusively conservative, the paper was now less partisan.

During the 1983 federal election campaign the *Herald* came down marginally and unavailingly on the side of Fraser's conservative government. At the next election, in December 1984, it concluded that the Hawke Government was entitled to a second term. This was the first time the paper had advocated a vote for Federal Labor since 1961, when it lent editorial support to the luckless Arthur Calwell. It did so again in 1987, arguing that on the strength of the Government's economic record it should be given a third term.

At State level, however, the *Herald* had grave reservations about the long-serving Labor Government. In 1981 it refrained from taking any electoral side; but in 1984, predicting correctly that Wran would be returned with a reduced majority, it advised voters to give Labor the 'good kick in the pants' which the Premier himself expected. At the next election, in 1988, it supported the Liberal–National Party coalition with more confidence and had the satisfaction of seeing it elected.

In spite of the threats which had been made to Gardiner, relations between Fairfax and the State Government became more equable after the election of March 1984. But on 12 September the chief classified advertising manager of John Fairfax & Sons Ltd, John Newnham, was taken aback to receive a letter from the secretary of the Premier's Department, Gerald Gleeson, advising him that in five days time, for reasons of cost, the Government would transfer all its classified advertising from the *Sydney Morning Herald* to the *Daily Telegraph*. The columns affected were mainly Tenders, Employment and Public Notices. Two weeks later, on instructions from the Minister for Health, the State's public hospitals transferred their allegiance in the same way. The combined value of advertising lost to the *Herald* as a result of these two decisions was more than $3 million per year.

Protesting that the *Herald* had not been informed of any client dissatisfaction, Brenchley asked the Government to follow normal commercial practice by briefing all potential suppliers (in this case the *Herald* and *Telegraph*) to make submissions for future advertising business. Gleeson said the crux of the matter was simply that the *Telegraph* was cheaper. Newnham presented readership and cost effectiveness figures showing that the *Herald* did a better job, but at a luncheon in the directors' dining room at Broadway Gleeson held to his argument that it was a cost matter.

On 24 December the company was notified that tenders would be called for a new contract to begin on 1 December 1985. The *Herald* made every effort to ensure that it came in below the *Telegraph*. Newnham devoted much effort to canvassing public servants, and at Brenchley's suggestion he set up a State Government Advertising Unit to deal directly with the State Government, thus saving the Government a 10 per cent middle man's charge. Fairfax's tender was chosen, but the *Herald* had lost more than a year's worth of State Government advertising before the river of gold was again flowing at its usual rate. Fortunately, thanks to the beneficial effect of Broadway's new computerized typesetting system on multiple-day bookings, the river of classified advertising was in fact flowing faster than ever. In spite of the Government hiatus, the volume of classifieds in 1984–85 was up by 16 per cent.

Since the introduction of an adequate computer system, making multiple discounting possible, the *Herald*'s classified department had been marketing properly for the first time. This was just as well, for earlier the *Telegraph* had been encroaching upon the *Herald*'s classified dominance, particularly in the motor trade columns. Under the leadership of some new women executives, an enthusiastic sales staff soon regained much of that lost ground.

While the State Government and Senate matters were running their troublous courses—from September 1984 into the following year—John Fairfax Ltd was also in conflict with its magazine competitor and suburban newspaper partner, Kerry Packer. The conflict arose from two articles in the *National Times* based on confidential and highly controversial material from the Costigan Royal Commission. Not only did these give grave offence to Packer, but on the Fairfax side they exacerbated a worsening relationship between Suich and Toohey. The trouble with Toohey, as Suich saw it, was that after the promising first six months of his editorship he had become more writer than editor. He wrote particularly about corruption in New South Wales and federal spheres, Suich told the board, and as that became more important his editorial vision narrowed.

> Mr Toohey was a person of great integrity and honesty [said Suich]. Mr Toohey had been told before Christmas that we needed to know where he was taking the paper and that he needed to approach broader issues.
>
> However, Mr Toohey had become immersed in the *Age* Tapes and the possible involvement of Mr Wran and also major stories on defence. After Christmas, it was agreed that the paper would be reviewed and strengthened with greater attention to be given to improved reporting from Melbourne and improvement in the arts, books and consumer affairs reporting. That did not happen. In June, Mr Suich spoke to Mr Toohey from London and requested that preparations for a major promotion campaign be begun. Once again this

> did not occur. Mr Suich said a major article on Mr Kerry Packer had caused tension between him and Mr Toohey.
>
> Mr Suich said board policy was that all articles on media personalities had to be referred to him. Mr Toohey had telephoned him in London and advised him of the story. When he returned he saw it was a dramatic major story. It touched on a competitor of Fairfax and, as first written, some people might have thought Packer was being ganged up on by his rivals.
>
> There had been a lot of consultation between the chairman and the group general manager and he had instructed that anything written must be absolutely right and absolutely fair. The story was delayed some weeks because of legal problems and . . . [the] *National Times* staff became obsessed that the story was being suppressed.

The main question posed by this story was whether the recently established National Crime Authority would pursue all the matters brought to light by the Costigan Commission—matters much more varied than the Commission's initial concern with the Painters and Dockers Union. Among them were certain transactions involving Kerry Packer, which had occupied much of the Commission's attention during the last few months.

Suich approved the article for publication with two provisos: it should not be the lead story with a front-page splash, for that would seem spiteful; and certain references to hashish oil should be removed from it altogether. According to confidential material to which the *National Times* had gained access, a commercial quantity of hashish oil, concealed in the walls of a box addressed to Packer from Katmandu, would have been delivered to his city office had it not been detected by a Customs officer at the bond store. No one knew who had sent the box, or why. In Suich's view, publication could well have the effect of branding Packer as a drug trafficker, without any justification. Toohey argued against his ruling, but complied with it.

The article as it appeared on 3 August 1984—'Kerry Packer and the Costigan Commission', by Marian Wilkinson—dealt at length with various topics including Packer's withdrawal of $1 million in $50 notes from a city bank; his business dealings with a Brisbane property developer, Brian Ray; and the suicide of a Queensland bank manager. It was guarded and enigmatic in the way that dangerous stories often are. Wilkinson had submitted several questions to Packer before publication; but on advice from one of his lawyers, Malcolm Turnbull, Packer replied that it would be illegal for him to answer questions about proceedings in a confidential session of the Commission.

The staff of the *National Times*—a group of about twenty-four, including such writers as deputy editor Adele Horin, Canberra correspondent Geoff Kitney, Colleen Ryan and Robert Milliken;

sub-editors Bob Dempsey, Jim Craigie, Gus Edison and David Frith; the artist Michael Fitzjames, and the photographer Lorrie Graham—were now showing signs of what Suich termed 'siege mentality'. Aware that Wilkinson's story had been cut, they also heard unofficially that the paper was soon to receive a new editor—or rather a managing editor with authority over Toohey, who was to remain as editor. In these circumstances they concluded that an outsider was being brought in to tame the paper.

Suich's main concern, running in parallel with tension over the Packer story, was to bring in a managing editor who could complement Toohey's undoubted strength with a broader approach to the market. Toohey agreed with Suich that he did not possess the requisite skills to market the *National Times*. It was up to Suich, he felt, to provide funds for promotion by experts. Suich would not do that, however, until Toohey 'got the paper right'—an adjustment which Toohey took to mean dropping or at least reducing the paper's component of hard-edged journalism. Suich scoffed at that interpretation, and in later years drew vindication from the continued content of the paper. 'If I had withdrawn my support from Brian, he would have been gone in a month', he said.

In Toohey's unavailing view, ample scope for promotion already existed in the paper's excellent political, sports and arts writing as well as the hard edge which sometimes drew blood. For Suich's part, he did not concede that the writing in those fields was excellent.

Suich's choice for managing editor was Jefferson Penberthy, a former *Financial Review* writer and currently editor of *Business Review Weekly* under a managing editor of his own, Robert Gottliebsen. On Tuesday 7 August the staff of the *National Times* went on strike for 48 hours in protest against Penberthy's appointment. Only once before, on the *Australian* in 1974, had Australian journalists taken industrial action over an editorial issue. They resumed work in time to get the next issue out.

There was no repetition of the strike. Suich and Toohey assured the staff that their fears were groundless, and Penberthy showed himself anxious to keep publishing 'hard' investigative stories. At the board meeting which approved Penberthy's appointment on 16 August, most directors expressed their determination that the *National Times* should continue to provide the type of journalism which had made it famous.

It did so, and with more alacrity than might have been expected. On Tuesday 11 September Toohey informed Suich that he had obtained access to forty-two case summaries which the Costigan Commission had recommended for further investigation by the NCA. Next day he mentioned the matter again and said he was proposing to publish some of the material immediately. The story, under Toohey's byline, consisted mainly of five case summaries presented verbatim from reports by the Royal Commission, with anonymity preserved by code names. On Thursday morning, Suich heard from Penberthy that the story included material which had been deleted from the earlier article. This was an hour before press start (since March 1983 the paper had been printed on Thursdays, for sale on Fridays), and Suich was due to leave for New York later the same day.

Penberthy, who was still learning to edit on the electronic terminals, did not know exactly what Toohey was proposing to publish, but had become aware that one of the case histories dealt with Packer, the box containing hash oil and other matters. The Commission had referred to Packer by the code name 'Squirrel'. To achieve further anonymity, Toohey changed that to 'Possum', and at Penberthy's intervention and Adele Horin's inspiration it was changed again to 'Goanna'.

Unhappy though he was about the reference to drugs, Suich told Penberthy it was too late to pull the 'Goanna' summary out. When he eventually saw the paper several days later while flying home from New York, he made the judgement—as he informed the chairman—that if he had been consulted earlier he would have endorsed publication of everything in the article. Like Toohey, he thought the federal Government was trying to slow down the Costigan Commission and delay a smooth changeover of duties to the NCA. The story demonstrated the serious nature of Costigan's suspicions, said Suich, and the use of code names seemed to him an adequate protection for people who were not necessarily guilty. For all that, however, he angrily rebuked Toohey for not having kept him adequately informed.

The identity of the 'Goanna', although it soon became known to many people at Broadway and elsewhere, might have remained a mere subject of conjecture in wider circles had it not been for an outburst in federal Parliament at that time by the Leader of the Opposition, Andrew Peacock, during which he referred to the Prime Minister as 'a little crook'. As Peacock apparently lacked any substantiation for this charge, some of his Liberal Party colleagues let it be known privately that he had been referring to Hawke's friendship with the 'Goanna'. This stirred up speculation, and raised the possibility that the 'Goanna' might be named under parliamentary privilege.

On 28 September Packer himself took the initiative by issuing a 5000-word statement, published in full by the *Sydney Morning Herald* next day, in which he said he recognized that he was intended to be the person referred to as 'The Goanna':

> My identity as 'The Goanna' has become well known by word of mouth and veiled hint through the media. Initially I did not believe

Fairfax management 1980–87
G. J. Gardiner, group general manager, with J. B. Fairfax (left), deputy chairman 1985–87

M. V. Suich, chief editorial executive

F. R. Brenchley, general manager Broadway

The *Sydney Morning Herald* 1980–87: (left to right) V. J. Carroll, editor 1980–82, editor-in-chief 1982–84; C. J. Anderson, editor 1982–84, editor-in-chief 1984–87; Eric Beecher, editor 1984–87; John Alexander, editor 1987–88, editor-in-chief 1988–

Taking a page proof for the last hot-metal *Sydney Morning Herald* on 25 March 1984; (below) pasting up cold type pages

Max Suich, editor of the *National Times* 1973–78, Brian Toohey, editor 1984–86, and investigative reporter Wendy Bacon leave Parliament House, Canberra, after appearing before the Senate Privileges Committee and refusing to apologize for alleged contempt of that chamber.

The National Times

Australia's national weekly of business and affairs

70 cents*

No. 554 SEPTEMBER 13 to 19, 1981

ASKIN: FRIEND TO ORGANISED CRIME

LABOR COUP IN WA Page 3

WHAT'S ALLOWED IN YOUR WINE Page 46

By DAVID HICKIE

SIR Robert Askin was an underestimated man. The mark he left on this country was considerable — and has never publicly been discussed.

While Sir Robert Askin was in power, organised crime became institutionalised on a large scale in New South Wales: for the first time, Sydney became, and has remained, the crime capital of Australia.

Joh's Garbage Bin

By MARK PLUNKETT

A PETITION publicly handed to the Queensland Premier, Joh Bjelke-Petersen, by Queensland Aborigines calling for land rights was later found disposed of in a nearby rubbish bin.

THE SURVIVAL OF WHITE AUSTRALIA

ART HEIST

The trouble with Sir Harry

Holiday in Europe (at our expense) Page 28

Clancy Page 16

National Times on Sunday

SUNDAY, AUGUST 10, 1986

Nearly a billion cut from welfare, health

The Budget's human face: colour it grey

By KATE LEGGE

Sad man seeks his Weeping Woman

McCaughey waits for thief's call

By PHILIPPA HAWKER and HELEN THOMAS

Cup sails safe in Budget eddy

Continued on page 2

Not a weeping woman, but a grieving man. Patrick McCaughey in his gallery, where the Picasso isn't.

Cairns and Morosi embroiled in funds tango

By KATE LEGGE

BUSINESS

SPORT

The world of Warren Anderson — a special report 6

How Packer nearly joined the Herald and Weekly Times 17

What Australian men think of their women 26

REGULARS

The *National Times* (1971–87) (top right) lived dangerously, illuminating some dark recesses of Australian society, making enemies with stories such as its posthumous indictment of Sir Robert Askin, and in the end failing commercially. It was turned into the broadsheet *Times on Sunday* on 10 August 1986, but that paper was closed after Tryart's takeover in 1987.

Editors of the *National Times*, David Marr (1981–82) and Jefferson Penberthy (1984–85)

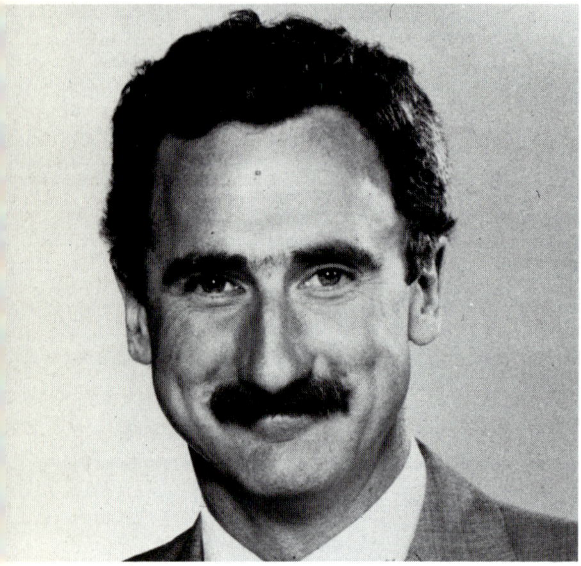

Editors of the *Times on Sunday*, Robert Haupt and Valerie Lawson

Some of the BRW group's business publications, and the group managing editor, BRW magazines, Robert Gottliebsen

> that one should dignify these sort of gutter allegations with any response, but sadly, I feel I owe it to my employees, my business associates and my friends to make an answer . . .
>
> These innuendoes and allegations emanating from the inquiries of the royal commission have caused immense suffering on the part of my wife and children for nearly a year. They have been fuelled by what I believe has been malicious rumour and innuendo in newspapers controlled by commercial rivals of mine, John Fairfax & Sons Ltd . . .
>
> Each and every one of the allegations made against me in the *National Times* article are false, and demonstrably false. It is extraordinary that this disgusting publication should place me in a position where I have effectively to prove my innocence. However, so ludicrous and misconceived are the allegations that my innocence is easily established.

So far as the box from Katmandu was concerned, Packer said that it had been opened at the airport by request from his own office, and been found to contain bronze statuary and some cricket books as well as the hashish oil concealed inside its walls.

> I was interviewed by officers of the Narcotics Bureau, as indeed were members of my staff. The universal conclusion was that somebody was either trying to embarrass me . . . or that somebody with access to the Consolidated Press building was importing drugs and hoped after the box had been emptied to take it away and remove the hashish . . . At no time did anyone suggest that I may have been involved in this importation. I imagine it would be a quite unusual thing for a drug importer to address his importations to himself.'

Packer replied to every point contained in the two *National Times* articles; he accused the Costigan Royal Commission of acting unjustly and irresponsibly in not recalling him to answer the sort of allegations that had been published about him; and he sued John Fairfax & Sons Ltd for defamation. After lengthy negotiations, the matter was settled in April 1985 by publication of an apology in which the company accepted and recognized that it had no evidence, and was not aware of any evidence, to support the allegations made in the Costigan case summaries. The company therefore 'sincerely [regretted] and [apologized] for the embarrassment and hurt caused to Mr Kerry Packer and his family . . .'

During the month this apology was made Consolidated Press set about dissolving its suburban newspaper partnership with Fairfax. As mentioned previously this embroiled the partners in a dispute about ownership of the Goss metro press at Bankstown. The dispute was largely ignored by the press—except for the *National Times*, which to Suich's discomfort took a close interest in it. Toohey and Bacon prepared a full report, mentioning that Fraud Squad detectives had taken sworn statements in which allegations were made that one executive of the Suburban companies had been found burning company documents. Reluctantly Suich agreed to publication during August, but only in the business section. A second story by Toohey reported that the case was likely to be heard in the Supreme Court before the end of the year; but the dispute was resolved before then, when Packer sold out of the second company.

Any impression that Penberthy might have softened the *National Times* was further dispelled by a special report on Sir Peter Abeles in the issue of 20–26 September 1985, written by Bacon, Kitney, Toohey and Geraldine Brooks. Entitled 'Empire of Influence', it dealt again with Sir Peter's so-called 'Brush with the Mafia' (the story quoted Sir Peter as saying he had not been aware that the Teamster official, Rudy Tham, who introduced him to other American union officials in 1972, and provided other services, had Mafia connections), Sir Peter's business associates, and his relations with the Askin and Wran governments.

While this report was being prepared, the public relations consultant Martin Dougherty telephoned Penberthy, with whom he was on friendly terms. Explaining that he was doing some work for Abeles, Dougherty went on to say, according to Penberthy, that Sir Warwick and the Fairfax board were unhappy with Penberthy at his failure to 'tame' the *National Times*, that Sir Peter Abeles was a close friend of Sir Warwick and Lady Fairfax, and that Sir Peter was disturbed at the prospect of another article about him in the *National Times*. Penberthy told Dougherty that he could not deal with him in this way, whereupon Dougherty contacted Suich. Suich did not interfere with the Abeles story, but grimly warned Penberthy that it had better be right.

Like his two immediate predecessors, and also Horin and Wilkinson, Penberthy encountered the full force of Suich's temper. After one such experience, he reported that the chief editorial executive's face had been so contorted with rage as to have been barely recognizable.

At a board meeting on 19 September, the day the issue containing 'Empire of Influence' went to press, Sir Warwick said he was considering what should be done about the *National Times*. Although not critical of Penberthy's performance as managing editor, he said that the paper's reputation had suffered, through people regarding it as a publication which wanted to capitalize on people's mistakes. He thought the ordinary person wanted a serious paper as against the present Sunday papers.

Suich replied that he and Brenchley agreed something dramatic had to be done with the *National Times*, which last year had lost $2.1 million. Since 1981 the circulation had risen only to 86 000. The total loss by the paper since its establishment in 1971 was $12.8 million. It might be best, Suich told the board, if the *National Times* reverted to being a Sunday paper and changed from tabloid to quality broadsheet.

The December board approved a re-launch along those lines and the appointment of Robert Haupt as editor of the paper from January 1986. Penberthy left to become editor of *Time Australia*, Toohey became a contributing editor of the *National Times*, and Valerie Lawson moved from the Good Weekend colour supplement to be one of Haupt's two deputy editors in charge of news. The other deputy was Russell Skelton, working in Melbourne and in charge of features.

Haupt and Lawson, although both outstanding journalists, were not well suited for editorial collaboration. Haupt, a former Canberra and Washington correspondent for the *Financial Review* and assistant editor of the *Age*, been hired away from the Nine television network, where he had been working as a political analyst. He was a graceful yet forceful writer, but apt to find the editorial chair rather cramping. Lawson, on the other hand, approached editing in deadly earnest. She drove herself and others remorselessly, priding herself on belonging to what she called 'the clenched teeth school of journalism'. Her reputation had preceded her, and when Haupt introduced her to an apprehensive *National Times* staff he began jokingly: 'This is Valerie Lawson, prisoner in the dock . . .'

Haupt and Lawson found they could not work together, and she left the paper shortly before the first issue of the *National Times on Sunday* on 10 August 1986. The main feature story in the first issue was a Toohey special written in collaboration with Wendy Bacon and Colleen Ryan—'The Multi-Level World of Warren P. Anderson'—and the following issue took this subject further by examining the property developer's friendship with the Federal Treasurer ('The Keating–Anderson Connection'). These two stories drew strong criticism from the Prime Minister at a two-and-a-half-hour meeting with Suich and Haupt, initiated by Suich in September with the hope of improving relations between the Prime Minister's office and the *National Times*'s Canberra reporters.

Discussing the various Fairfax publications, Hawke acknowledged the objectivity of the *Financial Review*, gave the *Herald* a pass rather than credit (though he praised its economic writer, Ross Gittins), and castigated the *National Times* as 'a bastard of a paper'. Suich and Haupt defended the *National Times*, but the Prime Minister said he could not be persuaded that attacks on himself, Keating, Wran and their friends Sir Peter Abeles, Warren Anderson and Kerry Packer were not motivated by a desire to destroy the most effective politicians in the Labor Party. In a note summarizing this conversation, Suich said that the Prime Minister seemed to derive considerable satisfaction from getting complaints off his chest, but remained strongly anti-*National Times*. He accepted that there was no Fairfax conspiracy, and while he did not acknowledge that there was no co-ordination to attacks, he recognized the force of the evidence that Fairfax papers had treated his government fairly.

The circulation of the *Times on Sunday* ('National' was dropped from the overly long title after four months) began at about 150 000, then dropped to 119 000. This was a distinct improvement on the *National Times,* whose circulation had been 86 300 under Penberthy/Toohey; but the figure soon dropped below 100 000. In November Suich told the board that the paper was in trouble. Its quality was not good enough, he said, and this was accepted by Robert Haupt.

In December the editor-in-chief of the *Sydney Morning Herald,* Chris Anderson, assumed the additional responsibility of being editor-in-chief of the *Times on Sunday*. Despite all efforts, the circulation continued to fall, reaching an average of 86 400 for the six-month period ending March 1987. In April Haupt's brief editorship came to an end. The immediate reason for this was an article by Brian Toohey, a Philippic full of vehement rhetoric against the new style of ALP leadership:

> The Australian political landscape is being redrawn. The last traces of egalitarianism have been scrubbed out. New colours are appearing, more dazzling than Thorstein Veblen, the chronicler of conspicuous consumption, could have imagined.
>
> Hawke and Keating see only hope in this display. Tax cheats become nation builders. Designers of exquisitely useless yachts are lauded as economic saviours. Hawke and Keating do more than enjoy the company of the new tycoons: they share their values. It is the distinguishing characteristic of their era. The Labor Party is an irrelevancy—an embarrassment that can be explained away to the people who count; a vehicle to deliver votes from those who don't . . .

Jenna Price, who had been brought from the *Herald* to take charge of features, felt that the proper place for this article was not on the front of the magazine section, where Haupt was planning to run it under the heading 'The Death of Labor', but further forward in the paper, opposite the editorial page. Haupt instructed her to leave it in the magazine section. Finally, on the day before going to press, Anderson told Haupt he had been thinking about the Toohey piece and did not want it used at all. Haupt accepted that, and the article was replaced. On Sunday night Haupt telephoned Anderson at home, said that he regarded the incident as a withdrawal of confidence, and offered his resignation. He went on leave and later joined the *Herald* as a feature writer. Toohey also resigned, and founded a satirical-revelatory monthly, *The Eye*, the first issue of which gave pride of place to 'The Death of Labor'. Valerie Lawson returned to the paper as editor and grimly threw herself into what some now regarded as a losing battle.

One of the paper's lesser troubles at this time was a sharp increase in the number of defamation claims being made against it. During the first half of the 1980s the *National Times* had received an average of six such claims each year. In 1985–86 there were eleven, and in 1986–87 another eleven. Furthermore, in 1986–87 there were settlements of two actions brought against the paper—one by Det-Sgt Rodney Moore in 1985, and the other by three members of the Ananda Marga sect in 1986. Both these cases were settled on terms not to be disclosed.

Considering the hazardous form of journalism practised by the *National Times* and the rigours of defamation law in New South Wales, it was surprising that between 1980 and 1987 only four other substantial claims against the paper succeeded, either in court or by financial settlement out of court. The first of these was an action brought by the author Lennard Bickel over a book review in 1980. Bickel was awarded $180 000 at trial, but after Fairfax lodged an appeal the matter was settled on terms not to be disclosed. The other three actions, arising from articles published in 1987, were also settled out of court by payments to a Sydney solicitor, Philip Polack; Mrs Gai Waterhouse; and Professor Geoffrey Blainey and his wife.

Otherwise, in spite of the risks it took, and the enemies it made, the paper had been remarkably free of settlements and adverse verdicts, though not of legal costs. The latter, including the six substantial settlements already mentioned and fourteen lesser settlements, amounted to $1 692 800 in the period 1980–87. This was a burden familiar to all Broadway papers and to the company's legal manager, Adrian Deamer. Legal costs incurred by the five papers during this period in connection with defamation, contempt and privilege proceedings amounted to $7 022 600. The *Financial Review* came off lightest with $750 860; the *Sun* with $1 125 680; the *Sun-Herald* with $1 174 760; and the *Sydney Morning Herald* with $2 188 800.

II

While the *Times on Sunday* struggled for survival, a more clearly defined battle was being fought in Sydney's highly competitive evening newspaper field. Two tabloids, the *Sun* and Rupert Murdoch's *Daily Mirror*, were pitted against each other and against the indifference of readers and advertisers brought about by competition from the electronic media and by changes in the structure of retail trade. Both papers were losing circulation, and both were losing money. In effect the two combatants were starving, yet the battle continued to rage.

Murdoch, who had bought the *Mirror* from John Fairfax Limited in 1960, told Falkingham in 1978—during a heated conversation about the *National Times*, which Murdoch believed had been conducting a campaign against him at the behest of Fairfax management—that he would destroy the *Sun*. He would turn the *Mirror* into a raffle ticket, he said, and the *Sun* would not be able to survive. This was a reference to high-prize contests requiring virtually no skill other than collecting the maximum number of coupons by means of buying multiple copies of the newspaper running the contest. If Fairfax did not match whatever the *Mirror* did, said Murdoch, the circulation gap would open to horrendous proportions; if it did match the *Mirror*, it would destroy its own credibility, thus forfeiting its main advantage of seeming the more conservative and responsible of the two tabloids. Falkingham was not intimidated. If Murdoch turned the *Mirror* into a raffle ticket, he said, Fairfax would turn the *Sun* into two raffle tickets. Everything Murdoch did, Fairfax would double. It would use the whole of its group resources: television and radio commercials, and rotogravure pre-prints every day to publicize the *Sun*. Murdoch did not yet own a television station. He said he was negotiating to buy Channel Ten, and had a second-hand rotogravure plant which he was going to install at Botany. Once he achieved those things he would have parity, and the *Mirror* would become a raffle ticket.

The contest war began sooner than Murdoch had threatened, in response to a reduction in the price of the *Sun*. This reduction brought the *Sun* back to the *Mirror*'s price of 10 cents, depriving that paper of an advantage which it had been enjoying for the past three and a half years. If there was one lesson to be learned from the history of Sydney's evening papers it was that serious circulation disadvantage was suffered only when one paper fell out of step in price, content, production or distribution. Otherwise the customers, dwindling in number though they were, seemed willing to share their allegiance more or less evenly between these two down-market products—one perceived as having more family appeal than the other, and the *Mirror* perceived as being slightly the more sensational and spicy of the two.

Ignoring accepted wisdom, the Fairfax board had decided in 1975 to raise the *Sun*'s price unilaterally, from 10 to 12 cents. Not only did this make the *Sun* dearer than its competitor, but its customers had to find two coins instead of one. The *Mirror* stoically held to 10 cents, and within a year the gap between the papers widened from a mere 5000 to 25 000. By 1978 it had increased to 60 000 in the *Mirror*'s favour.

There was nothing for the Fairfax board to do but let the *Sun* rejoin the *Mirror* at 10 cents, and to this long-overdue acceptance of reality in January 1979 the *Mirror* responded with a contest called Whoppa Swappa. Entrants merely had to send in coupons from the *Mirror*, and the greatest number of coupons won. The *Sun* responded with Sun Swap (a more dignified version of Whoppa Swappa) and a Find-the-Ball type of contest. The *Mirror* hit back with Triple Swappa and Mirror Ball. One day in March the two papers virtually engaged in an auction from one edition to the next. In the first edition the *Mirror* was offering a prize of $78 000, and the *Sun* $80 000. Next edition the *Mirror* raised the ante to $82 000, but the *Sun*, in its late final, had the last word with $84 500.

There was a lull for a while, and then it all broke out again with KISS rock concert tickets being given away by both papers in exchange for coupons, a Cars Giveaway by the *Mirror*, and Placewords in the *Sun*, with enough ambivalent clues to invite multiple entries.

In October 1979 the *Mirror* raised its price to 15 cents, and the *Sun*—rather to the surprise of some at Broadway, who expected it to take a leaf out of Murdoch's book by staying at 10 cents—quickly followed suit. In price strategy, many factors had to be taken into account. 'When News Ltd signalled in the *Mirror* they were going to 15 cents', wrote Fairfax's chief circulation manager, J. H. Flower, in a memo to other executives,

> we knew they would pull back to 10 cents in a month's time if the *Sun* did not follow. And with their greater resources they could have held the *Mirror* at 10 cents for perhaps years, leaving the *Sun* in an untenable position. Furthermore, our name would have been mud right through the newsagency and city vendor selling systems as being the people responsible for depriving them of additional commission. Even if we had held off for a few weeks to improve our circulation at the *Mirror*'s expense it would only be putting off the inevitable. We would have had to face the double shock of being second cab off the rank with an unpalatable move and risk losing even more reader confidence at a time when the *Mirror* had established itself at the new price.

The *Mirror*, with its higher circulation (400 000 as against 373 000), was better able to take a price rise than the *Sun*. For that reason the rise in price could be seen not merely as an augmenting of revenue but also as an act of war, intended to hurt the *Sun* more than it hurt the *Mirror*. In 1980 the two papers went to 20 cents, and in 1981 to 25 cents. They lost circulation at each rise, but the effect was not as damaging to the *Sun* as might have been expected. Under the editorship of Ron Ford, a shrewd and pragmatic Derbyshire journalist who had been with the *Sun* for fifteen years, the abnormally wide gap narrowed quickly after the restoration of price parity.

Ford met raffle with raffle, and beat the *Mirror* repeatedly on such news stories as the murder of John Lennon, the attempted assassination of President Reagan and the wedding of Prince Charles and Diana. When the news of Lennon's death arrived, the *Sun* put out a late extra edition at 4 p.m.; for the Royal wedding it printed in colour at 4 a.m., and put on an extra 60 000 sales.

In 1981 Rupert Murdoch had the gall to claim in his annual chairman's speech that 'on days of important news events, such as the shootings of President Reagan and Pope John Paul II, solid, reliable coverage had induced the public to turn overwhelmingly to the *Daily Mirror*'. In fact, the *Sun* had outsold the *Mirror* each time, going up by 58 204 with the President (the *Mirror*'s circulation rose by 28 063), and 32 573 with the Pope (*Mirror*, 23 530). The matter was later set to rights by a house advertisement in the *Financial Review*.

By mid-1981 the circulation gap had narrowed to 7700 and it seemed quite possible that the *Sun* would soon overtake its rival on half-yearly average figures for the first time in fifteen years. In the vital Sydney metropolitan area, it actually held a lead of 15 000. Then, on Friday 17 July, the *Mirror* escalated the contest war by announcing a series of Bingo games, starting the next Monday. Bingo had been doing wonders for the circulation of Murdoch's own *Sun* in London, but it was expensive. The London *Sun* had already spent $2 500 000 on it, and the Sydney *Mirror* promised prizes of $10 000 every week. The game was to be played with numbered cards distributed by letterbox drop. A selection of numbers would be printed each day in the *Mirror*, and players would cross off matching numbers on their cards in the hope of claiming a full house.

The *Sun* responded quickly with a Bingo game of its own, offering prizes of $25 000, which the *Mirror* had to match. By inserting game cards in the newspaper, the *Sun* avoided heavy expenditure on letterbox drops, but also limited its chances of building circulation.

'Frankly', said Ford, speaking on radio about Bingo,

> I don't think these games have got much to do with journalism. The *Daily Mirror* set out to buy circulation at a cost of $200 000 because they are losing in the straight news war with the *Sun*. We have followed on with our own contest simply because the *Mirror*'s stablemate in London gained big circulation advantages when it launched Bingo over there. We felt we had to match the *Mirror* and in fact we have produced a simpler, more straightforward game. But we still have news on page one and we haven't gone crazy about the game like the *Mirror*.

Next day Ford received a letter from the editor of the *Mirror* saying: 'It is obvious you are worried stiff about the unpopularity of *Sun* Bingo. I have enclosed a *Mirror* Bingo card so you can join in with the rest of New South Wales and have some REAL Bingo fun'. Although Ford regarded Bingo as a gross devaluation of the product, the *Sun* eventually had little option but to become more deeply involved in the costly game its rival had started to play.

'Bingo transformed the Sydney *Mirror*'s margin of 7,700 over the Sydney *Sun* into a margin of 62 000 in the first week', said Suich in a telex message to the editor of the *Chicago Tribune*, Maxwell McCrohon, himself a former *Sydney Morning Herald* journalist, who had sought advice about Bingo.

> [It dropped to] 54 000 in the second week, 50 000 in the third, 45 000 in the fourth, 40 000 in the fifth and 42 000 in the sixth. This notwithstanding the *Sun*'s own Bingo competition which increased its sales by 20 to 30 thousand once Bingo was launched. Without our own Bingo competition, modest as it was, the *Mirror* would have creamed us. There is no point in being high-minded about this. The goddam thing works.

After a relatively short involvement, however, Fairfax decided that Bingo was too expensive a means of putting on circulation. Leaving the field to Murdoch, it none the less kept an anxious watch on how Bingo was affecting circulation and advertising. By this time Murdoch's *Telegraph* and *Sunday Telegraph* were also using Bingo, with consequent damage to the *Herald* and more particularly the *Sun-Herald*.

Reluctantly, Fairfax returned to the gaming tables. 'A Fairfax campaign could start an expensive new Bingo war with News Ltd', wrote Suich to the group general manager, 'which would last all of 1982 and bleed us all to death. This seems to be occurring in Fleet Street'. No decision was taken until April 1982, by which time it was clear that News Ltd intended to continue Bingo at least until the end of the year. The battle was rejoined on 31 May, with Fairfax running letterbox-dropped Bingo games in the *Sun* and *Sun-Herald* at a cost of $200 000 per week.

For the next two years the *Sun* and the *Mirror* pandered to their readers with different variations of the game—Super Bingo, Bumper Bingo, Instant Bingo, Criss Cross Bingo, Bid'n'Win and Scratch Bingo. It was a travesty of journalism which depressed those who had no wish to act the part of croupier, but found themselves obliged to do so in order to survive commercially. 'We were locked in with the *Mirror*'s competition', recalled Ford in later years. 'It's like sailing. If they tack, you've got to tack with them. If we hadn't followed them in Bingo we'd have been out of business.'

The 1982–84 campaign cost Fairfax $1.6 million, but this outlay was alleviated by an increase in cover charge (the *Sun* and *Mirror* went up to 30 cents in 1982) and by a prodigious though temporary effect on sales. On the first Monday a Scratch Bingo card was inserted in the *Sun*, sales rose by 103 000. On the second Monday, they rose a further 31 600.

'Bingo brought more good news on circulation figures', reported Ford, who was appointed editor-in-chief in 1982.

> The *Sun* once again contained a frenzied *Mirror* Bingo attack and we ran into the school holidays with a gap of around 12 000 compared with over 32 000 at this time last year . . .The *Mirror* put out three new cards in four weeks, but the *Sun* with good timing came on top of them with a better game and more prize money which knocked out their advertising promotion about 'the big one'.

The new editor was John Benaud, who had started his newspaper career as a *Sun* copy boy and worked for a time on *News of the World* in London. Benaud performed well under pressure, as for example when the Sydney home of a Family Court judge was bombed one morning in 1984, causing the death of the judge's wife. A news flash reached the *Sun* office at 8.20 a.m. and, although it takes 40 minutes to turn editorial copy into a press room plate, the first *Sun* with front-page news of the tragedy reached the street at 9.45 a.m.

Under Ford and Benaud, the *Sun* outdid the *Mirror* with its coverage of the 1984 Olympic Games, although the *Mirror* had many more pages at its disposal. 'The *Sun* scored on quality', said Ford in his August report to the Board.

> We had one of the leanest teams of any major newspaper at the Games, but they were among the best. We had Frank Crook, down from New York, and Richard Sleeman writing, with Bill Casey holding the reins in Los Angeles and liaising with Sydney. The result was a bright, human, newsy and relevant cover. The *Sun*'s sales position improved against the *Mirror* during the Games period.

News was in fact coming back into its own, for the Bingo war was now mercifully drawing to a close. The State Government, concerned to protect its lottery revenue from newspaper competition, prohibited Scratch Bingo in December 1984. There were a few unsuccessful attempts to obtain Government approval for such variants as Aussie Scratch Quiz and Criss Cross Cash; but both papers now seemed to feel that readers were tiring of contests anyway, and early in 1985 an armistice came into being.

When casualties were counted, there was no avoiding the fact that Murdoch had won the Bingo war. It was his kind of war, and Bingo seemed more attractive to his kind of readers than to the *Sun*'s. The gap between the two papers, only 7700 when the *Mirror* started Bingo in 1981, had widened to 60 000 by the time the *Sun* responded to the challenge nine months later. And after more than two years of all-out warfare the *Mirror*'s lead, although substantially reduced, was still four times greater (28 000) than before Bingo.

The long-term effect of Bingo seemed to be that it damaged both papers, but damaged the *Sun* more than the *Mirror*. For the next two years, both papers lost circulation, but the gap also widened in the *Mirror*'s favour—from 28 000 in the March 1985 period to 34 800 a year later and 38 300 in March 1987. This was in spite of determined efforts to stop the slide. The *Sun* spent heavily on promotion (it already had Sydney's best annual newspaper promotional event in the 'City to Surf' run, which attracted 29 700 entrants in 1985); it used more colour, though sometimes that was disastrously out of register; and it began printing earlier.

Ford and Benaud wanted to turn the *Sun* into a morning paper which would continue to sell all day. The idea of an early sports-orientated *Sun* to compete with the *Telegraph* was explored in 1981 and 1985, but nothing came of it either time. In February 1985 the paper did push its first edition lock-up time back to 8.45 a.m., but the sales advantage flowing from that was compromised by a long fitters' dispute involving frequent stoppages which caused huge shortfalls in the first edition. There were seventeen of these stoppages in 1985, with shortfalls as high as 80 000. 'It is hard to calculate the damage caused by the paper arriving hours late with depressing regularity and no explanation', reported Ford. 'The *Mirror* increased its lead by default on our part rather than any spectacular improvement on theirs. The long dispute with the fitters avoided outright strike action and the other [Broadway] papers were relatively unscathed. But the effect on the *Sun* was devastating.'

In 1985 new positions of publisher were created on the *Sun* and the *Herald*, the occupants of which—Don Farrow, a newcomer from an advertising agency; and Peter Gaunt, who had returned to Broadway the previous year—were made responsible for improving sales. Farrow developed five new supplements intended to give the *Sun* a different look each day, and spent $3 million on a press, radio and television campaign around the theme 'The daily newspaper especially for the family'. The 'family' portrayed on television was of the Godfather kind, a metaphor that could not be said to have met with universal approval.

The daily supplements were 'Sun Sport', 'Sun Certain Sellers', 'Wednesday Woman', a Thursday pop music lift-out aimed at the youth market, and on Fridays a full colour 'Sun TV and Video Guide'. Only the latter was demonstrably successful, adding 30 000 to Friday sales and catching the *Mirror* at a disadvantage because News Ltd could not respond in kind without damaging its own separate magazine, *TV Week*. It was therefore bitterly disappointing to Ford when in 1986 Fairfax decided to save $1.5 million a year by dropping the Friday Guide.

In a fax message to Suich, who was in London, Ford said:

> Killing the TV magazine would be a savage blow at this critical stage

of the afternoon newspaper battle. This magazine is one of the great successes of afternoon newspaper publishing. It has destroyed the big lead of the *Mirror* on Friday and played a big part in Murdoch's *TV Week* circulation losses. It sits at the heart of our fight to win the war in Sydney, which makes it far too valuable a prize to be bargained away . . .

His plea was in vain. The *Sun*'s projected loss for 1985–86 was $15.6 million ($6.5 million more than the year before), and the board was intent upon cutting costs and raising revenue by all possible means, including a higher cover charge and reduction of staff from 130 to 106. Farrow was replaced as publisher by Malcolm Stening, who had formerly been the group advertising sales manager. Stening brought strength to the sales side, but advertising revenue was an intractable problem. More and more advertisers were turning away from evening newspapers, and the *Sun*'s advertising revenue for 1985–86 was $3.1 million down against budget.

The paper's future was uncertain, and decidedly insecure. In 1985 the editor-in-chief of the *Herald*, in a report requested by Suich, recommended closure of the *Sun*. This caused embarrassment and annoyance at Broadway when the gist of Anderson's recommendation appeared in Packer's *Australian Business*. Closure was discussed at a board meeting in the following year, but there was no real support for it. Brenchley thought the net benefit if the *Sun* was closed would be only $700 000 a year, as other publications would then have to take up fixed costs now being borne by the *Sun*. Gardiner agreed, saying that according to figures taken out recently there was not much difference between closing down the *Sun* and keeping it on at a loss. Murdoch, he said, was hoping that Fairfax would make a tactical error by closing the *Sun*. He did not think Fairfax would ever do that because Murdoch would then attack the *Herald*'s classified advertising by joining the *Telegraph* and the *Mirror*.

The prevailing view at Broadway was that so long as both afternoon papers were losing money the best course was to keep the *Sun* going until agreement could be reached with Murdoch to merge the two losers into one jointly owned paper. In the meantime the mutually destructive battle continued to rage.

6

On the Edge of a Precipice

I

Now this narrative comes full circle, returning to its prelude at the juncture of 1986 and 1987, and pressing forward into an unpredictable future. Like some early navigator passing a forerunner's furthest point, our story is about to enter the kind of region where maps have nothing to offer except the distended cheeks of prevailing winds. Before proceeding, however, we should recall certain events dealt with in the opening chapter: Sir Warwick Fairfax's death on 14 January 1987, the change of rules governing media ownership, Rupert Murdoch's takeover of the Herald and Weekly Times, and John Fairfax Ltd's purchase of the Melbourne television station HSV7. Never before had the company encountered so many significant events so close together in time. They were soon to be surpassed by events of even greater magnitude, but that was something still unknown to most of the voyagers.

Sir Warwick, who was then approaching the end of his eighty-fifth year and succumbing to fatal illness, attended his last board meeting in October 1986. The main topic of discussion was the Herald and Weekly Times. Since 1973 HWT and David Syme had been joint publishers of the Melbourne *Sunday Press*, an indifferent paper of limited circulation (176 000) competing only with the independent *Sunday Observer* (100 000) and Sunday papers flown in from Sydney. The two companies had agreed that neither would publish a separate Sunday paper without prior advice to the other, and now HWT was signalling such an intention. If it went ahead, said Gardiner at the October board meeting, Fairfax would have to launch a Melbourne Sunday paper of its own, at a cost of some millions of dollars.

Alternatively, suggested Sir David Griffin, Fairfax could make an offer for HWT. Certainly that company was vulnerable, for the circulation and advertising base of the once powerful Melbourne *Herald* had virtually collapsed and the paper was losing money heavily. On the other hand, a takeover by Fairfax was bound to provoke Government intervention. James Fairfax, recalling earlier discussions of this kind, thought the only part of the HWT group which might interest Fairfax would be its Queensland component—Queensland Press Ltd, the publisher of Brisbane's *Courier-Mail*. Sir Warwick agreed with him, saying Fairfax would not want the whole of the empire, only Queensland.

Before HWT had time to launch a new Sunday paper, that crumbling empire came under attack by News Ltd. On 3 December Murdoch offered $1.8 billion for all the company's issued capital. As already recounted in Chapter 1, Robert Holmes à Court then made a counter-bid of $2 billion. Fairfax, opting to work in tandem with Holmes à Court, made a $910 million offer for Queensland Press.

It would have been possible to frustrate Murdoch if Queensland Press had still been obliged under its 1981 agreement to give Fairfax first option to buy its HWT shares, but that agreement had lapsed. Murdoch bettered the Holmes à Court and Fairfax bids; Holmes à Court sold all his HWT and Queensland Press shares to News Ltd (in return, Murdoch promised to sell him two provinces of the HWT empire: West Australian Newspapers Ltd and Television Broadcasters Ltd, the licensee of HSV7 in Melbourne); and Queensland Press accepted Murdoch's offer for all its own shares, even though the offer was lower than an improved Fairfax bid. Fairfax then made a $2.5 billion bid for HWT, but the board of that company would not recommend it to the shareholders over Murdoch's earlier improved bid of $2.3 billion.

So Murdoch won. In the subsequent sale of some of News Ltd's newly acquired assets, Fairfax surprised many by outbidding Holmes à Court for the Melbourne television station which Murdoch had earlier promised him. The price was $320 million, and for a further $45 million Fairfax also acquired sixteen country newspapers in New South Wales, most of which had been purchased by HWT from Consolidated Press in 1985. The country papers were passed on to and paid for by Fairfax's partly owned associates Rural Press and Macquarie Publications.

Westpac and National Australia Bank funded the HSV purchase, bringing Fairfax's corporate debt to $450 million. The consequent gearing (borrowing in relation to shareholders' funds) was 0.41, a modest enough figure compared with Murdoch's, which often exceeded 1.00. But John Fairfax Ltd was not accustomed even to this level of debt. In the preceding four years its corporate group borrowing had risen from only $81 million in 1983 to $105 million in 1984, $155 million in 1985, and $201 million in 1986. Now suddenly the figure was more than doubling.

It was said by some—not least by Kerry Packer, who had sold his Nine Network television stations and radio interests to Alan Bond in January for $1050 million—that Fairfax had paid far too much for

HSV7. It was said also, and not only by competitors, that this was no time for a print media group to be expanding its investment in television. Impending changes to the rules governing media ownership—announced by the Government with effect from November 1986, but not yet enacted by federal parliament—seemed likely to enforce a choice between print and television.

In place of the long-standing two-television stations rule, any company would be able to own any number of stations providing access to no more than a certain percentage of the national audience. This deregulation would be counterbalanced to some extent, however, by a cross-media restriction propounded by the Treasurer, Paul Keating: the owner of a newspaper would not be able to acquire a television station in the same city, and vice versa. Fairfax's ownership of both print and television media in Sydney would be preserved by a grandfather clause exempting earlier generations of ownership; but if the proposed legislation were to be enacted, Fairfax would either have to sell the Melbourne station which it was now acquiring, or sell the *Age*. The same would of course apply to News Ltd's ownership of the *Herald* and ATV10 in Melbourne.

Gardiner defended the purchase of HSV7, insisting that far from being an extravagant consolation it had been a commercially sound decision. Unlike Packer, Fairfax had not previously owned stations in Melbourne as well as Sydney, the axis regarded as an essential prerequisite for network success. HSV was an operating partner in the Seven Network, but under HWT's ownership it had been a partner which seldom pulled its weight, and on which Fairfax could exercise little influence. With Holmes à Court as the owner, there would be no certainty of any improvement in this unsatisfactory situation; and, with Holmes à Court controlling HSV, it would probably be harder to find a buyer for the Sydney and Brisbane stations, should Fairfax ever wish to sell them. So Gardiner decided to buy. If the cross-media legislation were to be rejected by a closely divided Senate—as some, including Gardiner, thought it might be—Fairfax would have a fully effective network for the first time. And if the rules did change, Fairfax could either sell HSV or sell the entire Melbourne-Sydney-Brisbane network.

Several weeks later, during a five-hour interview with the Treasurer, Max Suich gained a better understanding of the HWT takeover, at least from Paul Keating's point of view. According to Suich's record of this interview, Keating said that while in America for a meeting of the International Monetary Fund in September 1986 he had outlined to Rupert Murdoch his proposals for limiting cross-ownership, and that Murdoch had pronounced them 'fair'. He had spoken in similar terms to Kerry Packer, but not to HWT or Fairfax.

HWT had been ruled out, said Keating, because of a campaign run by the Melbourne *Herald* against the assets test and rules concerning lump sum superannuation; Fairfax had received the same treatment because of attacks in some of its publications on Keating, his friend Warren Anderson, the Prime Minister, Kerry Packer and Sir Peter Abeles. Keating also complained bitterly to Suich about references to his house in Sydney which had appeared in the *Sydney Morning Herald*, making it clear that the house was empty. Since then, he said, graffiti had been sprayed on the walls, part of the external area had been vandalized, and he had been obliged to engage a security service in order to keep the house safe from prowlers.

In mid-November Murdoch told Keating he had come to the conclusion that it was better to be in newspapers than in television, if that was the choice. For this reason Keating, in his conversation with Suich, took credit for putting HWT 'into play'. He believed Murdoch had made his bid with confidence that he would have no difficulties with the Foreign Investment Review Board or the Trade Practices Commission, although he (Keating) had given Murdoch no personal assurances of that kind. He had, however, sought a report from the FIRB on the implications of the News Ltd bid in view of Murdoch's American citizenship, and the Board's advice to him had been that the takeover should be approved because Australians were the majority shareholders in News Corporation. Neither he nor, as far as he knew, any other member of the Government had sought to influence the TPC.

On 4 January, the day Fairfax made its bid for Queensland Press, Keating and Warren Anderson had been visiting Holmes à Court at his thoroughbred stud outside Perth. On occasions, said Keating to Suich, he had been present in the room while Holmes à Court took phone calls from Gardiner about the bid. He thought Holmes à Court had purposely given him this insight into the deal, and as a result he had left Perth with a good understanding of Holmes à Court's tactics and Fairfax's objectives. Arising out of that, he said, he warned Murdoch that Holmes à Court was serious and that Murdoch would have to do a deal with Holmes à Court over West Australian Newspapers to take him out of the bidding for HWT.

> Keating's point [wrote Suich in a board report] is that this intervention by him was critical to persuading Murdoch to ultimately do a deal with Holmes à Court. This, he says, left Fairfax exposed and ultimately cost it control of Queensland Press. Keating believes that as he successfully intervened with Murdoch to make a deal on West Australian Newspapers he could similarly have intervened to force Murdoch to deal with Fairfax over Queensland Press . . . Keating says his motives for getting involved in the HWT takeover were a desire to see the [Melbourne] Herald broken up and a desire to hurt Fairfax.
>
> On reflection it would seem to me the only significant disadvantage the company suffered from the Treasurer in the HWT takeover

> was in not receiving detailed briefings on plans for the legislation such as those received by Murdoch and Packer . . . The Treasurer is a product of the NSW right wing of the ALP and his conversation is littered with threats, references to getting even, doing deals and assisting 'our crowd' in business, the press and within the ALP. He is very blunt about the fact that the NSW right are 'deal makers' and that they provide favours to 'our crowd' in return for favours given.
>
> He also has a very strong feeling about what he calls old money or establishment money, which he describes as dead money stultifying the economy, and he sees great advantages in new money—in which he includes Murdoch and Packer—being given opportunities to knock off old money. This I guess is the last glimmer of the class warrior.
>
> Our meeting ended on friendly terms when he asked that I organise a lunch for him with Greg Gardiner, Fred Brenchley, Chris Anderson and myself. Unless some deal can be made to the Treasurer's advantage (and he acknowledges that Fairfax does not do 'deals') I think the venom will remain, although the meeting did allow him to let off steam.

There could be little doubt that the Treasurer saw himself in the role of landscape architect, a new Capability Brown reshaping the hills and dales of Australia's media industry. In March 1987, while attending a dinner given by Mary Fairfax at Fairwater, he responded on behalf of the guests in generally warm terms—warmer, at least, than was his custom with Fairfax management. He described the *Age* and the *Sydney Morning Herald* as 'the crown jewels', and later, in separate conversations with Lady Fairfax and James Fairfax, suggested that the company should consider selling part if not all of its television interests.

Next morning, in a departure lounge at Sydney airport, Keating spoke to John B. Fairfax along the same lines. Several people were prepared to pay big money for television stations, he said; indeed one of these had been prepared to pay Murdoch $100 million more than he had received recently for his Ten Network from Westfield Capital Corporation/Northern Star. He also remarked that Mary Fairfax was good at getting people together, and said it was likely, with Sir Warwick no longer living, that she would take a greater interest in Fairfax company affairs. John said that might be so, but that the Treasurer should be aware that Lady Fairfax did not speak for either the board or the management.

II

Relations between Fairwater and the rest of the family, touchy at the best of times, had come under further strain after Sir Warwick's death, when his second son and principal heir, 26-year-old Warwick G. O. Fairfax, had set about increasing the family's holding in John Fairfax Ltd. And here we touch upon events which are still to come. Warwick had returned for the Christmas holidays from Boston, where he was completing his Master of Business Administration at Harvard Business School. Late in December he had lunch at a Bondi Beach restaurant with one of his parents' advisers, Martin John Dougherty.

Dougherty, a 43-year-old former newspaper editor amply endowed with Irish-Australian shrewdness and sociability, lived in Buckhurst Avenue, Point Piper, only a few buildings away from Fairwater at the eastern end of Seven Shillings Beach. Born in Casino and educated at St John's College, Woodlawn, near Lismore, Dougherty obtained a cadetship on the *Sydney Morning Herald*, where his grandfather had once worked as a proofreader. Resigning after two years, he worked on several other papers, eventually becoming production editor of the Melbourne *Herald* and editor of Murdoch's *Truth*. Later Murdoch sent him overseas, to the London *Sun* and the *New York Post*, then brought him back to become editor of the *Daily Mirror*, a post which he held little longer than most of its previous occupants.

He joined a Melbourne public relations firm, and in 1982 established his own firm in Sydney. Tall, sanguine and easygoing, Martin Dougherty was adept at bringing people together for good commercial purpose. His clients included Murdoch, Packer, Abeles and his near neighbours at Fairwater, to whom he had been introduced by a mutual friend from Melbourne, the wife of businessman Richard Pratt. Dougherty helped Sir Warwick and Lady Fairfax in various ways, notably as a campaigner against the PIPS proposals, a lobbyist for the urban rezoning of Harrington Park, and a sounding board for their misgivings about the company. Young Warwick had sometimes been present at discussions between his parents and Dougherty about the Fairfax family's various shareholdings in John Fairfax Ltd, and the Kinghaven parcel of shares which would eventually pass from James to Warwick. He was well aware that his parents valued Dougherty's advice and trusted him.

At their lunch together in December, Dougherty and Warwick discussed the quality of management at Broadway. Each expressed concern about the way in which the company had acquitted itself in the recent struggle against Murdoch. Their subsequent recollections of this conversation differed considerably. Both agreed, however, that they talked about the prospect of Warwick soon having to take the kind of action which, as mentioned at the start of this narrative, had been contemplated for some time at Fairwater.

According to Warwick's account he said to Dougherty: 'It will be twenty years before I will be in a position to do anything about the mismanagement'. In that remark he was referring to the approximate time he could expect to wait before obtaining control of the Kinghaven shares upon James Fairfax's death, thus presumably becoming the company's largest single shareholder. At the time of this conversation Sir Warwick's branch of the family controlled 13.2 per cent of the issued capital; Sir Vincent's and John B. Fairfax's, 15.7 per cent; and James Fairfax, including the Kinghaven parcel, 19.7 per cent. Together, the three holdings amounted to 48.6 per cent.

'You might have to make a takeover bid for the company,' replied Dougherty.

'A takeover? That is a bit drastic and, besides, how can it be possible?'

'At some stage in the next three or four years you will probably have to do something like that.'

Dougherty, on the other hand, would later insist that the subject was by no means a new one. On earlier occasions, he claimed, Warwick had spoken to him in the following vein:

> Our general manager, Greg Gardiner, is a bigger threat to our family than Henderson was. He and James, Vincent and John Fairfax have completely shut my father out of the business. And they (the other Fairfaxes) are too stupid to see that Gardiner might bring us all down. My mother and father believe he is in league with Holmes à Court and that he will do whatever he can to help Holmes à Court split the family and take over the company. John Fairfax is the big worry. He wants to succeed James as chairman and he sees me as a big threat. He's also close to Gardiner. I think I may have to make a move to take over the company before these fools lose it.

At the Bondi lunch, according to Dougherty's recollection once again, Warwick returned to the same subject in words to the following effect:

> I am most concerned about the situation. Vincent, James and John have very little business ability. The company has some very good assets but there is no leadership and no direction. I cannot accept a life where I am tucked away in a minority position watching the business being mishandled. I am going to see if I can make a bid as soon as possible. I simply have to try and take over the company. I could not forgive myself if I did not try. The management is totally incompetent . . .

At the end of the Christmas holidays, after his father's funeral on 30 January, Warwick returned to Boston; but during the next three months he kept closely in touch with Dougherty by telephone. In mid-February they discussed a sudden rise in the price of Fairfax shares, from about $13 to more than $17, and the possibility that in the wake of the HWT upheaval and Sir Warwick's death someone was planning a takeover bid. They agreed that the best way to stop speculation and discourage any takeover bid by an outsider would be to lift the combined family holding from 48.6 per cent to more than 50 per cent. Warwick also discussed this with his mother and the family solicitor, Carnegie Fieldhouse.

On Saturday 14 February he made telephone calls from Boston to his half-brother James, at Retford Park, and his second cousin John, who was trout fishing near Queanbeyan. To each of them he proposed the purchase of a further 1.5 per cent of Fairfax shares, to be split into three equal parcels, so that the combined family holding would become 50.1 per cent. James rejected the proposal. John was enthusiastic, but questioned the wisdom of buying at such a historically high price.

In spite of that misgiving, John arranged a meeting of his own family during the coming week to consider Warwick's request that they meet half the cost of buying 1.5 per cent, which would probably cost them about $15 million. The most they could afford to contribute, according to their advisers, was $6 million—and that would involve a degree of borrowing which might cause financial uncertainty for some members of the family. The feeling of the meeting was that in the interest of family harmony they should participate to the extent of $6 million. But in view of the borrowing which would be necessary, they also expressed the hope that in the event of any serious economic downturn Warwick would be prepared to buy the shares from them at purchase price.

The latter was a suggestion, not a condition, and John Fairfax made this clear to Warwick when telephoning the offer of $6 million. Warwick said he would consider it, and call back. John expected him to accept the offer and decline the suggestion, but when Warwick phoned back it was to say that he would purchase the entire 1.5 per cent himself.

Before making that decision, Warwick had also telephoned Dougherty to tell him of the responses from James and John. Speaking in the same vein as at the Bondi lunch, Warwick said, according to Dougherty: 'It is time for me to do something drastic and my choices are either to sell out of the company entirely or to make a bid for the company . . .'

As Warwick recalled it, however, this conversation was confined to the purchase of 1.5 per cent of the share capital. 'If that is John's attitude', said Dougherty, 'what is the harm in doing it on your own? You will get the publicity. You will be seen as doing something in relation to the company and it will make it easier for you when you come back'. Dougherty, for his part, later denied having said that.

Warwick authorized Fieldhouse to arrange the share purchase through one of his late father's investment companies, Rockwood Pastoral Co Pty Ltd, and the financing of it through the Midland Bank. The purchase, made in the third week of February at $20 per share, cost $30 million. Admittedly this confirmed the family's control, but the way the purchase was made also affected family relations adversely. Warwick may be assumed to have felt let down by his relatives, and John later made no secret of his own feeling. 'Until that time', he said,

> I had great hopes for not merely a good family relationship but a good future working relationship with Warwick within John Fairfax Ltd. I shared many of his thoughts about the company and agreed with many of his ideas for the future. Warwick, in my view, had brought a degree of balance to what was potentially a fairly precarious family situation. The negative response to our proposal was totally unexpected and quite shattering, considering the urgency of it all over the previous few days and the great trouble we had taken to go out of our way to commit $6 million.

Within a matter of days the question of family control came up again, when Gardiner tentatively put forward for discussion another capital-raising scheme to improve the company's gearing. The need for capital was demonstrably greater than at the time of the PIPS attempts, for HSV7 had now been paid for and interest had started to run. The scheme—prepared by Dominguez Barry Samuel Montagu, the underwriters who had handled PIPS—was a complex one requiring family members to sell part of their John Fairfax Ltd shareholding to a pyramid structure of companies.

Gardiner asserted that the Fairfax family would retain control of both the existing company and a new company which would issue convertible notes to the public; but others were not so sure. When Warwick received a summary of the so-called Newco scheme in Boston he telephoned Dougherty, asking him to obtain advice from Baring Brothers Halkerston and Partners. It appeared to him that Newco would weaken the family's control, and Baring's advice provided no reassurance. James Fairfax arranged a telephone conference between Warwick, members of the family in Sydney, the solicitor Rod Halstead and other advisers. Warwick acknowledged the need for more capital, questioned whether Newco was the right way to raise it, but accepted that the board needed to make its own decision.

At a board meeting on 19 March, the Fairfax directors considered a criticism of the Newco scheme by Keith Halkerston, and an alternative proposal put forward by Warwick from Boston—that of selling the Seven Network. Another option, considered without much enthusiasm, was the floating of David Syme or Federal Capital Press; and Sir Eric Neal, perhaps because he was a newcomer to the board, wondered if there should be another attempt at PIPS. The chairman and the group general manager thought the latter would be just as difficult as before.

Sir Eric—managing director of the building and construction materials group Boral, and soon to be appointed Chief Commissioner of Sydney City Council—had joined the Fairfax board in September 1986, eighteen months after the death of Arthur Lissenden. At this meeting he said his first reaction to the Newco proposal had been that it was very complex. There were possibly some dangers as far as the family was concerned, and serious consideration would need to be given to establishing Newco in such a way as to protect the family. The meeting authorized Gardiner to investigate the proposal further. On closer examination, however, it was found to be even more complex and therefore less acceptable than had first been realized.

At the April board meeting Sir Eric again suggested another try at PIPS, and Gardiner said he would consider it. Sir David Griffin asked whether Warwick Fairfax's opinion of PIPS was known. Gardiner replied that he had discussed the matter with Warwick, who had appeared not to have a view on it.

Of more immediate concern than Newco or PIPS were rumours reported by Sir Eric Neal and Max Suich that Holmes à Court would make a bid for John Fairfax Ltd later in the year. Gardiner said that Holmes à Court's nominee companies had begun appearing on the company's share register again, and that Sir Peter Abeles was also building up his holding through a subsidiary of TNT. Fairfax was a very attractive target, he said, but if the family stayed together a bid could not succeed.

John Fairfax Ltd was indeed an attractive takeover target, despite its shortcomings as perceived by some outside the company, including Warwick Fairfax. From 1980–81 to 1985–86 its total assets had increased from $315 million to $845 million, and total liabilities from $196 million to $402 million. In 1986–87 bank borrowing for the HSV7 purchase raised the total liabilities to $729 million; but this, as we shall see, would be more than adequately covered by asset revaluation.

Between 1981 and 1987 John Fairfax's annual turnover increased from $379 million to $927 million. Operating profit before income tax rose from $20 million in 1981 to $78 million in 1985, dropped to $74 million in 1986, but then rose to $81 million in 1987.

So what shortcomings were perceived by the company's critics? The main criticism from commercial rivals and media observers was that in a decade which valued profit maximization above all else John Fairfax had been under-performing. Although it had been notably fortunate during the past seven years of sustained economic boom, and had achieved abundant growth, the company had not borrowed and gone global as spectacularly as Murdoch had; nor had it rewarded shareholders as generously as it might.

Thanks mainly to the fortuitous but shrewdly conducted David

Syme buyout (and the full *Age* cash flow which that brought into the group), sustained profits from the *Herald* and *Financial Review*, and repeated windfalls from AAP's sale of Reuter shares (capital dividends of $14 million in 1984, $12 million in 1986 and $96 million in 1987), the company had not been short of cash. Yet the dividend payout had risen only from $5.5 million in 1981 (48 per cent of net profit) to $11 million in 1985 (25 per cent), $12 million in 1986 (28 per cent), and $16 million in 1987 (39 per cent).

With the exception of 1981, when the sesquicentenary of the *Sydney Morning Herald* inspired a bonus dividend, these figures fell substantially short of the 50 per cent to which shareholders of most companies were more accustomed. But John Fairfax Ltd was not like most companies. It was controlled by a family which, except for such aberrations as HSV7, preferred defence to attack and prudence to audacity. Rather than maximizing profit, the directors accorded first priority to protecting the company's core assets. Profits went into capital expenditure rather than higher dividend rates. Rupert Murdoch paid low dividends too, but his attitude to debt was utterly different from Fairfax's conservatism.

In 1984 when Murdoch borrowed $300 million to acquire the Ziff-Davis chain of technical publications in the United States, Gardiner was trying unsuccessfully for a capital raising, and thereby incurring Fairwater's suspicion that he had no commitment to family control. The Fairfax board and management came off badly in that embarrassing PIPS affair, and were perceived as having been defeated by Sir Warwick and Lady Fairfax.

If the company wanted venture capital for some bold stroke or other, said the critics, why not borrow like anyone else? In the not too distant future, Gardiner would indeed persuade the board to depart from its traditional policy of low gearing in order to buy HSV7—a purchase regarded by many as the height of folly.

Apart from that, and the losses still being made by the *Sun* and *Times on Sunday*, the company was in excellent shape, and well able to service its unaccustomed level of debt. The major profit earners were all manufacturers of John Fairfax's original product, the printed word. In order of their contribution to group profit, they were David Syme ($45.6 million in 1986–87); John Fairfax and Sons Ltd, publisher of the Broadway papers ($19.4 million); Fairfax Magazines ($3.6 million); and the regional newspapers published by Newcastle Newspapers, Federal Capital Press, Illawarra Newspapers and Fairfax Community Newspapers ($3.58 million). After these came the electronic media: Amalgamated Television Services ($3.51 million), Brisbane TV Ltd ($3.1 million) and Macquarie Broadcasting Holdings ($980 600).

John Fairfax Ltd had every reason to be satisfied with its full ownership of David Syme. That thriving company's contribution to group profit was actually greater than its pre-tax profit, for the figure of $45.6 million included some extraordinary items, notably a substantial capital dividend of $26 million from the sale of Reuters shares. David Syme's operating profit before tax had risen from $30.42 million in 1985 to $34.14 million in 1986 and $37.9 million in 1987. The bulk of this was earned by the *Age*, thanks partly to the paper's editorial excellence and its smooth transition to cold type. The *Age* picked up much of the display advertising lost by the ailing Melbourne *Herald*, and by means of extensive pre-printing the paper had broken free from its 160-page limit, reaching an Australian record of 242 pages in April 1987.

Although by this time the *Age* had grown physically larger than the *Sydney Morning Herald*, the *Herald*'s circulation (256 000, compared with 254 000 two years earlier) still exceeded that of its Melbourne counterpart (230 400). Like the *Age* it was no longer restricted to 160 pages, and was steadily adding more pages to the Saturday edition. Chris Anderson was still editor-in-chief; but the editor, Eric Beecher, with the easy mobility of conspicuous achievement, went over to Rupert Murdoch in February to become editor-in-chief of HWT and editor of the Melbourne *Herald*. Beecher had played an important part in the revival of the *Sydney Morning Herald*, and his farewell luncheon at the Sydney Opera House restaurant was attended by more than a hundred of his former colleagues. He was succeeded as editor by the 35-year-old business editor, John Alexander, who had come to the *Herald* from *Australian Business* in 1984.

During the past three years Alexander had produced highly readable and well respected business pages by drawing together a group of relatively inexperienced but talented journalists, including Alan Deans and Deborah Light, and by developing new ideas such as the CBD gossip column, edited in succession by Hamish Fraser, Andrew Main, Mark Westfield, Glen Burge and Ian Verrender. In his new editorial post Alexander was to be assisted by a deputy editor, Max Prisk, and a news editor, Richard Glover.

Elsewhere in the Broadway building, Brenchley had enabled the *Financial Review* to strengthen its market position by achieving early morning delivery in Brisbane and Perth as well as Sydney and Melbourne. In 1985 the company had installed facsimile units to transmit page formes to Melbourne for printing at David Syme. Copies of the paper were at first flown to other capital cities, but in 1986 the facsimile network was extended to Brisbane and Perth by satellite link. This helped to lift the *Review*'s circulation from 67 400 to 76 600 in the space of twelve months. Under the editorship of Alan Kohler, the paper was substantially redesigned. In 1987 it was challenged by a Herald and Weekly Times publication, *Business Daily*, but that survived for only a few weeks.

The *Sun-Herald* had lost its formerly substantial lead over the *Sunday Telegraph*. Since 1981, when their respective circulations had been 702 795 and 663 411, the margin had narrowed, widened and narrowed again. Both papers had lost circulation, dropping back into the five hundred thousands, and for the last two years the *Sun-Herald*'s lead had been only about 3000. In April 1986 Suich appointed a well known former *Age* journalist, Peter Smark, to edit the *Sun-Herald*. Smark stayed for ten months, then chose like Beecher to join the Melbourne *Herald*, and was replaced by the deputy editor, Ray Odlum.

In the aftermath of Murdoch's victory, good journalists received very tempting offers to change their livery. The Melbourne *Herald* poached the *Age*'s widely read financial columnist, Terry McCrann, a senior *Sydney Morning Herald* reporter, Ben Hills, and the editor of the *Herald*'s 'Good Living' and 'Style' sections, Shelley Gare. The *Sydney Morning Herald* for its part hired John Edwards and the caricaturist Ward O'Neill from the *Bulletin*; and Janet Hawley, who had resigned from the *Age*.

'This is a curious and at times hysterical period in Australian journalism', wrote Suich in his April 1987 board report.

> Those who have not had offers look for them, those who have had recent discussions with Beecher refer to them as offers, and those who have really had offers agonise about taking the money but working for Murdoch. All this feeds on itself and provokes some overheated gossip. The amount of time that people like Chris Anderson and Alan Kohler have had to spend counselling staff, reassuring them and offering them encouragement becomes very onerous, not to say downright irritating on occasions.

The other two Broadway papers were in much worse trouble than the *Sun-Herald*. The *Sun* was trailing the *Mirror* by a weekly average of 45 000, and, as John Fairfax remarked at a board meeting, its financial results 'screamed out that something had to be done'. Gardiner responded by saying 'this would be more so next year'. In July the *Sun* launched a new production campaign with an old slogan ('Where the Action Is'), to coincide with the introduction of new typography and new layouts. The *Mirror* had a larger promotion budget, and it was gaining circulation with a weekly eight-page Rugby League lift-out, to which the *Sun* had responded with only four pages.

Compared with the *Sun*'s loss of more than $17 million in 1986, the *Times on Sunday* was a relatively small loser; but its latest annual loss of $3.5 million, under the former *National Times* masthead, brought its total loss in the previous fifteen years to $16.3 million. Since the re-launch in August 1986 sales had been disappointing, in spite of printing in Melbourne as well as Sydney and the secondment of such *Herald* journalists as Ian Hicks, Paul McGeough, Jenna Price and David Jenkins to help Valerie Lawson in her restructuring of the paper. Jenkins, the *Herald*'s foreign editor, was later appointed deputy editor of the *Times on Sunday*. He acted as editor when Lawson went on maternity leave in July 1987, though Lawson remained closely in touch with the paper during her absence.

Circulation rose to just over 100 000 for the federal election issue in July, but soon afterwards declined into the low eighty thousands. The Prime Minister, commenting appreciatively on the *Herald*'s editorial support for his government at the election, regretted that the Fairfax stable still contained one 'wonky shonky nag'. The *Times on Sunday* made the best of this jibe by offering its readers 'Wonky Shonky Nag' T-shirts designed by Michael Fitzjames. The description was bizarre enough to be taken lightly, but the word 'wonky' was not far off the mark.

In electronic media Fairfax's wholly owned Macquarie Broadcasting had greatly improved during the last six years, moving from an operating loss of about $1.5 million in 1981 to group profit contributions of $1 043 600 in 1985, $2 035 200 in 1986 and $980 600 in 1987. Two-thirds of the 1981 loss had been incurred by Macquarie Network's premier station, 2GB Sydney. That station was eighth in its market with a rating of only 5 per cent when R. A. Johnson, a former executive editor and manager of communications technology at Broadway, was appointed group general manager of Macquarie in January 1981. Bob Johnson's first Macquarie board meeting was interrupted by the arrival of the latest rating results. 'Good heavens', said the chairman, R. P. Falkingham, 'they're worse than ever—4.5 per cent'.

There was nowhere to go but up, and the successful climb to the top was presided over by a new chairman, John B. Fairfax, Johnson and an assistant group general manager in charge of marketing, Nigel Milan. Their strategy was to concentrate on the network's Melbourne station 3AW, which was third in its market; lift that to No 1; then use Melbourne's earnings and those of 4BH Brisbane and 5DN Adelaide to resuscitate 2GB. Under the management of Brian White, 3AW soon rose to first place with a more or less conventional format of talk and music. 2GB, on the other hand, became the first all-talk radio station in Australia.

'NewsTalk 87', so numbered because of 2GB's wavelength on the dial (873), was a combination of news and views, backed up by a staff of forty journalists and enlivened by the wit and mimicry of Mike Carlton and the resonant authority of John Laws. Laws joined the station from 2UE, bringing with him more than his astronomical new salary in the form of advertising revenue. Johnson was apprehensive about the format, but it worked. 'NewsTalk 87' went to air in 1982. By the end of 1983 the station had a rating of 10.4, and in 1985–86 it re-established itself as the market leader.

During that year Macquarie made pioneering use of Australia's first communications satellite, Aussat, launched in August 1985. Satellite dishes began relaying news and programme material between Sydney and Melbourne, and by the end of 1986 this facility was available throughout the network, including 2CA Canberra, 2WL Wollongong, 4AY Townsville and the partly owned 6PR in Perth. With the rise of FM radio, the surge in Macquarie's profit tapered off. But 2GB continued to dominate AM radio, leading all rating surveys for 1987.

In television, Amalgamated Television Services was still contributing well to group profit, though not so strongly as it had been earlier in the 1980s. Like other channels, it experienced a decline in profit as costs rose because of the Australian Broadcasting Tribunal's insistence on local content, and as colour lost its novelty with viewers. Nevertheless this station, owned 94 per cent by Fairfax (the residue being owned by the Albert family) was expected to make a pre-tax profit of $5.5 million in the current year.

Under the chairmanship of James Fairfax and the general managership of E. F. Thomas since the mid-1970s, ATN led the Seven Network in local production and in commitment to advanced television technology. Establishing its own drama unit at Rydalmere in 1983 to avoid having to use other facilities, it produced the series 'Rafferty's Rules' and later 'Home and Away'.'Rafferty's Rules', about a magistrate named Rafferty with a humane approach to the law, was funded entirely by Amalgamated Television Services until it proved itself a success and other network stations began contributing to the cost. The very successful early production, 'A Country Practice', was sold widely in Europe.

During most of the 1980s ATN7 came off second-best in the ratings to TCN9 which, mainly because of its ascendancy in the 6 p.m. to 7 p.m. news time, dominated the whole 6 p.m. to midnight period. Seven's news began at 6.30 p.m., half an hour later than Nine's and Ten's, and its successive news readers during the 1980s (Ross Simons, Richard Zachariah and Roger Climpson) proved no match for Nine's veteran Brian Henderson.

In April 1983 Amalgamated Television Services began a satellite service, using its own ground station at Epping to link ATN with its studios in London and Los Angeles via the international satellite Intelsat. Three years later it formed a joint venture with other Channel 7 stations, known as the Australian Television Network, and began satellite operations using the network's earth stations and a low-powered transponder on Aussat.

The wholly-owned BTQ7 in Brisbane was expected to make a pretax profit of $2.3 million for 1986–87. But HSV7, also wholly owned, at least for the time being, was a very different matter. The Melbourne station had made no money for the past three years, and if its previous network performance had seemed less than satisfactory to Fairfax, bad now turned to worse in the aftermath of the purchase. Several things were wrong with HSV. Its news service was poor, and it concentrated too much on sport, at the expense of more broadly based programming. Recently, however, the station's VFL contract had not been renewed satisfactorily, leaving some seventy employees redundant during the football season. Under Fairfax's ownership, appropriate retrenchments were made. Although redundancy payments were well above normal, an ugly industrial situation developed. In an unsuccessful attempt to secure reinstatement, the Theatrical and Amusement Employees' Association mounted a public campaign, to which State politicians and Murdoch's new Melbourne papers lent their support.

There was an element of interstate xenophobia in this, despite the fact that HSV's new management expanded the station's news service from 30 to 60 minutes, thus permitting a greater Victorian news content. When the station's main news reader was downgraded as part of the change in format, the Melbourne *Herald* and *Sun News-Pictorial*—once loyal allies of HSV—gave the matter front-page prominence.

In Sydney, Kerry Packer cheerfully estimated the current market value of HSV at no more than $70 million. In a rare display of journalism for *Australian Business*, he wrote that the $320 million purchase had made little sense at the time. 'It looked then as though Fairfax was aiming to shoot itself in the foot. Now it turns out Fairfax has blown off a kneecap.'

Although its prime-time ratings showed some improvement, HSV continued to worry its new owners for both operational and political reasons. The Broadcasting (Ownership and Control) Bill containing new media ownership rules was introduced in the House of Representatives on 29 April. Until that passed both Houses, Fairfax would not know for certain whether it would have to sell HSV. But already it knew that certain buyers were interested.

Holmes à Court had spoken all around the point to Gardiner, without making a definite offer; but in any case, the board regarded him as its last option. Two other West Australians, Kevin Parry and Kerry Stokes, had shown greater interest. The latter—who owned Canberra's only commercial channel (CTC7) and a licence to operate Perth's third commercial channel, and had bought Adelaide ADS7 during the dismemberment of HWT—seemed the more likely prospect. Stokes had offered $330 million for HSV, but Gardiner did not regard that as acceptable. In any case, until parliament had its say on the broadcasting bill, HSV's future would of necessity remain in abeyance.

This uncertainty provided ample scope for a paper on Fairfax's strategic and funding position, which Gardiner prepared for directors in May 1987. The paper examined options for a partial or complete withdrawal from television, but was basically another attempt by Gardiner to achieve a capital raising. Observing that both the PIPS and Newco proposals had been unacceptable to one major shareholder, he returned to a familiar refrain:

> The company is therefore in the unique position of not having raised capital for 21 years. During that period it has had a significant level of growth essentially generated by a retained cash flow and a conservative level of borrowings. It is now in the position that it is a major player in the media industry in Australia and it competes directly against News Corporation in the print media area, and Bond Media and Northern Star Holdings in the television area. Holmes à Court also straddles both media areas, but to date at least only in Western Australia.
>
> The significant point now is that each of these competitors are all of a very substantial size and, as opposed to Fairfax, seem to have no significant restrictions on either raising substantial additional equity capital or gearing themselves much more extensively than has been the more prudent Fairfax policy to date . . .
>
> At the moment the company's borrowings are at historically very high levels totalling approximately $450 million. As a consequence of the high interest rates currently applying and the negligible earnings of HSV, the company's profit has been substantially reduced each week and this will continue until such time as the ultimate HSV ownership position is resolved.
>
> Regardless of how the HSV position is resolved, it is fair to say that the most difficult problem facing the company, at least from the perspective of myself as chief executive and my senior personnel, is that we seem to be very substantially restricted in our growth, in Australia and overseas, in our existing industry or by diversification until such time that we can satisfactorily resolve our inability to raise capital from the market in a way which allows us to finance future growth.

So far during 1987, in addition to its plunge on HSV, John Fairfax Ltd had availed itself of one growth opportunity in Britain—the purchase by BRW Group of a business magazine publisher, Money Magazine Ltd, for $A2 039 000. Other opportunities had arisen recently in the United States and New Zealand, but no firm decisions had yet been made.

In March, Fairfax Magazines Pty Ltd sought board approval to commence publication of a magazine in the United States, to be called *Sassy*. This venture—developed by the assistant general manager of Fairfax Magazines, Sandra Yates—was to be an American version of the company's very successful *Dolly*, which enjoyed the highest per capita teenage girl sales of any such magazine in the world. Yates assured the board that there was a niche in the American market for *Sassy*. At first the board decided to defer any decision until it had dealt conclusively with the issue of capital raising. Then in April it gave approval for Yates and her team to continue preparing for a multi-million dollar launch in October, with the proviso that a final decision on whether to proceed or not would be taken later in the year on the basis of further market research.

The New Zealand opportunities concerned Wilson & Horton Ltd, publisher of the *Auckland Herald*; and Sir Ron Brierley's New Zealand News Ltd, publisher of the competitive *Auckland Star*. There were share-buying indications that someone was preparing to bid for Wilson & Horton, and Fred Brenchley had been talking to Brierley about the *Star*. Such acquisitions would be very useful strategically to Fairfax's existing interests in New Zealand, and as a counterpoise to Murdoch's activities there. But the combined cost would have been anything from $A150 million to $A350 million, and in view of Fairfax's current borrowing that was taken by Gardiner to be out of the question. 'This is very disappointing to me personally', he reported to the board, 'and I know it will be to other senior executives of the group. This is one further implication of why we must find some acceptable form of capital raising'.

In his board paper on funding, Gardiner presented the options of selling HSV into the hands of a group which would be a constructive network partner; floating the three stations as a separate company, either entirely or by retaining a cross-holding; floating David Syme & Co Ltd; and raising funds on an unsecured floating rate or redeemable note (UFRN) basis proposed by the brokers Ord Minnett. A combination of the latter two, he said, would raise sufficient funds to repay existing debt. It would result in two totally ungeared separate public companies which could then borrow in their own right.

III

The board meeting which considered these options on 21 May was attended by Warwick Fairfax, who had recently returned to Sydney after gaining his MBA degree at Harvard. Attending by invitation, for he was not yet a director, Warwick found the agenda packed with weighty and urgent business. Before coming to capital raising, the meeting increased the authorized capital of the company from $75 million to $250 million, by the issue of a further 350 million shares of 50 cents each; and made a special capital bonus dividend of $100 million, increasing the issued capital from 100 million to 300 million shares; and authorized a massive revaluation of the *Herald* and *Age* mastheads.

The masthead of a newspaper is an intangible fixed asset, not easy to measure, but nevertheless valuable in much the same way as goodwill. It is composed of editorial and advertising content, format, readership reputation and public influence, all of which attract revenue and consequently endow the masthead with value. Until recent years, the Fairfax group had made no use of this quite permissible accounting practice. In 1985, following the lead of News Corporation, David Syme attached a very conservative value of $34 million to the *Age*'s masthead. John Fairfax & Sons followed suit in 1986 by giving the *Herald*'s masthead an even more modest value, bringing the group's masthead valuation to $55.5 million. Now that figure, credited to the asset revaluation reserve, was being increased more than ten-fold to a commercially more realistic although still very conservative $650 million. Calculated on a 15-times earning basis, the valuations arrived at by Touche Ross & Co were $263 million for the *Herald*, $248 million for the *Age*, $74 million for the *Financial Review*, and $65 million for the *Sun-Herald*. For obvious reasons the *Sun* and *Times on Sunday* were not treated in this way.

The revaluation and share proposals were prompted on the one hand by concern to counterbalance the company's increased total liabilities, and on the other hand by an imminent change to the Income Taxation Act. After 30 June bonus issues made from the asset revaluation reserve would no longer be tax free. This was a last chance, and like other companies all over Australia John Fairfax Ltd was making hay for its shareholders while the sun shone. The increase in authorized capital was necessary for the making of a large bonus issue, and the increase in issued capital would eventually bring two benefits in addition to the obvious one conferred upon shareholders. It would improve the company's gearing, and strengthen its ramparts against the likes of Holmes à Court.

Here was food for thought for the board's quiet, bespectacled young guest. Apart from his American accent, Warwick bore some resemblance to his late father at the same age. He had a similarly lean figure, long face, thick hair and studious appearance. Not a lot was known about him at Broadway. The few executives who had made his acquaintance thought him intelligent, though apparently either shy or circumspect.

Those who had received Christmas cards from Fairwater over the years would have followed Warwick's progress through childhood and adolescence, for Lady Fairfax's carefully composed cards usually contained one or more photographs of the growing boy. At the age of seven he had been seated astride one of the Venetian stone lions in St Mark's Square; at eight he was holding the silver cup for Endeavour at St David's School in London; at thirteen, playing tennis at Cranbrook; at nineteen, brief-case in hand, starting his the J. Walter Thompson advertising agency before going nd at twenty-one, lunching *al fresco* with the family at while *en route* from his second job (personal assistant to an of Gordon Berg and Co Inc, investment bankers in complete his final year at Oxford.

At Balliol as at Cranbrook, Warwick kept to a limited circle of friends. He was secretary of table tennis, but was also a conscientious student. Like his father fifty-eight years earlier, he took a Second in Politics, Philosophy and Economics. Perhaps more importantly, he gained a strong Christian faith. Warwick had already been confirmed at St Mark's, Darling Point; but in England his religious commitment developed rapidly under the influence of Canon Michael Green, the rector of St Aldate's, Oxford.

Green was well known as a leader of evangelistic missions in Britain and elsewhere, and as the author of many popular religious books: *Choose Freedom, I Believe in Satan's Downfall* and *New Life, New Lifestyle*, to name only three. He spoke at the Oxford Union, and St Aldate's was always well attended by students. During the summer vacation it was Canon Green's custom to take a party of students to Lee Abbey in North Devon, and on one of these retreats during his second year at Oxford Warwick experienced if not a conversion then certainly a quickening of faith.

From 1983 to 1985 he worked at the Chase Manhattan Corporation, first completing its course of credit training and then joining the bank's media and entertainment group which financed such clients as the New York Times and Time Inc. To one of his colleagues in that group he seemed exceptionally bright, possessed of a dry sense of humour, but inclined to keep his own counsel.

While living in Manhattan Warwick attended a Baptist church to which he had been introduced by friends of his half-sister Annalise. Annalise Thomas was closer to Warwick than any other member of the family outside Fairwater. Only a few years older, she was an active parishioner of St Mark's and her husband, David Thomas, had for a time been Warwick's history master at Cranbrook. Writing to Annalise from New York, Warwick said that he had decided, as part of his Christian commitment, to involve himself wholeheartedly, as his parents had always hoped he would, in family and company affairs. Previously he had not been certain about his future; but this was something ordained by God, he said, and in the spirit of the Parable of the Talents he was going to give it his best.

Part of that best, as he saw it, was to gain a postgraduate degree of sufficient worth to persuade others that he was more than merely his father's son. Sir Warwick, wanting his son back in Sydney, tried to deter him from this; but in September 1985 Warwick began the two-year course at Harvard's Graduate School of Business

Administration, widely regarded as the best of its kind in the world. During one of the summer vacations he also worked at the *Los Angeles Times,* in its marketing department.

Warwick returned to Sydney, but not to residence at Fairwater. Feeling the need for independence, he moved in with some friends of his own age and religious conviction at a house in the grounds of St Augustine's Church of England, Neutral Bay. Two of these friends, one of whom had shared accommodation with him in America, were sons of Jim Cameron, who was a former Speaker of the New South Wales parliament, a political and moral conservative, and a committed Christian.

Like the Camerons, Warwick was already associated with an international prayer movement, a non-denominational fellowship centred in Washington and numbering in its fold many politicians and business people. Members of this movement came together for prayer meetings, including an annual prayer breakfast at the White House. In Sydney, Warwick also attended a North Shore church of the Christian and Missionary Alliance, the Australian branch of a long-established evangelical community with headquarters in Nyack, New York.

The Alliance had grown from a nucleus founded during the 1870s by a Canadian Presbyterian minister, A. B. Simpson, who preached first in Louisville, Kentucky, and later in New York City. During the twentieth century it became a global network of 'New Testament-type churches giving pre-eminence to Jesus Christ in personal experience and universal witness'. Although originally concentrating on countries of the Third World, the Alliance later began taking its message into Western urban societies as well. Since 1969, when the first C & MA service was held at a private home in the Sydney suburb of Naremburn, twenty-eight churches and a theological college had been established in Australia.

There was something about Warwick Fairfax's religious commitment that brought to mind his great-great-grandfather—the first John Fairfax, that 'man of business and the faithful servant of Christ', ever busy for both worlds. According to some of those who knew Warwick, he was 'a person of great integrity', 'never interested in flashy clothes and flashy cars', and 'a Christian in everything he does'. He had worked hard to prepare himself for business, and now that ordained career was about to begin.

The board meeting in May provided directors with their best opportunity so far to observe the young man who would doubtless be joining them formally before much longer. During discussion of the bonus share issue the acting chairman, John Fairfax, invited him to comment.

Mr Warwick Fairfax asked how the issue would affect individual

> shareholders. Mr Gardiner said the shareholder, after the issue, had the same percentage holding in the company and, therefore, had achieved very little but it would reduce the market price of the shares and these shares would be more easily within the reach of the smaller would-be shareholder.

Another matter on the agenda was a tentative proposal by Gardiner for an executive share scheme similar to some operating in other media companies. What Gardiner had in mind was not a scheme for all staff but one designed to keep senior executives with the company. Fairfax retirement funds already owned 11.3 per cent of the issued capital, and under the proposed scheme senior executives would hold an additional 5 per cent. Sir Vincent said that every share issued in this way would erode the family holdings, but there was a considerable need for such a scheme. Warwick Fairfax asked whether more shares would be issued as time went on, and Gardiner said he would prefer that not to be the case. He was not seeking an immediate decision, and indeed the proposal did not come up again.

Then discussion turned to ways of raising capital: floating some or all of the television interests as a public company, floating David Syme, unsecured floating redeemable notes, and even another go at PIPS. The discussion was inconclusive, for Gardiner drew attention to difficulties or shortcomings in all the options. It might be better, he said, to look at selling off assets, and in that context he advocated selling out of television entirely. Now was the time to sell, he said: even if television really fired, it could never justify the figures now being paid for channels.

> Mr Gardiner said he believed we were on the edge of a precipice. We could not find a solution to our problem. He said we were now in a position that unless we did something very positive we would be in a slump.
>
> The market, he said, believed we were about to do something very smart. A capital raising was expected by the market and the question was would we do something before the market fell away . . .
>
> If we sold both ATN and BTQ [as well as HSV] we could expect to get rid of all our borrowings and still have money in the bank. He believed we could get $650 million and possibly this figure could go to $800 million.

Sir Vincent said he did not believe the company had to be as big as Murdoch in order to continue creating quality products. Agreeing with that, Warwick Fairfax said he had nothing against the floating of David Syme, but if the company resorted to floating off subsidiaries it would eventually reach the point where there were no subsidiaries left to float. He could see no solution in the long term and agreed that the company had a great problem. Sir David Griffin and Sir Eric Neal said they would not be at all worried about getting out of television. John Fairfax spoke in similar vein, but wondered also whether such a course, producing a very cashed-up company, might further encourage a takeover bid by Holmes à Court. Gardiner replied that this could not happen if the family stayed together.

Although directors were clearly amenable to the idea of selling the television stations, no resolution was passed at this meeting. The only firm decisions taken were to revalue the mastheads, increase the authorized capital (this was ratified by an extraordinary general meeting of shareholders on 12 June), and declare the capital bonus dividend of $100 million. This dividend increased the company's issued capital from $50 million to $150 million. It had little effect on the market's valuation of the company, however, because although the number of issued shares trebled, the share price immediately fell by inverse proportion—from about $15 to about $5.

The 1987–88 group budget was presented at the next board meeting, on 17–18 June, which was also attended by Warwick Fairfax. Given the uncertainty surrounding the television channels, this budget was of limited practical value. But its general tone was optimistic. Broadway newspapers were budgeting for a profit increase of 44 per cent; David Syme for 8.76 per cent; Macquarie Broadcasting, 113 per cent; Fairfax Magazines, 20 per cent; Fairfax Community Newspapers, 41 per cent; Federal Capital Press, 21 per cent; Newcastle Newspapers, 31 per cent; and Illawarra Newspapers, 152 per cent. Group profit before tax was expected to be $114 million, compared with the previous year's target of $81.5 million. The 1987–88 estimate would have been much higher, said Gardiner, had it not been decided to take the loss-making HSV into budget reckoning. In the four months since its purchase, that channel had lost $2 413 000.

By the time Fairfax's budget was approved, however, it had become clear that the company would indeed have to dispose of HSV, for on 2 June the Broadcasting (Ownership and Control) Bill had scraped through the Senate with its cross-ownership provisions intact. The Opposition had at first sided with the Democrats to oppose the bill, but the Government had managed to do a deal with the National Party. In return for a reduction in the permitted television audience reach, the Nationals joined with Labor to produce a bare majority of 37–35.

Gardiner's negotiations with Kerry Stokes had now entered a new phase with the object not of selling HSV alone, as Stokes had earlier suggested, but of forming a jointly owned network managed by one chief executive. This would return Fairfax the price it had paid for HSV, but would not repay all its corporate debt. It was a complicated scheme involving the establishment of a company controlling five television stations, including 100 per cent of HSV and ADS, and

40 per cent of ATN. Fairfax would retain ownership of the balance of ATN and 100 per cent of BTQ.

At the July board meeting—once more attended by Warwick Fairfax, who by this time was gaining work experience at Broadway—there were two proposals for consideration: one from Stokes, and another from Christopher Skase, a 37-year-old Queensland entrepreneur, originally from Melbourne. After an early career as a financial journalist on the *Sun News-Pictorial* and *Financial Review* he had in the past twelve years created the Qintex group of companies with substantial property, tourism and media interests, including television stations in Brisbane and Maryborough. Now he wanted to buy the Seven Network.

Gardiner felt that both proposals were acceptable, and that first past the post would be the winner. He had been close to agreement with Stokes after Skase had interrupted negotiations by going overseas. Then on 16 July, the day of the board meeting, Skase telephoned Gardiner from Mt Kenya Rifle Club, where he was about to go on safari. He proposed a scheme of deferred payment under which Fairfax would return part of the purchase price as an investment in the purchasing company—Universal Telecasters Ltd, a subsidiary of Qintex. This investment was crucial to Skase, for his funding was touch-and-go, and from Fairfax's point of view it would provide a welcome opportunity to keep an interest in television. Admittedly that interest would be less significant than a joint venture with Stokes, but on the other hand Skase's proposal, unlike Stokes's, would eventually extinguish all of Fairfax's debt, and leave the company with more than $200 million in cash.

Although no resolution was passed, the feeling of the meeting inclined towards Skase. All directors expressed varying degrees of preference for his proposal, and Max Suich—when Gardiner sought his opinion of Skase—said that he had known him since Skase had been on the *Financial Review*, and thought he would make a good partner. The only support for Stokes came from Warwick Fairfax. Both schemes were good, he said, but Stokes's offered more flexibility. If he had an opportunity to choose, he would be inclined to go that way but he had no strong view.

The matter was left in the hands of the group general manager, the chairman and John Fairfax for further negotiation and final decision. Neither Stokes nor Skase knew of the other's bid, and as negotiations continued with both of them during the next few days they were running neck and neck. In the end, however, Gardiner went cold on the Stokes deal. He became disturbed at the influence which some of Stokes's outside investors and directors seemed to have, and began to worry that Fairfax might once again find itself in an unhappy network partnership. More importantly, the Stokes deal would have left Fairfax in debt to the tune of $250 million, and

Gardiner doubted that television could service a long-term debt of that size. His doubts about the future of television had been reinforced that week by Channel 10's decision to break an industry agreement on programme buying, thus signalling a potentially disastrous rise in costs. Gardiner and the two Fairfax directors decided to go with Skase. After a ten-hour meeting between Gardiner and Skase, the deal was concluded at 2.30 a.m., Friday 24 July.

For the three companies owning ATN, BTQ and HSV, together with related production operations, the cash price was to be $780 million, consisting of $25 million on signing, $470 million on 30 November 1987, and $285 million to be paid in July 1990. From this total, $21 million would go to the Albert family for its minority shareholding in ATN; $100 million was to be paid for shares in Universal Telecasters on 30 November 1987; and $55 million for Telecasters shares in July 1990.

To assist Skase in funding the deal, Fairfax agreed to an unconditional call option under which, in the event of Qintex defaulting on repayment to its banks, Fairfax could be required to buy back the network at a maximum price of $285 million, according to how much of the purchase price Qintex had paid at the time of defaulting. There would be no risk to Fairfax in this. Should Skase default, his bankers would surely seek some other buyer at a higher price. In the unlikely event of them not doing so, and the call option being invoked, the network would be a bargain at such a price.

Some aspects of the sale were singled out for criticism by journalists in the Packer and Murdoch groups. Packer himself ventured the opinion that the Fairfaxes had 'kicked themselves in the groin', and according to his *Bulletin* the network had been sold to 'effectively smother' the 'spectacular losses' incurred by Fairfax in its 'ill-judged' purchase of HSV. Terry McCrann, the former *Age* columnist now writing for the Melbourne *Herald* under the heading 'A $780 million Fairfax Folly', stressed the interest-free nature of Skase's deferred payments, the effect of that on the purchase price, and Fairfax's obligation to repay the money it had borrowed to buy HSV.

> Mr Skase has really paid closer to $650 million in today's dollars . . . [Fairfax] spent $360 million on [HSV] and will emerge with only $40 million in cash until the final payment in 1990.
>
> It gets $495 million [this year], but $100 million goes back into Qintex and $360 million goes to the bankers (ignoring the interest bill). And for that it loses its prime Sydney station and the Brisbane station.
>
> It may book an accounting profit, but the reality is that it has had to do a very poor commercial deal to avoid the more unpalatable prospect of having Melbourne's Seven taken from it under the new TV rules.

Another line of attack was that John Fairfax Ltd could have obtained a higher price by calling tenders for the network. On 27 July one of the earlier potential buyers, Kevin Parry, wrote to James Fairfax attempting to re-open negotiations and claiming that his company would have been willing to pay 'at the very least $100 million more' than Universal Telecasters. His overture was rebuffed, and the Sydney Stock Exchange, to which Parry also made representations, declined to intervene.

As with the HSV purchase, Gardiner vigorously defended the network sale. Skase was the preferred buyer, and the price was right. 'We take our ownership of assets, particularly media assets, very seriously', he told one interviewer.

> And we would not be prepared to put them in the hands of, necessarily, the highest bidder. We would want to put them in the hands of a person that we think can really take them on, look to the interests of the employees and form a long-term association with us.

Among Gardiner's critics in the Murdoch press were some who wrote with what purported to be reliable knowledge of feelings inside the Fairfax family about the network sale. Readers had to judge for themselves the worth of unnamed sources; but even after allowing for ulterior commercial motives, some would have been left suspecting that the reports had a certain amount of foundation in fact. One week after the sale, a columnist in the *Australian* wrote:

> The continuing saga of the sale of the Seven Network is taking on all the aspects of an episode of *Dynasty*. Observers of the Fairfax family are now tipping a major upheaval right at the top of the diminished media group.
>
> The Fairfaxes have a fine tradition of supporting their general manager to the hilt—and then ditching him. And that is the fate predicted for Greg Gardiner, whom the family is blaming for what has become an embarrassing debacle.
>
> Already, some shareholders are demanding to know why the Seven Network was not put up for general bidding.
>
> Kevin Parry, Robert Holmes à Court and Kerry Stokes have all intimated they would have paid more than did Christopher Skase in the sweetheart deal he thrashed out with Gardiner . . .
>
> Certainly Parry, who dined with Lady (Mary) Fairfax at Fairwater last Saturday night . . . made sure members of the family knew he would have paid more than Skase.
>
> It must be assumed that the chairman, James Fairfax, was fully informed of the Skase negotiations, but this will not help Gardiner avoid the blame.
>
> The whole mess may, in fact, serve to speed up the elevation of Warwick Fairfax, Mary's 27-year-old son, into the chief executive's chair.

Warwick is perfectly trained and ready to be the first operational Fairfax in a couple of generations.

If he moves into the hot seat, it will make his mother very proud and make life a little easier for his half-brother, James.

By the time the Fairfax board met again, on 27 August, this kind of sniping had ceased. The Corporate Affairs Commission and National Companies and Securities Commission, like the Stock Exchange, had decided not to examine the circumstances of the sale; and on the stockmarket, Fairfax shares had risen from $4.50 before the sale to $5.40. Holmes à Court was reported to have offered Skase a profit of at least $20 million to on-sell the network to him, but apparently Skase was not interested.

In the Fairfax boardroom it was as if the company had inched its way back from the precipice to safer ground, where vertigo could subside. Problems of television and gearing had receded, leaving the welcome prospect of a company freed from debt, with $200 million in the bank and still some residual financial interest in television through Skase's company. This feeling of respite was disturbed only by reports that Holmes à Court had lifted his holding in the company to 3.2 per cent, and by suspicions of commercial espionage. On Gardiner's instruction the boardroom and other rooms at Broadway were swept for 'bugs', but nothing was found.

Gardiner and John Fairfax were just back from a business and holiday trip with their wives. In the course of their travels to Paris, the South of France, Venice, Helsinki, London and New York, John had asked the group general manager what his ambitions might be now that Warwick had joined the company, presumably to become chief executive in due course. Gardiner's response was that if necessary he would move aside. He had already said as much to Warwick, in fact, and had expressed the view that Warwick should be a director. Warwick's Toyota was now to be seen regularly in the executive car park. He was working in the *Herald*'s marketing department, and consequently getting to know the middle management of every division in the company.

Warwick did not attend the August board meeting, perhaps because the television crisis had passed. Gardiner reviewed the sale, and discussion then moved to other matters. Brenchley reported on negotiations for the launching of a real estate paper in Adelaide, which he hoped would be 75 per cent owned by Fairfax. Gardiner also brought the board up to date on two proposed property developments connected with Broadway and the company's presence in the central business district.

The property developments were still at a preliminary stage, supervised by the administration manager, Philip Allen. One was a multi-storeyed Media Centre at the corner of Broadway and Jones

Street. Linked to the existing building, it was initially intended to accommodate ATN7, radio station 2GB and Fairfax Magazines, with room for future press expansion. Now that ATN had left the group, the nearby University of Technology had shown interest in renting space there. The cost would be from $40 to $50 million, but against that the company would be able to sell Macquarie's downtown building and the Fairfax Magazines building in Waterloo. Plans had been submitted to the City Council for approval.

After selling its triangular building at the corner of Pitt, O'Connell and Hunter streets to the Bank of New South Wales (Westpac) and moving to Broadway in 1955, the company had maintained offices in an old building at the corner of Hunter and Hamilton streets. In addition to that property, Fairfax had eventually acquired all of the block defined by Hunter, Hamilton, Curtin and Little Hunter streets. This was perhaps the most prestigious undeveloped site in Sydney, and in 1986 the company had undertaken a feasibility study for a $32 million office building, to be known as Fairfax House. It was to be built by Lend Lease Corporation and designed by Harry Seidler. The project was abandoned, however, because of a conservation order placed upon the site by the Heritage Council, requiring preservation of the Hunter Street façade.

The company was instead now inclined to sell the Hunter Street site and either buy into a building which was then under construction in George Street near the GPO, or—better still—buy back the old Sydney Morning Herald building. The latter possibility, suggested by Gardiner in June 1987, was taken up by the directors with some enthusiasm. At the August board meeting Gardiner reported that a reasonable price for the building would be about $55 million, and that according to architect's advice an additional $30 million would need to be spent on it. All directors supported an approach to Westpac, and Sir Eric Neal, who was also a director of that bank, undertook to bring the matter up at board level.

At the conclusion of this meeting James Fairfax, who had been a director for thirty years and chairman for ten of those years, advised the board that he would be taking sabbatical leave for six months the following year: he would be writing an autobiography. No one in the boardroom that day realized quite how much the chairman would have to write about.

7

The Gates of Paradise

I

For several months, unknown to the directors and executives, Warwick Fairfax had been preparing to privatize and restructure the company. Such a bold venture—likely to cost one or two billion dollars, depending on how many shares would need to be acquired—was not entered upon lightly. But neither was it accorded the degree of diligence and caution which might have been expected with so much at stake. Instead, there was a heady sense of predestination about what was happening. At every turn the young venturer displayed supreme confidence. Or was it fatalism? Win or lose, and at whatever cost, it seemed Warwick Fairfax's destiny to play the game through.

The game may be said to have started, and to have imposed its own compulsion, when Warwick bought 1.5 per cent of the issued Fairfax shares in order to lift the combined family holdings from 48.6 to 50.1 per cent as further security against hostile takeover bids. To make that purchase in February 1987, and to provide spare capacity for some capitalization of interest, he had borrowed $35 million at 18 per cent interest. The projected annual interest bill for this debt was $5.4 million, while the dividend income from the purchased shares was unlikely to be more than $187 000. Clearly something had to be done about the matter, and soon.

In March Warwick requested Baring Brothers Halkerston, the corporate advisory firm counselling him against the Newco proposal, to advise him and his mother generally about their investment in John Fairfax Ltd. As Warwick was in Boston, he dealt with Barings by telephone, and kept closely in touch with his mother and Martin Dougherty. What he expected from Barings was a scheme for the takeover of John Fairfax Ltd, but instead they advised against that course. At the current level of value placed on media stocks, the report concluded, Warwick and Lady Fairfax had little chance of acquiring control in a manner which would ensure their financial viability. While asset sales or the inclusion of a friendly partner would reduce financial risk, such measures would seriously undermine the rationale for a takeover bid.

It would be better, reported one of the principals at Barings, Mark Burrows, to wait for an opportunity to put forward proposals which would be in the best interests of family and other shareholders. Fairfax management was clearly under pressure to produce an answer to the ownership problem of the *Age* and HSV7, and to rebuild the company's earnings despite its enlarged corporate debt. Any proposed solutions might well be to the detriment of shareholders, thus providing Warwick with the kind of support he needed to mount a successful offer. For the meantime, Barings recommended certain steps to reduce the imbalance between interest and dividends—notably by establishing new private companies from which preference shares could be issued to a friendly partner.

According to Dougherty, Warwick interpreted this advice to mean: 'There, there sonny. When you have finished your degree and grown up a bit and got more shares, come back and see us. In the meantime just put your head down; nothing is going to happen while you are out of the country'. It was not the sort of advice Warwick was prepared to follow.

'Where do we go from here?' he asked Dougherty.

'From what Barings say, you need a partner. Maybe someone from the West could help.'

Dougherty's first suggestion was a client of his in Perth, Kevin Parry, who had already shown tentative interest in buying HSV. Parry met Lady Fairfax at Fairwater, and later his son met Warwick in New York. Time passed, however, without any specific proposal being made. Then, in April, Dougherty had a chance meeting with another West Australian—Laurie Connell, managing director of Rothwells Ltd—at an investment bank dinner in New York.

As he told Warwick in Boston, Dougherty was impressed by the 'decision-making ability' of this 41-year-old merchant banker—another Irish Australian, but more pugnacious than Dougherty. Although not so well known as some of his contemporaries, Connell had achieved sufficient prominence to be the subject of an illuminating profile in a recent issue of the *Sydney Morning Herald*'s Good Weekend magazine, entitled 'King of the Bare-Knuckle businessmen'.

> They are the new generation of bare-knuckle businessmen, men who fought their way into the *Business Review Weekly* millionaires' directory (their *Debrett*'s) before they were 40, men who made it in that Dallas Downunder where the Indian Ocean scalds the Western Australian desert, men who think that Robert Holmes à Court is Establishment Money, and Alan Bond a bit past it at 49. Twenty years ago they were builders' labourers, office boys and golf caddies, kids from the wrong side of the tracks whose education was briefly interrupted

> by their schooling. Today they control billions of dollars worth of Australia . . .
>
> The newest of the *nouveaux* and well on his way to becoming the richest of the *riches* is Lawrence Robert Connell, banker, developer, dealmaker, a man who has built the $5 stakes he used to win in sideshow boxing tents to a personal fortune of more than $300 million . . .

The article made clear that Laurie Connell was no ordinary banker. For one thing, this nuggety boxer and hockey player owned more than four hundred racehorses. In 1975—after a breach of the racing rules, which he denied but which nonetheless became widely known as 'The Kalgoorlie Sting'—he had been barred for two years from attending race meetings. Twelve years later one of his prize-winning horses, Brash Son, tested positively for a drug known colloquially as 'elephant juice'. The trainer was barred for failing to ensure that the horse was not drugged, but no charges of any kind were brought against Connell, who denied knowledge of the affair.

In matters more strictly commercial, Connell had been very successful. After putting himself through night school accountancy by caddying during the day, he worked first as a money-market dealer, then set up his own business in that market. In 1982 he took over Rothwells, a small Brisbane merchant bank which was the only one of its kind listed on the Australian stock exchanges. Within five years Rothwells was earning $90 million a year, and Connell ('Last Resort Laurie', as he was known in the high-risk end of the corporate lending spectrum) was talking about consolidating his various interests in a public float of $800 million.

Even though Rothwells had not given much takeover advice in the past, Dougherty on his brief first acquaintance with Connell felt that he would make a good partner for Warwick. Without identifying the target company, he asked Connell whether he would have any conflict of interest in giving advice about a media company in Australia. 'East coast or west?' asked Connell, and when Dougherty replied 'East' Connell said, 'None whatsoever'.

Connell had recently tried without success to acquire Perth's third commercial television licence, and also to buy the afternoon *Daily News* from Holmes à Court. That was the extent of his media experience, but Dougherty judged him 'smart enough and tough enough to handle the major predators we would be likely to encounter' and 'rich enough to help my young man seize the prize he was looking for'.

'[Connell] is Alan Bond's merchant banker', Dougherty told his young man.

> He was responsible for Bond's deals, and rescued him in the 1970s.

My impression is that he is tough but honest—but not the sort of man you would want to double-cross. He is a merchant banker, used to the ethical standards of that profession but still acts as a principal, owning his own companies, and therefore is a good negotiator.

With Warwick's approval, Dougherty met Connell again on 22 April at the Regent Hotel in Sydney. This time he identified the target company, if Connell had not deduced that already, and was pleased to discern a positive if wary response. After Dougherty had explained that Warwick and his mother owned about 14 per cent of the issued shares between them, the rest of the family about 36 per cent, and the Fairfax superannuation funds another 12 per cent, Connell said he saw no great difficulty providing that Warwick had a powerful investor with him and the rest of the family either retained all their shares or sold only a small proportion of them. He doubted that the rest of the family would oblige in this way, for he could not see why it would be in their interest to do so. If they insisted upon being fully bought out, he said, Warwick would have to sell a high proportion of the company's assets. But even in that event, he felt a takeover was achievable.

Several days later Dougherty, accompanied by the solicitor Fieldhouse, met Connell again in his Perth office overlooking the Swan River. By this time Connell had enlisted the help of Bert Reuter, a former lieutenant to Holmes à Court, but he postponed any final commitment to the Fairfax undertaking until ascertaining the availability of other consultants. Willem Bertus Reuter was the same age as Connell, of similar but more compact build, and more jovial by nature. The two of them had known each other since the days when they studied accountancy together.

Although born in Amsterdam, Reuter had come to Western Australia at the age of ten and was as much at home on Perth's Rialto as any of his bare-knuckle contemporaries. His personal stationery was embossed with the figure of a white knight. A black or green one would have been more appropriate, for in the nineteen takeovers Reuter had been through with Holmes à Court before they parted company, his role had been that of predator. He was a veteran of corporate jousting, and also had a good understanding of the media.

On 22 May Warwick saw Connell for the first time at a meeting in Fieldhouse's office attended also by Dougherty and Reuter. Connell proposed that ownership of the bid vehicle—a company to be used for making the offer—should be split equally between himself and Warwick. When Warwick said he wished to have control of John Fairfax Ltd, Connell replied that he himself had no such wish; all he wanted was 50 per cent of the shareholding. Warwick, he said, could have control of the bid vehicle's board by four members to three.

As for capitalizing the bid vehicle, Connell proposed that he and Warwick should each contribute $25 million. When Warwick said he had no available cash, having already over-extended himself by purchasing the 1.5 per cent parcel, Connell swept that difficulty aside. He would advance Warwick's share of the capital against the final outcome of a takeover.

After this meeting Warwick became increasingly uneasy about the joint venture proposal, particularly about the effect which it might have upon perceptions by other members of the family. He asked Dougherty whether he thought Connell would be willing to act for a fee rather than equity. Dougherty—whose company Tabulum Holdings Pty Ltd, trading as Dougherty Communications, had now been retained by Rothwells for public relations work in the eastern States—was doubtful. At Warwick's urging, however, he explored that possibility during the next few weeks.

Eventually the matter was resolved by offering Connell a fee which he could hardly refuse. There would later be irreconcilable differences of opinion as to who first suggested this prodigious payment. According to Warwick Fairfax, Dougherty told him early in August:

> 'I have discussed it again with Laurie Connell, and he is willing to do it for a $100 million fee, and not a joint venture. He says that it is a take it or leave it fee, that he will do it for you for that and that is the price.'
>
> I said: 'That's a lot of money.'
>
> Dougherty: 'It is a take it or leave it fee. It's firm. Where else can we go?'

Dougherty, on the other hand, claimed that Warwick had nominated the fee during a discussion with him in June, using words to this effect:

> My inclination is instead of having a 50/50 partnership with Connell, at the eleventh hour I will tell him that I want 51 per cent of the venture with Connell to have 49 per cent. Or alternatively I would offer Connell a tremendous return for his involvement, say a $100 million fee. Then if what Connell is after is influence, he would certainly have it with me. I would be very happy for Connell to be a director. The fee relationship might satisfy Connell, yet give me the full control of the company which is what I really want.

When Dougherty mentioned this figure to Connell, in late July by his recollection, Connell replied:

> I will consider that proposition because my feeling about this fellow has changed somewhat since our meeting. I do not have as much confidence in him or in the position in which I would be left in the [joint venture] company, so I think I might agree to do it on a fee basis.

The fee was agreed upon in the second week of August. According to Reuter, Connell said at a meeting in Fieldhouse's office on 12 August: 'We seek a fee of ten per cent of the purchase consideration of the bid to a maximum of $100 million. If you sell out at a profit to an over-bidder, we would seek a proportion of the profit so made'. Fieldhouse expressed surprise at the figure, and so did others at a meeting held without Connell the next day.

Among those present on 13 August were Ron Cotton and Peter King. Cotton, the former chief financial executive of John Fairfax Ltd who had resigned in 1985 after four and a half years of uneasy working relationship with Greg Gardiner, was then general manager finance and administration at the National Mutual Royal Savings Bank. He had kept in touch with Sir Warwick and Lady Fairfax after leaving Broadway, and had now been invited by their son to join the takeover team. King had no previous connection with the Fairfax group, the family or the media industry. He was a member of the executive board of Royal Packaging Industries Van Leer B.V. in Amsterdam, one of the world's largest manufacturers of industrial containers and food packaging—everything from 210-litre drums to papier mâché egg cartons and polystyrene hamburger packs.

Although born in South Africa, King had acquired Australian citizenship while running Van Leer's Australian subsidiary during the early 1980s. Knowing that King was unhappy in Holland, a mutual friend who was aware of Warwick's need for a chief executive mentioned his name. The suggestion was providential, for it happened that King's eldest daughter was about to marry one of the friends with whom Warwick was then sharing accommodation at St Augustine's. Warwick met King for the first time on 7 August, but it was not until October that he formally invited him to become chief executive officer, and not until early December that King accepted.

At the meeting on 13 August, Warwick Fairfax raised the matter of the fee.

King: That's an incredible fee. I've never heard of a fee like that.

Dougherty: If Warwick wants to proceed then Laurie Connell is the best man to do it and Warwick, you've got no alternative than to go with Laurie . . . If it's not done soon, then somebody else will proceed with a bid and it may be that that will be Holmes à Court.

Fairfax: I feel the fee is an incredibly high figure and I wonder whether we can't negotiate a lower rate.

Dougherty: Connell is prepared to walk away from this if he doesn't get the $100 million . . .

Fieldhouse: What would Connell charge if the bid failed?

King: It should be an all or nothing fee. Either he succeeds and he gets paid or he fails and he doesn't.

At another meeting with Connell next day the matter was settled in principle: a fee of $100 million would be payable by John Fairfax Ltd within six months of success, which would be attainment of a prescribed minimum percentage of the target company's shares. In the meantime Connell agreed to lend Warwick the commitment fee required for a bank facility to carry out the takeover plan which Reuter was developing.

The earliest plan, produced in May, had been code-named 'Giornale Dynasty'—presumably because it had been sent to Connell while he was in Italy, where 'giornale' means 'newspaper'.

> The objective [wrote Reuter] is to acquire control of the Dynasty empire in association with the ultimate heir of the empire. The Heir does not wish to wait for his inheritance as he believes that the value of his inheritance is depreciating under the present management.
>
> He wishes to join with interests associated with [Connell] to acquire a controlling interest in the Dynasty Corporation to allow him to make those management changes that he feels are long overdue . . .
>
> [Connell] is planning a major public float in the main to consolidate his current operating interests and investments in the one public vehicle. It is intended to utilise this newly structured public vehicle to develop the investment in Dynasty Corporation.
>
> A preliminary bid proposal has been developed after consultation with [Dougherty] and [Fieldhouse] to assess Dynasty families' attitudes and possible requirements.
>
> At this stage it appears that the most cost efficient and effective bid is to seek the family's support or at least provide an attractive situation for them to remain shareholders in Dynasty Corporation.

In place of a joint venture, Reuter produced at least four successive plans for a takeover by the Heir alone. One of these—'Dynasty Corporation', dated 3 August—set the following objectives:

> 1) The Heir to acquire effective control of Dynasty Corporation without retaining long term exposure to a high level of debt.
> 2) Although it is preferable for the remaining family members and [superannuation funds] to retain their shareholding, if possible a bid to be structured and financed for the potential situation that the family do not wish to remain shareholders.
> 3) Because of the synergy of the Dynasty print media, to structure the bid financing in such a way as to minimise losing control of the various divisions of the print media.

Synergy, it should be explained, was a term much in vogue with corporate strategists, denoting the familiar concept of a whole being greater than its parts. The Heir would undoubtedly need to sell off some of Dynasty Corporation's assets in order to pay the price of victory; but, as Reuter was pointing out, he would be well advised, in the interest of collaborative benefit, to preserve as far as possible the production, editorial and advertising advantages of owning four such papers as the *Sydney Morning Herald, Age, Australian Financial Review* and *Sun-Herald*.

The offer was to consist of $7 cash for each Fairfax share, but with an alternative to cash in the form of scrip in David Syme. That subsidiary—strengthened by acquisition of the *Australian Financial Review*, Fairfax Magazines, and full ownership of the Business Review Weekly group—was to be floated as a public company again. To preserve some degree of synergy, the privatized John Fairfax Ltd would retain at least 45 per cent of the new David Syme.

There is no point in lingering over the various 'Dynasty' proposals, for they changed by the week and in any case bore little resemblance to what would eventually happen. Basically they were estimates of how many shares the bid vehicle would have to buy, how much it would need to borrow for that purpose, and by what means it could repay the debt.

Warwick already 'spoke for' about 14 per cent—the 12.8 per cent held by Rockwood, and 1.1 per cent by his mother's investment company, Acrux. If all his relatives remained in the company, as he believed they would, and the superannuation funds retained half their present shareholding, the bid vehicle ought to buy 140 500 000 shares. That would leave Warwick with 60.7 per cent of a company owned exclusively by himself, the rest of the Fairfax family and the John Fairfax Ltd superannuation funds. At $7 per share the cost would be $980 million.

But what if $7 was not enough? In the third week of August the market price rose above $6. Holmes à Court was said to be buying again, and the price was still rising. And what if some or all of the relatives and funds sold out? If it became necessary to bid for all 224 150 000 shares not under Warwick's control already, the bid cost at $7 would be $1569 million; at $8 it would be $1793 million. As the relatives and superannuation funds between them controlled 48 per cent, what was to prevent them from aligning themselves with another 2 per cent, thus denying Warwick his control? Holmes à Court, Packer and Abeles were all known to have small holdings, and could be expected to seek some advantage from the struggle.

So many factors were unpredictable that the evolving plan consisted more of hope than confidence. The most important variable was the family, and on that account the plans prepared in August included substantial inducement for all the Fairfaxes to stay in. At first they were to be offered a large return of capital from the proceeds of asset sales, in the form of special dividends and redeemable preference (non-voting) shares in the bid vehicle. James Fairfax, whose holding amounted to 17.9 per cent (Kinghaven's 11.3 per cent held in trust for Warwick, and 6.6 per cent under his own control), would receive a capital return of $69 million, half in cash and

Warwick Geoffrey Oswald Fairfax, aged nineteen, as he appeared on Fairwater's Christmas cards in 1981, ready for work experience at an advertising agency; (right) his mother, Lady Fairfax

Laurie Connell and Warwick Fairfax at the Rothwells office in Sydney in 1987

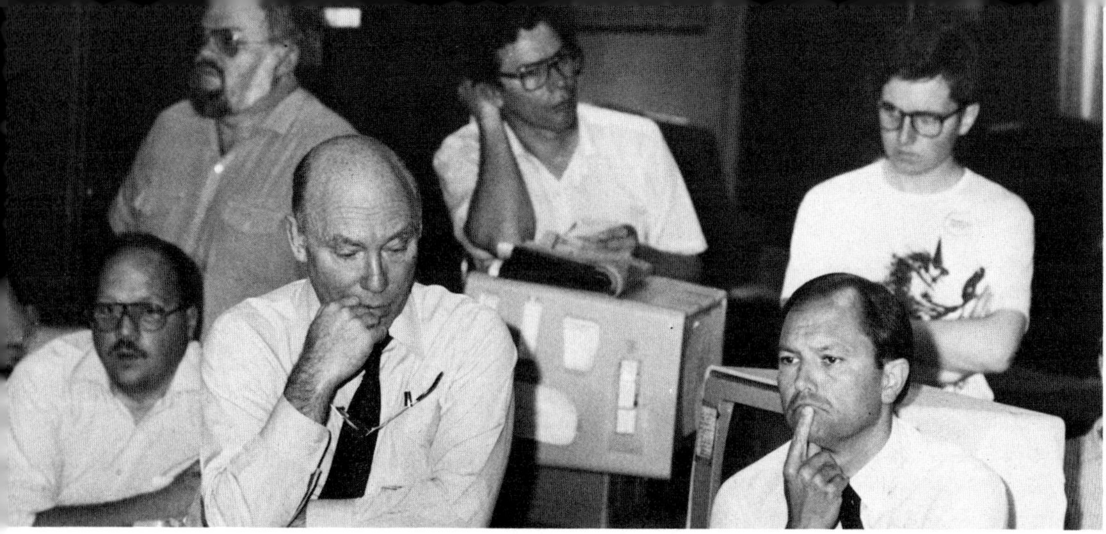

With Visigoths at the gate: (above) Max Suich and Chris Anderson at a meeting of journalists at Broadway during Tryart's takeover bid, September 1987; (below) James Fairfax delivers his chairman's address at the last annual general meeting of John Fairfax Ltd, September 1987: seated, left to right: Sir Eric Neal, Sir Vincent Fairfax, company secretary Ian Cumming, Greg Gardiner and Sir David Griffin.

After the takeover a visual display terminal installed in Martin Dougherty's office became a contentious industrial issue, and was removed.

half in preference shares. 'Dynasty Cousins', the code-name signifying Sir Vincent and John Fairfax and other members of that branch of the family (15.6 per cent), would receive $164 million divided the same way. Other Dynasty members apart from Warwick's branch (2.8 per cent) would receive $32 million, but no preference shares.

In the next version of the plan, however, the preference allotments for James and John were not mentioned. James would merely be offered $36 million as a special cash dividend, and the 'Dynasty Cousins' $31 million. Warwick's bid vehicle would be paid $93 million as a special dividend on its newly acquired Fairfax shares, and he and his mother would receive $28 million for their 14 per cent.

These special dividends would be paid out of capital profits from the sale of several assets: the payments still to be made by Universal Telecasters from the Seven television network; the Macquarie radio network; and shares in the new David Syme, by which means that company's assets and such other Fairfax assets as the *Financial Review* would be partly sold to the public. Reuter estimated the proceeds at $2012 million.

After repaying $300 million of Fairfax's $481 million corporate debt, the amount available from asset sales for distribution would be $1712 million. Of that amount, $200 million would be absorbed by the special dividends, and at least $900 million would be used to buy preference shares in the bid vehicle, thus enabling it to repay its borrowing for the takeover. If the bid price had to be raised, John Fairfax Ltd could subscribe for more preference shares. Another option to extinguish the bid vehicle's bank loan, according to the plan, would be for the superannuation funds to subscribe for preference shares too.

As further incentive for James and John to retain their shares, they would be made welcome on the privatized Fairfax board. James would also be invited to remain chairman of both the privatized company and the refloated David Syme. At one early meeting, Reuter said to Warwick: 'Laurie and I think that you should begin immediately the process of bringing the family up to a comfortable feeling about your plans'. Warwick persuaded them, however, that the rest of the family should not be forewarned. 'They have difficulty in making decisions', he said. 'If it was sprung on them at the last moment they would be paralysed by indecision and unable to come up with a sensible counter plan.' On another occasion, Warwick remarked to Connell that the approach to the family should be like a 'dawn raid'.

With dawn almost at hand, the raiding party assumed greater reality for those who were aware of its existence. It now had a name, for Fieldhouse had purchased a shelf company from Corporate &

Personal Planners Pty Ltd, a company 'factory' which registered about 7000 corporate structures a year, complete with articles of association and temporary directors.

As the name of each shelf company had to be unique, Corporate & Personal made maximum use of each prefix by tacking on to it as many suffixes as possible. Fieldhouse might easily have bought a company by the name of Tryarn, Tryarp or Tryash. As it turned out, the corporate vehicle for the Fairfax bid was Tryart Pty Limited. Its capital consisted of two $1 shares, held for the time being by Carnegie Fieldhouse and his son Simon.

Tryart went into operation at Rothwells' office in the AMP Centre, Bridge Street; at Fieldhouse's office in a building at Circular Quay East owned by one of his clients, the West Australian mining Croesus, Lang Hancock; and in Connell's and Reuter's suites at the Regent Hotel. At the centre of this rapidly accelerating activity during August, Reuter continued to revise the plan as new information came to hand. His knowledge of the target company, though incomplete, had been supplemented to some extent with board papers passed on by Warwick.

Reuter also negotiated a bank facility considerably larger than the estimated cost of share buying—in case Tryart had to buy more shares than expected, or raise its bid. Through his past association with Holmes à Court, Reuter had good personal relations with senior executives of the ANZ, and it was to that former banker of John Fairfax Ltd that he turned for assistance. On 19 August he went to Melbourne for a half-hour meeting with the bank's deputy chairman and chief executive officer, Will Bailey, and the general manager corporate banking, John McConnell.

How times had changed since 1956 when the ANZ had refused to honour some John Fairfax Ltd cheques because of a temporary liquidity crisis! Bailey and McConnell were favourably disposed, primarily because of their confidence in the target company's assets, and perhaps also because one of the bank's customers, Christopher Skase, had undertaken to buy the Seven Network. After another meeting between Reuter and two ANZ officers, Bruce Maisey and John Conn, a management paper was prepared for a loan of up to $1.31 billion. The term was to be six months, and as security the bank would hold charges over all the Fairfax shares acquired by Tryart and all those already owned by Rockwood and Acrux.

At a meeting in Fieldhouse's office on Friday 28 August, lasting most of the day and into the night, the principal members of the takeover group finalized their preparations. In view of the continued buying pressure on Fairfax shares, which had now pushed the price up to $7, it was decided to offer $7.50, and to obtain an even larger bank facility so that Tryart could if necessary buy all Fairfax shares not already owned by Warwick and his mother. Reuter phoned the bank, and the amount was promptly increased to $1750 million. As this was $70 million more than the maximum purchase would cost at $7.50 a share, it may have been that the possibility of a still higher price was being taken into account, or that some provision was being made for the payment of Rothwells' fee. The size of that fee, incidentally, was not mentioned to the ANZ.

Enlarging the bank facility affected the size of the commitment fee, which now rose from $6 million to $10 million. Although Connell had already agreed to cover this fee, and in the event was as good as his word, he nevertheless debated the point, arguing that unless Warwick was at some personal risk he would not be sufficiently dedicated to endure the ordeal ahead of him. 'On some days', said Connell, 'you will feel like it is not worth it, that you just can't go on. Unless you too are deeply committed then it won't succeed'.

'My experience with takeovers', said Reuter,

> is that you start off with a plan, but then events force you to deviate from it and often to such an extent that you end up proceeding very differently from the way you planned . . .There will be a lot of trials and tribulations during this takeover and I don't want a situation where you wake up one morning and decide that it's just too hard and that you don't want to press ahead with it. Some days you'll feel like you have a blow torch on your belly.

This admonishment was probably unnecessary, for Warwick Fairfax had already given ample evidence of his resolve. 'If the family sell', he was asked on one occasion, either by Connell or Reuter, according to Dougherty, 'then you will have to sell more assets. What is your attitude to that? What are the break points?'

'There are no break points', he replied.

> I'll go as far as I have to go. If I have to sell more assets, then I'll sell more assets. I would be happy if I ended up with the *Sydney Morning Herald*—if I owned it outright. If I can't retain the *Sydney Morning Herald*, then I would sell my shares and take my money and go and invest it in the United States.

At the Friday meeting Tryart's two shares were transferred to Warwick Fairfax and Rockwood, and the Fieldhouses were replaced as directors by Warwick, Reuter and Dougherty. Warwick and Connell also signed an agreement between Tryart and Rothwells under which Tryart, in the event of its becoming entitled to a 'minimum acceptance number' of shares in John Fairfax Ltd, would, within six months of that success, pay Rothwells the lesser of two amounts—$100 million, or 10 per cent of the price paid for shares in the target company.

For its part, Rothwells agreed to act as consultants and financial advisers to Tryart in all matters connected with the takeover offer:

instructing a leading firm of solicitors in Sydney, Blake Dawson Waldron, to prepare all legal documentation; arranging finance for the takeover offer; attaining the minimum acceptance number; and, if the takeover offer was successful, advising on the manner in which Tryart might deal with any debt incurred for that purpose. The minimum acceptance number was defined as being 36.15 per cent of the issued shares in John Fairfax Ltd. Combined with the 14 per cent already held by Warwick and his mother, this would constitute a majority of the company's shares.

With all major issues apparently squared away, Warwick was understandably elated. After leaving Fieldhouse's office he said excitedly, according to Dougherty: 'Laurie does not know it but I would have gladly paid him $200 million to get control of the company in my own right'.

Fearing a bid by someone else—probably Holmes à Court, as Connell kept saying—Warwick decided next day to announce the Tryart bid on Monday morning, and break the news to his relatives as late as possible before then. He telephoned his mother, who was in Salzburg, to inform her of this, and telephoned James Fairfax, Greg Gardiner and John Fairfax, making appointments to visit them in that order on Sunday evening.

On the Saturday he also met Aleco Vrisakis, a mergers and acquisitions lawyer from Blake Dawson Waldron, who had joined the group. Vrisakis told him to be sure to ask James and John whether or not they would accept the offer. If they were not going to sell they could be classed as 'associates' under the takeover code, thus clearing the path to compulsory acquisition, if that became necessary.

On Saturday night Warwick attended the 21st birthday party of Kerry Packer's daughter, Gretel. The party was held at Packer's mansion on Bellevue Hill, not far from Ginahgulla, which was now part of Scots College. Among the guests were Prime Minister Hawke, Premier Wran and Rupert Murdoch.

Next day, D-Day, Warwick received some last-minute instruction from Connell at the Regent. At first Connell had been doubtful about the young man's ability to deal with his relatives unaided, but he acquiesced when Warwick insisted on making those visits alone. It was agreed, however, that Reuter should be present at the meeting with Gardiner. Connell's advice to Warwick was to tell James and John that the offer was being made for the good of the family, to keep John Fairfax Ltd together, and to stop it being taken over by others. He should reassure them that they would continue to be involved in their corporate roles, and point out the benefits they would receive by way of special dividends. Finally, he should tell the family there was a strong possibility that Holmes à Court was going to bid the next day.

II

Soon after 5 p.m. Warwick left the hotel in a chauffeured white hire car, bound for his appointment with James at Darling Point. James Fairfax was not entirely unprepared for the news now to be imparted. He was aware of the other two appointments, and Gardiner had already telephoned him to compare notes, saying he guessed from the tone of Warwick's voice that the visits would be to do with a takeover bid, probably by Warwick himself. When Warwick broke the news, James's first reaction was relief that his half-brother was not proposing to join forces with someone outside the family. According to Warwick, his own first words were: 'I am planning to launch a takeover bid for the company'.

'Why are you doing this?' asked James.

Warwick then mentioned his fear that Holmes à Court would launch a bid next morning, and that some members of the family might sell. He covered all the points suggested by Connell, including the special dividend, and said: 'I assume that you will not sell'.

James at first said that he would not. But later, after Warwick had explained that although he wanted the rest of the family to retain their shares he himself would control more than 50 per cent, James said: 'I will not say that I will support the privatisation. Please wait for at least 24 hours so that the board can discuss this proposal'.

'I cannot wait another 24 hours.'

'Please reconsider.'

'I will not reconsider.'

At about 8 p.m., accompanied by Reuter, Warwick arrived at Gardiner's home in Vaucluse. He outlined his intentions and, according to Gardiner, invited the group general manager to continue in his present role, offering him an improved salary, an incentive scheme and a contract for whatever duration he wished. Reuter then expanded on details of the takeover scheme. When the visitors had finished explaining themselves, Gardiner said carefully that he was in favour of anything which would entrench the family's position in the company, providing it did not disadvantage minority shareholders. From what they had told him, however, he foresaw real difficulties for the other family shareholders. He also said that, in view of the proposed takeover, the offer of a contract for himself was inappropriate. (Reuter subsequently denied that any such offer had been made. Gardiner stood by his recollection, however, and although sceptical of the sincerity behind Warwick's offer he reported it to the board.)

Finally, at about 10 p.m., Warwick was driven to Lang Road, Centennial Park, where John Fairfax and his wife Libby, having returned that evening from a weekend spent with friends near

Cootamundra, were waiting up for him. The Fairfaxes had been intending to ask him to a small family dinner with Sir Vincent and Lady Fairfax. John now thought it better to wait until they heard precisely what Warwick had to say; but his wife, less cautious, raised the subject while chatting with their visitor. Warwick seemed nonplussed by this, and the Fairfaxes later attributed his nervousness to apprehension that his news was not likely to be well received. John and Warwick retired to the study, each with a glass of apple juice.

John, who had not heard from James or Gardiner, was taken aback by the news, and did not commit himself to any course. According to Warwick, he said: 'There is no way that I will support you. You will be tearing the family apart. I am not prepared to say that I will not sell as I have to consider my position'. By his own recollection, John said that as far as he could see the share offer would not be privatization involving family unity but rather a takeover by one member of the family. His own branch of the family would keep all options open—including selling, staying in, and even making a counter-bid.

Leaving his apple juice untouched, Warwick made an uneasy departure and was driven back to the Regent for a debriefing session with Connell, Reuter, Dougherty and Vrisakis. According to the driver, who later spoke about that evening to another passenger, Warwick said to Reuter, who was still in the car: 'My father said this is what it would be like'.

Back at the Regent, Warwick told Connell and the others: 'I do not think they will sell. They could, but I think that because of the 150 years of family history they will not'. Connell and Dougherty agreed. 'I think you are right', said Connell.

> For the first few weeks they will probably be aggravated and annoyed, but they are not going to actually sell out. There is a lot of cash here for them, so why would they sell out? It is very important to stay close to them during the first week, call them every day and try to explain things to them. Explain that the takeover is not directed against them personally.

After further discussion the meeting agreed to proceed as planned. 'Nobody could take you seriously if Holmes à Court makes the first bid', Connell told Warwick. 'If we get into a bidding war with Holmes à Court, don't count on the ANZ to support you. We now have the ANZ financing. You have the chance now, it might not be there again, I think you should go for it.'

Earlier in the evening Connell had telephoned Sir Peter Abeles with a view to securing TNT Ltd's 3.4 per cent parcel of Fairfax shares. That was easier said than done. When Connell told him of the intended bid, Abeles said that he had an appointment next day with Holmes à Court, whose holding was thought to be 3.2 per cent.

Connell asked Abeles not to deal his shares without seeing him first, and arranged a meeting for the morning.

Tryart's offer—announced to the Stock Exchange at 9 a.m., 31 August—was $7.50 cash per share, three David Syme shares plus $4.50 cash for every two Fairfax shares, or fifteen Syme shares for every two Fairfax shares. The cash option valued John Fairfax Ltd at $2.25 billion. This almost equalled the $2.3 billion of Murdoch's successful bid for the Herald & Weekly Times—though not, of course, his combined bid of $3.32 billion for HWT and Queensland Press. So feverish had the sharemarket become that this figure of $2.25 billion was about four times greater than the value conferred by the market only twelve months earlier.

Tryart's offer applied to all shares not already controlled by Warwick Fairfax and was conditional upon 90 per cent minimum acceptance. The market price immediately soared to a peak of $9.06, closing at $9. Next morning the *Herald* and the *Australian* predicted a counter-bid.

The *Australian*'s main front-page headline ('Fairfax bid too low for the markets') ran below a commentary by Bryan Frith entitled 'High risk strategy to buy back the jewel'. 'Mr Warwick Fairfax jnr has embarked on a high-risk strategy', wrote Frith, 'with his attempt to buy back the family's "birthright," the 156-year-old The Sydney Morning Herald; if it fails, the family could instead lose control of the Fairfax media empire'.

The *Herald*'s front-page lead ('Market tips fresh bid for Fairfax'), written by the Investment Editor, Alan Deans, concluded that the prospects for Tryart's bid had been diminished by the stock market's reaction. It also quoted Rupert Murdoch as saying that he thought the bid would succeed, although 'maybe not at this price'. 'It's a very courageous move', said the enigmatic owner of the *Australian*, Sydney *Daily Mirror* and *Daily Telegraph*, Melbourne *Herald* and *Sun News-Pictorial*, Brisbane *Courier-Mail* and Adelaide *Advertiser*, 'and I think it's the right move for him and his family. I wish I'd had the guts to do it when I was 26'.

It was said later that James and John Fairfax could have defeated Warwick at the very start by announcing publicly that under no circumstances would they sell their own shares. That would have denied him the 90 per cent acquisition which was a pre-condition not only of his bid but also of his bank funding. The takeover would have stopped in its tracks.

There were two reasons why the rest of the family did not react that way to Warwick's bid. Firstly, they did not initially rule out the possibility of staying in the company as associates in the takeover, for perhaps Warwick would end up settling for less than a controlling interest. James and/or John might well have agreed to a genuine family partnership, but not to one in which their young relative held more than 50 per cent of the shares. Secondly, a precipitate announcement by Fairfax family directors would have been detrimental to the interests of non-family shareholders intending to accept Tryart's offer.

Bert Reuter's prediction that events would force Tryart to deviate from its plan was borne out sooner than expected. Response from institutions to the all-share component of the offer was immediately so enthusiastic that Tryart, obliged to recognize that there would not be sufficient shares in the Syme float then being underwritten by the stockbrokers Rivkin James Capel, abandoned that alternative on 1 September. The offer of three shares plus $4.50 was retained, and any shortfall in the allocation would be offered to Fairfax shareholders.

No counter-bid was made, but before the week was out Connell knew that somehow he would have to deal with two particularly dangerous adversaries. On Wednesday Holmes à Court confirmed that he was still buying Fairfax shares; on Thursday it was reported that Abeles had sold his parcel to Kerry Packer. The market price closed on Friday at $8.80, and for the next two weeks was never far below $9.

As soon as possible Connell began what he called a game of bluff poker with Holmes à Court, Packer, Abeles, James Fairfax and John Fairfax. As he saw it, there were four obstacles. To start with, anyone who acquired more than 10 per cent of the Fairfax shares would be able to block a 100 per cent takeover, because Tryart would not be able to gain the 90 per cent necessary for compulsory acquisition. By now Holmes à Court probably owned about 5 per cent, and Packer's holding, depending on whether the report about Abeles could be believed, was between 3 per cent and 7 per cent.

The second obstacle was that Warwick 'spoke for' only 14 per cent of the stock. His holding was dwarfed by that of the rest of the family and was only marginally larger than that of the Fairfax superannuation funds, whose trustees were to some extent influenced by the Fairfax board. Thirdly, Warwick was in no position to service the loan which he had incurred to purchase the parcel of 1.5 per cent. Finally, he did not have the financial resources to engage in a bidding war. The other players had much deeper pockets.

Connell's basic strategy was, firstly, to convince the non-family players and other potential players that the Fairfaxes were a united bloc which would always act as such to prevent anyone but a Fairfax from gaining control; and secondly, as a corollary of that, to stop any section of the family making a counter-bid. Not only would such a bid destroy the perception of family unity but Warwick would be hard pressed to match it.

With those objectives in mind, Tryart resumed discussions with the family as soon as possible. Dougherty, in his dealings with the media during the first two or three weeks of September, managed to convey an impression that the Fairfaxes were staying together; and the Fairfaxes themselves, either as family members or company directors, did nothing to counter that.

On 3 September Warwick, Connell, Reuter and Vrisakis conferred with James and John Fairfax, Gardiner, and the company's solicitor, Rod Halstead. At Gardiner's suggestion they met in James's office at Broadway, but when Reuter began going into detail about the proposed restructuring of Fairfax and Syme they moved to a conference room equipped with a whiteboard. The scheme which Reuter outlined diagrammatically differed in some respects from the last 'Dynasty' plan. For example, Tryart was now to borrow $1.2 billion from the bank. This would be repaid with $1.2 billion subscribed by John Fairfax Ltd for preference shares in Tryart, derived from Fairfax's sale of the *Financial Review*, Fairfax Magazines and half of BRW to David Syme; its discounted sale of the Seven Network; and the sale of 50 per cent of the Macquarie Network.

David Syme, the present issued capital of which was only $12 million, would revalue its existing assets by $362 million and make a bonus issue for that amount out of the asset revaluation reserve. Tryart would lend $450 million to Syme on condition that Syme use it to purchase the specified assets from Fairfax and satisfy repayment of the loan by issuing 900 million 50-cent shares in Syme, thus absorbing the full $450 million. The bonus issue of $362 million would be designed to give John Fairfax Ltd a 45 per cent holding in the relisted company. Syme would issue shares to an estimated value of $450 million either to acceptors of Tryart's cash and scrip alternative offer, or to underwriters, and Tryart would pay an estimated $750 million in cash to accepting Fairfax shareholders.

Connell thought the Fairfax people 'did not seem to comprehend', and indeed they did find it difficult to see how the scheme could work. After the meeting broke up, Gardiner and Halstead were joined in the conference room by Barry Taplin—a senior partner of Touche Ross, auditors to the company—who was also an adviser to John B. Fairfax. Going over Reuter's diagram again, Gardiner came to two conclusions, with which the others concurred: the restructured company appeared more than likely to be non-viable; and for that reason, if no other, James and John would be unlikely to remain shareholders. In any case the meeting had left James and John in no doubt that if they remained they would be minority shareholders.

There had been no mention of Fairfax's existing $481 million corporate debt. If Skase's repayments were to go towards extinguishing Tryart's indebtedness to the ANZ, how could the cash-flow from Fairfax's reduced assets satisfy Westpac and NAB? Interest charges on $481 million would be $72 million, and that could hardly be met from a reduced annual profit estimated at $29 million. The only possible explanation, thought Gardiner and the others, was the existence of some other element yet to be revealed by Tryart.

The Fairfax board was bewildered. Not only did the available arithmetic of the takeover bid fail to make sense, but the intentions of the three Fairfax directors were as yet unknown to the other two members of the board (Griffin and Neal) and the management. At a board meeting on 16 September, Halstead raised the possibility of a conflict of interest for himself as the bid progressed. As well as being the company's solicitor, he had for some years past been adviser to James, John and Sir Vincent.

> He said at this time [the board] did not know where the affair was going to lead and, in fact, some of the family may align themselves with Mr Warwick Fairfax. He was concerned that independent shareholders should have access to advice from a solicitor other than the one advising the family. He believed another solicitor should be fully briefed.

The company did brief a legal understudy, who attended one board meeting. Before much longer, however, it became clear that Halstead would not have to stand aside. This was not for want of trying by Warwick and Connell. During the early days of the bid Warwick did his best to reassure the rest of the family. On the first Monday morning he telephoned Bill Anderson, Sir Warwick's stepson by his second wife. Anderson, a close friend of John Fairfax, had often tried to improve relations between the Fairwater and Elaine Fairfaxes, though not with much success. He now urged Warwick to telephone Sir Vincent about the bid, which Warwick did.

John had already broken the news to his father, who was recovering from a bout of pneumonia and a fall in which he had broken two ribs. 'If you think your ribs are giving you trouble', said John, 'I've got something to tell you that will make it much worse'. Later that week a bunch of flowers intended for Mary Fairfax at Fairwater was delivered next door by mistake. When Nancy Fairfax rang to let her neighbour know, Mary explained that she was not very well. '*You're* not well?' said the other Lady Fairfax. 'You can imagine how *we* are!'

On the day after the whiteboard meeting, Warwick was in the middle of writing a conciliatory letter to John when his telephone rang. It was John, inviting him back to Centennial Park that evening. He finished the letter and sent it ahead before going to see his cousin. Here, for once, Warwick lowered his habitual screen of reticence.

> John, I respect you a great deal [he wrote]. Your commitment to the company and family heritage is probably stronger than any of the rest of us in the family . . . I know that you feel very hurt now. You had a vision of another Fairfax who cared about the business coming

home. You wanted those two Fairfaxes to work side by side, as Geoffrey Fairfax and James Fairfax did before. Yet, no sooner does he come home, than he stabs you in the back and tramples on you. John, I understand how you feel. I am at a loss at how to get across that this was not an attack against you.

I have a vision that has been burning a hole in my heart for some time now. It has grown during the time that I have been away. It has come from reading many cases over the last two years about successful companies. It has come from working at Chase Manhattan Bank, where I felt like a very small unimportant cog in a big machine. It has come from working at The Los Angeles Times last year, where there was a tremendous feeling of loyalty and team spirit.

I want John Fairfax to be a company where there is a real sense of leadership and vision. I want people to be able to say that they know where the company is going for the next 10 years . . . In the three months since I have been back, I have found that the employees are very loyal to the company and that they would much prefer to work for us rather than Murdoch. But I want more than that. I want them to feel that senior management cares about their opinions and wishes to help each employee be the best that they can be.

Your vision for the company is probably not that different. However, I am afraid that I have not taken the time to learn about your vision . . .

Though we may differ on the business side at times, let us not let the decisions we make there impact on our relationship, which is far more important. What I did last Monday was for business reasons and I felt that despite the risks, that I had no choice . . .

Their second conversation was ineffectual. Asserting that the takeover scheme did not add up, John asked Warwick to 'come clean with us' and explain what other element was involved. Warwick insisted there was none, and went over the same ground again. Five days later he had a similar conversation with his brother at Lindsay Avenue. James said he had not decided what to do, but at the moment was not happy about staying. Warwick was glum but stoical.

Meanwhile John's branch of the family had been taking advice from Peter Mason and Brian Wilson of the corporate advisory service at Lloyds International merchant bank. James relied on Hungerfords, a firm of accountants, but it was understood that negotiations by Lloyds on John's behalf would have James's support. Rod Halstead provided legal advice to both groups.

After much preliminary discussion, the adult members of John's family met on 7 September in the offices of Touche Ross. Those present were Sir Vincent and Lady Fairfax; John and his wife; his brother Tim, who was a grazier in Queensland; his sisters Sally and Ruth, and their husbands Geoffrey White and Jonathon Armytage. The options before them, as written on a whiteboard by Brian

Wilson, were: '(1) Go along with Warwick. (2) Make a counterbid. (3) Accept Warwick's offer. (4) Attempt to buy some of the assets for ourselves. (5) Start an auction for the company by making it known that we have split with Warwick and will sell to the highest bidder'.

The decision of this meeting was to sell, and to try to buy some assets. John and his family were unwilling to start an auction, for fear of damaging the company; but they felt none the less that $7.50 was too low an offer. Mason and Wilson informed Rothwells of their involvement on 10 September, and negotiations began the following day. Martin Dougherty was still busily assuring the press that the family would 'continue its 150-year tradition of unity', and on 14 September the *Herald* reported that Warwick Fairfax would soon be issuing shares in Tryart to James, John and Sir Vincent Fairfax in exchange for their combined shareholdings in John Fairfax Ltd. This was totally wrong. On 16 September Lloyds advised Connell that James and John would be willing to sell for $9 per share.

Why the chairman and deputy chairman neither retained their shares nor mounted a bid of their own against what Sir Vincent termed 'the viper in our midst' perhaps needs further explanation. James knew that his shareholding would eventually become Warwick's, at least for voting purposes. The Kinghaven parcel (11.3 per cent) was a non-discretionary trust, destined for Warwick upon James's death, and under a codicil added to James's will in 1986 Warwick would also inherit the voting rights (though not the income) of the remaining 6.6 per cent fully owned by James. So why fight, James asked himself, if his own shares would eventually reach Warwick anyway? He would sell, and not attempt to buy any assets.

With James non-combatant, a fight would be too risky for John on his own. Of course he was not alone, but carried responsibility for all his branch of the family—some twenty beneficiaries in all. A share-buying contest was too expensive for them to contemplate, and in any case it might well leave them with a larger but nevertheless still subordinate shareholding. Their 15.6 per cent may have been a critical part of the wider family's 51 per cent, but on its own, or even united with James, it would be irrelevant after a successful takeover by Warwick.

For John and James alike, the prospect of being the minority in a company controlled by Warwick was intolerable. John was also aware that some members of his own family, richer in assets than cash, would welcome acceptance of Warwick's offer. 'This was an opportunity that was inevitable anyway', he said later. 'The company was going to be broken up one day—it had to be. This was the day, it had come, so therefore let's look at other opportunities.' At first it did not seem out of the question that even the *Age* or the *Financial Review* might end up with his branch of the family.

Connell was relieved to learn of John's interest in assets, for that would be a bargaining point in share price discussions. He had to argue Lloyds down from $9 while at the same time negotiating whatever asset sales seemed most appropriate for the conciliation of John Fairfax, Holmes à Court and Packer. John was in a strong position, for there was always the possibility that he might sell to someone other than Warwick. Consequently he could probably take first pick of whatever assets his branch of the family could afford, and then Connell would deal with the other two contenders.

Holmes à Court and Packer were out for all they could get. Both spoke to Connell about taking over the whole of Fairfax if they could. Alternatively, if the family stayed together, as Connell and Dougherty kept assuring everyone it would, they were prepared to be bought off for less. Both were keenly interested in the *Financial Review*. John Fairfax ruled out that possibility for himself when Gardiner and Suich persuaded him that it would be folly to separate the *Review* from its present advertising advantages and economies of scale within the Fairfax organization.

> A national Murdoch advertising sales network has been established [wrote Suich to John] and there are already moves to offer discounts . . . if Fairfax is excluded from the buy. We can resist this while we can offer the *Age* and the *Herald* together with their ancillary products such as The Good Weekend as a joint purchase of the key markets. We can similarly resist the *Australian* while we have the efficiencies and economies of scale of the *Age* and the *Herald* to support the *AFR*. But if the *Herald* or the *Age* or the *AFR* should become isolated from the main trunk of the Fairfax publishing group, or worse still become competitive with each other at the same time as they have to face the onslaught from Murdoch, then their current levels of profitability are just not sustainable.

As for the *Age*, John soon came to the conclusion that even if it was not to be floated publicly the price would be far too high for his family. He therefore opted for several less expensive but none the less attractive assets, and reached agreement to buy them in a telephone conversation with Warwick. Then Connell was free to finalize sales with the other two parties.

Holmes à Court was interested in the *Age*, and Packer in the *Sydney Morning Herald*; but Connell soon dispelled those illusions, saying that only a few assets would be sold. He regarded Holmes à Court as the more formidable of these two adversaries, and expected him to exact the highest possible price for his co-operation. This meant that the *Financial Review* would probably have to be withheld from the relisted David Syme, and sold to Holmes à Court instead.

And so it was, at least for the time being. According to Connell's account, he managed to divert Packer away from the *Financial Review* by convincing him that others were offering considerably more for it than he was. Packer then focused his attention on the *Canberra Times* and Fairfax Magazines. Connell also suggested that Packer take up $100 million worth of preference (non-voting) shares in John Fairfax Ltd, but this he declined to do.

Although negotiations with Holmes à Court had been proceeding by telephone from the start of the bid, Connell did not meet him face to face until 21 September. The assets under discussion then included the *Financial Review, Times on Sunday* and Macquarie Broadcasting. On 23 September Holmes à Court flew Connell and Vrisakis with him from Sydney to Perth in his Boeing 727. They negotiated all the way, and for another hour or so on the tarmac at Perth. It was a typical Holmes à Court fencing bout, replete with the usual feint, lunge and parry.

Next day the talks continued in Connell's office, broke down, and resumed at Holmes à Court's mansion in Peppermint Grove, where the three of them bargained into the early hours of Friday 25 September. From Tryart's point of view it was imperative, because of concurrent negotiations with Packer and the Fairfaxes, that the deal be concluded urgently. Holmes à Court was protracting matters by insisting that he needed to put some of his own people into Macquarie Broadcasting to establish the true worth of its assets. As Connell lacked the kind of information which might have reassured Holmes à Court, he agreed for the sake of expediency to a put option under which Bell Group could, if it so decided, require Tryart to buy back the radio network in six months time.

At about 3 a.m. an agreement was signed for the sale of the *Australian Financial Review, Times on Sunday, National Business Review* in New Zealand and Macquarie Broadcasting to Bell Group, and small portions of the Fairfax shareholdings in Australian Associated Press Pty Ltd, AAP Information Services Pty Ltd and Australian Newsprint Mills Ltd (6.3 per cent, 5.7 per cent and 7.1 per cent of the total issued capital of those companies respectively) to Bell's newspaper subsidiary, West Australian Newspapers Ltd. The price was $475 million. Because the deal was negotiated as a package, the component values were uncertain. Depending on whether the price for the *Australian Financial Review* was taken to be $350 million or $300 million (in different contexts, Connell later used both figures), Macquarie and the two lesser assets could be priced at either $125 million or $175 million, and Macquarie itself at either $100 million or $150 million. Under the put option signed with the sale agreement, Bell was entitled to sell back Macquarie for $157 812 500.

Although the interests in the news service and paper mills were relatively small, the selling of them involved certain difficulties of which Tryart did not seem to be fully aware. Since Murdoch's takeover of the Herald and Weekly Times, the two dominant shareholders in Australian Associated Press (which was merely a holding company for shares in the British-based newsagency Reuters Holdings Plc) and AAP Information Services (the operating news service) had been Fairfax, with 38 per cent of the shares in each company, and News Corporation with 45 per cent. West Australian Newspapers was already a minor shareholder with 15 per cent. Under the articles of association of both companies, any shareholder wishing to sell shares had to offer them first to all existing holders. A similar situation existed at Australian Newsprint Mills, where News Corporation had a pre-emptive right to prevent Fairfax from selling shares.

In addition to pre-emptive rights, the facts of life at AAP included a collaborative agreement between Fairfax and News, one term of which provided that if existing shares were offered for sale the Fairfax and News groups should each take up their entitlements so as to maintain respective levels of holding in AAP and AAPIS.

Tryart's deal with West Australian Newspapers was probably in breach of the AAP articles, and was certainly in breach of the Fairfax–News agreement. At one of the last meetings of the old Fairfax board, Max Suich, who was still a joint managing director of AAP, expressed dismay at what Tryart was doing. It was blundering into an area it knew nothing about, he said—an area very sensitive, and commercially important to Fairfax. Suich had spoken to Cowley of News Corporation, and had done all he could to ensure that the sale went ahead and that the relationship between Fairfax and News at AAP would not be impaired. Cowley had replied that he would facilitate the transaction providing Tryart satisfied him that it had no intention of working with West Australian Newspapers against News Corporation.

News of the Tryart–Bell–West Australian Newspapers deal began to leak almost immediately. The *Herald* prepared a story for Saturday's paper, but it was held out for want of confirmation. The *Times on Sunday* did the same. On Sunday the acting editor of the *Financial Review*, Glenda Korporaal, rang Suich at home to say that the investment writer Martin Peers had strong sources to confirm the sales of the *Review* and Fairfax Magazines. She read him the story. Suich checked with Rod Halstead, found that the story was basically correct, and rang Korporaal back, telling her to publish it. Korporaal, who had been expecting a denial and a direction not to publish, was shocked when she realized that her own paper had been sold. Before hanging up, she said to Suich: 'What a rotten way to find out!'

First thing next morning Korporaal went to the foyer of the AMP Centre, hoping to waylay Warwick Fairfax on his way up to the Rothwells office. He arrived at about 8.20 a.m. with two other men, who entered a lift as Korporaal introduced herself to Warwick. They had met at a dinner in New York. Were there any alternatives to selling the *Review*, she asked him. 'Oh no', he said, backing into the waiting lift, 'wait till it's all over, you'll understand later'.

The news came as an even greater shock to the editor, Alan Kohler, who was holidaying with his wife in Tuscany. Kohler had told his secretary that he would be phoning his parents, and through them Suich made contact with him on Monday afternoon. When Kohler heard the news he fell down in the phone box.

The way now seemed clear for Tryart. On Monday 28 September it announced the asset sales and a revised share offer which James and John Fairfax had accepted subject to there being no higher one. The new offer, with a reduced minimum acceptance level of 75 per cent, was $8.50 cash for each Fairfax share (valuing the company at $2.55 billion, which was more than 55 times the company's latest annual operating profit after tax), or $40 cash plus eleven Syme shares for every six Fairfax shares. James Fairfax elected to take cash—$141 million for his personally owned 6.6 per cent, but only $22 700 000 for the larger Kinghaven parcel, which at the full cash offer would have fetched $288 million. The price for Kinghaven was based not on $8.50, but on a net calculation of the dividends which James might reasonably have expected to receive from those Fairfax shares in the future, given the company's past performance and taking taxation into account. 'I thought he was crazy to accept it', said Connell later. As James saw it, he was simply abiding by the trust agreement which he had entered into at his father's request. As a secondary consideration, he also felt that holding out for a higher price might incur the penalty of being left as a minority shareholder in a much reduced company.

John B. Fairfax's family also took cash for its 15.6 per cent. The price was $397 million, but from that amount the family would pay $78 million for the Fairfax interests in Rural Press Ltd, Macquarie Publications Pty Ltd, the Eastern Suburbs Newspaper Partnership in Sydney, Stereo FM Brisbane Ltd, and the *Queanbeyan Age*.

In a third assets deal announced at the same time Kerry Packer's Consolidated Press Holdings agreed to pay $250 million for most of the Fairfax magazines (including *Woman's Day, Dolly, Pix-People* and *Australian Property News*, but not *BRW*, Good Weekend or *Spectator*), the *Canberra Times* and the free weekly *Canberra Chronicle*. The magazines were a logical acquisition for the publisher of *Women's Weekly* and the *Bulletin*, but rumour already had it that Packer might on-sell the Canberra papers to News Corporation.

'Fairfax empire split up', declared a seven-column headline on the front page of next day's *Herald*. A diminished John Fairfax Ltd was apparently going to consist mainly of the *Herald, Sun, Sun-Herald* and the regional newspapers in Newcastle and Wollongong, with a

45 per cent holding in David Syme. Syme would still be relisted on the Stock Exchange, but because of the sale of the *Financial Review* to Bell it would be capitalized at $500 million instead of the $824 million proposed earlier.

In a prepared statement Tryart said it had obtained agreement from Bell, Consolidated Press and John B. Fairfax that continuity of employment would be offered to all editorial and commercial staff of the papers, magazines and radio stations which had been sold. As originally drafted, this statement contained no reference to staff. That reference was included after intercession with Warwick by James and John. James Fairfax, in a separate statement, said he would continue as chairman of John Fairfax Ltd 'because [of his commitment] to the continuity of the business, both in the interest of the readership and the staff'. John Fairfax and his father would also remain directors of the privatized company, and John would remain a director of Syme.

On the evening these announcements were made, John was addressing a dinner for 25-year and 35-year employees at Broadway. 'You can well imagine how difficult it is for me to stand here and tell you this', he said. 'Everything I have worked for [has been] sold off or acquired by another member of the family . . . From your point of view you must now wonder what on earth is happening. I am just as shocked—totally shattered.'

The dawn raid had turned into a four-week-long siege, and although the main defenders had parleyed successfully with the enemy, and final surrender seemed inevitable, no one could say with certainty what the future might hold. A siege mentality prevailed at Broadway. Some executives began referring to 'the Visigoths'. On the editorial floor, rumours swarmed around the terminal network: Tryart intended to close the *Sun*, Tryart had a hit list, Murdoch was about to make a counter-bid . . . Finance reporters recorded every leak, and cartoonists lampooned the takeover bid without restraint.

'How do you start a small business?' asked a Patrick Cook cartoon in the *Financial Review*. Answer: 'Give Warwick Fairfax a big one'. Another cartoon was in the form of a film poster, by Pryor of the *Canberra Times*, showing Warwick on horseback in Mongol garb, with the flames of war behind him. 'A Tryart Production', it said. '"Young Genghis Fairfax" . . . In one afternoon he destroyed an empire which had taken a hundred years to build.'

On the *Financial Review* there were mixed feelings about Holmes à Court. No one relished the prospect of being controlled by one of Australia's largest market speculators, but at least under Bell's ownership the paper would be able to compete more vigorously with the *Sydney Morning Herald* and the *Age*.

From Tuscany, Kohler rang Holmes à Court in Washington, where he was attending a meeting of the International Monetary Fund. Holmes à Court invited the Kohlers to meet him in London and return home in his Boeing. When they met, he asked if they would like to see 'Phantom of the Opera'. The Kohlers had already tried, but it was booked out. 'That's all right', said Holmes à Court, 'I own the theatre, and I always keep a dozen tickets for my friends'.

On the flight back to Perth, Holmes à Court had a cold. After an hour's small talk he retired to one of four rooms on the aircraft and did not reappear for twenty hours. At Perth Kohler insisted upon some sort of discussion before disembarking. The running of the paper should be vested in the editor, he ventured, and the editor should hire and fire. 'That's all right', said Holmes à Court, 'as long as you understand it's not a right. You can determine the editorial content and hire and fire, but it's not a right. I own the paper'. With that to think about, Kohler flew on to Sydney.

Later Holmes à Court spoke to Suich and others, who reported their conversation in question and answer form to the employees. This was in sharp contrast to the level of communication from Tryart. On 10 September the 'Chanticleer' column of the *Financial Review* had published the contents of an 'information document' prepared by Rivkin James Capel about the forthcoming Syme float. Assuming annual cost savings of about $7 million, and circulation increases of 2 per cent for the *Age*, 15 per cent for *BRW*, and 9 per cent for the *Financial Review*, the document set a highly optimistic growth path for David Syme—18 per cent growth for 1987–88, and 39 per cent for the following year. According to the Melbourne *Herald*, the document also said that Syme publications would be 'even leaner', and that Bert Reuter 'would replace the already cost-conscious Syme chief Greg Taylor'.

Taylor reported angrily to his board that the document had created major morale problems:

> Internally, the report has created fears about future employment and career opportunities. The same fears surfaced after the 1983 Syme family decision to quit the company. They were suppressed by the sensitive handling of the ownership change by the Fairfax company and public assurances given by the Fairfax chairman, Mr James Fairfax. The present situation is aggravated by the prospect of a lengthy period of uncertainty before a final resolution . . . I am concerned particularly for my senior executives who must deal daily with the fears of middle level managers and their staff . . . Having pushed the value of the company up by more than 1000 per cent in the past four years, executives are now told by the Rivkin report that the restructuring would involve a major new round of cost-cutting.

In Sydney the Fairfax board faced similar morale problems. Executive service contracts were issued in order to preserve management and editorial stability, and Gardiner persuaded Warwick Fairfax, who had already apologized to Taylor for the aspersions cast by the Rivkin report, to telephone Max Suich. Warwick told Suich that he was prepared to talk to the editor-in-chief of the *Herald*, Chris Anderson, the editor, John Alexander, and Alan Kohler; but nothing came of this during the next few weeks. Warwick also arranged to meet Suich and Brenchley, but that meeting was cancelled and in spite of several phone calls from Suich it was never rescheduled. Not surprisingly, Suich and Brenchley concluded that they would not be welcome in the restructured company. Gardiner had been of the same opinion about himself from the start.

In his October report to the board, Suich wrote:

> The manner in which Tryart has behaved in relation to staff has been both out of character with past practices in [John Fairfax Ltd] and ultimately of likely disadvantage to Tryart and this company. The readiness with which Mr Holmes à Court has spoken to editors and given reassurances has been in considerable contrast with the difficulties management and editors at Fairfax have had in obtaining any kind of positive communication from Mr Warwick Fairfax . . .
>
> Details of the arrangements with Mr Holmes à Court are better known to Alan Kohler, because he had Mr Holmes à Court as his source, than they are to Fairfax management . . .
>
> The sale of *Australian Property News*—which is an important part of the BRW group—was not advised to Mr Gottliebsen in a conversation he had with Mr Fairfax in the days immediately after the Tryart announcement of the sales. He learned of it in the end from a leak—and the news came as a great blow.

BRW Publications in Melbourne had been particularly shaken by the Rivkin document, which set steep profit targets for the group and earmarked *Triple A* for closure. Robert Gottliebsen, the group managing editor, and three of his senior colleagues—Steve Congerton, Stuart Simson and David Koch—immediately renewed an earlier request to Broadway for equity in the business. 'Unstated but nevertheless very real', wrote Suich in a memo to James Fairfax and Gardiner, 'is the fact that if the board refuses the BRW team equity when the dust settles, they will probably depart'. The board noted the proposal, but felt unable to take such action. It did, however, issue service contracts to the four BRW executives.

Business Review Weekly was at that time under greater pressure than any other Fairfax enterprise, for on 1 October its competitor—Packer's fortnightly *Australian Business*—also went weekly. The first weekly edition carried on its cover a smiling portrait of Warwick Fairfax superimposed on the figure of Gainsborough's 'Blue Boy', with the legend: 'Young Warwick has claimed his estate. And driven some good, hard deals in the process'. The story was sympathetic, as might have been expected from the Packer camp, and it reflected the sense of satisfactory achievement then being savoured by Tryart.

Connell, satisfied that matters were 'stitched up' for the time being, departed on 4 October for 'a well-earned break in Hawaii'. Soon afterwards Warwick also left on a week-long trip to see Peter King in Amsterdam and Lady Fairfax, who had been overseas since August and was then in London. Tryart's Part A statement, containing information about the takeover offer, was served on John Fairfax Ltd on 9 October. It was dated 24 October, allowing Fairfax time to prepare a complementary Part B statement containing directors' advice and recommendations to shareholders. Before that date arrived, however, the Part A statement was overtaken by calamity.

III

On 19–20 October 1987 the world's stock-market, swollen by gluttony, suffered the worst crash in history on all major exchanges except Tokyo. In the first half-hour of trading on Tuesday 20 October the Australian market, reacting to events of the previous day in New York and London, lost one-quarter of its value. Fortunately the economies of Europe, North America and Japan were strong enough to resist a slide into world-wide depression; but for several weeks, as share prices continued to fall, the future remained in doubt.

The crash could not have come at a worse time for Tryart. Had it occurred only a few weeks earlier, the share offer could have been set at a much lower price. But the offer had been accepted by family shareholders, and the Part A had been served. The proposed relisting of David Syme was now in doubt, and among the crash's more conspicuous casualties were Tryart's chief adviser, and one of its main asset purchasers, Connell and Holmes à Court.

The only saving grace of calamities like Black Tuesday is that they visit nemesis upon greed and overweening pride. Rothwells and Bell Group, highly geared, and up to their necks in the stock-market, were suitable cases for retribution. Rothwells' shares, which had been selling at $3.40 in August, dropped to $1 in October. Bell Group dropped from $9.40 to $1.50, and Bell Resources, the group's investment company, from $4.70 to $1. Connell rapidly became preoccupied with his own commercial survival, and so also to a lesser but none the less substantial extent did Holmes à Court.

From here on the story of Tryart becomes steadily more abstruse as one difficulty or embarrassment is heaped upon another, like Pelion upon Ossa to reach heaven. As we shall see, Warwick Fairfax resolves to press ahead with the takeover; he gains full control of John Fairfax Ltd, but remains heavily encumbered with debt. Asset sales fall through, friends fall out, journalists go on strike, banks threaten to foreclose, plaintiffs go to court, and the company is eventually restructured and refinanced. And one other event, coincidental to our narrative yet strangely in harmony with it, should be noted from this tumultuous period. 'The Gates of Paradise' open within a stone's throw of the Fairfax building at Broadway.

After many years in storage at the Art Gallery of New South Wales, the plaster cast of Lorenzo Ghiberti's famous Baptistery door from the Florence cathedral, purchased in 1890 by Sir James Reading Fairfax, reappeared in the Neville Wran building of Sydney's new Powerhouse Museum of applied arts and sciences. This huge bronze-painted door—eight metres high and four metres wide, with ten bas-relief panels, each depicting a very detailed Old Testament scene—was erected in the entrance hall of the museum during November, and unveiled on 1 December. The *Herald*'s report of the unveiling ('Gates find new home') quoted the curator of ceramics as saying that plaster copies of important European works of art had been popular in the nineteenth century as a refresher to memory. 'They lost appeal this century', he said, 'but now they are back in fashion'.

The first panel showed Adam and Eve eating from the Tree of Knowledge, their Fall from innocence, and finally their Expulsion from earthly paradise by the Angelic Host. In other panels Ghiberti displayed some of the consequences of that first Fall and other Old Testament scenes: the murder of Abel by his brother Cain, the separation of Noah's three sons after the flood, rivalry between the brothers Isaac and Ishmael, Esau bartering his birthright to his brother Jacob, Joseph sold into slavery by his envious brothers, Joshua's conquest of Jericho, David slaying Goliath, and the judgment of Solomon. The impression of so much happening at once was overwhelming, and in a sense was not unlike that of the turmoil to which we now return.

In deciding to proceed with the takeover in spite of the crash, Warwick Fairfax chose to ignore an entreaty by his mother to withdraw the offer. Tryart's Part A statement provided for withdrawal with consent of the National Companies and Securities Commission, and the Commission might well have regarded the Stock Exchange crash as ground for consent. Furthermore, ANZ's funding offer contained a provision that, in the event of a significant change in the financial markets materially affecting the facility, the parties could seek a mutually acceptable solution. But did Warwick want to withdraw? On Black Tuesday, or very soon afterwards, he and Martin Dougherty were in Bert Reuter's suite at the Regent when the manager knocked on the door to say that Lady Fairfax was downstairs wanting to see her son. According to Reuter, Warwick said: 'Don't send her up because I don't want to see her'. Shortly afterwards he received a letter apparently written by his mother in the foyer. He showed it to Dougherty, then threw it in a wastepaper basket, from which Reuter later retrieved it. The letter asked Warwick to withdraw his offer because of the effects of the share market crash.

Soon afterwards, perhaps on the same day, Warwick said to Reuter: 'I don't want to withdraw. What do you think?' Reuter replied: 'One normally only gets one chance in a lifetime at a major objective such as this. This is a fact which has to be taken into account because you may not be able to come back again later because factors by then would have changed, particularly in respect to the family's position and attitude. You have agreements in place for the sale of assets and the bid is largely self-financed by these'.

On another occasion at about this time, and again according to Reuter, Warwick said to him: 'I want to be in control. My birthday is on the second of December. It would be a great birthday present if I was in control by then'.

On or about 21 October a meeting was held in Connell's office to discuss the implications of the crash. According to Dougherty, Warwick said: 'I am determined to proceed. The crash has been helpful in that it has guaranteed a speedy acceptance of the offer. There is no chance that any of the predators will double-cross me or of any new predators emerging'. Warwick gave a rather different account of this meeting. Connell, he said, advised against persevering with the Syme float, but at no time suggested to him that, because of the crash, he should reconsider the viability of the takeover proposal.

'The underwriting agreements are firm', he quoted Connell as saying about the float proposal,

> but we should not test them as this is not the sort of thing that one does to underwriters. The underwriters would take us to court to get out of the agreements. Besides, the Syme stock price will plummet, which would look bad. It would hurt Syme's future ability to raise capital.

At this meeting decisions were taken to proceed with the takeover but to delete the Syme share option from the offer, making it 'cash only'. There would be no float, and to compensate for that loss of capital Reuter suggested selling Fairfax's remaining news service and paper mill shares to the Murdoch group. As Connell was returning to his floundering bank in Perth, negotiations with News Ltd were entrusted to Dougherty. He contacted Ken Cowley, and on 26 October an agreement was signed for the sale of all Fairfax's shares in Australian Associated Press, AAP Information Services, Australian Newsprint Mills and Australian Newsprint Mills Investments Pty Ltd except those already sold to West Australian Newspapers. The agreed price for 38.3 per cent of the issued capital in AAP and 37.6 per cent in AAPIS was $120 million, and for 44.5 per cent of the ANM companies it was $150 million. News Ltd was also given an option to buy the suburban *St George Leader* for $5 million.

There was not likely to be any pre-emptive difficulty within AAP and ANM. But almost certainly there would be much public concern about the prospect of Australia's news agency and newsprint industry being almost completely controlled by one man, and an American citizen at that.

In Perth, Rothwells suffered the ultimate indignity of its trade—a run on the bank. As the *Herald* reported in its Page One lead on 24 October,

> Angry clients gathered in the foyer of Rothwells merchant bank and demanded to see its chairman, Mr Laurie Connell, or other executives.
>
> The clients were believed to be seeking funds owned by the merchant bank. It is believed that Rothwells' troubles stem from a clearing bank it dealt with which was taking a conservative stance in the wake of the stock market crash. Many clients are known to have been paid yesterday.

Next morning Martin Dougherty rang Max Suich at home to protest angrily at the report, which he said was likely to cause panic and worsen Rothwells' situation. Suich replied that it was legitimate news and, far from being sensationalized, had consisted of only two paragraphs buried in the main story of the day.

The run subsided. Several of Australia's leading entrepreneurs, including Alan Bond, joined forces with the West Australian Government to try to rescue Rothwells from collapse. The merchant bank Whitlam Turnbull set about discounting Tryart's $100 million fee, which would mean accepting less for the sake of obtaining it quickly, and Martin Dougherty applied his public relations skill to the rescue operation.

In early November, Whitlam Turnbull negotiated a deal by which the State Bank of New South Wales would make a cash advance of $75 million to Rothwells in exchange for full entitlement to the Tryart fee when that became payable. As a prerequisite, however, the State Bank required an unconditional undertaking from Warwick Fairfax that the fee would be paid. Reuter, at some cost to his personal relationship with Connell, advised Warwick not to give such an undertaking, as it would oblige him to pay the fee no matter what might happen in the future. This was sound advice, for the ANZ facility agreement had not yet been signed, and as already mentioned Tryart had not told the bank about the size of Rothwells' fee. Just what the bank's reaction would be to that information if it became known, as might easily happen during discount negotiations, was a matter of some concern to Warwick.

The State Bank decided not to proceed. Whitlam Turnbull then tried TNT Ltd, but Sir Peter Abeles's idea of discounting was more than Connell was prepared to forego. Finally, on 9 November, the fee was assigned to Bond Media for $68 million. Warwick signed a memorandum of understanding in which Tryart acknowledged itself bound by the agreement of 28 August with Rothwells, agreed that it was not presently aware of anything which would entitle it to refuse to pay the fee, but did not commit itself unconditionally. The fee was made payable directly to Bond Media, and at a somewhat later date than in the August agreement—29 June 1988, instead of six months after the acquisition of majority control, which had already occurred.

Such substantial discounting inevitably upset certain arrangements which had been made for sharing the fee. Originally Connell and Reuter were to have received $45 million each, and Dougherty $10 million. After the discounting, however, it was agreed that Reuter and Dougherty should receive between them only $10 million—Reuter, $8 million; Dougherty $2 million.

At some stage Warwick Fairfax became aware of this payment to Dougherty; but precisely when he heard about it, and how it was represented to him, would later come into dispute. Dougherty would assert that he had told Warwick about the fee-sharing arrangement, and that Warwick expressed his approval of it. Warwick, on the other hand, would maintain that he knew nothing about fee-sharing. Dougherty had said to him that he was receiving a fee of $2 million for his public relations work in connection with the Rothwells rescue operation.

As Warwick had feared, the enormity of the Rothwells fee did leak out. John McConnell rang Reuter to say that Will Bailey was 'very annoyed'; but this did not impede Tryart's access to the ANZ facility.

The ANZ had agreed in September to another increase in its proposed loan to cover the possibility of family acceptance. It had not invoked the 'significant change' clause over the Stock Exchange crash, and it was not likely to jib now over a mere $100 million. It was a case of 'in for a penny, in for a pound'.

Before the facility agreement could be signed, however, a rather delicate matter had to be resolved. It concerned Warwick Fairfax's mother, who was understandably alarmed by the crash, and offended by the brusqueness with which Warwick had dismissed her plea for caution. Lady Fairfax's personal shareholding in John Fairfax Ltd was larger than most of the Tryart participants realized. Warwick may have 'spoken for 14 per cent' before the takeover; but apart from his contingent interest in the Kinghaven parcel, his only personal shares were the 1.5 per cent which he had purchased earlier in the year and half (not all, as Connell and others believed) the 12.84 per cent owned by Rockwood. Rockwood's Fairfax shares were held by Tailer Investments Pty Ltd—half of them in Tailer's capacity as trustee of the Jones Trust, which meant Lady Fairfax, and the other half in its capacity as trustee of the Oriolo Trust, which meant Warwick.

According to a submission made several months later, during legal proceedings which will be explained in due course, Warwick was originally to have inherited the full 12.84 per cent from his father. But late in Sir Warwick's life, so it was submitted, Lady Fairfax prevailed upon her husband to alter his will so that she and Warwick junior would share Rockwood between them. These submissions were made in support of an application for access to Sir Warwick's will. As the application was denied, and Sir Warwick's will was not subsequently filed for probate, the facts of this matter remained confidential.

Whether or not the will was changed, however, Lady Fairfax's holding was now 7.53 per cent—6.42 per cent through Rockwood, and 1.11 per cent through Acrux. Worried that the substantial Fairfax dividends of the past might not continue, she declined to allow her Fairfax shares to be mortgaged to the ANZ under the proposed facility agreement until she was appointed a director of Tryart and John Fairfax Ltd.

As Warwick would not agree to that, his mother had to be reassured by other means. The matter was eventually resolved by an agreement dated 27 October 1987, between Lady Fairfax, Warwick

Fairfax, Tryart, Acrux, Rockwood and other family companies. In consideration of Lady Fairfax supporting Tryart and Warwick by leaving her Fairfax shares in the company, and of Acrux and Rockwood agreeing to mortgage their Fairfax shares to the ANZ, the parties gave several undertakings. Among other things, Warwick undertook to discharge all encumbrances upon Acrux within a year. Tryart and Acrux agreed to a put and call option on the Acrux shares, which provided that until November 1988 Tryart could require Acrux to sell the shares, and Acrux could require Tryart to buy them, at a price of $8.50 per share adjusted for cost of living.

More importantly, Warwick indemnified Tailer Investments, in its capacity as trustee of the Jones Trust, against any loss of Fairfax dividends for the rest of Lady Fairfax's lifetime. This would be done by payments of $2.9 million per year to Lady Fairfax, tax free and adjusted for cost of living, starting in 1989. The intention was to ensure that whatever happened at Broadway there would be no adverse effect upon the present rate of income earned by Lady Fairfax's shares.

Finally, Warwick agreed to help his mother acquire full ownership of the Grand Hotel at the corner of Pitt and Hunter streets. The hotel had been bought in 1985 for $3.1 million, 72 per cent of which was paid by Tailer and 28 per cent by one of Lady Fairfax's companies, 137 Pty Ltd. Under the 'Grand Settlement', Warwick provided his mother with $3.91 million for the purchase of Tailer's interest, and indemnified her against any loss which she might incur on selling the hotel. With Lady Fairfax thus reassured, the Rockwood and Acrux parcels were mortgaged. On 10 November Warwick signed an ANZ facility agreement for a maximum of $2.115 billion, to be repaid within six months of the first drawdown.

Two weeks earlier, on 27 October, the National Companies and Securities Commission had given its blessing to a 'cash only' offer. Tryart immediately dispatched the offer to shareholders, and on 30 October John Fairfax Ltd issued its Part B statement, in which directors unanimously recommended acceptance of the offer unless a higher one was forthcoming. On 5 November Tryart passed the minimum acceptance level, and its offer was declared unconditional. In five more days its shareholding reached 90.4 per cent, opening one of the two gates to compulsory acquisition.

With writing plainly on the wall, John Fairfax Ltd held its annual general meeting of shareholders in the Broadway auditorium on 28 October. It was a melancholy occasion. The cover of the annual report was a sombre grey out of respect for the late Sir Warwick Fairfax, and the chairman, as well as reviewing the events of the past financial year, permitted himself a few valedictory remarks. He and the deputy chairman, and Sir Vincent as well, had by this time decided to sever all connections with the company when Tryart formally took control. 'In the context of the takeover bid', said James Fairfax, 'I would like briefly to say something of the overall Fairfax family involvement with the company and its products spanning 146 years'.

> With my brother, Warwick Fairfax, joining the group in June this year, he became the thirteenth Fairfax to have a direct involvement with the company.
>
> It will be clear to you all that the family's sesquicentenary of publishing the *Sydney Morning Herald* will be celebrated in 1991. But the company itself will not be today's company. It will be vastly different.
>
> I cannot help but reflect on the significant and sometimes dramatic events which led to developing new products and acquiring existing ones. Editors, management and the directors have spent painstaking hours worrying about the various stages of development of both the *Australian Financial Review* and the *Times on Sunday*. They are both products of which we can be immensely proud . . .
>
> They reflect, just as the *Sydney Morning Herald* does, the objectives and purpose which first led John Fairfax to purchase an interest in the *Sydney Herald* in 1841.
>
> Both the *Financial Review* and the *Times on Sunday* are to be sold if Tryart's offer becomes unconditional.
>
> Macquarie, the magazines and the *Canberra Times*, all products which have been carefully but not aggressively acquired over many years, are also to be sold.
>
> Overall, the company has a leading edge, backed by a group of executives and employees dedicated to the application of their professional skills.
>
> It would be dishonest not to say that many of us associated with the company for so long are very sad to see a great organisation built up to be a world force in publishing, dismembered.
>
> Australia needs an independent press—a press that is prepared to stand aloof from Government and vested interests. To do that it must be strong and impartial. With the privatised John Fairfax Ltd that need not change, and indeed I hope and trust that it does not.

The events of 1986–87 reviewed by the chairman seemed to belong further in the past, for in spite of their importance at the time they had all been eclipsed by the intervention of Tryart. Thanks mainly to a huge AAP capital dividend from the sale of Reuters shares ($96 107 000), the total group profit was $133 190 000—99.6 per cent more than in the previous financial year. This was the first time in the company's history that profit had exceeded $100 million.

The most significant and controversial event of the year had been the purchase of HSV7. Referring to the subsequent sale of the Seven Network, the chairman announced revised terms of deferred payment. The sale agreement with Universal Telecasters had not been signed until 13 October, and Christopher Skase had managed in the meantime to reduce the first tranche due on 30 November from $470 million to $440 million.

'Directors considered the sale price to be most satisfactory', said the chairman,

> and certainly, on a proportionate basis, substantially above that which would have been obtained if the company had sold only ATN and BTQ. The significant decision to move out of television was designed to lead to a total elimination of the Group's debts and leave a substantial cash surplus. This cash surplus, together with the borrowing capacity supported by the ungeared nature of John Fairfax Ltd, and the powerful cash-generating assets it owns, had been planned to allow substantial growth by the company in its traditional newspaper and magazine field.

As if to show that the takeover bid had not sapped the company's initiative, the board had approved a proposal to purchase the prestigious but unprofitable American feminist magazine, *Ms*. Established in 1972 as a joint venture between Gloria Steinem, Patricia Carbine and Warner Communications, *Ms* had started out successfully. For the past few years, however, it had been incurring an average annual loss of $700 000.

Sandra Yates—who was supervising the launch of *Sassy*, now scheduled to begin publication in March 1988—had developed with Anne Summers, who was managing Fairfax's New York bureau, a plan to update and relaunch *Ms* as 'a good-looking, glossy news magazine for women'. The present owner, Ms Foundation, was looking for a buyer or partner, and on 17 September the general manager of Fairfax Magazines, John Hemming, and Summers made a full presentation to the Fairfax board.

Although Gardiner had doubts about it, most of the directors were favourably disposed to the project. In all likelihood it would be their last fling. Gardiner said the project was 'little better than a gamble, but he could go along with the view that such a gamble would expose the company to other opportunities should they arise in the United States'. Suich expressed the hope that *Ms* would form the basis of a larger group of publications, as *BRW* had done. Sir Vincent Fairfax thought the timing was bad, but as the other directors reacted with various degrees of enthusiasm, Hemming was authorized to pursue negotiations. Seven days later agreement was reached to purchase the magazine for $US10 million.

Gardiner, Suich and Brenchley resigned during the week Tryart's offer became unconditional. They were paid out generously by the board, and continued working for another two weeks. In this transitional period, the company provided certain information requested by Tryart—notably the facility agreements with National Australia Bank and Westpac for the HSV7 purchase, and the Seven Network sale contract. The board also agreed to give Australian Consolidated Press access to information about Fairfax Magazines, and to supply Tryart with copies of the service contracts recently entered into with thirty-four executives and editors who intended staying with the company.

These contracts allowed their holders to resign on advantageous terms in the event of 'material adverse change in the authority or status of the executive' or of 'persistent editorial disagreement between the executive and the company'. They reassured those fortunate enough to receive them, but were in themselves no guarantee that valued employees would choose to remain with the company.

Chris Anderson and John Alexander were both approached by News Ltd. Anderson, who had previously made known his wish to be considered for any future senior management vacancy at Broadway, was tempted by just such an offer from Ken Cowley in early November. He was invited to become an equivalent of Murdoch's chief executives in Melbourne (John D'Arcy, chairman and chief executive officer of the Herald and Weekly Times) and Brisbane (Keith McDonald, chief executive and director of Queensland Newspapers), reporting directly to Cowley, supervising all the Sydney newspaper operations, and joining a restructured News Australia board of directors.

Attracted by the offer, and uncertain of his future with Tryart, Anderson discussed Cowley's approach with Dougherty and Warwick Fairfax, who did their best to dissuade him from going. Anderson was 'the key to the building', said Dougherty during one conversation; nobody else at Broadway had his experience, and the new management would operate through him in any dealings with the editorial staff.

Max Suich, who was kept closely informed by Anderson, told the board at its next meeting, on 19 November, that he believed the editor-in-chief would choose to stay at the *Herald* and build upon his past seven years of hard work there. Suich was not certain of this, however, for one of Anderson's terms—that he report to the private company board—had been definitely ruled out. On editorial matters he would have to report to Dougherty. Warwick and Dougherty also spoke to Alexander, seeking to assure him of his future with the company.

The board meeting on 19 November was the first to be attended by representatives of Tryart–Dougherty and the lawyer Vrisakis, but not Warwick Fairfax. It was also the last meeting to which Gardiner, Suich and Brenchley reported. 'I would like to take this opportunity', said Gardiner, 'on my own behalf and that of Mr Suich and Mr Brenchley to thank the board'.

> No executive team could possibly have wished for a better, more productive or more supportive board to work with over the years. As a consequence of this outstanding board/management environment which was created, the company has benefited enormously during seven years since the board exercised its authority to appoint the new management team.
>
> The company at that time was capitalised on the market at a total value of $74 million. It was not even listed within the top 100 companies and it had just achieved earnings of $9 million after tax in the previous year. At today's date it is earning at the rate of $45 million per annum, its market capitalisation in the Tryart bid is $2.55 billion and it is the 12th largest company listed on the Australian Stock Exchanges. Even at half the Tryart bid price, it is capitalised at $1.275 billion and would be the 20th largest capitalised company in the country . . .
>
> I would particularly like to thank the chairman for the very productive relationship which he engendered between himself and myself as chief executive and even more importantly throughout the whole board and senior management team . . .
>
> I wish the staff who will be remaining with the company the very best for the future. I extend also to Mr Warwick Fairfax the best wishes of those senior executives, including myself, who will be leaving. He assumes control and stewardship of a great company with fine traditions and outstanding journalistic performance.

This was not an occasion for counting mistakes as well as achievements. But if it had been, anyone so inclined could have found fault with the stewardship of Gardiner and his fellow executives. It was said, for example, that the *National Times/Times on Sunday* and the *Sun* had been allowed to go on losing millions far too long. They were weakening the group. Gardiner knew this, of course, but argued that the company could continue to bear the *Times*'s tax-deductible losses until it would, as he trusted, eventually grow into profit like the *Financial Review* and *BRW*.

As for the *Sun*, he feared that closure would allow the *Mirror* and *Telegraph* to undermine the *Herald*'s advertising revenue. His strategy was to persevere with the *Sun* until a merger with the *Mirror* could be achieved, and negotiations to that end were already under way. At Brenchley's suggestion, Gardiner had raised the possibility of a merger while dealing with Murdoch over the purchase of HSV7. Since then Brenchley and a senior executive at News Ltd, Bob Muscat, had held several meetings to discuss such matters as production, editorial content, and cost of redundancy for a paper which they referred to as the *Smirror*. By mid-1987 Brenchley was optimistic that it would be printed at News Ltd, thus freeing more press capacity at Broadway for the *Herald*'s growing classified volume.

A second criticism was that the Arsycom débâcle had not been tackled as quickly as it might have been after the new management team took office. Gardiner acknowledged that he was 'slower off the mark' about Arsycom than Suich and Brenchley, citing heavy capital investment in the old system as the reason for his initial conservatism. Once the Arsycom débâcle was acknowledged, however, a new system was chosen and installed with great expedition. Broadway's plant had also been improved during the 1980s, but not as thoroughly as it should have been. And the problem of colour printing had not been dealt with satisfactorily.

As for expansion overseas, the company had made sound investments in New Zealand, designed to repeat the BRW exercise over there, and certain smaller investments in the United Kingdom. Buying the London *Telegraphs* would have been a triumph with which to silence the critics who expected more of the company globally. But that missed opportunity was more disappointing to Fairfax's management than it was to the board. Sir Warwick and James Fairfax both had doubts about the London *Telegraphs*.

The purchase of HSV7 and sale of the Seven Network were regarded by many as commercial mistakes of major proportion. Gardiner, however, continued to defend both the purchase and the decision to get out of television altogether.

Finally, it was said that the management had let Fairfax journalists get out of hand in their pursuit of the Wran Government, and that the company had suffered accordingly. Whether vengeful politicians had really tried to get their own back on Fairfax was difficult to decide. But a belief that they had—and had succeeded—most certainly existed both inside and outside the company.

Before the end of the November board meeting, Suich reported on the present condition of the main publications. The *Sydney Morning Herald* had finally broken through its long-standing 160-page production barrier on Friday nights, and the most recent Saturday edition contained 204 pages.

The average circulation, 258 684, was slightly below that of 1981, but the *Herald* had none the less consolidated its position as Australia's biggest selling quality daily newspaper, with a margin of 28 000 over the *Age* and 123 000 over the *Australian*. Its market share of classified advertising was 80 per cent, the highest for some years.

The editor-in-chief of the *Sun*, Ron Ford, had retired, and John Benaud was in full control. Ford's retirement had tended to strengthen rumours that the paper would be closed when Tryart took over.

The *Financial Review*, which had recently celebrated its twenty-fifth anniversary as a daily publication, was enjoying record circulation (86 000 immediately after the crash) and revenue. The *Sun-Herald* was trailing behind the *Sunday Telegraph* by anything from 10 000 to 20 000 per week, and the *Times on Sunday* was in the low

80 000s. It was rumoured that Bell would not retain Valerie Lawson as editor. If that happened, said Suich, she would be a considerable acquisition for Fairfax.

Brenchley warned of the many production difficulties which would be involved if, as seemed likely, Bell continued to publish the *Financial Review* and *Times on Sunday* at Broadway for some time. It was not possible, he said, to physically divide the computer typesetting system into *Financial Review/Times on Sunday* and *Herald/Sun/Sun-Herald* systems without disrupting its ability to cope with peak levels of the *Sydney Morning Herald* on Friday nights. This and other problems of partition were under constant discussion between Bell executives and the assistant general manager finance and administration, Max Pride; the assistant general manager operations, Frank McMahon; the editorial manager, John Richardson; the editorial administration manager, Crystal Condous; and the editorial production manager, Graham Stevenson.

Seven days later Tryart passed through the second and final gate to compulsory acquisition (acceptance by 75 per cent of shareholders), and on the closing day of the share offer, 8 December, it began to acquire the 4 113 766 shares still owned by 663 recalcitrant investors. The physical takeover had already occurred on Monday 7 December, when Warwick Fairfax arrived at Broadway for the inaugural meeting of his own board of directors. First, in company with Connell, Dougherty, Cotton and Vrisakis, he attended the last meeting of the outgoing board.

At the chairman's invitation Warwick nominated himself and Connell to fill two vacancies already existing on the board, and they were duly elected. Given the desperate plight of Rothwells, and Connell's less frequent contact with Tryart of late, his appointment had not been a foregone conclusion.

'Should I appoint Laurie Connell to be a member of the board of John Fairfax Ltd when we take control?' Warwick had asked Dougherty and Cotton at lunch in late November. 'What do you guys think?'

Cotton advised against such an appointment on grounds that it would impair the company's relations with bankers, who tended to have little sympathy with any of their own kind who were in financial trouble. Dougherty, on the other hand, sprang to Connell's defence, accused Cotton of hitting a man when he was down, and urged Warwick in the strongest terms to have Connell on the board. Warwick agreed to think about it, and ended by accepting Dougherty's advice.

After Warwick and Connell had been elected to the board James Fairfax tabled letters of resignation from all five directors of the old board, and these were accepted. James asked his brother to assume the chair, and Connell proposed the appointment of Dougherty,

Peter King

Ron Cotton

Martin Dougherty and Laurie Connell

HOW WHIZKID BEAT THE SCHOOL RULES
Full story – Page 3

The Sydney Morning Herald

Late Edition No. 46 724 First Published 1831 Tuesday, Sep

WHEN JUDGES DISAGREE
FEATURES

TEEN MOVIES
AGENDA

Financial Review, radio network, magazines sold

Fairfax empire split up

MEDIA DEAL: WHO WINS WHAT

WARWICK FAIRFAX	JOHN FAIRFAX	KERRY PACKER	HOLMES à COURT
The Sydney Morning Herald, THE AGE, BRW, The Sun, The Sun-Herald	THE LAND, Wentworth Courier, The Fairfax interest in: Macquarie Publications, Eastern Suburbs Newspapers, Rural Press	The Canberra Times, WOMAN'S DAY, COSMOPOLITAN, Dolly, people	FINANCIAL REVIEW, TIMES on SUNDAY, 2GB, Macquarie Radio Network

It's 3 am and deal is signed

INSIDE

Governor swears to defy coup

Tearful end to new life

Parents, children who make a bad mix

Asset buyers, real and illusory: according to the *Sydney Morning Herald* on 29 September 1987 (top right) Tryart had financed its takeover mainly by selling assets to Robert Holmes à Court (top left), Rupert Murdoch (below) and Kerry Packer. The Holmes à Court deal disintegrated, and those with Murdoch and Packer had to be re-negotiated.

Christopher Skase (below left), who bought the Seven Network, and Tryart's adviser, Bert Reuter

Cotton and Peter King as directors of John Fairfax Ltd. King was not taking office as chief executive until March. He flew out from Amsterdam for the handover, but did not attend this board meeting. At the conclusion of proceedings Dougherty—designated as group managing director editorial—congratulated James Fairfax on the dignified manner in which the handover had taken place. James and John Fairfax also resigned from the David Syme board, and the deputy chairman of that board, W. G. Bland, succeeded James Fairfax as chairman.

Later on 7 December a second Fairfax board meeting resolved to convene a general meeting of members of the company (which for practical purposes meant Warwick Fairfax) to approve the granting of financial assistance by John Fairfax Ltd to its holding company, Tryart. The assistance would be a loan of up to $1115 million, derived by Fairfax from the sale of assets, and passed on to Tryart for the purposes firstly of enabling that company to repay the ANZ loan with which it had bought Fairfax shares during the takeover, and secondly of enabling Rockwood to repay its borrowing (initially from the Midland Bank, but now refinanced with ANZ) for the earlier purchase of 1.5 per cent.

Formerly, in more moderate times, the New South Wales Companies Code would have prohibited this kind of assistance. In 1981, however, Section 129 of the Code helped set the stage for the takeover boom which was to assume such monstrous proportions in that decade. Henceforth—provided that creditors were properly informed, and so enabled to take legal action if considered necessary to protect their interests—any company could resolve in general meeting to approve the granting of assistance to another company, even a $2 shelf company such as Tryart, which had taken it over with borrowed money.

Hence the general meeting, held on 11 December and attended only by Warwick Fairfax, Dougherty and two Fairfax executives.

In compliance with Section 129, the new Fairfax directors had also resolved on 7 December that in their opinion the granting of assistance to Tryart would not be likely to prejudice the interest of creditors. This was widely advertised, as required by the Code, and any creditors choosing to object could apply to the Supreme Court within twenty-one days to oppose the resolutions of the general meeting.

In his new capacity as proprietor—a title last used by his great-grandfather, Sir James Reading Fairfax—Warwick Fairfax issued a statement of principles for publication in the *Herald* and the *Age*. This caused some concern on the editorial floors. A draft of the statement was first shown to John Richardson on the evening of 7 December by Martin Dougherty's brother Paul, who was joining the company as executive editor planning and projects. Richardson, whose responsibility included industrial relations, said he thought the statement reflected badly on past journalistic practices and consequently might provoke industrial action by journalists. He suggested several changes.

Chris Anderson was similarly concerned when Richardson showed him the draft, and Creighton Burns, the editor of the *Age*, let it be known at one stage of the evening that he would not necessarily be publishing any of it. Nevertheless the statement, incorporating most of the changes suggested by Richardson and one by Anderson, appeared in both papers next morning:

> What we are trying to do is nothing new. Rather we seek to maintain the company and its newspapers firmly within the tradition started by John Fairfax and continued for much of the past 150 years.
>
> Editorially, we seek to report the facts. Nothing more, nothing less. We should strive to keep opinions out of the news reports in our papers and we must not allow the news to be slanted in any way.
>
> When one set of views on an issue is reported, we will continue to ensure fair representation is given to opposing viewpoints. In the same way, we will continue to ensure that our published commentaries cover a variety of opinions.
>
> Our editorials will continue to strive to be balanced and thoughtful. We do not seek to favour any political party or viewpoint.
>
> We do not see it as our role to change Australian society. That would be gross arrogance. It is our more modest goal to equip people with the information they need to make their own judgments.
>
> Within this charter, we will also try our best to be bright, readable and—where possible, and appropriate—entertaining.
>
> Our management philosophy is simple. We seek to create a caring and supportive company, where excellence at all levels is encouraged. It is a rather old cliche, but the success of the company depends on its people . . .
>
> We will treat all people with honesty, openness and respect.
>
> These are the goals for which we will strive. They provide a benchmark for what we are trying to do.

On this eventful day Bert Reuter composed a position paper for the new Fairfax board. It assumed that the objective of the Tryart-Rothwells agreement had been attained, and that the two advisers, Connell and Reuter, would now enter an 'as required' phase.

> The bulk of the day-to-day requirements relative to the contract settlements, refinancing requirements and company restructuring will be handled by the company executives under the management control of Ron Cotton and in liaison with the legal team at Dawson Waldron. The next 12 months period will be the most critical in respect of achieving the financial structure both from a gearing and ongoing operational basis to ensure maintenance of group viability.

After reviewing outgoings for share acceptances and the Rockwood loan settlement (total: $2026 million) and the expected income from asset sales and the Universal Telecasters settlement (total: $1970 million), leaving a shortfall of $56 million, Reuter listed several financial commitments facing the company in 1988. These amounted to another $809 million. 'The [shortfall] will require refinancing to achieve the optimum long term borrowing structure for the new Group', he wrote.

> Borrowing ratios will need to be closely scrutinised to ensure normal banking requirements are achieved. The failure to achieve this will require the sale of further assets . . .
>
> In conclusion, may I wish the new Board of Directors and management the highest level of success in the building of a new dynamic media organisation.
>
> 'They said we wouldn't make it . . .'

Reuter's jaunty allusion to Bond Brewing's television commercial was more than a little premature. His congratulatory tone may have been understandable in the flush of success. But the way ahead was beset with many dangers, some already manifest, others vaguely discernible, and still others not suspected.

8
The Fall

I

On Tuesday evening, 8 December 1987, Lady Fairfax held a victory dinner at Fairwater to celebrate her son's assumption of board and management control. Not everything in the garden was lovely, but at least all the known problems seemed solvable. Universal Telecasters Ltd was running several days late with its $370 million instalment for the Seven Network purchase, but according to the ANZ, which was banker to Christopher Skase as well as to Tryart, the money would soon be forthcoming. Tryart intended using the Skase payment to help discharge its own obligation to the ANZ, but Fairfax's chief accountant, Barry Moore, had recently drawn Ron Cotton's attention to a difficulty about that. The Skase payment due in November had already been earmarked for the two banks which had funded Fairfax's purchase of HSV7, the National Australia Bank and Westpac.

'Ron, you would be aware that I am not rolling over the NAB and Westpac bill facilities for $150 million each', said Moore at a meeting with Cotton on 27 November to discuss the company's financial position. Cotton, the new group managing director, was in charge of the company's business affairs, as the chief executive officer, Peter King, was not expected to take up his post until 1 March.

'Barry, just wait a minute, that's $300 million', said Cotton. 'Why do you say you're not rolling them over?'

'Because our arrangement with NAB and Westpac is that when we receive the Skase monies the banks will immediately receive these funds.'

'At this end', said Cotton, 'that is not my understanding. It is expected that both banks will continue to maintain those lines to Fairfax'.

'Well, I am not aware of it. In fact, I have a letter drafted which I am about to send telling NAB and Westpac that they will be repaid at the end of the month.'

On Cotton's instruction, Moore delayed sending the letters until Cotton could speak to Reuter. There had been no discussion with

NAB and Westpac, said Reuter, seemingly unperturbed, because they were the company's bankers and Tryart saw no reason why they would not continue the facilities. 'Well Bert, I don't think the banks will see it that way', replied Cotton, 'and this is an issue that we will need to clarify quickly. I will advise Barry Moore not to send his letters and to contact the banks indicating to them the expectation that [the facilities] will be rolled over'.

Reuter and Cotton drove to the victory dinner together, and on the way they discussed some of the points raised in Reuter's position paper, which Cotton had received earlier that day. By way of general advice to Cotton, Reuter stressed the need for Peter King to take charge as soon as possible. He said there might be some difficulty with Dougherty, who was relatively inexperienced in corporate management; and Connell's presence on the board could pose a problem. The company had tremendous potential, but would require a lot of hard work from Cotton and his colleagues. 'You are in for a very tough year', said Reuter.

Apart from such considerations as Skase's tardiness, bankers' precedence and human compatibility, the outlook was auspicious for those dining at Fairwater on Tuesday evening. Cotton, who was seated at a table with Lady Fairfax, Warwick, Connell and Vrisakis, made a short speech thanking everyone for their efforts. He referred to the 'clever way' in which Tryart had been able to achieve 'the impossible', and said that it was now up to Warwick Fairfax and his executive team to get on with the job of restoring Fairfax to its 'former glory'.

Warwick spoke even more briefly. 'A lot of people thought this could not be done', he said, 'but it has been and I would like you to drink a toast to the future of the company'.

Next day Cotton received three pieces of unwelcome information. First, one of Tryart's proposed asset sales appeared to be coming undone. According to the morning papers, Holmes à Court had declared his intention to exercise the put option concerning Macquarie radio network. This was the first Cotton had heard of any option, and he rang Reuter in some alarm.

'What's this about a put option that Holmes à Court is going to exercise?'

'What put option?' asked Reuter. 'I don't know about a put option.'

'It's in all today's papers that Holmes à Court has announced that he will put back the Macquarie Network to us for a price of $158 million.'

Dawson Waldron sent Cotton a copy of the option agreement, and he rang the beleaguered Connell. 'Leave it to me', said Connell, 'I have a lot of things to sort out with Robert and will be talking to him about this'.

The second piece of bad news was that one of Fairfax's unsecured creditors, Chase AMP Bank Ltd, had written asking for reassurance about its loan. This was the first request of its kind, but was unlikely to be the last. Cotton quickly sent a circular letter to the twenty banks to which John Fairfax Ltd owed its existing corporate debt of $481.7 million, seeking to assure them of the company's stability.

As a third blow that day, Barry Moore told Cotton that the Fairfax superannuation funds were Section 23F funds under the Income Tax Assessment Act. This implied a serious shortfall in one of Tryart's basic financial assumptions—that the retirement and welfare funds, which collectively held 11.7 per cent of the Fairfax shares, would reinvest a substantial part of whatever financial benefit might accrue to them as a result of the takeover. There were six funds: the main John Fairfax Retirement Fund, the John Fairfax Supplementary Retirement Fund, the Fairfax Long Service Retirement Fund, the Fairfax Staff Provident Fund, the Sydney Morning Herald Centenary Fund and the Fairfax Foundation. All but the first of these were non-contributory. The last two were endowed for selective welfare purposes, and had no memberships.

Traditionally, all six funds invested in Fairfax shares held in trust for them by Vident Pty Ltd. This was a strategic advantage for the company, and profitable for contributors. But not all companies were such good investments as Fairfax had been, and in 1985 the Commonwealth parliament legislated to prevent superannuation funds from putting too many eggs in their employers' baskets. This was done by amending the Income Tax Assessment Act to impose a limit of 10 per cent on the extent to which superannuation trustees could invest members' funds in employing groups and still retain full tax concessions. Investments of this kind made before 1985 were exempt for the time being, but would have to be reduced to the prescribed percentage by 1994.

The trustees of all Fairfax funds, contributory and non-contributory alike, resolved on 4 November that acceptance of Tryart's cash offer would best serve the interests of members and, where there were no members, the interests of the funds. For their Fairfax shares, which had previously been written up at only $2 each (total book value, $70 200 000), the funds collectively received $299 million. The main contributory funds, John Fairfax Retirement Fund and Fairfax Long Service Retirement Fund, received $95 300 000 and $70 915 000 respectively. To reinvest any of this in Fairfax would have meant the loss of tax concessions, and, in the unanimous view of the trustees, would not have served the interests of members. Instead of passing most of the bonanza back to Fairfax, and so to Tryart, Vident put it straight on to the money market pending pro rata allocation to members and payment to them upon retirement.

Exactly how much Tryart had expected from the funds varied

according to Reuter's successive working papers. The latest assumption had been about $200 million, and it was a shortfall of this size that Cotton discussed, first with Moore and then with Reuter. Reuter had mentioned the problem in his position paper of 7 December, but not so bluntly as Moore had. 'As previously advised', wrote Reuter,

> the new legislation in force at present relative to superannuation funds prohibits company funds investing an amount greater than ten per cent of the total net worth of the fund with the employing group. To achieve the required position relative to the reinvestment will require a negotiated position with the trustees . . .

Perhaps, in the confusion of taking up his new position in Greg Gardiner's old office, Cotton had not read this part of Reuter's paper, for Moore's warning seemed to come as news to him. 'Barry Moore tells me', he said to Reuter, 'that in the takeover financing estimates it is assumed that the superannuation funds will be used, and they cannot be, with the exception of ten per cent, because they are Section 23F funds. We have a shortfall of about $200 million'.

'Yes, I am aware of that', replied Reuter, 'but I don't see it as a problem because we should be able to negotiate with a financial institution, such as AMP or National Mutual, to invest the superannuation funds' money with them and then for them in turn to lend it back to Fairfax'.

But it was a problem. Indirect investment proved to be impractical, and newly appointed trustees were no more inclined to reinvest funds than their predecessors had been. In the long run only $48 million came back to Fairfax—$10 million in the form of a loan from the Fairfax Foundation and $38 million from the Centenary Fund, under deeds of covenant requiring the company to use the loans for the purpose of maintaining its superannuation contributions, even in adverse economic circumstances.

These three set-backs—the brandished put option, the nervous creditor, and the superannuation shortfall—were like drops of rain portending a downpour. More aptly, they portended a fall; a falling away from ambition and innocence; a Fall distantly but none the less pertinently related to that ancient myth depicted by Ghiberti on the Gates of Paradise. As Sir Warwick Fairfax had written in *The Triple Abyss*, the story of Adam and Eve is an account not of events but of principles. 'Genesis', he wrote,

> is not saying that two ancestors of the human race were at one time perfect and fell from perfection. What it is saying is that the human organism, unlike the rest of creation, embodies within itself the principles of perfection in the image of God, but continuously and inevitably through its own choice and its own frailties falls away from this.

Others, including theologians, have viewed the Fall of Man not as religious dogma or myth but as a universal expression of the human predicament. 'In a certain sense all life is a falling', said one writer, '—a falling below and away from one's aspirations, one's ideals, one's hopes, one's intentions. Falling short is a reality even if the ideas of an aboriginal Fall and inherited guilt seem unimaginable and are virtually meaningless'. It matters little, according to another,

> whether the Fall occurs by choice or by act of destiny, whether it comes at adolescence or birth or even old age, whether it takes place quietly within the self or dramatically and in public view. Everywhere testimony of the Fall surrounds us . . . However altered by psychology and behaviourist thought, by technology and scientific determinism, [the Fall] still offers an appropriate metaphor for what it means to be human. And the very pattern of the Fall—the movement from a garden state to temptation to self-knowledge to consequences—remains an apt description of the human drama.

Warwick Fairfax the younger had dwelt in the garden states of Fairwater, Cranbrook, Balliol, Harvard and Chase Manhattan, and had eaten from the tree of self-knowledge. Now, dramatically and in public view, he was falling away from the vision which had been burning his heart. His was a Fall brought about equally by choice and act of destiny. He had chosen to seize control of the company without proper consultation with his relatives, and they had not acquiesced as he had expected them to. He had also dared outrageous fortune by choosing to proceed in spite of the stock exchange crash.

In theological terms, the Fall is not a break, but an imperfect fulfilment. It is the prelude to a re-birth, for as Sir Warwick put it, 'without a Fall there could not be a Redemption'. This comforting thought may conceivably have occurred to the son, who was well versed in such matters; but more likely, amid the distractions of adversity, it did not. The slings and arrows were beginning to fly.

One after another, the asset sales fell foul of legal and other troubles. On 14 December Kerry Packer sought to renegotiate his agreement on grounds that Connell had misrepresented the profitability of the *Canberra Times*. Until then, the sale had seemed sufficiently certain for the retiring general manager of Federal Capital Press, Graham Wilkinson, to deplore the change of ownership. In a candid farewell speech, reported on the front page of the *Canberra Times*, Wilkinson accused Warwick Fairfax of 'wrecking' the Fairfax group of companies. Of the *Canberra Times*, he said:

> Let us pray that Mr Packer will recognise that the responsibility of being a publisher is to give the editor clear guidelines that are acceptable to the editor's standards and leave him alone to carry out his or her duties.
>
> Proprietors should feel free to sack editors who fail to carry out their duties to their satisfaction, but they must not interfere.
>
> The Fairfax family have always understood this and their understanding has led to their being regarded as the greatest newspaper family—not only in Australia but on the world stage.
>
> Will Mr Packer be able to withstand the temptation not to try and repay a prime ministerial favour through the columns of the *Canberra Times*?
>
> I won't bet on it.

When Consolidated Press gained access to the Canberra trading figures, it was disappointed to find that the *Times* was not doing as well as Connell had given Packer to understand. Rothwells had prepared projections of the paper's profitability from Fairfax's 1987–88 budget papers, without regard to the board papers for July and August, which noted that profitability was being substantially reduced by competition for advertising from a new Canberra real estate paper. When Packer raised this objection, Connell tried a blunt approach by saying that Tryart and Consolidated had an agreement, and it was going to have to proceed. This was not the right way to approach Packer, who replied: 'Well, good luck old mate, we will see you in court and I hope you have a happy Christmas in the meantime'.

Packer's insistence upon a lower price was well founded, and at Connell's suggestion Dougherty, who had dealt with Packer before, reopened negotiations with him. This resulted in a considerably lower price ($211.6 million instead of $250 million) for a somewhat reduced package. The main exclusions were the Fairfax Magazines building at Waterloo, *Australian Property News*, and 80 per cent of

Homes Pictorial which Fairfax had purchased in 1986 for $2.4 million. The latter, a Sydney-based home-buyers' guide, had not been specifically mentioned in the first sketchy agreement with Packer, but it was assumed to have been covered by the catch-all phrase 'and any other magazine . . . produced or published by Fairfax'. So careless was this wording that some mistakenly assumed that it also covered *Time* magazine.

One difficulty with the Packer negotiations seemed likely to affect the $11 million sale of Fairfax's 49 per cent interest in Macquarie Publications, as part of the package of assets going to John B. Fairfax's family company, Marinya Media Pty Ltd. The Macquarie plant at Dubbo did part of Fairfax's magazine printing, and a condition of Marinya's purchase was that Fairfax should ensure that the sale of assets would not deprive Macquarie of any of that work. Consolidated Press would only agree to have its newly acquired magazines printed at Dubbo if Macquarie guaranteed levels of price and quality.

According to some press reports, this was causing John to have second thoughts about the Macquarie purchase. He was indeed having second thoughts, but for other reasons. He withdrew from purchase of the half-interest in Macquarie, and this reduced the price of his asset package from $78 million to $67 million.

On 24 December—after three agreed postponements and almost daily contact between Skase, Reuter and Cotton—Universal Telecasters Ltd paid $282 million of the $370 million instalment which had been due on 30 November. Skase was allowed to delay the repayment of another $60 million until March 1988, and the $100 million worth of convertible notes in UTL which Fairfax was to have taken at this time was reduced to $40 million, with the balance of $60 million delayed until March. Cotton agreed to this renegotiation as the most practical commercial solution. The only alternative would have been legal action to enforce full payment of the money due. That would probably have brought UTL's parent company, Qintex, into default with its bankers, leading to further and perhaps indefinite delay. Given Qintex's difficulties in the aftermath of the crash, and Skase's awareness of Fairfax's own vulnerability, the renegotiation was probably inevitable. But the delay from November was bound to complicate the task of discounting further UTL payments due in 1990, as originally proposed by Reuter.

Three days before UTL paid its diminished November instalment, the agreed sales to News Corporation of Fairfax's interests in Australian Associated Press, AAP Information Services and Australian Newsprint Mills had met some not unexpected obstacles. If the sales were completed, News Corporation—then controlling 58 per cent of Australia's daily newspaper market in terms of circulation—would hold about 82 per cent of the AAP companies and 93 per cent of

ANM. This was more than the non-Murdoch press could stomach. 'It is now time to stop Rupert Murdoch', declared the *Australian Financial Review*, still in limbo between Fairfax and Bell.

> The hint of desperation in this sale is inescapable. In broad terms, a controlling interest in Australian Associated Press or Australian Newsprint is of real commercial interest only to Fairfax's biggest competitor, News Corporation Ltd . . .
>
> Both these enterprises represent entire industries in the Australian context and their opportunities for price fixing are obvious.
>
> In the past, the existence of two major partners [Fairfax and the Herald and Weekly Times] has ensured that pricing policies would remain under strict control. But if News Corporation emerges as virtually the sole proprietor, what kind of control will there be on the pricing of either newsprint or news?
>
> Quite simply, the sales of the two stakes must not go ahead. For Mr Murdoch to get a controlling interest in the operations in question would give him undue control over two major sources of supply to the Australian newspaper industry.
>
> The Murdoch takeover of the Herald and Weekly Times was barely acceptable because it left in place at least one powerful rival in the form of Fairfax and a potentially powerful rival in the form of Robert Holmes à Court's Bell Group.
>
> Both these rivals are emasculated to varying (and so far unknown) degrees by the unpredictable course of events.
>
> The obvious development of weaknesses in the Murdoch group's rivals makes it even more necessary in the public interest to block his further expansion.
>
> The Trade Practices Commission has this responsibility under law . . . If it cannot see this responsibility clearly and act decisively, then it is up to the Australian Government to intervene in the Commission's due processes just as it does when the national interest is threatened by proceedings before the Arbitration Commission.

Intervention soon came in two ways. On 21 December the Trade Practices Commission obtained an interlocutory injunction in the Federal Court restraining John Fairfax & Sons Ltd from selling any interest in the AAP and ANM companies to News Corporation, as it believed such sales would contravene the Trade Practices Act.

Eight days later the Federal Treasurer, Paul Keating, signed an order under Foreign Investment Review Board regulations prohibiting the acquisition of shares in AAP Information Services by News Corporation. The Treasurer made no objection to Murdoch's increased holdings in AAP or the ANM companies. The first, he said, was a company whose major asset was its stake in a foreign company, Reuters. In the case of ANM, further market concentration would be offset by the ready availability of newsprint from abroad, particularly New Zealand.

The Trade Practices Commission remained doubtful about all

three transactions, and at least for the time being Tryart would be denied a badly needed $275 million. Murdoch answered his critics, but failed to convince them. In a letter published by the *Financial Review* he revealed a hitherto unsuspected streak of altruism by declaring that his sole motive for the AAP and ANM purchases was 'to help Mr Warwick Fairfax keep his newspapers together'.

'Neither company is really profitable', he wrote.

> We have always preferred the media service of AAP to be owned, operated and financed as a co-operative and intend that this will be the case . . . Australian Newsprint Mills has a long history as a co-operative of the two Heralds, and one from which News was long excluded! Some people have even suggested we would refuse to supply other papers. Nothing could be more counter-productive to our interests. The problem will be to get them to buy the product.

To complete the unhappy sequence of events confronting Tryart, Holmes à Court's intentions were becoming more enigmatic than ever. Negotiations were proceeding on the basis that the *Financial Review* and *Times on Sunday* would still be sold to him. Operational agreements were being drawn up to separate—or, where separation was not feasible, to charge for—such services as computerized type-setting, accounting, editorial support (library) and distribution. But who could be sure that Bell Group, having already invoked an escape clause for Macquarie Broadcasting, would not also prove unable to buy the newspapers? This uncertainty was damaging to staff morale and to the quality of both products.

It was also worrying the ANZ. As early as November, Reuter received a call from one of its senior executives. 'The bank is concerned about Holmes à Court', he said. 'What if he is unable to pay?'

'I couldn't imagine Rob defaulting on a contract', replied Reuter. 'I'm sure he will pay because he really wants those assets.'

'Yes, but what if he can't pay?'

'Warwick fully understands that if he gets into trouble, he will have to sell the *Age*.'

Throughout December the ANZ and other banks became increasingly nervous—about the total lack of finality in Tryart's asset disposal programme, and about the eventual destination of proceeds from sales whenever they might be concluded. First, the National Australia Bank and Westpac laid claim to their share of the forthcoming Skase payment. At a meeting with Cotton, Moore and Reuter on 1 December, an NAB executive complained that Tryart had 'taken us for granted' by assuming that the facilities would continue to be rolled over. The funds had been lent for the specific purpose of buying HSV7. That purchase was now reaching culmination, and the bank expected repayment. The bank was also concerned, he said, that the security of the company upon which the funds had been advanced had changed substantially as a result of the planned asset sales.

Westpac made similar representations. It offered to extend its $150 million facility for two more months, but warned that it would require full repayment or renegotiation of residual debt by 28 January 1988. The level of bank concern rose sharply after the publication of Section 129 notices on 12 December. This announcement of Fairfax's intention to pass funds to Tryart so that the holding company could repay the ANZ provoked a flurry of letters and urgent meetings between the ANZ, NAB, Westpac and Fairfax. Smaller creditors also made their concerns known.

Reuter's prediction that Cotton was in for a very tough year was amply borne out during the Christmas holiday season. The group managing director was virtually on his own, for on 21 December Dougherty and Reuter left Australia—Dougherty for Hawaii, and Reuter for a long-arranged holiday with his family in the United States. On Christmas Eve, Cotton spoke to Dougherty in Honolulu. 'Marty', he said, 'we are in a hell of a mess here'.

> I have all the merchant banks threatening to take action or expressing concern in relation to the recovery of their funds. NAB, Westpac and ANZ cannot reach agreement as to how we will handle the Skase payments. The asset sale contracts are not proceeding and the ANZ are very nervous particularly about the effect on their cash flows and our ability to service the debt. Marty, I can't get hold of anybody: you are in Hawaii, Warwick is not around, Bert is in the States, where I don't know, I can't get Laurie, I can't get Aleco. Where are we going? Marty, it's all very well for you to ring up every day, and take ages wanting an update, which I am also doing for Peter King and Warwick, but where are these people who we are supposed to be paying to put this takeover together? We need Laurie Connell here. I can't get him, will you do something . . .

Dougherty said he would try to make Connell aware of the situation, but by the end of December Cotton was still complaining that Connell had not returned any of his calls. Connell had more than enough trouble on his hands in Perth, for the rescue of Rothwells had not gone according to plan. On 21 December that bank had been obliged to relinquish its securities dealing licence. Connell himself had resigned as executive chairman, but remained a non-executive director.

In Sydney, Fairfax's creditors had lost patience, and were going to law. On 29 December a Westpac official told Cotton that the bank was not prepared to extend its facility beyond the January expiry date, and was in fact considering lodging a Section 129 notice to stop funds leaving John Fairfax Limited to Westpac's disadvantage. 'We will do our best', he said, 'but we are not prepared to reduce our security and we do not wish to rank behind the ANZ'. Later that day Westpac lodged an objection in the Supreme Court of the Australian Capital Territory, opposing the giving of the financial assistance referred to in the Section 129 notices. This was designed not to prevent Fairfax from selling assets, but to prevent Tryart from receiving the proceeds of such sales. NAB took similar action two days later, and simultaneously one of its subsidiaries, First National, made a demand under its facility with John Fairfax Ltd for the immediate repayment of $13 million.

News of this kind posed some delicate problems of journalistic objectivity at Broadway. The *Herald*'s report of the Westpac notice, written by Ian Verrender, produced an anxious telephone call from Martin Dougherty in Hawaii, protesting that the story had not been in the best interests of the company. A similar report on the NAB notice was then being prepared for next morning's paper. Dougherty suggested to the acting editor, Max Prisk, that the notices were 'just a fight among the banks' and the report might be misconstrued. It was published nevertheless, and next day Dougherty called back to apologize for any testiness he might have shown. He also said that in his view the bank story was not as interesting as Prisk seemed to think.

During the first week of January, Section 129 claims were lodged by six more creditors: National Mutual Royal Bank, Bank of America Australia, Banque Nationale de Paris, BNP Banking Group, Australian Industry Development Corporation and Hong Kong Bank. At the same time Cotton was scouting for buyers who might be interested in Fairfax assets which had either come back on to the market, or might soon do so. The Hong Kong publisher Sally Aw Sian was interested in Macquarie Broadcasting, and in the *Australian Financial Review* if that should become available. The Pearson group in London, publisher of the *Financial Times*, was also interested in the *Financial Review*, and Lord Rothermere of the London *Daily Mail* rang to inquire about Australian Newsprint Mills. Asset memos prepared daily by Max Pride for distribution at Broadway and faxing to King in Amsterdam and Connell in Perth recorded the progress of negotiations. The Bell, Packer and J. B. Fairfax deals were still simmering, but for one reason or another none had yet come to the boil.

On Wednesday morning 6 January two emissaries from the ANZ, McConnell and Conn, attended a meeting with Warwick Fairfax, Cotton, Connell, Dougherty and Vrisakis in the boardroom at Broadway. The only comfort which McConnell had to offer was that the bank had 'no desire or intention to pull the plug', and was still fully committed to the privatization. Otherwise his remarks were a grim recital of anxieties all too familiar to everyone else in the room.

The bank was very concerned, he said, at Tryart's slow rate of progress in reducing its debt, and at the effect of this upon community perception of the ANZ. The ANZ board was also concerned about the sudden emergence of the Macquarie Broadcasting put option, of which it had not been aware; about Fairfax's failure to settle the NAB and Westpac facilities; and about the size of the debt which would remain even if all the proposed asset sales were completed. As far as the bank could see, the residue would be about $645 million. The last thing the ANZ board wanted to do was create acute nervousness, or put good assets on the line. But Tryart/Fairfax should realize that it needed to get the Section 129 objections rescinded, and needed to have some fall-back lines in place.

Connell then assured the bankers that the Bell and Consolidated agreements were under control. '[Holmes à Court] will settle, don't worry', he said. 'He has got the money and it will happen soon. The Packer agreement will also settle. There is no problem there.' Cotton went through the list of Section 129 objectors, and mentioned First National's letter of demand for $13 million, which had to be paid the following day. On a more hopeful note, he said that News Corporation had found a replacement buyer for the newsprint shares affected by the injunction—Fletcher Challenge Ltd, the dominant force in New Zealand's pulp and newsprint industry. The price was $25 million more than the $150 million agreed to by News, but the New Zealand company still had to pass scrutiny by the Foreign Investment Review Board and the Trade Practices Commission.

In addition to the requirements mentioned by the ANZ, Tryart/Fairfax urgently needed more consultative assistance than Connell was providing. Cotton had hoped to discuss the Universal Telecasting contract with Connell after the ANZ meeting, but before he could do so that worried entrepreneur had left the building and was on his way back to Perth. Later the same day, either by chance or initiative, another merchant banker made a timely appearance at Broadway.

Malcolm Turnbull, a young solicitor-barrister-banker, had come to see Cotton about the possibility of providing legal services for Fairfax. Turnbull was a jack of all the legal, money and media trades. A former Rhodes Scholar, protégé of Kerry Packer, son-in-law of the august T. E. F. Hughes, QC, and a principal in the merchant bank Whitlam Turnbull Ltd, Turnbull had lately been in the public eye as solicitor for the author Peter Wright in hearings before the New South Wales Supreme Court concerning the British Government's efforts to stop publication of Wright's book *Spycatcher*.

Cotton was at a meeting, and while Turnbull waited in the fourteenth floor reception hall he was recognized by Warwick Fairfax and invited into his office. After hearing Warwick's account of the company's predicament, Turnbull offered the assistance of Whitlam Turnbull in handling the banks.

In a later conversation with Cotton, he said: 'Is there anything we can do to help you? As I understand it Bert Reuter is overseas and you are trying to handle all of the banks yourself, which must be an impossible task'. Cotton conceded that he could do with some help of that sort (Shearson Lehman was looking for someone to take out the Westpac NAB facilities, but had found no one), and said that his most immediate problem was finding $13 million by noon the next day to satisfy First National. The ANZ would not help any further, so the money would have to come from somewhere else. 'As you can hear', said Cotton, 'the phones are just not stopping and if I don't speak to the banks they will get more uptight'.

John Fairfax Ltd was now technically in default of its borrowing covenants, and could have been sent into liquidation or receivership by creditors at any time. Only prudence prevented the ANZ from exercising its power of sale over the company's shares and against such guarantors as Rockwood and Acrux.

Next morning, 7 January, Whitlam Turnbull presented John Fairfax Ltd with a cheque for $13 million, an unsecured 60-day loan with which the company paid out First National. This help was rich in irony, for it could hardly have come from a more improbable source. Just as Sir James Reading Fairfax's Gates of Paradise had come to rest in the Neville Wran Building, so also was John Fairfax Ltd now beholden to a merchant bank partly controlled by two of its one-time adversaries. The chairman of Whitlam Turnbull was none other than Neville Wran, and the major shareholder was Kerry Packer. It would hardly have been surprising if these two, remembering past wounds, had thought to themselves how sweet were the uses of adversity.

On 8 January Tryart retained Whitlam Turnbull to raise a new facility of $500 million to replace the funds provided, and now being clamoured for, by John Fairfax Ltd's original lenders. This was attended to by Nicholas Whitlam, eldest son of the former Prime Minister and himself a former managing director of the State Bank of New South Wales. At Tryart's request Whitlam Turnbull also began formulating options available to reduce the Tryart/Fairfax debt. It looked into the feasibility of revaluing mastheads, reviewed the ability of superannuation and non-contributory funds to reinvest in the Fairfax group, and proceeded to deal with the discounting of Skase's remaining instalments, the sale of the AAP and newsprint shares, and later the increasingly dubious Bell contract.

Tryart also asked Wardley Australia to seek a buyer for Macquarie Broadcasting. This merchant bank was already aware of interest by Sonance Ltd, a Queensland-based consortium led by Sir Frank Moore and including Sally Aw Sian, and before long it was also negotiating with Trypool Ltd of Canberra and an Adelaide group headed by Jeremy Cordeaux.

In the third week of January Bert Reuter, back from the United States, telephoned Cotton to ask what had been happening. 'Well, Bert', said Cotton, 'where the hell have you been, because we're in a state of total disarray'. This was not as true as it would have been earlier in that desperate month. Cotton's exaggeration was understandable, however, for he had been in the forefront while others had been on holiday.

The outlook, though still very bleak, had in fact improved. Consolidated Press had settled on 11 January for $211 million, and four days later Marinya settled for $67 million. The price paid by Consolidated had been reduced by $39 million mainly because of the misunderstanding about profitability. In the course of negotiation with Packer, Dougherty had managed to remove *Australian Property News* from the list of magazines being sold. This came as a relief to Robert Gottliebsen and his colleagues at BRW, for they regarded that publication as one of their key assets.

Even better than the completion of these two sales, Whitlam Turnbull was well advanced in negotiation with Citibank Ltd for the formation of a syndicate to refinance Fairfax's existing bank facilities. There was little time to spare, for on 12 and 15 January Westpac and NAB had demanded repayment in full, the latter within seven days. With these and all the other banks apparently deadlocked over priority, the only alternative to receivership seemed to be a refinancing which would permit Tryart/Fairfax to pay Paul without having to rob Peter.

Citibank Ltd was a subsidiary of the New York-based bank of that name—the world's largest private lender and, according to some, the most aggressive of all multi-national banks. The Australian subsidiary had been a finance company for twenty-five years until it obtained a formal banking licence in 1985 as part of the Hawke Government's deregulation of Australia's banking system. As the result of negotiations between Whitlam and Citibank's general manager and chief credit officer, Gerry Van der Merwe, terms were settled for a 12-month facility of $500 million. Citibank would underwrite that amount and arrange its syndication; it would take security over all Fairfax's core assets, such as the *Herald* and *Age*, but would have no objection to all the planned asset sales proceeding, and proceeds being pushed up to Tryart to repay the ANZ. If Fairfax wanted to sell any of the secured assets—the *Age*, for example—Citibank would have no objection so long as the proceeds were split fifty-fifty for debt repayment to Citibank and the ANZ. Another condition of the loan was that Fairfax's cash flow should service Citibank first and the ANZ second.

The ANZ gave its approval to this arrangement on 20 January.

Admittedly the bank was surrendering some of its own security and priority, but the arrival of this third lending force would break the deadlock between old and new creditors. The ANZ could see about $600 million of asset proceeds, either waiting for it in John Fairfax Ltd, or likely to be available soon; yet, because of the other banks' Section 129 objections, the proceeds could not be transferred. So the ANZ, with security over Fairfax's shares, gave its blessing to Citibank.

Formal approval of the Citibank facility for John Fairfax Ltd had a salutary effect on the impatience of creditors. Nine banks which had been ready to take legal action against Fairfax on 5 February now desisted, although Westpac later threatened to resume legal action when payment took longer than expected. The facility was to last a year from first draw-down on 28 March, and on that date all old creditors were paid out and their Section 129 proceedings were withdrawn. At the same time ANZ's facility, due to be repaid on 30 June 1988, was extended to 31 December on condition that further asset sales should be made before then.

Although Bert Reuter played some part in this battle of the banks, through his ANZ contacts, Whitlam Turnbull had unmistakably taken over the consultancy function originally performed by Rothwells. Little more would be seen or heard of Connell and Reuter at Broadway, and the directors of John Fairfax Ltd became dubious about the $100 million fee which would become payable in June to Rothwells' assignee, Bond Media Ltd. At a board meeting on 18 January, at which the fee was discussed, directors agreed that it was a success fee, and that success would have to be judged by future events.

By mid-February Whitlam Turnbull had made good progress with some of its tasks. Perhaps most importantly, the Bell agreement was rescinded. This deal had been predictably difficult, for as Mary Fairfax had warned on one occasion, Robert Holmes à Court was a destroyer of tranquillity. In addition to the difficulties of separation, which Max Pride and Frank McMahon were trying to solve in Perth, there was uncertainty about Holmes à Court's intention (in January he was reportedly negotiating with Pearson Group to sell it a 50 per cent interest in the *Financial Review*, *Times on Sunday* and *National Business Review* in New Zealand) and about the Tryart/Bell agreement. On 21 January, Bell Group entered a summons in the West Australian Supreme Court seeking a decision on certain parts of the agreement dealing with the amount of equipment to be included in the sale of the three publications under negotiation with Pearson. This dispute was resolved out of court, but there were other contractual problems as well.

The terms of the agreement were such that Fairfax could probably not force Holmes à Court to settle unless News Corporation agreed to his acquiring more shares in AAP and ANM. News would not agree to that, and Holmes à Court knew it. 'John Fairfax Ltd faced a real risk', reported Whitlam Turnbull to Cotton, 'of Holmes à Court exploiting the inadequacies of the agreement to tie up the assets which were the subject of it in litigation, at which time he would no doubt have made us a very reduced offer to purchase them'.

On the other hand, Holmes à Court had difficulties of his own arising from the Broadcasting Act, and would probably not be able to complete the deal even if he wanted to. This meant that although Fairfax might not be able to settle, Holmes à Court's similar inability would preclude him from having an action against the company. On 2 February the contract was mutually terminated.

This was a set-back to the asset disposal programme, but there were two consolations. Fairfax would not have to let the *Australian Financial Review* go for the bargain price which Holmes à Court had been able to exact because of his strong bargaining position five months earlier. And, secondly, recovering the AAP and ANM shares would allow Whitlam Turnbull to negotiate better prices for Fairfax's whole stakes in those companies.

The sales were finalized on 15 March. News Corporation was to pay $67.5 million for Fairfax's 44.6 per cent of AAP Pty Ltd. In a separate deal at the same time, News also arranged to buy Bell's original 8.3 per cent, which would bring its own AAP holding to 89.3 per cent. As Fairfax was retaining its AAPIS shares, the Foreign Investment Review Board made no objection. The Trade Practices Commission still had its injunction in the Federal Court, but after satisfying itself that News was not buying AAPIS shares from either Fairfax or Bell it also approved the sales. As it happened, Fairfax's AAP shares were paid for in May not by News Corporation but by Reuters Holdings Plc, to which News had on-sold the shares, together with half the Bell stake.

For the time being, News and Reuters were equal partners in AAP (48.5 per cent each), with the remaining 3 per cent held by two Tasmanian newspaper companies. But in the following year, when Reuters converted its A class shares to B shares and became a one-class company, News and the Tasmanians sold out of AAP. The name 'Australian Associated Press' reverted to AAPIS, and the company which had once borne that name became a dormant company under the nondescript name of Reuters Investments (Aust) Pty Ltd.

As for the news agency itself, AAPIS, Fairfax and News Corporation were equal partners with 43.4 per cent each. The remaining shares were held by West Australian Newspapers, which later came under the control of Bond Media (8 per cent); the two Tasmanian companies (1.1 per cent each); and AAP Nominees Pty Ltd, owned by AAP staff (3 per cent).

At an early stage of Whitlam Turnbull's negotiation with News, Murdoch was also going to purchase the masthead of *Business Review Weekly*. Better judgement prevailed at Broadway, however, and the BRW group remained intact. Under the original agreement with News, the *St George Leader* was to have been sold at about one quarter of its real value. Fortunately this sale, which would have impaired the value of the rest of Fairfax Community Newspapers, was not part of the new agreement negotiated by Whitlam Turnbull.

Fairfax's 50 per cent holding in Australian Newsprint Mills was sold to Fletcher Challenge for $221.1 million. That New Zealand company also bought Bell Group's 11.6 per cent holding, thus accumulating a 61.6 per cent stake in Australia's newsprint industry, with the balance held by News Corporation. As part of the Fairfax and Bell agreements, Fletcher signed long-term supply contracts with options to extend.

The Trade Practices Commission was in two minds. Initially it was inclined to block the sales on grounds that they would remove Fletcher Challenge as ANM's most significant competitor. In spite of its earlier opposition to Murdoch, the Commission at first preferred an industry dominated by him, but still competing against Fletcher, to one operating without Fletcher's competition. Finally, in June, it swung around to granting permission for the Fletcher/News merger, giving as its reason potential benefits under Closer Economic Relations (CER) with New Zealand. On balance, the Commission said, a $400 million investment plan proposed by Fletcher for ANM, combined with public benefits under CER, would offset ANM's dominant position in the market.

Macquarie Broadcasting Holdings Ltd was sold to Sonance on 26 February for $97.5 million. Within six months Sonance on-sold six of the company's eight radio stations, retaining only 2GB in Sydney and 4BH in Brisbane, and sold the 2GB building to Mary Fairfax for $15 million.

Whitlam Turnbull's efforts to find a third party willing to discount the final Universal Telecasters instalment of $285 million, due in 1990, were unavailing. Fairfax needed to obtain as much of that amount as it could, and as quickly as possible. As no one else was prepared to take the risk it seemed logical for the company to renegotiate the terms of payment with UTL itself. Skase was willing to negotiate: he knew a vulnerable opponent when he saw one, and early release from the 1990 obligation would give him greater control over the Seven Network.

After extensive negotiations between Whitlam Turnbull and Skase, the principal contract was amended. In lieu of the $285 million, UTL would make cash payments of $130 million on 30 June 1988 and $64 million on 31 December 1988. In addition, or rather subtraction, Fairfax would make eight quarterly $3.5 million payments to UTL, starting on 30 June 1988. Fairfax agreed to forego its right to $55 million of convertible UTL notes in 1990; it sold to the AMP, for $55 million, the UTL shares and notes which it had received under the original agreement; and it was released by UTL from the put option over the network. The net effect of all this made sorry reading for Fairfax management new and old. Instead of the $780 million which Skase had originally agreed to pay for the Seven Network, Fairfax would by the end of 1988 have received a much reduced total of $567 million.

Excluding the last two UTL payments scheduled for June and December, but including the ANM shares, the asset proceeds by March amounted to just over one billion dollars. On the debit side of the ledger stood ANZ's $2.1 billion and Citibank's $500 million, and in the middle, figuratively speaking, was Fairfax's cash flow from its remaining assets. The imbalance between asset sales to date and bank facilities could be corrected to some extent by further sales, but each sale would have its own diminishing effect upon the cash flow with which Fairfax was paying its horrendous interest bills. Further refinancing was another option, perhaps to be used in conjunction with more sales. But having just consolidated its pre-Tryart debts in the Citibank facility, Fairfax for the time being was concerned mainly with selling.

So what else should be sold? 'Before any further asset sales are made', wrote Whitlam Turnbull to the ANZ,

> it is essential that a number of important strategic questions be addressed. Are the New South Wales and Victorian regional and suburban newspapers essential to protect the flanks of the *Sydney Morning Herald* and the *Age* respectively? On what if any terms should John Fairfax Ltd agree to merge the *Sun* and the *Daily Mirror*? Or should the *Sun* simply be closed? Is it better to sell all of the Victorian papers and keep all of the New South Wales papers, or to sell half of the *Age* and keep only the *Sydney Morning Herald* in New South Wales?
>
> These issues are complex and will require considerable analysis and review. At this stage, it is simply too early to make definitive decisions. Moreover if some or all of the *Age* is to be disposed of, a fire sale is not the best way to achieve an optimum price.

On 15 February Whitlam Turnbull submitted to Fairfax the results of its analysis and review: four possible scenarios for further asset disposal. Scenario A assumed the sale of all assets except the *Sydney Morning Herald, Sun-Herald,* the newspaper insert business, David Syme and the Good Weekend colour magazine. In Whitlam Turnbull's view this was 'certainly financeable in the short term' but had the disadvantage of selling the *Financial Review*.

Scenario B retained all profitable New South Wales publications—including the *Newcastle Herald, Illawarra Mercury* and

Fairfax Community Newspapers—and sold half of Syme. This was also regarded as being financeable for the short term, and had the attraction of Fairfax remaining the dominant New South Wales newspaper publisher.

Scenario C sold all assets, including the whole of David Syme, except the profitable New South Wales newspapers. This was seen as 'eminently bankable', providing both a long-term solution to the debt problem and flexibility for the future.

Finally, Scenario D assumed the retention of only four newspapers: the *Sydney Morning Herald, Financial Review, Sun-Herald, Age* and the insert business. This was thought to be 'the toughest scenario', and most unlikely to be bankable. 'To undertake this', reported Whitlam Turnbull,

> the board would need to be confident of its ability to substantially increase earnings and more importantly of its ability to persuade the banks that it can achieve these increases. From a banker's perspective, it is difficult to see where a quantum leap in earnings can be found . . . Without these there will be no prospect of reducing the level of debt even in the long term.

In spite of the merit which it saw in the third scenario, Whitlam Turnbull recommended that Fairfax should adopt the second one—that is, retain all profitable New South Wales papers, close the *Sun* and sell half of David Syme. 'We recognise that the task of finding appropriate partners for Syme, at the right price and on satisfactory terms, will not be easy', it said. 'However during the discussions over Syme we will no doubt receive many offers for all of Syme, which can be considered on their merits. The recommended announcement does not foreclose on Scenario C.'

During the last few weeks there had been rumours of interest in David Syme from several quarters in Australia and overseas. The most impressive of these possible contenders, and the first to make a firm offer, was Maxwell Communication Corporation Plc, a London-based group including Europe's largest printing operation, Britain's second largest newspaper (the *Daily Mirror*), and the world's third largest publisher of academic journals. Its chairman, Robert Maxwell, had come to Britain in 1939 as a 15-year-old Czech refugee named Jan Hoch. He was now Rupert Murdoch's main rival in Fleet Street, and in the course of expanding globally he was anxious to establish MCC's presence in Australia.

Early in February MCC sent to Australia a six-man negotiating team led by its senior deputy managing director and including Maxwell's son. On 8 February, after gathering information and holding preliminary discussions with Whitlam Turnbull, the negotiating team made a written offer for much more than David Syme. The offer was $1.2 billion for 100 per cent of David Syme, the

Australian Financial Review, *Times on Sunday*, BRW Publications, the Good Weekend, Fairfax Community Newspapers, the *Newcastle Herald*, *Illawarra Mercury*, and all Fairfax's shareholdings in AAP, AAPIS and ANM—that was to say, virtually all of John Fairfax Ltd except the *Sydney Morning Herald* and the *Sun-Herald*. If Fairfax wished to retain 50 per cent of Syme, the revised offer price would be $835 million. The revised offer put a value of about $730 million on the *Age*.

Fairfax rightly interpreted this as an opening gambit. Four days later, when the negotiating team had returned to London, MCC offered $1.4 billion for a smaller package consisting of all David Syme, 50 per cent of the ANM shares, 100 per cent of the AAP and AAPIS shares, 50 per cent of the *Financial Review*, and all of the *Times on Sunday*. On 3 March Fairfax responded by offering David Syme, with the exclusion of a few minor assets, for $1.1 billion. MCC came back with three offers—$650 million for that package, $1 billion for all of Syme plus half the news agency and newsprint shares, or $350 million for half of Syme. And there, for the time being, the matter rested.

II

While refinancing and asset-selling proceeded on one level of the company's fevered life, reporters still went about their rounds, sub-editors click-clacked on the keyboards of Coyote terminals, and the presses at Broadway continued to roar day and night. Yet it was not 'business as usual', as Fred Brenchley had prescribed in a staff memo after the first announcement of asset sales at the end of September. Staff morale had been seriously shaken by the sudden turn of events. The newspapers may have seemed unaffected by this, but before long production was being affected by stop-work meetings and short-term strikes over redundancy terms for some thirty magazine journalists who were not required along with their magazines by Consolidated Press.

There was also trouble about editorial matters. 'Whilst all sectors of the company have had to make major readjustments to the Tryart takeover', Martin Dougherty reported to the board in January,

> the impact has been most traumatic on the editorial staffs—not least because they were quite shamelessly drafted by sections of the previous management to do battle on its behalf. As a result, we have faced a good deal of residual hostility from some sections of our own papers, and a degree of confusion from those whose fate has been in the balance for so long as a result of the lengthy negotiations with the Bell Group.

This hostility, which at times reached almost hysterical levels and

> resulted in some very bad reporting, is now receding; but some changes in personnel will probably be necessary before it is eliminated . . . We have begun a policy of contacting and briefing key opinion leaders on the editorial staffs to further improve the climate. It's a slow process, however, as the departing editorial management did a very effective job of poisoning the wells.

This kind of suspicion resembled, and was probably no more surprising than, the siege mentality which had prevailed at Broadway when the 'Visigoths' appeared. Dougherty's older brother Paul, a former journalist who had followed Max Suich as *Sydney Morning Herald* correspondent in Tokyo during the early 1970s, felt the same. In a memo to Martin in December he urged him to have Chris Anderson's service contract examined and 'fight it to the wire'.

'I don't believe his contract would stand up in Equity', he wrote.

> It encourages him to act badly in the hope of attracting a payout. I believe it would be open to a judge to conclude that the contract was a landmine [laid] by the outgoing administration to disadvantage the incoming one . . . He would seem to have sought to prevent your playing any role in the editorial process, and has sought to define any attempt by you to do so as 'interference' under the terms of his contract.

From this it may be seen how quickly relations between the managing director editorial and the editor-in-chief of the *Sydney Morning Herald* had deteriorated in the short time since Martin Dougherty had referred to Anderson as 'the key to the building'. The two of them were natural opposites: one tall, amiable, open faced, though more calculating than he looked; the other, about the same age (early forties), shorter, dark visaged, and quietly but incisively spoken. Whereas Dougherty was returning to journalism after years of public relations, Anderson, although qualified as an economist, had been a journalist all his working life. He was a consummate editorial administrator; bureaucratic, but not to the detriment of journalistic flair and professional skill. Accustomed to the high degree of editorial independence which Fairfax editors had won from board and management during the last few years, he was instinctively suspicious of the executive to whom he would now be responsible if he remained at Broadway.

Administratively, this responsibility would be no different from some of the earlier editorial channels at Broadway (for example, Suich's surveillance of the *National Times*), but it would certainly differ from the free hand which editors of the *Herald* and *Financial Review* had exercised in recent years. Although Suich had been chief editorial executive, Anderson's contact with him had usually been confined to broad matters such as budgets. Anderson had provided a monthly report to the board, and had seen the chairman once a week.

Henceforth he would report only to Dougherty, who would in turn report directly to the proprietor. Peter King had reserved the right to have some say in editorial matters, but only if they seemed likely to affect his proper management of the company. In any case, King had not yet arrived at Broadway. If there were to be difficulties in the first few weeks of Tryart's management, they would be primarily between Dougherty and Anderson. And there were indeed some difficulties.

As was his usual practice, Anderson recorded the tentative understanding which he had reached with the proprietor in light of the offer made to him by News Ltd, of which the proprietor was aware. In a letter to Warwick Fairfax on 11 November he noted that the proprietor and Dougherty wanted him to continue as editor-in-chief, and that the proposed method of reporting through Dougherty was 'a detrimental change in my authority and status with which I [am] most unhappy'.

> You noted my objections, but said that was how at present you intended to operate . . .
>
> For my part, I am committed to making the changeover as professional and smooth as possible. Assuming that I stay, I will use my authority, expertise and position in the company to ensure the new team is enthusiastically received at Broadway—and elsewhere in the Group.
>
> I would use the legitimacy of my position—in the Company and the community—to maintain our reputation of independence and integrity. I will reassure everyone those standards will be enhanced by the new owners.

With colours thus hoisted, Anderson began working vigilantly under the new dispensation while nevertheless keeping the News offer open. Trouble began even before Dougherty took office. In mid-November Anderson sent two reporters—financial writer Colleen Ryan and crime reporter Andrew Keenan—to look into the Rothwells rescue operation, particularly into how that was affecting Laurie Connell. The subject was newsworthy, and it was also one which would serve to calibrate 'independence and integrity'. In sanctioning the assignment, Anderson was showing as clearly as possible that he took those words seriously. He was also challenging Dougherty.

Late on the night of 17 November Dougherty rang Anderson at home to say that he had received a call from 'the west'. He wondered whether doing such a story was wise, for it might reflect on the proprietor; and he wondered whether some 'smart arse' at Broadway was singling Connell out for special attention. Anderson replied that the assignment was a totally appropriate piece of journalism and consistent with what readers expected of the *Herald*. He would make sure that, if published, the article was balanced and well judged. Dougherty replied that he would leave it in Anderson's 'capable hands'.

'It is early days', wrote Anderson in a file note next day,

> in what is (hopefully) a long relationship with Marty and Warwick. However, after the call I feel on reflection it was a fundamental questioning of my authority and judgment. It was also an attempt to influence my judgment on a story of some moment that could affect a friend [Connell]. Certainly, in my 10 years or more as an editor, no one has ever asked me whether sending reporters to seek information for possible preparation of an article was, in any way, an attempt to 'get' an individual or an entity. I will put this down on file, but, as a sense of record and fairness, will send a copy down to Marty.

In reply nine days later, Dougherty disclaimed the motives imputed to him in the file note, said he had made clear to Anderson that he would have no objection if the story was 'accurate, fair and reasonable', and wondered whether Anderson was 'simply building a case to invoke the editorial independence clause in [his] contract'.

'I am not a barrack-room lawyer', replied Anderson,

> and I don't 'build cases.' If I had wanted to leave Fairfax the perfect opportunity was presented a month ago and I decided to stay. Naturally I'll keep you informed. But it wouldn't be usual practice in newspapers for an Editor-in-Chief to discuss stories with management, or the directors, before publication. Without in any way seeking a confrontation, that would, in my mind, constitute a significant downgrading of confidence in my professional ability. I presume that my original record of our conversation—and your reply—were shown to Warwick. I'd appreciate if you would pass this on to him as well.

Whether sought or not, a confrontation was developing. On 9 December, the third day of Tryart's management, Anderson protested to Dougherty about a proposal to install visual display terminals on the fourteenth floor, linking some of the new directors with the editorial system. This would be seen as a vote of no confidence in editors, he wrote, if it were thought that directors needed to monitor, before publication, the words that went into the company's newspapers. There was also a risk, he said, that it would provoke industrial action by journalists.

The journalists at Broadway had already expressed concern about editorial independence in a resolution passed on 28 September at a meeting called by the AJA House Committee. A threat to the professional independence of journalists arose, said the resolution, through the ownership of media by proprietors who had wide non-media business interests, and significant conflicts of interest were inevitable if journalists were to cover their own proprietor's business activities.

This referred to Holmes à Court and Connell rather than Warwick Fairfax, but clearly there might also be a conflict of interest in reporting Tryart's increasingly complex affairs. The resolution called for urgent talks between company and union on several matters including a charter of editorial independence incorporating the AJA Code of Ethics to ensure 'total editorial independence, particularly when covering the owner's business interests'; and establishment of joint AJA–publisher committees in each major company of the group to monitor and resolve disputes concerning editorial matters.

On the day Anderson protested about the VDTs, Dougherty told him that he had offered a well known Australian journalist in New York, Andrew Clark, a position on the *Sydney Morning Herald* as associate editor (finance). Dougherty had mentioned Clark some weeks earlier, but Anderson had understood then that Clark—the former investigative reporter on the *National Times,* founding editor of Packer's *Australian Business,* formerly assistant managing editor of Murdoch's *New York Post,* and now a freelance executive with News Corporation—would probably be joining the BRW magazine group.

Although Anderson did not know Clark well, he knew of his reputation as a strong but, as Brian Toohey once put it, 'explosively temperamental' editor. Clark was a big, urbane and vehement man. Being 'clarked', as the saying went on *Australian Business,* was an experience not easily forgotten. The editor of the *Herald,* John Alexander, the business editor, Deborah Light, and the investment editor, Alan Deans, had all worked under Clark at *Australian Business* before moving to Broadway. Anderson told Dougherty that to have made such an offer to Clark without first clearing it with himself was a blow to his authority. He feared that Alexander, Light and most of her staff would resign as a consequence. They agreed to discuss the Clark matter later, and Dougherty said that in future he would not appoint people to Anderson's staff without prior consultation.

At about the same time Dougherty invited the former editor of *Australian Women's Weekly,* Ita Buttrose, to become editor-in-chief of the *Sun-Herald.* Against the forebodings of some at Broadway, including Anderson, she took up that position on 9 February, with Ray Odlum continuing as editor. Dougherty also had in mind a new editor for the *Age*—Patrick Boyce, formerly an assistant editor of the paper, who had been press officer for the 1986 Papal Tour. He arranged for Boyce to be placed on a monthly retainer, but for the time being Creighton Burns remained editor.

On 11 December Dougherty raised the Clark matter again. Anderson said that appointment without consultation placed him in an intolerable position. If Clark were to be associate editor (finance) he would have to report to the editor-in-chief, the editor and the business editor. Dougherty replied that the first two would be all right, but reporting to Deborah Light was out of the question.

Anderson countered by suggesting that Clark be made New York correspondent. Dougherty thought that was a possibility, but he also revealed that he wanted the associate appointment made so that Clark could be available to take over as editor should Alexander prove unsatisfactory. Anderson said he had full confidence in Alexander's ability. Privately he also concluded that an editor-in-waiting could just as easily become an editor-in-chief.

On Sunday morning 13 December Dougherty rang Anderson at home to express his concern about a Page One story in Saturday's *Herald*. The story reported that, according to an ABC radio programme to be broadcast that day, Dr William McBride, the man credited with having discovered the adverse effects of thalidomide, had committed scientific fraud. Dougherty was worried about the legal implications, and asked whether the *Herald* had sought McBride's side of the controversy. Anderson replied that the report had been extensively checked by the company's lawyers, and that Dr McBride had been approached. Again Dougherty said he would leave the matter in Anderson's 'capable hands'.

It was at this point that Anderson decided to leave. 'I wasn't used to people phoning up editors asking why did you publish that piece', he recalled later.

> I didn't question his right to do it per se, because he obviously had the new owner's ear. It was just that it was a different type of journalism, and clearly one of us would have to go. It wasn't going to be him, so it would have to be me.

On 16 December he told Dougherty of his decision, saying that he expected the full terms of his contract to be honoured, and would try to make the next few weeks as smooth as possible. He would go overseas until the end of January, and finish up in mid-February. He would not make a public issue of Clark's appointment, and would help to ease him into the paper. Dougherty generally concurred, but according to his later recollection the termination date was moved to March or April.

On 18 December two hundred Fairfax journalists held a stop-work meeting to discuss the Clark appointment, which was common knowledge by then, and the VDTs on the executive floor. Addressing the meeting, Anderson successfully appealed for a return to work. Clark's appointment could not be construed as a breakdown of editorial independence, he said, for Clark would answer to the editor and editor-in-chief. As for the terminals on the fourteenth floor, he understood they were to be used for 'messaging'. The meeting passed a motion calling on the management not to hire staff against an editor's wishes.

Anderson's decision was as yet known to few people apart from Alexander, Dougherty and the proprietor. Although his future was uncertain, he had not lost touch with News Corporation and was now more interested than before in that option. The interest was mutual—so much so, indeed, that Rupert Murdoch invited Anderson, his wife Gaie and their teenagers Simon and Shauna to stay with him and his wife at the ski resort of Aspen, Colorado.

The Andersons left Sydney on Boxing Day, bound for Denver and then Aspen. As it happened, Warwick Fairfax was part of the same check-in queue, seeing his mother off on a flight to London. This required a certain amount of caution on the editor-in-chief's part. The same applied in conversation with a passenger on the Andersons' flight—Kerry Packer's chief executive, Trevor Kennedy, who was going to Detroit. While chatting with Kennedy at Los Angeles airport, Anderson managed to give the impression that he was on his way to London—which in any case he was, via Aspen.

Anderson was charmed by Rupert Murdoch, whom he found to be a 'most interesting, involved man', but also overpowering. Some nights the two families would play scrabble. Other times Murdoch would produce the London *Times* which, like all his papers, was flown in for him. He would ask Anderson's opinion about typefaces and stories. Or perhaps it would be the *South China Morning Post*. What should we do with that? They went to Little Nell's cafe; to a party given by Barry Diller, the impresario of Murdoch's film and television interests in America; and to lunch with the television presenter Barbara Walters. At the end of their stay Murdoch brought in his private jet to fly the Andersons to New York.

When Anderson reached London, he was very much interested in News Ltd, but still undecided. He and the family visited his mother-in-law in Dublin, then went to Egypt for a trip up the Nile. At Luxor he received a message to ring Max Prisk, who was acting editor while Alexander was on holidays in Sri Lanka. Dougherty had objected to a story prepared by Ian Verrender about complaints to the National Companies and Securities Commission that Tryart was late in paying out some former John Fairfax Ltd shareholders. Anderson authorized publication, and the story appeared on 9 January. The *Australian* ran it too.

Back in London Anderson rang Dougherty offering not to return to the *Herald*, where he might become a focal point for dissent. Dougherty disagreed, saying they had a deal that Anderson would not leave before March. On the morning of 18 January, after a jog along the Thames embankment, Anderson returned to the Fairfax flat to find the London manager, Alan Dobbyn, waiting for him with Mary Fairfax. Lady Fairfax said she was alarmed to hear that Anderson was planning to leave the company. She believed her son was in the hands of Martin Dougherty, and if Anderson resigned the integrity and authority of the *Herald* would be damaged. The level of Fairfax debt scared her, and she was worried that if the new chief executive officer knew of the real situation he might be reluctant to come.

Next morning Lady Fairfax telephoned Anderson, renewing her criticism of Dougherty and imploring him not to leave. She said she had 'hocked [her] all' to support her son's initiative and was desperately concerned about the outcome.

But Anderson's intentions were now firm. Returning to Sydney late in January, he accepted News's offer and had several meetings with Cowley in Murdoch's apartment at Elizabeth Bay. They discussed the job and it was understood that several Fairfax executives, editors and journalists would follow Anderson to News Ltd.

Dougherty knew nothing of this. He did become aware of Anderson's meeting with Lady Fairfax in London, and asked him for a full memorandum about it. Anderson complied with more candour than perhaps Dougherty had expected. 'I should add', he concluded,

> that my view is that Lady Mary has only the best intentions at heart and is genuinely concerned about the debt situation and about her son's welfare.
>
> At all times when she has spoken to me, the newspapers' integrity, the financial future of the company and her son's welfare have been at the forefront of her concern.
>
> Of course, I knew Sir Warwick early in my career and saw him regularly when he was a director . . . Lady Fairfax once told me that Sir Warwick was a great supporter of mine and would protect my position (and the *Herald*'s) whether I was right or wrong.
>
> Thus, I don't find it terribly surprising that she would lobby me about her son and the welfare of his company.

At this time Lady Fairfax was also lobbying another director, Ron Cotton, who later described himself as 'a respectful but intolerant listener'. She telephoned him frequently with advice, as he recalled it later, about 'finances, who around the world if I rang them straight away would fly out and sort us out, what my diet should be . . . the position of Mr Dougherty, her concern about Warwick leaving the business . . .' She also sought to enlist Cotton's support for her appointment to the Fairfax board, which she said Dougherty had been opposing. Cotton's impression was that she aspired to fill a vacancy which might be created by Dougherty's removal from the board.

Andrew Clark started work at Broadway on Monday 1 February. The first person he met was Anderson, who told him of the friction between himself and Dougherty. On Thursday Dougherty informed Clark that Anderson had decided to resign, and offered him the position of editor-in-chief, which Clark accepted. Clark spent the rest of the week working amicably with Anderson, who was serving out his notice. The resignation and appointment were not as yet announced.

Events now began to accelerate. Journalists at Broadway were already taking intermittent industrial action related to negotiations then in progress about the terms of retrenchment for magazine journalists. News Ltd was simultaneously negotiating terms for employees whose jobs were threatened by the pending closure of the Brisbane *Telegraph*. In its negotiations with the AJA, Fairfax was trying to prevent 'leap-frogging' between the two companies, and also to avoid industrial action of a more drastic nature. Industrial feeling was running high because of the AJA's claim that the company had earlier given an assurance that no journalists would be compulsorily retrenched.

On Monday 8 February the journalists at Broadway held a two-hour stop-work meeting, and on Tuesday the *Herald*'s sub-editors stopped work briefly. On Wednesday this continuing dispute was overshadowed by another one. The news of Anderson's resignation and Clark's appointment spread quickly that morning, and a meeting called by the House Committee at 12.30 p.m. heard with amazement that the editor and a number of senior journalists had resigned in sympathy. Those who resigned with Anderson and Alexander were Glenn Burge, Alan Deans, the news editor Richard Glover, the business editor Deborah Light, Anne Lampe, Deirdre Macken, the chief-of staff Paul McGeough, the deputy editor Max Prisk and Colleen Ryan. They were not fully aware of Anderson's arrangement with News Ltd, but had been advised by Alexander not to seek other employment as there was something in the wind. Others were also believed to be considering resignation.

After long debate, the meeting passed several resolutions. The first expressed 'profound lack of confidence in the senior management of John Fairfax Ltd, specifically Martin Dougherty, and. . . concern about the continuing risk to editorial independence in [the company's] newspapers'. A second resolution said that Anderson's and Alexander's positions should be filled only by candidates who had the confidence of the staff, and a third one called for establishment of a joint committee to consider candidates for those positions.

The Committee should consist of two journalist-elected members, two company appointees, and one 'senior independent person acceptable to both sides'. Voting on this motion was less overwhelming than on the others. There were 125 votes for, and 69 against.

Finally, and of most concern to management, the meeting

resolved that *Herald* journalists should stop work until the first shift on Saturday. Not without some difficulties and omissions, but without any missed editions, the *Herald* was produced by non-union editorial labour for the next three days. Clark worked strenuously and conscientiously, but because of his unfamiliarity with the paper and its electronic system he naturally relied to a considerable extent on Alexander, Prisk, the assistant editor Ian Hicks, and others.

Brief though it was, this strike had a crucial effect on the company and its bankers. On Monday 15 February Whitlam Turnbull reported to Cotton that Citibank had so far been unable to syndicate any part of the $500 million facility. 'It is underwritten, of course, and hence not dependent on syndication, but the higher Citibank's exposure the less flexible it will be when flexibility is called for. This is largely driven by the uncertainty within Fairfax which has manifested itself in industrial disruption.'

Peter King, who was visiting his mother in South Africa, first heard of the strike on Thursday from a friend in Holland, who telephoned him about it. Earlier that day King had spoken to Dougherty, who told him there were no major problems. Some of the natives were restless, said Dougherty, but that was part of journalistic character. Then came the call from Amsterdam saying that the *Wall Street Journal* and the *Financial Times* were carrying reports of a strike at Fairfax. King rang Cotton, who urged him to come to Sydney as quickly as possible.

Cotton was by then aware that resignations might not be confined to the editorial department. The group publisher of the Sydney newspapers, Peter Gaunt, had complained to him about his marketing staff receiving directions from Martin Dougherty, usually conveyed through Paul Dougherty. Gaunt was considering joining Anderson, and others in his department were in the same frame of mind.

Peter King also rang Warwick Fairfax, who had gone to the United States for a Presidential prayer breakfast, and it was agreed that they should meet urgently in Sydney. King managed to get the last seat on a plane from Johannesburg to Hong Kong, connecting with a flight to Australia on Saturday. The proprietor, King and Cotton conferred in King's Sydney hotel room on the Sunday, and on Monday morning 15 February Warwick decided in consultation with King to terminate Dougherty's employment.

It was done that day. The proprietor saw Dougherty with King, who had formally taken office. Warwick said he did not think Dougherty had performed adequately in his position, and nominated a termination payment of $2 million. Later in the day Dougherty told the proprietor that he wanted $5 million. Warwick demurred, but agreed to pay $3 million—$2 million as a fee for the

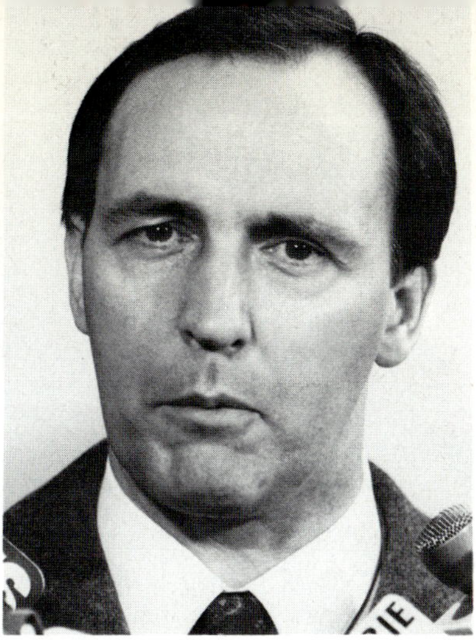

Maintaining the *Age*: the British newspaper proprietor Robert Maxwell (top left) tried hard to buy David Syme & Co Ltd. It seemed possible that the Treasurer, Paul Keating (above), might look favourably on that foreign ownership in spite of his own past differences with the Fairfax Group, and vigorous opposition from a 'Maintain Your *Age*' Committee (below), whose members included (left to right) Simon Crean, Ian Macphee, Frank Costigan, and the *Age*'s Canberra correspondent, Michelle Grattan. Unknown to the protesters, however, Warwick Fairfax, Peter King and Chris Anderson had decided to seek additional borrowing to avoid selling or floating David Syme.

(top right) Greg Taylor, managing director of David Syme

Thirty-eight days and 646 000 words in court: during the hearing of *Bond Media & Anor* v. *John Fairfax Group Pty Ltd & Ors* in the Supreme Court of New South Wales in October, November and December 1988, Warwick Fairfax spent 24 days in the witness box under examination by Fairfax Group's senior counsel, Neil McPhee, QC (below, left), and the plaintiffs' senior counsel, Tom Hughes, QC (right), and other counsel. He came through the ordeal with flying colours.

takeover, and $1 million as compensation for Dougherty's loss of income through leaving his public relations business. Other entitlements brought Dougherty's payout to $3 625 000.

At 6 p.m. Peter King broke the news of Dougherty's resignation to a meeting on the fourteenth floor attended by the editors of the *Financial Review* and *Times on Sunday*, Alan Kohler and Valerie Lawson; the new editors-in-chief of the *Herald* and *Sun-Herald*, Andrew Clark and Ita Buttrose; John Richardson, who was about to retire; and John Newnham, the former chief classified manager, whom Dougherty had appointed in Richardson's place. As soon as Clark returned to his office, he telephoned King and asked: 'How does this affect me?'

'You will be judged on your performance', replied the new chief executive officer.

The *Herald* reporter who was doing a news story about Dougherty's resignation, Jenny Curtin, came in to question Clark. 'What are you going to do?' she asked her editor-in-chief. 'Are you going to resign?' Clark responded with 'No comment', but off the record he said no.

On Tuesday he met Anderson twice, before and after lunch; and although he was still carrying out his duties as editor-in-chief, he had started thinking that his days in the job were probably numbered. Anderson already knew that was the case, for by the time he attended a farewell luncheon for himself and others on the Tuesday, he had been invited by Peter King to withdraw his resignation. The invitation was not too late to bring about a change of mind, for the strike and its sequel had left Anderson feeling, as he said, a prisoner of his own rhetoric. The reasons for his resignation no longer existed. Furthermore, he felt beholden to those who had resigned with him or gone out on strike, and he now wondered how life at News Ltd, under a proprietor who made no bones about interfering with editors, would compare with life in altered circumstances at Broadway.

Terms satisfactory to Anderson were agreed upon in negotiation on Wednesday. At 11.30 a.m. on Thursday 18 February Andrew Clark was called up to King's office to be told by Anderson and King that Anderson had been appointed group editorial director and a member of the John Fairfax board in place of Dougherty. (Five days later Anderson became a director of David Syme, as also did Warwick Fairfax, King and Cotton.)

John Alexander would become editor-in-chief of the *Sydney Morning Herald*, Anderson told Clark. There was nothing personal about it, he said, but he was asking Clark to accept an assistant editorship under Max Prisk, who would become editor. Clark had until 2 p.m. to consider the matter.

In spite of Clark's 'explosive' reputation, there were no raised voices. Those who dealt with him during that period were impressed by the manner in which he took the disappointment of having a great opportunity snatched away so soon after making a satisfactory start in extremely difficult circumstances.

King invited him to lunch, but he preferred to go back to his office, where he telephoned his father, the historian Manning Clark. Anderson came in to repeat that Alexander wanted him to stay as number three, and Alexander himself came to talk about it.

Clark said the offer was an attempt at humiliating him. He suggested returning to New York in charge of Fairfax operations in the United States; but Fairfax Publications (US) Ltd, rather than expanding beyond *Sassy* and *Ms*, would soon be contracting. In May 1988 Fairfax sold the two magazines for $A18 million to Matilda Publications Inc, which had been formed by the president and vice-president of Fairfax Publications (US) Ltd, Sandra Yates and Anne Summers.

The answer for Clark was London. Operations were contracting there too (the *Spectator* was sold to Conrad Black in April for $5.6 million, and *Money Magazine* for a lesser sum in the following month); but the London manager was about to retire, and Clark undertook to combine that post with writing for the *Financial Review* and *Sun-Herald*.

Peter King, Anderson and Cotton announced Anderson's appointment and several other board decisions to a meeting of Fairfax staff in the auditorium on Thursday afternoon. The position of Ita Buttrose on the *Sun-Herald* was reaffirmed (she resigned four months later, however, and was succeeded by David Hickie with the title of editor, Ray Odlum having resigned some weeks earlier) and Peter Gaunt was installed as general manager of the Sydney newspapers.

Richardson resumed his duties for the time being, and Anderson asked Newnham to return to his former position. It was inevitable that Newnham's recent appointment would be rescinded as part of Dougherty's eclipse. Newnham recognized this, but was unhappy with the way it was done and advised the company that he was going to consider his position. The classified staff came close to taking industrial action in sympathy with Newnham, just as the journalists had done with Anderson, and certain key members of that department were ready to go to News Ltd if Newnham took that course. Peter Gaunt intervened, and over the weekend he negotiated conditions on which Newnham agreed to return as chief classified manager.

Paul Dougherty left the company at the same time as his brother, and in Melbourne Peter King put an end to the retainer on which Martin Dougherty had placed Pat Boyce. (Boyce later took legal action against Fairfax over this. Creighton Burns retired as editor of the *Age* in October 1989 and was succeeded by the assistant editor, Michael Smith.)

As the *Herald*'s front-page headline put it, peace had broken out on Broadway. Resignations were withdrawn, and the contentious VDTs were removed from the executive floor. In the flush of victory the journalists' demand for a joint committee to select editors was set aside. So also were similar proposals which had been discussed at strike meetings—a charter of independence, and inclusion of the AJA's Code of Ethics in the company's articles of association. The new appointments had the confidence of journalists, and there was every reason to believe that editorial independence was secure. 'I really think we should stop making news', Anderson told the mass meeting on Thursday, 'and get back to reporting it, which we are good at doing'.

Terms of payment for the retrenched magazine journalists were settled to the union's satisfaction on 16 February, and a second redundancy package was agreed upon one month later without resort to industrial action. This time the number of redundancies was much higher, for the loss of employment was caused by closure of the *Sun* and the *Times on Sunday*. The closures were not unexpected, for the *Sun* was carrying an annual loss of more than $20 million and the *Times on Sunday* about $9 million. The decision to close both papers was forced through by Anderson as part of a board review of company strategy, and was announced to the staffs by him on the afternoon of 14 March. The news preceded him, as Malcolm Brown reported in next morning's *Herald* under the heading 'Shock, horror in the Sun newsroom':

> 'Broadway Horror. Paper Bashed To Death,' was the joke poster circulating in the *Sun* newsroom yesterday morning as journalists fidgeted while waiting for the pronouncement of doom.
>
> Someone tried to remember the song the men sang on the decks of the Titanic when, having put the women and children on the available lifeboats, they prepared for the end.
>
> It was a period of high emotion. Graham Davis, *The Sun*'s police roundsman, who for decades had pursued firemen, ambulances and policemen with a zeal that made him a legend, waited with eyes as ever alert.
>
> 'Hey Graham, where's your beeper, there's a fire at Oatley,' someone yelled, and Davis appeared to jump momentarily before seeing the joke.
>
> The announcement by the editorial director, Chris Anderson, was meant to be at 1.15 pm. But he was late. The news was already circulating on the AAP wires and journalists were reading it. . .
>
> There had always been a brooding bitterness among *The Sun* staff about other papers such as *The Sydney Morning Herald*, which shared the same floor and had at times had spats with its afternoon cousin.

> It came out yesterday when [the editor, John] Benaud said the Fairfax company had always put its quality papers such as the *Herald* and *The Australian Financial Review* before *The Sun*.
>
> They came to consider whether they would publish just one more edition, and a sub-editor yelled out: 'No, it'll only be a botched job if we do.' And that decided it. At four minutes to two. No more work, ever, on the *Sun*.

The *Sun* had first risen in 1910, under the auspices of Hugh Denison, and had been published by Fairfax since 1953. Some of those gathered in the news room had full-sized photocopies of the paper's first front page. This had been the first Australian front page to carry news, and, in the prevailing mood of 'shock, horror' seventy-eight years later, one of its reports still seemed facetiously relevant. The headline was: 'Harvard Wins; American Varsity Boat-race'.

Of course the real winner was News Ltd. Difficulties faced by afternoon papers everywhere—the declining use of public transport, greater popularity of television sports and news programmes, and changes in newspaper reading patterns as morning publications were being read later into the day—had cost the *Sun* nearly 130 000 in daily circulation since 1981. The *Mirror* had suffered too, but its circulation of 270 000 was still about 58 000 ahead of the *Sun*. Rupert Murdoch attended a victory dinner for the *Mirror* staff. According to popular report the editor remarked in his speech that 'we are all journalists, and no-one is gloating about the demise of the *Sun*'. Whereupon Murdoch, who had once danced an impromptu jig after acquiring the *Mirror* from Fairfax, said: 'I am'.

Undoubtedly there were also some who gloated about the demise of the *Times on Sunday*, for in its eighteen months of broadsheet existence this paper had made its own share of enemies as well as having inherited others from the *National Times*. The paper was falling further and further away from its long-term circulation goal of 200 000 (the latest figure was about 88 000, compared with more than 100 000 regularly achieved by the *National Times* in the late 1970s), and its advertising content had fallen from 40 per cent in 1986 to less than 20 per cent.

When Anderson arrived at the *Times on Sunday* to perform its obsequies he was asked whether there could be one more issue for the approaching State election. 'No chance', he replied. 'I know how you feel. It's just awful.' Five hundred and four jobs were made redundant by the two closures, but because many editorial and production employees elected to take early retirement the number of retrenchments was approximately 370.

There was one more redundancy, and a conspicuous one at that. Among the conditions set by Anderson for his becoming a director was that Laurie Connell should cease to be one. Whitlam Turnbull had also been advocating this, citing various inadequacies in Rothwells' performance and arguing that Connell's presence on the board was an impediment to refinancing. In spite of efforts to rescue Rothwells by Western Australia's entrepreneurial Labor Government, Connell's troubles seemed to be mounting. One of the first meetings which Anderson attended with his new co-directors—Warwick Fairfax, King and Cotton—considered the matter of Rothwells' fee. King repeated his earlier view that it was a success fee, and said that perhaps by any standard one would now have to question whether the takeover had been a success. Cotton agreed. Anderson said the takeover had not been a success, and he would take a lot of convincing that the fee was payable.

Although reserving final judgement on the fee, the directors decided to request the resignation of their absent colleague. On 4 March Warwick Fairfax sent Connell the following brief letter, composed by Queen's Counsel:

> Dear Mr Connell,
>
> I have spoken to our co-directors and we are in agreement that we have no longer any confidence in your contribution as a director of this company.
>
> I might add that your reputation is such that your position on the board is a serious embarrassment to the Company attaining suitable financial accommodation.
>
> I therefore ask you to sign and return the enclosed Notice of Resignation. In the event that you do not wish to do so, I shall convene an Extraordinary General Meeting to pass a resolution seeking your dismissal.
>
> Yours faithfully,
> W. G. O. Fairfax
> Proprietor.

As if to emphasize this parting of the ways, the *Herald* three days later devoted the top of its front page to a report by Andrew Keenan and Colleen Ryan, entitled 'How Laurie Connell lent money to super board head'. Their earlier report on the Rothwells rescue operation had not been published. This was attributed by the authors and other journalists to editorial caution, but Anderson maintained that the story had simply not come up to expectation. The story on 7 March, done by telephone from Sydney, revealed that a company controlled by Connell had lent $30 000 to the head of the West Australian State Superannuation Board at a time when Connell was involved in multi-million dollar negotiations with that Board. 'Mr Connell', it said, 'who was appointed late last year to the board of John Fairfax Ltd, which publishes this newspaper, has declined to answer any questions put to him by the *Herald*'.

On the other hand John Fairfax Limited, in the person of its proprietor, declined to have any further dealings with Connell. On

9 March Connell wrote to Warwick Fairfax saying that he was astounded by his letter. 'It is offensive and unwarranted and comes out of the blue', he wrote. 'You have never made a request of me that I have not complied with . . . I believe that I am entitled to a better and frank explanation.' In reply, Warwick declined to discuss the matter. Connell then faxed a short letter of resignation to the company's secretary, and his departure from the board was announced on the day the *Sun* and *Times on Sunday* were closed.

III

Perhaps those three closures marked the end of the Fall, the rock bottom from which things would at last begin to look up. At any rate, that was the impression conveyed by Peter King at a press conference held on 14 March to announce several decisions reached after detailed strategic assessment of the company's operations. 'The decisions', he said, '—perhaps the most difficult in the company's 150-year history—are aimed at consolidating Fairfax's position as a quality Australian publisher and setting a platform for growth and future expansion'.

Apart from the closures announced earlier in the day, Fairfax planned to maintain ownership of its New South Wales base: the *Sydney Morning Herald, Sun-Herald, Newcastle Herald, Illawarra Mercury* and community papers. It would also maintain and develop the *Australian Financial Review* and the *Business Review Weekly* group; seek equity participation in David Syme; sell its surplus property holdings in Australia and overseas; and consider offers for such non-publishing interests as Datamail and Planned Communications.

This was essentially Whitlam Turnbull's Scenario B, and as mentioned earlier Fairfax already had one firm offer from Maxwell for 50 per cent equity in David Syme, or alternatively 100 per cent. Rumours of a foreign purchase, probably by Maxwell, had begun to circulate almost as soon as the offers were made. The effect upon the *Age* staff was similar to the unrest at Broadway, though it did not lead to industrial action. On the day after Maxwell's latest offer, 13 February, the staff paid for a display advertisement in the *Age* placing on record its support for 'the continuing independence and integrity' of the paper, and declaring its complete confidence in the managing director and the editor. It said: 'We believe the best interests of the newspaper and you, its readers, will be served if The Age continues to be run by an independent, Melbourne-based board of directors'.

The *Age*, no less than the *Herald*, had become aware of Martin Dougherty's interest in editorial content. When the paper had put some questions to Connell about the Rothwells rescue, Dougherty telephoned the managing director, Greg Taylor, to say that the proprietor was upset about it. With ardour reminiscent of 1975, a 'Maintain your *Age*' committee was elected. It met almost every day, and often late into the night, to discuss new developments and ways of alerting the staff and public. Talks were held with several potential local buyers; but these, although more eligible in many ways than Maxwell, lacked his financial capability.

The union was not involved in this campaign, and the campaigners were not concerned with job security or improvement of wages and conditions. Their main objective was to ensure that no one should buy the *Age* for its cash flow and masthead, then strip it of integrity.

With touching faith in the efficacy of charters, the committee drew up an 'Age Charter' codifying certain well-established editorial practices on the paper. On 18 March a second advertisement appeared in the *Age* signed by forty prominent Australians, ranging from the Anglican Archbishop of Melbourne to the chairman of BHP and the president of the ACTU. A meeting of editorial staff unanimously approved the charter, which was intended for endorsement by any buyer of the paper.

The main points of the charter were that 'journalists, artists and photographers must record the affairs of the city, state, nation and the world fairly, fully and regardless of any commercial, political or personal interests, including those of any proprietors, shareholders or board members'; that editorial staff 'shall not be required to work other than in accordance with the AJA's Code of Ethics'; that 'full editorial control of the newspaper, within a negotiated, fixed budget, be vested with the editor of 'The Age'; that the editor alone shall determine the daily editorial content of the newspaper'; and that the editor alone 'shall hire, fire and deploy editorial staff'.

In an early draft shown to Creighton Burns, the charter had also provided that the editor should be a member of the board. 'Not on your life', said Burns, who had been a Reader in Political Science at Melbourne University before joining the *Age* in 1964. 'God made managing directors to protect editors from the board.' In its final form, the charter provided that 'the editor shall not sit on the board . . . and shall not be directly responsible to the board but to its appointed management'. Apart from that modification, Burns and Taylor took no part in the campaign. Taylor, who saw his job as keeping the company on a steady course, said later he would have gone public only if he had felt the *Age* was at risk.

The Federal Government's attitude to purchase by Maxwell, or any other foreign buyer, was a matter for speculation. The Treasurer had been invited to lunch with Maxwell and some of his editors while visiting Europe in February, but he later denied having discussed the fate of the *Age*, insisting that conversation had been about the state of the Australian economy. Towards the end of March Keating said publicly that he had reservations about foreign ownership of strategic areas of the news media such as the *Age*. It was not hard to believe, however, that he and his party might find some saving grace in Robert Maxwell, who had himself once been a Labour MP, and whose newspapers were consistently pro-Labour.

Chris Anderson—who was on better terms with the Treasurer than Suich had been—discussed the matter informally with Keating. The Treasurer gave no undertakings; but, according to a memorandum from Anderson to King on 18 March, he did say that if the *Age* was going to be sold to Maxwell it should be done quickly, and that he should be kept informed so the Government would not be taken unawares. Fairfax and Keating might find common cause, said Anderson's memo, in the fact that Maxwell would be a countervailing force to Murdoch.

With thoughts such as these in mind Peter King flew to Paris with Nicholas Whitlam and Malcolm Turnbull for more negotiations with the Maxwell organization. He wanted to establish what David Syme was really worth, in part or in whole, and for that purpose he was open to offers from Maxwell or anyone else, if only to determine market value. In negotiations at the Ritz Hotel on 22 and 23 March the two parties defined a package comprising 100 per cent of David Syme, the Fairfax-Syme electronic publishing ventures, part of Fairfax's shareholding in AAP Information Services, and continued publication of the *Financial Review* in Melbourne by Syme. But for what price? Robert Maxwell, who joined the proceedings with great bravura on the second day, proposed a form of bidding in which he would write his highest offer on a piece of paper and the Fairfax side would write down the lowest price it was prepared to accept. The figures would then be exchanged, and if Fairfax's was lower than Maxwell's a deal would be struck half way between the two.

Malcolm Turnbull persuaded Maxwell to forgo a public exchange of envelopes, and in further private negotiation it emerged that Maxwell's top figure was $805 million, to which Turnbull replied that Fairfax could not accept less than $850 million. The two parties then agreed to adjourn for three weeks, and meet again in London on 13 April.

This adjournment was a godsend to King, for in the last two days he had begun to doubt whether he personally, and John Fairfax Ltd corporately, would be able to work closely and harmoniously enough with a Maxwell-owned Syme to ensure the kind of co-operation and synergy which would be required to resist the stronger Murdoch group. It might be better, he was coming to think, if Fairfax held on to all its core assets including David Syme.

Since joining the company, Peter King had quickly become its main public figure. The proprietor, although taking part in some decision-making, eschewed public appearances and statements to such an extent that Robert Holmes à Court was moved to wonder publicly whether he actually existed. Warwick Fairfax took the view that he employed executives to run the company and represent it in public.

Peter Frank Sheard King, then aged fifty-two, may have been a newcomer to the media industry; but he was experienced in personnel management, and he inspired confidence. Warwick Fairfax was said to have remarked, perhaps only half seriously, that the ideal person for chief executive would be someone from outside the industry who was a Christian, and who was not an Australian. Peter King very nearly filled this bill, though in spite of his slight southern African accent he was now an Australian citizen.

Born at Kokstad, in what was then the Cape Province of South Africa and was now Transkei, homeland of the Xhosa nation, King grew up from the age of four in Southern Rhodesia, where his father was a maize and beef farmer. After the Federation of Rhodesia and Nyasaland came into being, he took citizenship there. In 1956 he joined the Anglo-American Corporation of South Africa Ltd, working on the copper belt, mainly in personnel management, and when the Federation was dissolved in 1963 he became a citizen of Zambia. Transferred to South Africa by Anglo-American, he reverted to the citizenship of his birth to obtain a work permit, and in 1969 joined the Van Leer group as personnel manager in Zambia.

Royal Packaging Industries Van Leer is an unusual company in that all its shares are owned by a philanthropic organization, the Bernard Van Leer Foundation, established under the will of the company's late founder and sole proprietor for the purpose of educating under-privileged children. Van Leer's thirty-three operating companies around the world retain what they need out of consolidated profits and pay the rest (currently more than $A20 million a year) to the Foundation. Basically the Foundation endeavours to help children 'impeded by the social and cultural inadequacy of their background', in any of the countries where Van Leer operates, 'to achieve the greatest possible realisation of their innate intellectual potential'. In Australia, it has funded endeavours of this kind with Aboriginal children in New South Wales and Victoria.

Peter King served as group personnel manager in Amsterdam, transferred to London and Johannesburg, and ran the Australian company for two years until, in 1985, he was invited to join the executive board in Amsterdam. A graduate of the senior management programme at Harvard, his management style was open, and his personal manner informal and jovial.

After the Paris negotiations, King telephoned Warwick Fairfax in

Sydney about his growing uneasiness at the prospect of selling David Syme to Maxwell, and asked him to come to London urgently. He also spoke to Anderson, who had already been advocating retention of David Syme and now reinforced King's feeling that as much of the group as possible should be kept intact.

In London, King and the proprietor agreed that they should be thinking in terms of additional borrowing in order to avoid selling or floating part or all of the *Age*. They felt, however, that the latter options ought to be kept open in case sufficient refinancing could not be arranged. To that end they did not confide in Whitlam Turnbull about their incipient change of mind, and they sounded out the London *Daily Telegraph* as a possible equity partner in David Syme.

On Saturday 26 March they flew to New York. This was to be partly a research trip, for King wanted to inform himself about the newspaper industry through contact with the *New York Times* and *Los Angeles Times*. More to the point, though, the United States was an abundant source of debt capital.

9
Angels

I

If Tryart was to retain all the core assets of John Fairfax, including the *Age*, it would need to replace its present bank facilities with a longer-term arrangement capable of being serviced by cash flow. That was self-evident. And if, as seemed likely, the senior debt available from trading banks proved less than adequate for that purpose, subordinate help would have to be obtained as well. Debentures could be issued to investors willing to risk their money, but ministering angels of that kind did not come cheaply. As subordinate debentures ranked behind senior debt in the event of an issuing company's collapse, they naturally carried higher rates of interest than usual—yet not too high for the ambitious or the desperate. In America this form of high-risk, high-yield security had achieved a mixture of notoriety and orthodoxy. It had financed some of the country's most avaricious corporate predators, and more constructively it had rescued some worthwhile companies judged too risky by traditional lenders. Not surprisingly, given their exploratory purpose in New York, Warwick Fairfax and Peter King called on various Wall Street investment banks for advice about placing high-yield debentures.

At Ansbachers on 29 March 1988 they happened to meet the newspaper publisher Ralph Ingersoll II, chairman and chief executive of a chain of 32 dailies and 110 weeklies in Missouri and other States. Ingersoll empathized with the young Australian, for he had been Warwick's present age of twenty-seven when, thirteen years earlier, he had inherited his medium-sized but fast-growing company. He knew his way around the high-yield bond market, and his advice was: 'Go see Drexel'. By this he meant the investment bank Drexel Burnham Lambert: not the head office in New York, but the branch in Los Angeles presided over by a financier of almost mythical renown, Michael Milken. Since 1985 Milken's high-yield bond department had raised $500 million for Ingersoll, who now prided himself on being 'close to Mike'. There and then he telephoned Milken and made an appointment for Fairfax and King to meet that prodigy in two days time.

Before going to Los Angeles they kept an appointment in Palm Beach, Florida, with Conrad Black, the owner of the London *Daily Telegraph*. This was to talk about selling the *Age*, a subject now of only academic interest to the Australians, though they were still keen to assess the paper's real value. At Miami airport King received a telephone call from Malcolm Turnbull relaying a demand from Robert Maxwell that Fairfax either accept or reject his offer immediately. King said the two parties had agreed to a three-week adjournment, and the Fairfax side would adhere to that.

At Los Angeles they were met by John Barber, the young American merchant banker who had become a welcome visitor at Fairwater while working in Sydney for Morgan Stanley several years earlier. Sir Warwick Fairfax had taken a liking to Barber, whose father, Professor of Economics at Wesleyan University in Connecticut, had been a Rhodes Scholar at Sir Warwick's alma mater, Balliol. The two had different politics (while at Yale, Barber had worked for George McGovern, against Nixon, and he was still a registered Democrat), but on the esoteric PIPS issue, then of such great concern at Fairwater, they saw eye to eye. On home leave in 1984 John Barber had also met and befriended Warwick the younger, who was then at Chase Manhattan.

Returning to the United States in 1987, Barber went into financial consultancy with one of his former Morgan Stanley colleagues, Warren Schlichting. Barber worked in New York, advising Hooker Corporation on its acquisition of Bonwit Teller, while Schlichting was based at the other end of America's financial axis, Los Angeles. In October 1987, thanks to an introduction by Mary Fairfax, they became two of the nine senior vice-presidents of WSGP International Inc, a merchant-banking firm established in Los Angeles by William E. Simon (WS) and Gerald L. Parsky (GP).

Simon was a former bond trader and partner at Salomon Brothers who had become Treasury Secretary in President Ford's administration and, after returning to private business, had done extremely well with a takeover manoeuvre known as the leveraged buyout (LBO). The LBO had much in common with Tryart's originally intended strategy of borrowing money to buy a company and then selling off sufficient assets to repay the loan, though LBOs were usually mounted in equity partnership with the target company's management.

In 1982–83 Simon and a partner, Raymond Chambers, pulled off the most spectacular LBO coup to that date by acquiring the Gibson Greeting Card division of RCA. When they had reorganized this company and taken it public again, Simon's original stake of $US330 000 had turned into a phenomenal $US70 million. By the time he parted from Chambers and formed the merchant bank with Parsky, a prominent Los Angeles lawyer who had been one of his

Assistant Secretaries in Washington, Simon's personal fortune was estimated by *Forbes* magazine at about $US400 million.

Lady Fairfax might conceivably have encountered Simon sooner or later in Los Angeles, for she sometimes patronized the Pritikin health and fitness clinic at Santa Monica; but in fact their first meeting had taken place in Brisbane in 1986. She had flown there for lunch with Bruce Judge, executive chairman of the Queensland-based international conglomerate Ariadne Australia Ltd, with whom she had become acquainted through his fellow New Zealander, Sir Ron Brierley. Simon had formed a business connection with Judge, and was also present at this lunch. He had come to Brisbane on his new 125-foot ketch, *Freedom,* a sea-going office equipped with a facsimile-satellite system which plucked the *Wall Street Journal* out of the heavens for him each morning.

Simon predicted great things for the 'Pacific Rim', and in 1986 he had taken Judge into partnership with himself and Parsky in a forerunner of WSGP called International Merchant Banking Services. Ariadne provided some of the funding for investments by this company. Ariadne's disastrous losses in the 1987 crash put an end to that brief alliance, however, and Simon and Parsky went ahead without Judge.

One consequence of Lady Fairfax's meeting with Simon was a decision by her, announced in 1987, to donate 40 hectares of land at Harrington Park as the site for an Australian branch of the William E. Simon Graduate School of Business Administration at the University of Rochester, New York State. The Simon school already had one overseas campus, in Rotterdam, and the University and its benefactor were now planning another one on the outskirts of Sydney.

By 1988 WSGP owned five savings and loan associations (so-called S & Ls, similar to Australian building societies), four in California and one in Hawaii. The outlook for S & Ls, formerly rather sleepy institutions with assets tied up mainly in fixed-rate mortgages, had been enhanced considerably by Government deregulation permitting them to make industrial and consumer loans. WSGP also owned or controlled two commercial banks (the World Trade Bank, somewhat less grand than its name, and First Interstate Bank of Hawaii, the third largest of its kind in Hawaii), and was actively engaged in corporate acquisition and restructuring, real estate investment and institutional money management.

In WSGP, and particularly in 28-year-old John Barber, Warwick Fairfax and Peter King had a ready source of aid and counsel for their meeting with Drexel Burnham Lambert. WSGP's office was in the World Trade Bank building directly across Santa Monica Boulevard from the Beverly Hilton, where Drexel held its annual High Yield Bond Conference, a festive gathering of clients known in the high-yield bond community as the Predators' Ball. Fairfax and King moved into this hotel, which was also handy to Drexel's office complex at the corner of Wilshire Boulevard and Rodeo Drive, an address at the very centre of Beverly Hills.

El Pueblo de Nuestra Senora la Reina de los Angeles, to use the original name, is a difficult entity to describe, for the 'Village of Our Lady Queen of the Angels' is now an aggregation of several cities between the Pacific and a backdrop of mountains named after the angels Gabriel and Rafael. The smallest and most opulent of these constituent cities is Beverly Hills, about half an hour's drive from downtown Los Angeles, between Hollywood and Century City. Sometimes called 'The Wall Street of the West', Beverly Hills is a small enclave of banks and bond brokers, emporiums, boutiques, galleries, de luxe hotels, and mansions once illumined by such stars as Mary Pickford, Joan Crawford and Judy Garland.

Here the traffic is sedate, with a high incidence of stretch limousines, and the palm trees lining Wilshire Boulevard create a pleasing impression of languid holiday. The impression is false, for Beverly Hills never relaxes in its pursuit of the next billion. It is a sanctuary of Mammon, and on its skyline are inscribed the names of secular angels: Bank of America, First Pacific, Wells Fargo, Shearson Lehman Hutton, City National, Drexel Burnham Lambert . . .

At the time of Warwick Fairfax's visit to Beverly Hills, the angel of highest rank was undoubtedly Michael Milken, despite a perceptible tarnishing of his reputation by recent legal proceedings. The errant stock speculator Ivan Boesky, sentenced three months earlier to three years gaol and fined $US100 million for insider trading, had managed to lessen his penalty by agreeing to give evidence against Drexel and Milken, both of whom were now under investigation by the Securities and Exchange Commission and the United States Attorney's office in Manhattan. That was common knowledge, but as yet Milken had lost none of his power and confidence. Each day he was at his desk by 4.30 a.m., getting ready for the bond market to open on the other side of the continent.

Born into a middle-class Jewish family in the San Fernando Valley of Los Angeles, Milken had joined Drexel in New York after graduating from Wharton business school, University of Pennsylania, in 1970. He started in the bond-trading department. Another newcomer at about that time—Fred Joseph, destined to become Drexel's chief executive officer and Milken's staunchest ally—would later recall their first meeting. 'It was clear he was very smart', said Joseph, 'but it was hard to interpret his fast trader talk, and he didn't know anything about banking and I didn't know anything about high yield bonds . . . We both kept looking at each other, thinking, Gee, I could probably do something with that guy'.

What they did—or rather, what Milken did with Joseph's support—was to foster a new form of debt capital. Milken did not invent high-yield bonds, but he recognized their potential, dubbed them 'junk bonds', and did more than anyone else to develop a $US180 billion market for them. From the start of his career, Milken had been fascinated with corporate bonds that had been issued as investment grade (rated Triple A because of the issuing company's balance sheet strength and credit record), only to be downgraded later because of deterioration in the company's performance or reputation, and consequently traded at a discount from face value. These were known as 'deep discount' bonds, or 'fallen angels'. Although they were 'junk', selling for as little as twenty cents on the dollar, in the right circumstances they could be surprisingly good investments. There was empirical evidence, which Milken had come across at business school, to show that a low-grade bond portfolio—if large, diversified and held over a long enough period—would outperform a high-grade portfolio. Although junk suffered more defaults than high-grade, its high yields more than compensated for losses. In other words, yield outweighed risk. That was Milken's sales pitch, and it worked.

Drexel's next step was to issue bonds which started out as junk—that is, bonds making no pretence of ever being anything other than high risk and high yield. Another Wall Street investment bank, Lehman Brothers Kuhn Loeb, had written several issues of this kind in 1977. Drexel overtook Lehman, and continued to dominate the expanding market. Milken, who some said *was* the market, gathered around him loyal investors attracted by high interest rates and the comforting knowledge that if they had to unload at any time Milken would be willing to bid, at a discount of course.

In 1978 Milken persuaded the firm to let him move his entire high-yield group to Los Angeles, away from the relatively cautious ambience of the main office. There was one more stage in the evolution of the high-yield bond. In 1982, while Chambers and Simon were dazzling Wall Street with their Gibson Greeting Card deal, Drexel began raising subordinate or 'mezzanine' funding for LBOs. Usually LBOs were financed with about 60 per cent of secured debt from trading banks, a 'mezzanine' of about 30 per cent unsecured, and perhaps an issue of 10 per cent equity in the target company. Milken stepped on to the mezzanine level, using junk bonds in place of more restrictively covenanted private placements with insurance companies.

Other investment banks did the same, spurring the takeover frenzy of the 1980s. But once again Drexel led the field, financing such raiders as Carl Icahn, Nelson Peltz, Ronald Perelman and Henry Kravis. By the age of forty Milken was a billionaire living in a house once owned by Clark Gable. His annual remuneration from Drexel amounted to $US135 million in 1985, $US294 million in 1986, and $US550 million in 1987. No one who had worked with him for five years, he claimed, was worth less than twenty million. 'Someone like Mike comes along once every five hundred years', said one grateful disciple. Even allowing for adulation, and taking into account the shadow cast by Ivan Boesky, it did seem that Warwick Fairfax was coming to the right place.

With a mixture of hope and caution Fairfax and King, accompanied by Barber, Schlichting and Ralph Ingersoll, arrived at Drexel's trading floor on the morning of 31 March to meet Milken and the vice-president in charge of capital markets, Peter Ackerman. After hearing about Fairfax's situation, its proposed strategy, and its need of approximately $500 million in subordinate debt, Milken said: 'We can do this. We'll do it in a month'.

Milken had not previously taken many foreign clients, although he had raised some debt capital for an American brewery purchase by Alan Bond. In the case of Fairfax he was presumably influenced by the residual value and potential of what was still a blue chip company, and by his friend Ingersoll's introduction.

Fairfax and King were delighted with this encouraging response. At WSGP's urging, however, they returned to New York for a series of meetings arranged by William Simon at Salomon Brothers, Shearson Lehman, Merrill Lynch, Bear Stearns and Morgan Stanley. All responded positively, but at the end of this comparison shopping expedition the two shoppers decided to go with Drexel. They returned to Los Angeles for another meeting on 20 April, attended by Milken and the managing director, Bruce Raben, who had been out of town on the first occasion.

By this time Fairfax and King had decided in telephone conference with Anderson and Cotton definitely not to sell the *Age*, although the issuing of equity in David Syme would remain an option for the future. King received one or two telephone calls from 'Maintain Your *Age*' activists in Melbourne, but felt constrained from telling them yet that their fears were groundless.

The Melbourne anxiety had been heightened by reports of Maxwell's interest, an offer of $700 million from Conrad Black, and inquiries from three Australian syndicates, including the property company Hudson Conway and a consortium organized by Macquarie Bank. The negotiations with Maxwell were now in fact suspended, for in mid-April Fairfax had set a minimum price of $950 million—almost certainly too high a figure to be forthcoming. Whitlam Turnbull was instructed to refrain from trying to sell the *Age*, and restrict its efforts to such other asset sales as might be requested by Fairfax. The bank's remuneration from Fairfax, including a $3 million 'kill fee' for its efforts to sell the *Age*, amounted to about $10 million. Because Fairfax's greatest need of financial advice was now in the United States rather than Australia, the company entered into a service agreement with WSGP.

So far as the *Age* staff knew, that paper was still for sale. On 28 April a delegation consisting of the Business Age editor, Steve Bartholomeusz, the Father of the Chapel, Mike Duffy, and journalists Rod Usher and Peter Stephens came to Sydney seeking the Fairfax board's endorsement of the 'Age Charter'. They saw Anderson and King, but returned to Melbourne empty-handed. Four days later they faxed a letter to King, repeating their request and warning that 'if you do not [endorse it] the staff will suspect your motives and your already dented image here will suffer'. Later the same day a call from Broadway informed them that the board would endorse both the letter and spirit of the Charter which, in the board's view, represented 'the relationship that has long existed between the Fairfax management and the employees of the *Age*'. On 20 May, King and Anderson informed the staff that Fairfax's preferred option for dealing with its debt was now to refinance. A final decision on the future of the *Age* would be made in June, and although Fairfax might consider some joint-venture options it would most likely retain full ownership of that paper.

Drexel moved quickly on preliminary stages, but soon found that the project was going to take much longer than a month. On 25 April a party of three—Bruce Raben, vice-president Jim Zimmerman and an associate, Karen Shishino—arrived at Broadway for a week-long reconnaissance of the company. Their visit was disclosed by the television commentator Max Walsh on 8 May. Fairfax's two bankers had been aware that the company was in contact with Drexel, but they were none the less surprised that matters had developed so quickly. In April Peter King had told Gerry Van der Merwe about the decision to refinance using junk bonds for subordinate debt, and invited Citibank to be one of the senior lenders. He had also been to see Bailey and McConnell in Melbourne, with the result that the ANZ relaxed its earlier pressure for further asset sales.

As it happened, Citibank was Drexel's lead commercial bank in the United States. Van der Merwe consulted the bank's credit policy member for Asia and the Pacific, Fred Catterson in Singapore, then talked to John McConnell and Bruce Maisey of the ANZ. It was agreed that the two banks would go halves in providing a secured senior debt, notionally about $900 million and probably involving other banks by way of syndication. Citibank would be the agent for structuring the facility, and Van der Merwe, a South African who had previously worked for Citibank in Johannesburg, would lead the bank side in its dealing with Drexel. His main assistants at Citibank were Mary Reemst, Mike Gelhard and a specialist in leverage finance, Jim Featherstone, who was brought to Sydney from Citibank's office in Dallas.

Certain difficulties were obvious from the start, and others soon became apparent. Because Fairfax's annual cash flow (a healthy

$102 million though it was for 1987–88) would not be sufficient to service all senior and subordinated debt from the outset, either the banks or Drexel would probably have to make it possible for the company to postpone part of its interest payment by means of a 'zero coupon'. This would mean lending additional funds with which Fairfax could pay the interest on part of its refinancing. On that part (an accreting facility rather than an amortizing one) the company would have zero obligation for several years, but then of course the piper would have to be paid. At the end of the interest holiday, the accreting facility would convert to current pay with regular interest.

There was also the risk of disadvantageous fluctuation in the rate of foreign exchange between America and Australia. If Drexel's bonds were to be issued in American dollars, as was initially assumed, someone would have to cover the currency risk by means of foreign exchange swapping; and given the probable duration of about twelve years, this would be difficult to arrange. Also the amount of debt required was increasing as new contingencies arose. For example, Drexel was surprised to learn about the $30 million which Warwick Fairfax had borrowed to buy 1.5 per cent of John Fairfax Ltd in February 1987, and the option to buy his mother's Acrux parcel.

Finally, there was more than the usual amount of tension between the senior and subordinate lenders when these parties met in Los Angeles for the first time late in July. Drexel's credit committee had approved a subordinate debt offering of up to $500 million; but this was by no means a final commitment, and terms had yet to be specified. Some degree of mutual suspicion was only to be expected when the two lending tiers came to grips over covenants and risks, and in this case suspicion was heightened by the storm gathering around Milken and Drexel.

Shortly before Van der Merwe, McConnell and their fellow negotiators went to Los Angeles, a rather alarming book had been published about Drexel. This was *The Predators' Ball* by Connie Bruck, a senior reporter for *American Lawyer*. Van der Merwe made it compulsory reading for his colleagues, and what they read was enough to put them all on guard. Milken had transformed the face of corporate America, wrote Bruck. Admittedly his awesome bond machine had forced inefficient companies to improve themselves before others did it for them, but it had also caused managements to concentrate on takeover defences rather than productivity.

> Experts would long debate whether the value that Milken's onslaught had added to American business outweighed the damage it had done . . . What was not debatable was that Milken, some of his Drexel colleagues and his anointed players had made more money in

> a shorter period of time than any other individuals had done in the history of this country. And they may have broken lots of rules and perhaps even a few laws to do it.

Writing twelve months after Ivan Boesky's agreement to co-operate with the Government's further investigation of insider trading, Bruck said that Drexel was

> still in limbo—its likely indictment spelled out in great detail in the press many months before but not yet issued by any grand jury . . . It seemed plain that even if Drexel and Milken were to survive, their idyll—in which Milken could raise billions in a matter of days for a hostile bid, in which no company in America was safe from him—would be ended. It was a time for epitaphs.

No wonder, then, that Van der Merwe and McConnell approached their Drexel counterparts warily. They also thought that WSGP was too close to Drexel, and for its part WSGP had reservations about the banks. On the first day, at WSGP's office, Gerry Parsky launched an angry attack on Citibank's proposed covenant and the size of its structuring fee. 'He was throwing paper around', recalled Van der Merwe later. 'We got Peter and Warwick back into the room and said: 'We're putting together a billion and we're not going to take abuse like this. Either you straighten him out or we fly back to Sydney.' They calmed him down.'

The two-week-long conference at the Drexel building was acrimonious from the start. The banks were jealous for their rights *vis-à-vis* subordinate debt, while Raben and Zimmerman insisted that Drexel could not issue the zero coupon, and could not bear any of the foreign exchange risk. Raben and Zimmerman also suspected the WSGP advisers—Barber, Schlichting and Chuck Berg—of siding with the banks. 'It was nightmarish', Van der Merwe recalled. For Peter King the worst moment came as he was walking from WSGP's office to the Beverly Hilton. Taking the quickest route, he braved the traffic of 'little' Santa Monica Boulevard and opened a heavy wire gate giving access to the parallel and busier 'big' Santa Monica. The gate sprang back, hitting King full in the face and leaving him to cross the freeway with a bleeding forehead. That just about summed it up, for the July conference was a most painful rebuff to Fairfax hopes.

Believing the deal with Drexel to be dangerously near collapse, Citibank and ANZ spent most of August trying to put the sub-debt together in Australia. They came close to doing so with the AMP and some Japanese investors, but the amount required was simply too large. In the meantime, however, Peter Ackerman had been on the telephone to King, saying that he now thought Drexel could sell the currency risk to its investors. 'We told Ackerman we didn't appreciate the way he had put his gorillas on to us', said Van der Merwe later, 'and unless he was coming back with a live deal we wouldn't see him. He is a very polished individual, and we got it back on track again'.

Ackerman was a formidable combination of academic intellect and tough business instinct, with two master's degrees and a PhD in international relations. In his ten years at Drexel he had risen to become Milken's right-hand man on LBO financing, and in that capacity he now took a more active and conciliatory part in the Fairfax negotiations. To the banks' relief he agreed to make Payment in Kind (PIK) a feature of the subordinate debt. Under this provision, which could be triggered by the banks if they deemed it necessary to protect the borrowing company's cash flow, Fairfax would have the right to pay some of its semi-annual junk-bond interest instalments in kind—that is, by issuing junior subordinated debentures equal in principal to the amount of interest falling due.

Another feature of the subordinate finance took longer to settle. The company and its senior lenders realized that some sort of 'sweetener' would have to be used by Drexel in placing the debentures. This was customary in the high-yield market, and although the precise form of what were to become known as Equity Appreciation Rights (EARs) was not finalized until late in the talks with Drexel, the general idea was clear enough. Drexel would have at its disposal a certain number of equity warrants which it could attach to debentures in need of sweetening. The warrants would be quasi-shares, entitling their holders to non-voting equity in the company at some prescribed future date unless the company exercised its right to buy them back.

On 29 August Drexel at last sent one of its 'highly confident' letters to John Fairfax Ltd, declaring itself 'highly confident of its ability to provide [subordinate finance of $450 million]'. This was its customary way of making a penultimate commitment, and the firm claimed that it had never yet reneged on such a letter.

For the past few weeks, two of the leading law firms in Los Angeles—O'Melveny & Myers and Latham Watkins, acting for Fairfax and Drexel respectively—had been conducting 'due diligence', the investigative process required in America before preparation of a Private Placement Memorandum, or prospectus for a bond issue. Due diligence provides the only defence in United States law against heavy penalties for inaccuracy or omission in a prospectus. The Securities and Exchange Commission insists upon full disclosure of weakness as well as strength, and in all the documentation which John Fairfax would eventually have to file for public inspection in Washington the company would find itself submitting to a degree of self-exposure amounting almost to exhibitionism.

Lawyers play a crucial role in the issuance and registration of American securities, and in O'Melveny & Myers Fairfax was fortunate to have a firm with some knowledge of Australian conditions. When the need for counsel first arose, John Barber made a late-night telephone call to an Australian friend, Mary Molyneux, who was an associate at O'Melveny. She was able to arrange a meeting for him early next morning with one of the firm's senior partners, Edward J. McAniff, who not long before had spent a sabbatical year working in Sydney at Freehill Hollingdale and Page. Most of the legal work for Fairfax was done by Jay Herron at O'Melveny's Newport Beach office, and according to McAniff his role was crucial to the whole project.

At senior debt level, the banks had agreed to do the zero coupon, and Citibank was arranging interest rate swaps necessary to provide a fixed rather than floating rate for the bank facilities. 'A floating rate starting at say 13 per cent and rising to maybe 20 per cent could easily destroy a company in Fairfax's position', said Van der Merwe later. 'Rates began to rise during the due diligence period, so swaps were pre-condition Number One.' The management of swaps, in which two parties choose to exchange types of borrowings because the interest rate structure of each suits the other better, is one of the most arcane and sophisticated businesses in the world of finance. Citibank was well placed to do the interest swaps, for its 'warehouse' containing $28 billion worth of swap deals was the largest in Australia.

While financial matters were thus being resolved satisfactorily, Drexel's looming trouble with the Securities and Exchange Commission materialized in the form of a civil suit accusing the firm and four of its employees, including Milken, of securities fraud totalling an estimated $US100 million. Early in September John Fairfax Ltd received an explanatory letter sent to all Drexel clients by the chief executive officer, Fred Joseph, and the chairman of the board, Robert E. Linton. The tone was highly confident, but none the less disturbing to anyone whose trust had been reposed in that firm.

> We believe, based on information available to us, that the charges filed by the SEC are wrong. After an examination of 1.5 million pages of documentation and interviews of scores of Drexel Burnham employees, we continue to believe that neither Drexel Burnham nor any of our employees named in this matter have engaged in any wrongdoing. We expect to be vindicated.
>
> A thorough examination of the SEC complaint shows that the charges rely almost entirely on accusations by convicted felon Ivan Boesky . . . The linchpin in the complaint is Boesky's payment of a $5.3 million fee to Drexel Burnham in March 1986. The evidence indicated that this fee was payment for normal corporate finance, research and other advisory services furnished to the Boesky organisation prior to March 1986.
>
> Indeed, Ivan Boesky's allegations must be viewed in the context in

> which they were made: Boesky was desperate to settle with the SEC and to minimise his own punishment by accusing others. We are particularly eager to confront Ivan Boesky in the fair and open forum of a court to demonstrate that his charges are false.
>
> It is important to recognise, however, that the filing of these charges by the SEC does not necessarily represent the only front upon which Drexel Burnham and our employees may ultimately need to fight to prove our innocence. The US Attorney, as you are aware, has been conducting his own investigation which has yet to be resolved. In addition, various Congressional committees continue to pursue their own studies.
>
> We at Drexel Burnham have been operating successfully in a difficult environment since Ivan Boesky's criminal actions publicly surfaced . . . This performance is reflected in our strong financial position, with total assets of over $30 billion, total capital of approximately $2.3 billion, and excess regulatory capital of approximately $1.1 billion. The SEC complaint does not quantify the amount of monetary relief it seeks; however, it appears that the total amount is in the range of $100 million. Although we expect full vindication in court, the firm has provided generous reserves for any contingency.

Eight days after the arrival of this letter, on 20 September, John Fairfax Ltd announced that it had reached general agreement for a long-term restructuring of its debt, then amounting to about $1.4 billion. The ANZ and a syndicate led by Citibank would provide a total of about $1 billion, and Drexel would find buyers for high yield bonds amounting to between $400 and $500 million. No further details were announced, but Peter King said that he expected the package to be completed within three weeks. In that regard he was too optimistic.

II

If by this time Warwick Fairfax had been worn down by all his difficulties, he could have put an end to them by calling off the refinancing and selling out completely. Such an opportunity had already been presented by Alan Bond, whose Bond Media Ltd had paid Rothwells $68 million for the right to collect $100 million from Tryart on 29 June 1988. At a meeting with Peter King on 5 May, two go-betweens for Bond—none other than Laurie Connell and Martin Dougherty—conveyed an offer of $800 million for the *Age*, intimating that the figure was open for negotiation, and that Bond might also be interested in taking over all shares in John Fairfax Ltd. After passing this on to the proprietor, King informed Dougherty that neither the *Age* nor the whole company was open for negotiation. Dougherty tried again two weeks later with an offer of $1.8

billion for the whole company. A price like that would have permitted Warwick to extricate himself with up to $400 million left over for his own future use and his mother's recompense. But he was not interested.

The only assets disposed of at around this time were 50 per cent of Fourth Estate in New Zealand, which went to the Auckland-based Liberty Publishing Ltd on the undertaking that Liberty would finance it for two years; the Hunter Street property, for which Leda Holdings Ltd paid $35 million; and an agreement by Fairfax to allow its equity in *Time Australia* to be diluted in lieu of providing further loans to finance losses.

Time Australia, a fifty-fifty venture with Time Inc, was losing money without any sign of going into profit. The publisher, Steve Congerton, had found selling advertising for a composite American-Australian magazine much more difficult than expected. Despite the best efforts of the Australian editorial staff in Melbourne, readers and advertisers alike were chary of the Australian content, which was sometimes as much as 25 per cent. To some, the magazine seemed too much like the *Bulletin*.

Alarmed at the continuing losses, Fairfax arranged to pass half its equity to Time Inc over a period of two years from September 1988 in exchange for that company taking full responsibility for management and funding. BRW ceased to have any management responsibility for the Australian and New Zealand editions of *Time*, and Congerton's place was taken by an American, E. Bruce Hallett, who moved the magazine's headquarters to Sydney. Fairfax was then merely a shareholder, whose holding by September 1990 would be 25 per cent.

In addition to these three asset disposals, there was in mid-1988 one other prospect of substantial gain—or rather, of avoiding a very large outgoing. This was the $100 million fee which might or might not be owing to Bond Media Ltd. On or about 26 May the four directors of John Fairfax Ltd—Warwick Fairfax, King, Anderson and Cotton—took a firm decision not to pay, and to seek legal advice about the matter. King said that in view of all the company's problems he could see no reason why the fee should be paid. Anderson agreed. Cotton and the proprietor were not sure, but concurred in the decision.

Shortly before the due date Rothwells' solicitors wrote to Fairfax inquiring about the fee, and on 28 June Mallesons Stephen Jaques replied as follows:

> On our instructions, Rothwells Limited has neither fully nor properly performed its obligations under the Agreement made on 28 August 1987. Some aspects of the services which Rothwells rendered were seriously defective and other services which Rothwells

> was required to render were not rendered or were not completed. It follows that the fee of $100m referred to in the Agreement has not been earned and is not owing.

Legal battle was then joined between Bond Media and Rothwells on the one side, and Tryart—or more correctly, John Fairfax Group Pty Ltd, for Tryart had been thus renamed on 1 August. Matters soon became more complicated, for not only were there to be two plaintiffs and one defendant but also one cross-claimant and five cross-defendants. The proceedings began during July when Bond Media and Rothwells issued a summons in the commercial division of the Supreme Court of New South Wales, claiming an order that the defendant pay the sum of $100 million to the first plaintiff, or alternatively to the second plaintiff. Clause 5 of the Tryart Agreement had provided for a fee 'in consideration of and conditional upon Rothwells properly performing its services', and in the light of subsequent events, said the summons, that was now due and payable.

In its cross action, John Fairfax Group denied that the plaintiffs were entitled to the fee, and sought damages of at least $150 million because Rothwells had failed to perform its services properly. For various reasons adduced in the particulars of defence, the defendant submitted that all agreement between Tryart and Rothwells (including the Tryart Agreement) should be rescinded. To be binding upon the defendant, it said, that agreement must be an entire contract, under which Rothwells would have no entitlement to the fee unless there had been complete and proper performance on its part. Then followed a recital of alleged failures to provide complete and proper performance, to which the plaintiffs replied in a counter claim.

Firstly, Rothwells should have advised Tryart not to announce the takeover offer when it did, because of several known risks: that some or all of the Fairfax family would accept the offer; that the Fairfax superannuation and employee benefit funds would accept it; that members of the Fairfax family would not support the offer, or would actively oppose it; and that some or all of them, even if they did not accept the offer, would resist the sale of assets by John Fairfax Ltd and distribution of sale proceeds to the defendant. So far as the funds were concerned, there had been no proper basis for assuming, as Rothwells had done, that the trustees would—contrary to the interests of beneficiaries, and the provisions of the Income Tax Assessment Act—reinvest up to $216 million in John Fairfax Ltd.

For their part, the cross-defendants denied any failure to give proper service or advice. Each of the risks referred to had been well known to Tryart and Warwick Fairfax, and had been the subject of advice and consultation with him. On advice received by Rothwells at the time, it had believed that the superannuation funds could invest with some other company, which could in turn, without breaching the Income Tax Assessment Act, make an appropriate investment in Fairfax. Furthermore, the cross-defendants said that the risks would not have justified advice against proceeding with the offer.

Secondly, the August takeover proposal had made no provision for payment of the fee; and no disclosure had been made about the fee to the ANZ. The cross-defendants admitted this, but said the non-disclosure had been at Warwick Fairfax's instruction. All financial projections shown to him had taken the fee into account, but at his direction the projections sent to ANZ had not disclosed it.

Thirdly, the offer should not have included an alternative of fifteen Syme shares in payment for two Fairfax shares because there would have been insufficient Syme shares to satisfy acceptance of this alternative by all to whom the offer was made. The cross-defendants admitted this, but said the alternative had been promptly withdrawn.

Fourthly, the final offer of $8.50 per share had represented a multiple of sixty times earnings, which was grossly in excess of price earnings multiples for comparable companies at that time. At such a price, it was submitted, Tryart/Fairfax would be unable to service its residual consolidated borrowings and unable to repay its debts. The cross-defendants admitted the historically high nature of the price, but otherwise denied the allegation.

Fifthly, Rothwells had assumed wrongly that the current unsecured creditors of John Fairfax Ltd (National Australia Bank, Westpac and other banks, with total lending of more than $450 million) would permit $1829 million worth of asset proceeds to be used to repay the ANZ in priority to themselves. The cross-defendants admitted that this assumption had been made, but said it was reasonable.

Sixthly, Rothwells had again wrongly assumed that the whole of the discounted proceeds from the sale of the Seven Network to Qintex would be available to help repay the ANZ, notwithstanding that Fairfax board papers, to which Rothwells had access, recorded that the Qintex proceeds would be used to reduce the borrowings which had been incurred for the network purchase. Nor had Rothwells made any approach to John Fairfax Ltd's bankers or Qintex to clarify use of the Qintex proceeds. In reply, Rothwells denied having had access to the relevant board papers, and said that any approach to the banks had been precluded by the express direction of Warwick Fairfax.

Seventhly, Rothwells should have advised Tryart to seek to withdraw its offer, for several reasons. These included some of the failures already alleged, the decisions by James and John Fairfax to accept the cash offer in full, failure of the funds either to retain their shares or reinvest the proceeds of acceptance, the stock market crash, and its effects upon the proposed float of Syme shares and asset sales then in course of negotiation. The cross-defendants denied that they should have given such advice. Tryart and Warwick Fairfax had been well aware of all the matters referred to, and had decided to proceed nevertheless.

Eighthly, in the course of asset sales Rothwells had failed to investigate the articles of association of Australian Associated Press and Australian Newsprint Mills so as to become aware of their pre-emptive rights provisions. This was denied.

Ninthly, in negotiating the sale of Macquarie to Bell Group Rothwells had agreed to a put option rendering Tryart liable to a demand that it repurchase the radio network for $32 812 500 more than the selling price. Because of this option, considerable uncertainty had existed as to who the eventual owner of the network would be. This had created severe morale problems among staff, creating a danger that if Bell exercised its option the network would by then have become an asset of much lower value than at the time the put option had been agreed upon. Rothwells replied that the option had been negotiated with Warwick Fairfax's knowledge, consent and authority. It admitted that Bell's apparent profit from exercising this option would be $32 812 500, but said $25 million of that sum represented a mechanism for adjusting the price at which the *Financial Review* was to be sold, and the remainder represented the interest cost to Tryart of using Bell's funds. Given this, the cross-defendants denied that the put option price was in any way excessive or improper.

Tenthly, in negotiating the sale of the *Canberra Times* to Consolidated Press Rothwells had supplied profit projections without proper regard to the Fairfax board papers for July and August 1987, which noted substantially reduced profitability for the *Canberra Times*. Rothwells denied having had access to those board papers, saying that it had relied on information supplied by Warwick Fairfax.

There were many other allegations of non-performance, but the foregoing are more than sufficient to demonstrate the 'Byzantine perplexity and complexity' of the coming trial, as one of the participants described it. On 7 September John Fairfax Group broadened its counter claim by obtaining leave from the chief judge of the commercial division—Justice Andrew Rogers, who had listed himself for the case—to add Martin Dougherty, his company Tabulum Holdings Pty Ltd, and Bert Reuter to the list of cross-defendants. This action, so the cross-claimant informed the court, was being taken because it had recently come to Fairfax's knowledge that

Dougherty and Reuter had each had an interest in the Rothwells fee. As mentioned in an earlier chapter, the fee was originally to have been split between Rothwells ($45 million), Reuter ($45 million) and Dougherty ($10 million), although Dougherty was apparently unaware of the size of Reuter's share. But after Rothwells discounted the fee to Bond Media, the arrangement was revised to give Reuter $8 million and Dougherty $2 million.

According to Fairfax's amended particulars of defence, these expectations put a different complexion—amounting to breach of fiduciary duty—upon certain actions by Dougherty and Reuter while they had been directors of Tryart. In Dougherty's case, the cited actions included his advice not to negotiate with Rothwells for a lower fee, to enter into the Tryart Agreement, to announce the takeover offer, to increase the share price offer, and to enter into the Memorandum of Understanding for assignment of the fee to Bond Media. It was alleged that on all such occasions involving advice, agreement or action by Dougherty and/or Reuter, each had been in a position where his duties conflicted or may possibly have conflicted with his interest. At no time prior to the recent discovery had Dougherty, Rothwells or Reuter disclosed to Tryart or Warwick Fairfax the existence of those interests.

In consequence, John Fairfax Group was claiming additional damages of such magnitude that Mr Justice Rogers was moved to ask whether Dougherty would be 'horrified'. In Dougherty's case, the cross-claimant sought full repayment of the $10 million which had initially been due to him from the fee; $2 million, or such sum as may have been paid to him under the subsequent arrangement; and the sum of more than $3 million paid to him on his departure from Broadway. In Reuter's case the cross-claimant also sought repayment of both his initial and revised shares—$45 million and $8 million. Obviously there was some overlapping in these claims, but press reports stated simply that the damages sought against Dougherty and Reuter could total more than $68 million. At a preliminary hearing two days later Dougherty's counsel told the judge that his client was 'horrified and appalled' at the allegations, and would defend himself most vigorously against them. Warwick Fairfax had at all relevant times been aware that Dougherty was to receive part of the Rothwells fee, he said, and had 'consented and approved' the payment of $2 million to him. Reuter denied that he had been guilty of any breach of duty.

Four days before the case began, Justice Rogers was replaced by Justice Roger Giles, who had joined the Supreme Court bench only six months earlier. The chief judge offered no explanation for this last-minute change, but it was believed that he had disqualified himself because of his acquaintance with the lawyer Aleco Vrisakis, who might be called as a witness. Justice Giles was quietly spoken, benign in manner, yet always firmly in charge of the proceedings before him.

Bond Media & Anor v. *John Fairfax Group Pty Ltd & Ors* began on Monday morning, 17 October, at the steady pace of a cross-country run which was going to last a long, long time. The field consisted of six QCs, one of whom was reputed to charge $5000 a day, and another $4000; six assisting barristers; and an array of solicitors and clerks who each day wheeled trolleys full of documents in and out of the tiny courtroom 11E. More than a thousand documents had been produced, including prepared statements by Warwick Fairfax (56 pages), Dougherty (56), Connell (71), Reuter (74) and Cotton (100). Fairfax's solicitors were as usual Mallesons Stephen Jaques. The plaintiffs were using Bond's usual solicitors for media work, Allen Allen and Hemsley, who had briefed T. E. F. Hughes, QC, J. D. Heydon, QC, and two senior juniors. Hughes, the first to open, was one of the most redoubtable silks of his day, and the most theatrically accomplished.

His opening address began like the prologue for a play within a play, setting the scene and foreshadowing a cathartic re-enactment of past events. 'Your Honour', he began, 'this is a case about a very large debt, very large even by today's standards of appreciated currency'.

> First, however, let me etch in some of the necessary background. The catalyst of the immediate events which bring the parties to this court may be thought to be the death in January 1987 of Sir Warwick Fairfax . . . It would appear from the evidence that Mr Warwick Fairfax was at that stage and indeed had been for some time very concerned about the state of the management of the John Fairfax empire . . . Mr Warwick Fairfax had an ambition, a very strong ambition. The evidence will disclose that in his state of dissatisfaction with the management of John Fairfax Ltd he wanted to gain control of the company. He wanted to gain control of the company whatever the risk and virtually whatever the cost. He obviously held the view that if he did not move in that direction the empire might crumble or even worse be taken over by an acquisitive corporate predator. Apparently he nourished fears—and nobody suggests that they were ill-founded—that Mr Holmes à Court, Robert Holmes à Court, might be that predator . . .
>
> He became, if he was not one already, a young man in a hurry. A young man in a hurry to gain control for himself of the empire of which he regarded himself as the legitimate heir. It might be said when one reads some of the documents that will go into evidence in this case that he regarded the empire as his birthright and that he regarded the people presently in control of the company as open to severe criticism on the grounds of mismanagement. I am not saying that on the basis that we support any such perception. It may or may not have been correct. The point is that it was Mr Warwick Fairfax's

> perception of affairs . . . and the evidence will make it plain that [he] determined for himself that he would obtain control of the empire even if it involved making a bid for all the company, and reached that conclusion on the basis that if he had to incur a large amount of debt to acquire all or virtually all the company he would sell off some of the jewels in the Crown—and there were many, there was a treasury box full of jewels—so long as . . . in the worst case he finished up with control of the principal jewel in the Crown, the *Sydney Morning Herald*. That was his state of mind.

As a foretaste of what was to come, Hughes issued a gratuitous challenge to Warwick Fairfax, who was present in the courtroom. Speaking of the proprietor's refusal to discuss with Connell his written request for the latter's resignation, Hughes said, or rather declaimed:

> Unless Mr Warwick Fairfax gets into the witness box in this case and explains exactly why unfortunately he did not wish to meet Mr Connell man to man and face to face; unless he gets into the witness box and gives an adequate explanation, the view is open that he is a coward.

This brought strenuous objection from Fairfax's senior counsel, a Victorian QC, Neil McPhee, who realized that his learned friend was seeking to create an impression that Warwick would have to be forced into the box. As Warwick Fairfax's witness statement had already been filed, it was a foregone conclusion that he would be called to give evidence. 'That is a quite unnecessary remark, your Honour', said McPhee, 'and it is perfectly obvious that Mr Fairfax can give evidence in this case and Mr Hughes can try and tell him something then'.

> HIS HONOUR: In the light certainly of what Mr McPhee has said, I will be expecting to see Mr Fairfax in the box.
> HUGHES: I would like your Honour to see him and I will issue a challenge that unless he explains why he would not meet Mr Connell face to face and man to man, he is a coward.
> HIS HONOUR: Mr Hughes, I don't think cowardliness is an issue in this case.

Hughes then examined the scope of the obligations accepted by Rothwells in the Tryart Agreement. Firstly, Rothwells had accepted appointment to 'advise and assist' in several matters, principally the takeover offer and the manner of dealing with indebtedness incurred for that purpose. According to Hughes, 'advise' and 'assist' were two words denoting one idea, which was 'advisory assistance'. Another of Rothwells' obligations had been 'to use its best endeavours to ensure that the Take-over Offer is successful'. In Hughes's submission, 'success' meant nothing more than 'attaining the Minimum Acceptance Number'—that was to say, not less than 36.15 per cent of the issued Fairfax shares excluding those already owned by Rockwood and Acrux.

In his further submission, Rothwells' role had been specifically limited to one of advising and assisting Tryart, with no obligation to provide any such services to John Fairfax Ltd. If that view was correct, he said, it would follow that much of the defendant's case, seeking to raise allegations that Rothwells had performed inadequately in relation to the refinancing of John Fairfax Ltd's debt to various bankers, was quite misconceived.

Secondly, Hughes drew attention to Clause 9 of the Tryart Agreement, which precluded Rothwells from holding out to any person that it was an agent for Tryart. Because no relationship of principal and agent could arise under the Agreement, he submitted, any assumption by Rothwells of the role of Tryart's agent in the course of arranging asset sales could not have been the consequence of any contractual obligation.

> We say in short that in so far as Rothwells did those negotiations its actions in doing so were not actions taken under the Agreement. If Rothwells owed any legal duty to Tryart as Tryart's [agent] in relation to the conduct of such negotiations it was a duty outside the Agreement and non-fulfilment of that sort of duty cannot be pleaded in bar of the plaintiff's claim.

In concluding his opening address, Hughes submitted that the limitation of obligation to Tryart and the prohibition on agency left many of the defendant's allegations of non-performance very much open to question.

McPhee, who addressed the court next, was less rhetorical than Hughes. He ignored the gallery, speaking exclusively to the bench in a voice which did not always carry to the back of the court. Described by colleagues as 'laconic' and 'pugnacious', he was one of Fairfax's main defamation silks, best known for his victory in an action brought by the architect Harry Seidler over a cartoon by Patrick Cook in the *National Times*. McPhee was said to be good with juries, but in *Bond* v. *Fairfax* the only person he needed to persuade was the judge. He was assisted by W. G. Caldwell, QC, and two senior juniors, Stephen Rares and Michael Ellicott.

After a prologue of his own, McPhee dealt with the allegations against Dougherty before proceeding with Fairfax's defence and counter-allegations against the plaintiffs. 'We contend that there was a fiduciary relationship', he said.

> Warwick Fairfax regarded Dougherty as a friend. He regarded him as somebody who was on his side, and somebody who shared many of his views. He trusted him. He gave to Dougherty all the information that he had about the Fairfax organisation. He told Dougherty all about his own personal position. He told him of his aspirations. He

> told him what he would do and what he was not prepared to do. He turned to him for advice—advice about the takeover, advice about Connell and Reuter, and the $100 million, and he put his confidence in him and that was a confidence that was betrayed.

McPhee then cited some of the advice which Dougherty was alleged to have given on crucial occasions. For example, on the day the Tryart Agreement was about to be signed he had told Warwick Fairfax: 'We are being far too tough. We should not be this tough, otherwise Connell will walk away and if he does we have had it'. And again on the same day: 'The $100 million is cheap in comparison with the joint venture proposal'.

Dougherty had wanted to get a fee from both sides, said McPhee. Warwick Fairfax had always known and contemplated that Reuter would be receiving a substantial fee under the Tryart Agreement, but not that Dougherty would. 'Your Honour may think', he said, 'that the agreement to pay $100 million, and the existence of those two secret agreements [on sharing the fee] may assist to better understanding the events that took place subsequently in these transactions'.

Turning to the Tryart Agreement, McPhee took issue with Hughes's contention that 'advise and assist' should be read as 'advisory assistance' or, as McPhee put it, 'advise and advise'. 'In our submission there is no basis for considering the Agreement in that way', he said. 'One must start from the facts that existed at the time this agreement was entered into and they include Mr Fairfax's inexperience in the takeover field, the obvious experience of Mr Connell and Mr Reuter and the reasons that they were engaged . . .'

'Advise and assist' meant the rendering of assistance as well as advice, and 'that assistance would include negotiations with banks and negotiations with the persons who propose to buy assets. Indeed, that is what was done and what the parties contemplated would be done'. Clause 9 did not prevent Rothwells from acting as agents if that was the type of assistance which Tryart required and authorized.

> For example, when the Holmes à Court agreement was entered into, [Rothwells] were armed to enter into the agreement with the Bell Group and that is what they did. Mr Hughes suggests that most of the important work that they did was far outside the contract and I must say that . . . sent a chill up the spines of those instructing me because [Rothwells] say they are entitled to be paid for it and if $100 million is a measure of the work they did inside the contract, one hesitates to think what the cost will be for the claims . . . external to the contract. If there is one thing that is obvious, [it is] that everything these people did fell within the contract and the payment of $100 million.

In McPhee's submission, the fee was not merely 'substantial', as stated in the Tryart Agreement; it was nothing less than outrageous. Evidence would be given, he said, that competent merchant bankers would commonly have charged a fee of about 0.5 per cent of the money involved in the bid—which in Tryart's case would have amounted to perhaps $10 million.

The defendants based their refusal to pay on a variety of grounds, said McPhee, but particularly on Rothwells' failure to give proper advice in respect of the takeover offer, and failure to provide a range of calculations for asset sales. Tryart should not have been advised to make a bid unless the financial adviser was confident that the takeover was achievable—confident in terms of the enforcement of sales contracts that Tryart would finish up with a viable company capable of comfortably servicing its debt. And if the point was reached when, notwithstanding Warwick Fairfax's enthusiasm, the appropriate advice would have been not to proceed, then that advice ought to have been given. 'At no point throughout the whole history of this matter was that advice ever given', said McPhee, 'but an analysis of the transactions will show that at various points of time that advice should have been given'.

Furthermore, any competent merchant banker advising on a takeover offer would produce a projected balance sheet, profit and loss account and cash flow calculations for both the bid vehicle and the target company. Nothing less than that would suffice to indicate the eventual outcome, yet such documents had not been prepared by Rothwells. Speaking of one crucial proposal, dated 20 August 1987, McPhee said: 'If this document was a financial analysis prepared for the purchase of a small milk bar, it would be inadequate. As a basis for making a bid for one of the largest media organisations in Australia, it is pathetic'.

McPhee's second general criticism was that Rothwells had not prepared best case–worst case scenarios for deciding whether or not to sell certain assets. Figures used for this purpose had been optimistic and sometimes unrealistic, with the consequence that Warwick Fairfax had always been shown the upside but not the downside. Apart from the Kinghaven purchase, every proposed deal had fallen through.

Finally, McPhee submitted that Rothwells, Dougherty and Reuter had each owed a fiduciary duty to Tryart, and had breached it. Under the Tryart Agreement, Rothwells had been required 'to truly and faithfully perform its services hereunder in the sole interests of the Offeror and its directors and shareholders'. In McPhee's submission, the 'secret agreements' on the fee sharing had constituted breaches of fiduciary duty for all three cross-defendants, each of whom had been under a duty to make full and frank disclosure of their interests.

Dougherty's senior counsel, George Palmer, QC, told the court

Andrew Clark, editor-in-chief of the *Sydney Morning Herald* for eight tumultuous days in February 1988, before being succeeded by John Alexander

Max Prisk (top right), who followed Alexander as editor of the *Herald*

(left to right) Ian Hicks, assistant editor, and three of the senior *Herald* journalists who resigned in sympathy with Anderson and Alexander: the business editor, Deborah Light, Colleen Ryan and the investment editor, Alan Deans

Perceptions of Warwick Fairfax: as Genghis Khan in Pryor's *Canberra Times* cartoon, 29 September 1987; and as a rift in the family arms on the cover of the *Sunday Times* magazine, 20 November 1988

Gale Fairfax, who married Warwick in May 1989

that his client's case was, firstly, that no relationship of confidence and trust, such as described by McPhee, had existed between himself and Warwick Fairfax. Dougherty had no fiduciary relationship with anybody at all until he came into one with Tryart, upon becoming one of its directors. Secondly, it was Dougherty's case that at all relevant times he had informed Warwick Fairfax of his arrangements with Connell for participation in the Tryart fee.

Palmer acknowledged the contradiction between this defence and Warwick Fairfax's denial, in his prepared statement, that any disclosure of fee sharing had been made to him by Dougherty prior to discovery in the present proceedings. 'The accounts on each side are so clear and explicit', said Palmer,

> that there is no room in this case for the suggestion that there has been a breakdown in communications, a misunderstanding, or there has been faulty recollection. Your Honour will be driven to the conclusion that one side or the other is deliberately lying, and, unfortunately, it is of no use to engage in euphemisms, that must be the result. So that credit and the credit of witnesses is at the core of the case against Mr Dougherty and, to a very large extent, of the case of Mr Fairfax against the other cross-defendants.

Palmer went on to submit that in Dougherty's case there was nothing unusual or improper in his taking fees from both sides of a deal. He was a man with many contacts, who on occasion acted as a 'middleman or commercial marriage broker', receiving a fee from one or other of the parties and sometimes from both. His commercial marriage-broking function was well known to Sir Warwick Fairfax, Lady Fairfax and Warwick Fairfax, and it was a function which they perceived as being of use to them.

Reuter's defence was summarized as follows by his senior counsel, Bruce Oslington, QC:

> Your Honour, essentially and in summary Fairfax was aware of Reuter's interest in the fee arrangement and says so. Reuter's presence on the [Tryart] board was simply part of the takeover strategy, and Fairfax knew that. Even if there was an obligation of disclosure in the circumstances, that obligation was discharged. Mr Reuter disclosed his interest. Mr Reuter does not claim that during August 1987 he told Warwick Fairfax then of Dougherty's interest, nor did he have an obligation to do so. A director's obligation is to disclose his interest. Mr Reuter will say that Mr Dougherty told him during August that Fairfax was aware of his, Dougherty's, interest. Mr Reuter had no reason to believe that Mr Dougherty would not have told Mr Fairfax of his interest.

Rothwells' defence against the fiduciary allegation was even more succinct. During his address in reply Hughes said that the second plaintiff would deny standing in a fiduciary relationship with

Warwick Fairfax. It would also say there had been full disclosure of the arrangement for remuneration of Dougherty and Reuter, by one or both of them.

At the conclusion of Hughes's address in reply on the fourth day of the case, Warwick Fairfax entered the witness stand to be examined by McPhee and cross-examined by other counsel. As he had never yet granted a press interview, apart from answering one or two unavoidable kerbside questions, there was considerable public interest in how the young man would fare under prolonged legal questioning, and how much of his seclusive character might be revealed in the process. As it turned out, he came through twenty-four days of examination, cross-examination and re-examination without serious inroads on either his case or his privacy.

For fourteen of those days the cross-examination was conducted by Hughes, one of the bar's most incisive and persistent inquisitors. If Hughes had been expecting cowardice, he found instead a dogged refusal to be intimidated or flustered. Time and again the witness would ask for questions to be repeated, or the meaning of words explained. 'Neophyte', 'novitiate', 'remonstrate', 'advert', 'peremptory', 'pout' and 'furtive' all had to be defined. This may have been prevarication, and may have been intended to disconcert the questioner. Certainly it seemed to have that effect.

When the answer eventually came, it was sometimes couched in a form of words amounting to neither affirmation nor denial: 'I don't recall saying that, I think it unlikely but I don't deny it'. Or again: 'Though I don't specifically recall it, I also don't categorically deny it'. This might have been construed as wariness or even evasion, but the judge took no exception to it. Many of the questions seemed designed not only to bring out the facts of the case but also to disparage the witness, with recourse to such words as 'arrogant', 'selfish', 'dishonourable', 'cowardly', 'back-stabbing' and 'ruthless'.

In one exchange, Warwick Fairfax conceded that he had told Reuter that if his relatives actively opposed the takeover, with the effect that it could not succeed, he would sell his shares.

Q. Did Mr Reuter then say interrogatively 'Even to Holmes à Court?' A. I don't recall him saying that.
Q. Would you deny that he said it? A. No.
Q. Did you reply 'Yes'? A. Also—
Q. Did you reply 'Yes'? A. I am about to answer that question. I don't recall saying that and I won't specifically deny it.
Q. If you did say that, it demonstrates that you possess a streak of ruthlessness, doesn't it? A. No, I wouldn't say ruthlessness but perhaps an ability to face up to the situation that I would find myself in.
Q. Namely? A. An inability to implement my vision.
Q. In other words, if you could not implement your vision involving

you taking control of John Fairfax, you were prepared to bring the whole house tumbling down?

McPhee objected to the last question, and after Hughes had rephrased it the witness agreed that in such circumstances he would have sold out, even though that may have necessitated the family losing control of John Fairfax Ltd. '. . . [When] you say by doing this I would make the house fall down or whatever words you used, one must see it in the light of the fact that I thought in the sense of the house already going to come down, so at least I felt I could make an attempt to save it.'

Q. Did you not convey to Mr Reuter by words the idea that if the family united to resist your takeover bid so that you found yourself locked into a minority position, you would react by selling or doing your best to sell control to somebody like Holmes à Court or Packer? A. No, as I have said before I said that if they united together to oppose the bid that I would sell out.
Q. To anyone, including Holmes à Court? A. That is not what I have said that I have said.
Q. But you haven't denied saying it, have you? A. I haven't denied it, neither have I said that I said it.
Q. Did Mr Reuter say to you by way of a question 'You would cross the family'? A. I don't recall him saying that although needless to say I don't deny it.

Hughes also questioned Warwick Fairfax about criticisms which he had made of his relatives 'behind their backs':

Q. To whom did you criticise their performance behind their backs? I am talking about Mr James Fairfax, Mr John Fairfax and Sir Vincent. A. Well, one to whom I expressed these feelings would have been Mr Dougherty.
Q. And you expressed these feelings to him trenchantly, didn't you. A. I said I expressed those feelings to him.
Q. And trenchantly, I suggest to you? A. What does 'trenchantly' mean?
Q. Don't you understand the meaning of the word? A. Not precisely.
Q. You didn't pull any punches when you criticised your relatives behind their backs to Mr Dougherty, did you? A. Again, I would not use that phrase. I did criticise them to him, whether you say I pulled any punches—I criticised them as accurately and as fairly as I could.

At another stage of the cross-examination Hughes asked Warwick Fairfax about the nature of the 'vision' mentioned in his letter to John B. Fairfax, which had been tendered in evidence.

Q. And just what was that vision? Let me make a suggestion to you. It might help you to answer the question quickly. The vision was that

you would achieve total ownership of John Fairfax Ltd was it not? A. No, that was not the vision.
Q. It was part of it, was it not? A. Not a necessary part, no.
Q. A component part was it not? A. Not a necessary . . .
Q. What was this vision that was burning a hole in your heart and had been for some time? A. Right. The vision that I had had for, well, that evolved over the course of a number of years was not so much that I would control John Fairfax Ltd but that it would be run in a professional—I should say it should be managed professionally by executives of the greatest competence; that in line with the history of the company and its papers that it would have the highest editorial standards; and that that would continue, and indeed increase; that the company would be secure from outside predators, that the management . . . of the company would have the utmost integrity. These are some of the things that were part of the vision that I had, to name just a few.
Q. What else was part of the great vision you had, if anything? A. That is what comes to mind at the moment.

If the testimony of this first witness had occupied twenty-four days, how long would the entire hearing take? The answer seemed likely to be five months. On the day after McPhee's re-examination of Warwick, 1 December, Justice Giles informed the parties of his concern at the effect which *Bond* v. *Fairfax* was having on the rest of the commercial division. It was unfair to other litigants, he said, to allocate a quarter of the division's judicial resources to one dispute for months on end without the strongest reasons.

> Since the hearing began, the second plaintiff has suffered the appointment of a provisional liquidator, and the financial position of the first plaintiff put forward as the basis for the original urgency cannot provide the same basis for urgency where what is involved is not a three week sprint but a five month marathon.

Accordingly, he intended that when the hearing adjourned for court vacation in mid-December the adjournment should last until some date in the second half of 1989.

In the few remaining court days, evidence was heard from two merchant bankers, Malcolm Irving and Michael Smith of CIBC, and the group managing director of John Fairfax Ltd, Ron Cotton.

CIBC had been retained by Mallesons to review the advice and assistance received by Tryart. It did this, firstly, by furnishing the kind of advice which in its view a merchant banker exercising reasonable skill, care and competence would have given as to whether Tryart could reasonably make a takeover offer for John Fairfax Ltd, how such an offer should be structured, and when it should be announced. Secondly, CIBC compared Rothwells' actual advice to Tryart with that hypothetical model. Irving and Smith concluded that the comparision did not reflect favourably upon

Rothwells, and for seven days they were examined and cross-examined about that conclusion. Some of their evidence was given in closed court for reasons of commercial confidentiality.

Cotton then spent five days answering questions about the quality of advice and assistance from Rothwells after the takeover, and other aspects of that period, including Cotton's opinion of Warwick Fairfax's commercial ability. Questioned by Hughes about the proprietor's part in preparing the company's budget for 1988–89, Cotton said that Warwick would often ask questions about a premise upon which the budget was based.

> Q. Were they searching questions? A. I think some of the questions were quite perceptive . . .
> Q. And astute? A. Given his training, yes.
> Q. Given his training means his training as a graduate of the Harvard School of Business Administration? A. Correct.

Cotton apparently had second thoughts about this when, three days later, under re-examination by McPhee's associate, Caldwell, QC, he was reminded of his earlier answers.

> Q. And you were asked 'Were they searching questions?' and your answer [was] that 'I think some of the questions were quite perceptive.' I appreciate you do not wish to be offensive to your employer, but dealing with the other questions, other than those that you have dealt with in the answer, other than those that you have said were quite perceptive, what in your view was the answer to that question, 'Were they searching questions?' A. Some of the questions were, in fact, quite naive.
> Q. . . . you were asked about his probing and challenging as to whether it was astute and your answer was, 'Given his training, yes' and the next question referred to his training as a graduate of the Harvard School of Business Administration. Can you explain please what you meant by your description as astute given that training at the Harvard Business College? A. When I responded 'Given his training' as indicated there, from my experience the questions were typical of a person who spent a lot of years with very little significant working experience . . .

(No less surprising in an ambitious media entrepreneur, albeit a neophyte, Warwick Fairfax was not a regular reader of his newly acquired core asset, the *Sydney Morning Herald*. He admitted this in the course of his cross-examination.)

On 16 December, the thirty-eighth day in court, Cotton retired from the stand, and proceedings were stood over until 31 July 1989. The transcript by then amounted to 1292 pages, containing approximately 646 000 words. What it all signified was hard to say, for at many points the conflict of evidence was bewildering.

Was Warwick Fairfax astute or naive? Had Martin Dougherty

declared his interest to Warwick, or had he not? Was Rothwells at fault for not disclosing its fee to the ANZ, or was the non-disclosure at Warwick Fairfax's behest? What did 'advise and assist' really mean? None of these questions had been resolved by the time the case was adjourned.

Several months later it happened that a sculpture of stainless steel was affixed to the façade of the Supreme Court building. Entitled 'Order out of Chaos', this work depicted the legal process in idealized form: lower depths of meandering lines tied in knots but eventually ascending from the centre as straight, parallel verticals. Perhaps Justice Giles would have done something like that with the chaos of *Bond* v. *Fairfax* but the case was never to resume. His Honour had made no explicit suggestion, but for the plaintiffs and the cross-claimant, all of whom were in straitened circumstances, a wink was as good as a nod.

Bond Media had lost $14 million during the past six months; Rothwells was in the throes of Australia's biggest provisional liquidation, with losses amounting to $610 million; and Fairfax was approaching the culmination of months of laborious refinancing. All the circumstances were conducive to settlement out of court, and early in January Alan Bond and Peter King sat down together in Bond's Sydney office at the State Bank Centre, Martin Place. Several hours of negotiation led to a settlement under which John Fairfax Group paid $27 million to Bond Media and, at Alan Bond's insistence, dropped its fiduciary claims against Dougherty, Reuter and Rothwells. In addition to the $27 million, Bond Media had already been paid $25 million by Rothwells, and a further $25 million was expected from the Rothwells liquidator. Thus Bond would probably finish with $77 million, which would mean a loss of $23 million, plus legal costs. Fairfax lost $27 million plus legal costs of $3 200 000, but declared itself well satisfied with the outcome.

III

For reasons now to be explained, the refinancing of John Fairfax Group Pty Ltd took longer than expected. Difficulties kept arising in Los Angeles, but that was not all. It had soon become apparent that if the group was to be refinanced successfully it would also need to be restructured. These changes went hand in hand, and were still under way when *Bond* v. *Fairfax* lapsed into terminal adjournment. If the court case had been a complicated and costly play within a play, the concurrent restructuring-refinancing was a rival production that ran longer, cost more and had an equally labyrinthine plot. It was the largest refinancing ever undertaken in Australia, and from start to finish it took the best part of ten months.

Restructuring was needed to overcome two taxation difficulties, either of which could have ruined the company. The first concerned grouping of tax losses against income. Under provisions of the Income Tax Assessment Act, a holding company may group interest and other deductions against the income of tax-paying subsidiaries—but only if the subsidiaries are wholly owned. Grouping was absolutely essential to the survival of John Fairfax Group, a holding company with a huge interest bill but no income of its own against which to use that loss. The group's income was all earned down below, mainly by the former holding company John Fairfax Ltd and its subsidiaries John Fairfax & Sons Ltd and David Syme. So the first problem was this: JFG could not set its interest bill against the group's income because it did not wholly own John Fairfax Ltd.

It may have looked as if Warwick Fairfax owned everything, but the takeover had actually left Tryart holding only 224 032 355 of the 300 000 000 issued shares in John Fairfax Ltd. The rest were held as follows: Rockwood Pastoral Company Pty Ltd, 38 521 080, shared equally by Warwick and his mother; Kinghaven Pty Ltd, 33 994 116; Lady Fairfax's Acrux Holdings Pty Ltd, 3 333 333; the estate of Sir Warwick Fairfax, held on trust for Rockwood, 103 116; and the four directors of John Fairfax Ltd (Fairfax, King, Anderson and Cotton), 4000 each, held on trust for Tryart/JFG. Before there could be any tax grouping, these extraneous parcels would have to be acquired by the holding company. The problem, apparently unforeseen during the takeover, was identified by Touche Ross, auditors to John Fairfax Ltd, when they turned their attention to the privatized company.

There was another reason why Tryart/JFG needed to acquire 100 per cent of the shares in John Fairfax Ltd. In the Treasurer's mini-budget statement on 26 May 1988, Paul Keating announced the withdrawal of an existing tax rebate on dividends received by one private company from another. After 26 May the rebate no longer applied to private companies not forming part of a wholly owned group. The intention here was to prevent individuals from deferring tax on unfranked dividends (that is, dividends issued when full company tax had not been paid on profits in accordance with the dividend imputation scheme introduced in 1987) by paying them into their private companies. Hitherto, when dividends were passed between companies the recipient had been entitled to a rebate for the tax that would normally have been payable on them. As first proposed, the blocking of this loophole would have penalized some companies inadvertently—and none more onerously than Tryart/JFG.

The rationale of Tryart's leveraged buyout had been that the victor should pay back or at least reduce its massive borrowings by having the target company sell some of its assets and pass the proceeds up to Tryart for that purpose. Between the takeover and

30 June 1988 John Fairfax Ltd had made advances of this kind totalling $1 032 768 000—none of it liable for tax (so the company thought!) and all of it intended for the discharge of debt. Now, if the advances were deemed to be dividends, that sum would be taxable in Tryart's hands at 49 cents in the dollar, representing a horrendous tax liability of about $500 million.

Under Section 108 of the Income Tax Assessment Act, advances or loans made by a private company to associated persons are deemed to be dividends to the extent that the Commissioner considers they represent distributions of profit. Almost certainly the advances to Tryart would have been treated in this way; and 'deemed dividends', regardless of when they are actually paid, are deemed to be paid on the last day of the financial year. Thus it would make no difference that the bulk of the advance to Tryart ($889 511 000) had been transferred before 26 May. It would all be deemed to have been paid on 30 June, and thus all be liable for tax.

Chris Anderson made several telephone calls during June to the Commonwealth Treasurer, putting it to him that the apparent liability was an unintended consequence of the May proposal, which imposed retrospective taxation. Given Keating's own estimate that the change would increase revenue by only $50 million, it seemed clear, said Anderson, that the Government had not meant to involve Fairfax in this way. Other Fairfax representatives held more detailed discussions with the Australian Taxation Office, and when a bill to amend the Income Tax Assessment Act reached parliament late in August it contained a safeguard against unintended consequences. Section 54(6), known at the Taxation Office as the 'Fairfax amendment', provided that the denial of rebate applied to dividends paid after 25 May 1988, other than '(a) dividends declared on or before that date; or (b) dividends that are Deemed by Section 108 . . . to be paid after that date because of an amount having been paid or credited on or before that date'.

At about this time Paul Keating had a chance encounter with Max Suich at Tokyo airport. With mordant relish he informed his one-time antagonist that the Australian Government had 'just saved Fairfax $500 million'. No favours had been done, however; on any objective view, the Fairfax amendment had merely rectified a mistake. Although spared having to pay unexpected tax on $889 511 000, Tryart had also received other advances from John Fairfax Ltd between 26 May and the end of the 1987–88 financial year. These were exceeded by Tryart's interest expense of $120 million, and so the company's liability for 1987–88 income tax was nil.

But what of future tax years, when the group's operating companies would still be making payments from cash flow or asset sales to enable Tryart to meet its loan commitments? Such payment would certainly attract income tax unless John Fairfax Ltd became a wholly owned subsidiary of Tryart, and so, for that reason as well as the grouping of tax losses, the elimination of minority shareholdings was accorded urgent priority by the accountants at Touche Ross, notably Barry Taplin, Gavan Smith and Ross Doherty, all of whom had worked for years past on Fairfax matters. On 26 July Taplin called on Lady Fairfax's solicitor, Fieldhouse, to explain the need for sole ownership. Fieldhouse took the point, and requested that Warwick put forward a proposal setting out which shares had to be transferred by his mother, and the incentives offered. Lady Fairfax, he said, was most unhappy with the current situation.

Warwick's proposal, drafted by Freehill Hollingdale & Page (Mallesons had a conflict of interest with Citibank), pointed out that because of the minority shareholding JFG was unable to pay its accruing interest on the ANZ loan without incurring tax liability.

Tryart was now clearly in default of its ANZ borrowing. The facility had expired on 30 June, and was being extended informally with capitalization of interest until the refinancing was completed. It was indeed an unhappy situation for Lady Fairfax, the joint beneficiary of Rockwood and full beneficiary of Acrux. 'It should be recognised', said Warwick's proposal,

> that the original guarantees granted by Acrux, Kinghaven and Rockwood in favour of ANZ do not appear to be limited to the value of the shares in John Fairfax Ltd. In other words, the other assets and property held by these companies would be available to ANZ (as an unsecured creditor) to the extent that any unpaid moneys due from Tryart exceeded the value of the shares and assets in JFL and its subsidiaries mortgaged to ANZ. There is a risk therefore that the other family assets held by these companies would be available, albeit on an unsecured basis, to the ANZ in any enforcement situation.

The turning point came on 30 September, when JFG acquired all the issued share capital of Rockwood and all of Acrux's shares in John Fairfax Ltd. At the same time the authorized capital of JFG was increased from two shares to 300 million shares of $1 each, consisting of 200 million A Class ordinary shares and 100 million B Class ordinary shares. Only the A shares carried entitlement to vote. The B shares were non-voting, but had priority on winding up to receive the first $150 million ahead of the A shares.

In consideration of the proposed purchase price for Rockwood ($268 095 400), JFG issued 24 931 of its B class shares to Tailer Investments Pty Ltd as trustee for the Jones Trust (Lady Fairfax) and an equal number of A class shares to Tailer as trustee of the Oriolo Trust (Warwick Fairfax). Acrux's JFL shares were purchased, in accordance with the put and call option of November 1987, by cash payment to Lady Fairfax of $28 333 330 adjusted for inflation. This sum was to be incorporated in the refinancing, as also was Lady Fairfax's continuing annuity of $2.9 million after taxes, adjusted for inflation.

The only other substantial minority was Kinghaven, owned by the Guilford Bell Trust, via three interposed companies, of which Warwick himself was the primary beneficiary. James Fairfax had already transferred his interest in Kinghaven to Warwick for the relatively nominal sum of $22 700 000, but in the context of tax grouping Kinghaven was still an extraneous shareholding which had to be eliminated. This was not completed until December, when a further 50 136 A Class shares in JFG were issued to Kinghaven. As part of the consideration in this settlement, a loan of $26 960 000 to Warwick Fairfax—borrowed by Tryart as part of its ANZ facility, and on-lent to Warwick for the purposes of paying James Fairfax for the Kinghaven parcel and to make the Grand Hotel Settlement on Lady Fairfax—was removed from the accounts of JFG and transferred to Kinghaven, thus effectively extinguishing it. The JFL shares from the estate of Sir Warwick Fairfax really belonged to Rockwood, and so to JFG. This left only the qualifying shares held by directors, and they were held on trust for JFG.

As a result of the acquisitions completed in December all shares in John Fairfax Ltd were beneficially owned by Warwick Fairfax and his mother through their shareholdings in JFG. Rockwood still owned 12 per cent of JFL, but was itself wholly owned by JFG, which owned the rest of JFL directly. Warwick Fairfax, through Kinghaven, the Oriolo Trust and his original two shares in the shelf company, owned 75.069 per cent of the issued capital in JFG, and his mother owned 24.931 per cent. All the voting shares were held by Warwick or his associated companies.

So far as the ANZ was concerned, John Fairfax Group would be prepared to stand in the shoes of Acrux, Rockwood and Kinghaven in relation to the guarantees and securities previously given by those companies. If required by the ANZ, the holding company would provide, as additional security, a share mortgage over the additional shares which it had acquired in JFL. But that would hardly be necessary, the company thought, if the refinancing was completed without much more delay.

Restructure of the shareholding had been essential to solve Fairfax's tax problems; but, because grouping is permissible only if a company has been wholly owned for the full financial year, that advantage would not be felt until 1989–90. Fortunately another change to the group structure was made during the early months of 1989 by transferring to John Fairfax Group about $1 billion worth of assets belonging to John Fairfax & Sons Ltd, John Fairfax Ltd, David

Syme and Rydges Pty Ltd. This enabled JFG to use from the date of transfer all the interest deductions which might otherwise not have been applicable in that tax year. The main assets transferred were the Broadway newspapers. Their book value had been increased substantially by a recent board decision, taken with the approval of Touche Ross, revaluing the company's mastheads from $682 million to $1341 million.

A sale of this magnitude would normally have attracted New South Wales stamp duty of about $50 million, but Freehills ascertained beforehand from the Office of State Revenue that an application for exemption would be approved under the public interest provisions of the relevant legislation. There was ample precedent for exemption in the case of internal reconstruction, but that did not prevent the Opposition from raising a brief and ineffectual flurry about it.

While Touche Ross was eliminating the minority shareholdings, attending to various tax matters and finalizing an audit of the company, the refinancing was making erratic but definite progress. By mid-October a Private Placement Memorandum (PPM) for the high-yield bond issue was nearing completion and Drexel was organizing a road show or selling tour of several American cities by Fairfax executives, to be undertaken during the second half of November. Chris Anderson, who was due to go to the United States soon with Peter King, expressed serious misgivings about the latest draft of Drexel's PPM. On the morning of 19 October he sent the following memo to King:

> I've received the latest PPM from Drexel.
>
> I am still most unhappy about the disclosure values of the document and, in my view, the downplaying of risk to potential investors.
>
> It is, in my view, very much a selling—rather than disclosure—document.
>
> For example, talk of leverage, currency risk and [the Rothwells' fee] litigation has been downplayed to one page, wedged at the back of the document between a discussion of the Australian economy and photo-copies of covers of the company's products.
>
> There is also, in my view, not enough detailed discussion of the tax situation, nor of the operations . . . of the Equity Appreciation Rights.
>
> As a director, I'm concerned about the lack of such full disclosure to potential investors.
>
> I also believe that the Fairfax Foundation, the Centenary Fund [both of which were expected to make substantial loans to JFG] and the Kinghaven rearrangement must be off the table before the PPM goes out—and we commence the road show.
>
> We should also have assurance that the tax position has not

changed—and that Touche Ross are happy, subject to refinancing, to certify the company is a viable, on-going operation.

In a second memo to King later that day, Anderson went further. 'I hate to give ultimatums', he wrote, 'and I dislike doing this to you, but I'm loath to go to the USA/sign the accounts or the PPM—or participate in the road show—until we get a few issues clarified'. After reiterating the issues he had raised earlier—and stressing the need for ANZ, Citibank and Drexel to give the Fairfax directors and company officers indemnity against personal financial exposure, he concluded by saying: 'I know you are anxious to go—and I realise what my non-compliance would mean—but I think these basic issues must be clarified before we consider entering the final stage of our refinancing'.

Some of these issues were clarified before the road show. In final form the two-volume PPM gave more prominence to such matters as leverage, taxation, currency risk and litigation. They were presented briefly, but with sufficient candour to alert potential investors, and perhaps even to deter them.

About leverage the Memorandum said:

> The Company's operating cash flow may be insufficient to meet its debt service requirements. In such case, the Company may be required to refinance its indebtedness or sell assets. In addition, the Company presently anticipates, based on its projections, that portions of the Senior Bank Debt will be refinanced upon maturity. There can be no assurance that the Company's revenues will be sufficient to meet its debt service requirements or that any such refinancing or asset disposition could be effected quickly enough, or in amounts sufficient, to pay interest or principal on the Debentures.

About currency risk: 'The Debentures are Australian denominated obligations. Consequently, fluctuations in exchange rates between the Australian dollar and the US dollar could have a material positive or negative effect on the value, in US dollars, of the interest and principal payments to be made on the Debentures'. And about litigation: 'The Company is currently party to a lawsuit in Australia regarding investment banking fees. If a significant judgment is rendered against the Company, it would have an adverse impact on the Company'.

To cap it all, Drexel made full disclosure of its own legal difficulties. On the fourth page of the Memorandum, it said about the Securities and Exchange Commission's civil action:

> The complaint charges trading on inside information, market manipulation, fraud, improper disclosure, parking, aiding and abetting violations of the net capital rules, and margin and record-keeping violations. The complaint seeks an injunction against further

> violations of the securities laws, disgorgement of profits and fees received and losses avoided as a result of the alleged illegal conduct, treble any profits realised or losses avoided on insider trading, and all further relief, legal or equitable, that the court believes is warranted under the circumstances.
>
> The company has also been advised that Drexel and . . . several key employees are targets of a grand jury investigation being conducted by the United States Attorney for the Southern District of New York with respect to certain alleged violations of the federal criminal laws including, but not limited to, securities fraud, mail and wire fraud and racketeering . . . Drexel has advised [JFG] that no assurance can be given that the results of the SEC action or grand jury investigation will not have an adverse effect on Drexel and/or the market for 'highyield' securities, such as debentures.

With warnings such as these preceding them, the road show participants would clearly need to do some hard selling. Fortunately they had a reassuring story to tell about the company and its products. To compare only on-going operations—that is, to exclude from past fiscal years the income earned or losses incurred by assets sold since the takeover—JFG's earnings before depreciation, interest and income tax (EBDIT) had been $87.4 million in 1985–86 and $88.8 million in 1986–87. For 1987–88, a period in which Tryart controlled the company for seven months, the figure was $125.6 million; and the projected figure for 1988–89 was $161.9 million. The projection was in fact too conservative, and when results came to hand it would be seen that the Fairfax group in its first full year of new management had produced an EBDIT of $213.7 million.

There were various reasons for this spectacular and opportune improvement. The Australian economy—reflecting unexpectedly robust growth in the world economy, particularly in property, manufacturing and leisure industries—was improving in much the same way as it had earlier in the 1980s, when Fairfax's EBDIT rose from $32 million in 1982–83 to $63 million in 1983–84. Another reason for the surge in profit during the late 1980s was that advantages from closure of the *Sun* and *Times on Sunday* had been greater than expected. Economies became possible once the plant at Broadway was no longer running on a 24-hour cycle. Also, staff numbers were reduced as more employees took early retirement.

Above all, however, JFG had the flourishing *Sydney Morning Herald*, *Age* and *Australian Financial Review* to thank for its massive cash flow. Saturday's *Herald* had exceeded 200 pages for the first time on 27 October 1987, and in the following months such sizes became commonplace. The Saturday *Age* had been well over 200 pages since 1985.

In terms of readership measured in five market segments according to income, education and occupation, the *Herald* and *Age* could boast that 38 per cent and 48 per cent of their readers belonged to the AB segment, the one valued most by advertisers for its high disposable income. The *Herald* held 78 per cent of its classified advertising market and 49 per cent of display advertising, while equivalent figures for the *Age* in Victoria were 70 per cent and 47 per cent. These far exceeded comparable figures for any of Murdoch's Australian newspapers. The *Herald*'s revenue had risen from $154.9 million in 1986–87 to $190.7 million in 1987–88; the *Age*'s from $170.3 million to $198 million; and the *Financial Review*'s from $39.2 million to $49 million.

Although Touche Ross did not complete its audit until December, the issues raised by Anderson seemed to have been clarified sufficiently, for he left as planned with King. Their intention was to visit various American banks before the road show, in search of syndicate members for the senior debt. While in Pittsburgh, Anderson telephoned a friend in Sydney, Ray Greenshields, who was a senior executive at the AMP Society. Might the time now be right, he asked, for the AMP and certain other Australian institutions to take equity in the Fairfax group—perhaps as much as 50 or 60 per cent, if Warwick Fairfax would agree to reduce his own holding? This cut directly across the refinancing; but Anderson, still wondering whether Drexel was really the way to go, was sufficiently encouraged by his friend's response to return to Sydney before the road show began. After talks with Greenshields and the AMP's investment manager, Leigh Hall, and others on 8 November he asked John Barber and Warren Schlichting of WSGP to explore the matter further. They did so, but nothing eventuated. In Anderson's view this was a great opportunity lost.

And so to the road show, which began in the City of Angels on 15 November, then moved to New York, Chicago, Miami, Boston, Phoenix, Houston, Minneapolis/St Paul, Denver, Pittsburgh, Kansas City and San Francisco under the guidance of advisers from Drexel and WSGP. The Fairfax participants were King and Anderson; Peter Gaunt, general manager of the Sydney newspapers; Jerry Austin, a Rhodesian-born accountant, formerly with Touche Ross, who had succeeded Barry Moore as group chief accountant on the latter's retirement; and Greg Taylor, the managing director of David Syme.

Warwick Fairfax did not take part in the tour. He was still in the witness box, and in any case the pragmatists at Drexel did not want him on the selling operation. Drexel believed that the delicate task of reassuring investors would best be left to JFG's long-term executives, and that their chances of success would be improved by distancing themselves from the proprietor. Ackerman's harsh advice was: 'Trash the owner'. Drexel also insisted on editing the proprietor out of a promotional film which had been made about the company in Sydney.

Travelling between airports and hotels in two stretch limousines, the selling party addressed breakfast, lunch and dinner meetings of potential investors assembled by Drexel. Anderson and Gaunt delivered the main address, and the others answered technical questions. The main selling points were: 'Premier assets which dominate their markets; strong and growing cash flows; significant asset value with market value exceeding net debt by over $500 million; market value of equity underlying the debentures increasing to $1.7 billion in 1993; and equity participation through Equity Appreciation Rights'.

At the conclusion of the American tour, Anderson went to Hong Kong and Tokyo for more sales talking while King and Barber flew to London. The timing of the London presentation was unfortunate, for only two weeks earlier Rupert Murdoch's *Sunday Times* had published a malicious article about the proprietor and his current predicament. On the cover of the paper's magazine was a photograph of Warwick Fairfax superimposed upon the Company's arms, with the question: 'Would you let this man run your family business?' The ten-page article began with a tirade of personal insults, then proceeded in the following vein:

> . . . Motivated by greed, ambition and revenge, [Warwick Fairfax] has orchestrated the destruction of his own fabulous inheritance and the oldest established family business in Australia. In the space of six months, he transformed a large, successful, debt-free business into a small debt-laden business now struggling to survive. Warwick's debut as a businessman, a debacle unparalleled in the annals of Australian corporate history, stunned the country.
>
> Thus it is that [he] is lampooned, reviled, castigated, inculpated, pilloried and vilified throughout Australia. That he is a scion of the gilded Fairfax family, one of the most esteemed business dynasties in Australia, naturally adds irresistible piquancy to the affair.

Warwick Fairfax was indeed being subjected to an ordeal by denigration and ridicule, an ordeal perhaps unprecedented in Australian experience. Queen's Counsel called his character into question, cartoonists regarded him as fair game, satirical songs were written about him, he was the butt of jokes, and even the *Sydney Morning Herald* treated him with less respect than newspapers usually show their own proprietors. Having asserted its independence against Tryart, the *Herald*'s editorial management seemed unwilling to play the part of censor, even when a blue pencil was clearly needed.

One notable example of this *laissez-faire* approach was a report in the *Herald*'s back-page gossip column on 10 November that

Warwick Fairfax had become engaged to be married. His fiancée was an American, Gale Ann Murphy, who had come to Sydney from Chicago earlier in the year to study at the Australian branch of a Christian group with which Warwick was associated. The gossip item in the *Herald* was illustrated by an unprepossessing likeness of the proprietor wearing heart-shaped glasses, and the heading was: 'Love Is a Many Splendoured Cringe'.

The effect of all this upon a young man beset by a sea of troubles could only be guessed at, for the victim himself made no protest. Apart from what plaintiffs' counsel managed to prise out of him in court, he stoically maintained his policy of silence.

After a less than encouraging reception from investors in London on 5 December, King and Barber returned to Los Angeles, where Citibank and ANZ were engaged in a final round of talks with Drexel. Milken was not involved; he was preoccupied with his own worsening legal troubles. On 2 December the Fairfax talks had broken down, with Drexel backing away from currency risk and Payment in Kind. Raben and Zimmerman said they had taken the currency risk to their clients, but had not been able to sell it. Van der Merwe accused them of reneging on his earlier understanding with Ackerman.

Ackerman, who was working on the RJR Nabisco leveraged buyout for another client, Henry Kravis, rang from New York asking angrily what had gone wrong. The bankers thought it was all over, but Ackerman, back in Beverly Hills the following day, invited Van der Merwe to watch his son play football in a school match. Over lunch they agreed that somehow the deal must go ahead. Raben and Zimmerman maintained their intransigence. Ackerman told Van der Merwe it looked as if there was no longer any hope of success, and Van der Merwe agreed. Then Ackerman proposed a solution to the currency risk, in the form of Foreign Exchange Appreciation Rights (FEARs), and a modification to Payment in Kind. By the time King and Barber returned from London the banks and Drexel were back at the negotiating table.

FEARs, a financial instrument devised by Ackerman in a restaurant late at night, would place the currency risk with Fairfax by giving debenture holders the right to receive additional payments in the event of adverse change in the US/Australian exchange rate between date of issuance and redemption date. The subordinate debt would include finance for such contingencies down to a nominated low point in the value of the Australian dollar. By this means it was hoped that American investors would be reconciled to an Australian denomination. FEARs got the talks going again, but there were still other difficulties to be overcome.

While negotiations continued in Beverly Hills, sales presentations for the debentures were held in Sydney and Melbourne on 14 and

15 December, with no more success than in London. The anticipated settlement date was 10 January, but just before Christmas the ANZ gave vent to its growing concern that Drexel would not meet that deadline. The bank's concern was understandable. Its privatization support facility agreement had been breached for months past, and its commitment to provide half the new senior debt had expired on 8 November. Patience was running out fast.

In a letter to the Fairfax directors on 20 December, John McConnell listed several worries conveyed to him by John Conn, who had recently returned from Los Angeles. Even at this late stage, he said, Drexel had not provided any commitment to fund the amount to be provided by the subordinated notes on any fixed date. 'We therefore have to continue to face the implication of there being no certainty as to whether the funds will be provided and if so, when.' The ANZ had received no terms and conditions for the Equity Appreciation Rights, and was worried that they might erode the value of its share mortgages as security. Exposure to FEARs might also reduce Fairfax's future ability to work towards another refinancing package at lower interest rates.

'The Bank requires to be satisfied on the above issues', wrote McConnell.

> Pending such satisfaction the Bank is, on a daily basis, assessing the risks associated with the refinancing and the prudence of continuing to extend the Privatisation Support Facility . . . The Bank continues to reserve all rights, powers and privileges that it may have under the Privatisation Support Facility Agreement as a result of the breaches and Events of Default. The Bank does not waive, by any failure or delay on its part to exercise such rights power and privileges, nor does its acceptance of any interest . . . constitute any waiver on its behalf.

Anderson arranged a telephone conference next day with McConnell, Peter King (who was still in Los Angeles), Warwick Fairfax, himself and others. McConnell was assured of the company's commitment to a speedy conclusion by Drexel, but two days later he was on the phone to Anderson again saying the American documentation had arrived and was causing his officers grave concern. It was 'very sloppy in many areas', and a lot of the fundamentals were back to Drexel's original position. He wondered whether Drexel was seriously committed to the deal.

Certainly it would not have been surprising if Drexel had lost interest, for on 21 December it had capitulated to federal securities investigators. The firm agreed not only to plead guilty on six felony counts and pay a record sum of $US650 million ($A760 million) in fines and restitution, but also to co-operate in the US Attorney's continuing investigation of some of Drexel's clients and executives, including Milken. This was a costly way of settling its difference with both the Attorney and the Securities and Exchange Commission; but Drexel had no option, for the government had threatened to invoke the draconian Racketeer-Influenced Corrupt Organisations law. RICO—once reserved for organized crime, and now also used in cases of alleged white-collar crime—provided for heavy prison sentences and the freezing of corporate assets before trial.

Drexel feared that it might simply be RICOed out of existence. But there was more to its capitulation than that. The government's case against Drexel had been greatly strengthened by the granting of immunity to three Drexel employees, all close associates of Milken, in return for their co-operation with the government. No longer would the prosecution depend solely upon Ivan Boesky's testimony.

On 28 December Mary Reemst of Citibank rang Anderson to convey the bank's alarm at the slow rate of progress, asking Fairfax to see if Drexel could make its lawyers expedite their revision of the sub-debt documents. By the end of the month, however, the banks were more relaxed. 'A lot of action' seemed to be taking place, McConnell told Anderson, though he was still worried about the EARs—not so much their effect on the bank, but how they might affect Fairfax's long-term viability.

In mid-January, with the deadline exceeded but completion seemingly only a few days away, the Bond organization made another offer for all that remained of the Fairfax group. The offer was $2.1 billion, and it came to Peter King from a friend of Alan Bond's in London, Graham Lacey. No mention of the offer was made during the negotiations between Bond and King to settle the Rothwells' fee dispute, but the approach from London was treated seriously at Broadway.

It was not rejected automatically. Given the uncertainty still surrounding the Rothwells fee, an offer of $2.1 billion demanded careful consideration, even at this late stage of the refinancing. If the fee case went back to court, an adverse judgment could well put the company out of business. Warwick asked Michael Smith, one of the two CIBC consultants who had given evidence in court, for advice about the prospect of floating the company in the next few years to raise enough money for capital re-equipment, and to remain viable. He also sought opinions from King, Anderson and Barber as to whether he should proceed with the refinancing. King and Barber said yes, reposing their confidence in the company's long-term income projections.

Anderson was less confident, but none the less in favour of refinancing. 'I agree . . . that the projections are aggressive but achievable', he wrote in a memorandum to the proprietor.

But we have to recognise that we are pushing from an EBIT (earnings before income tax) of $28.4m in 1984 to an EBIT of $421.2m in 1998. It is no mean achievement. However, as John Barber and Peter King have pointed out—and have been proved right so far on the actual results—it is a lesser jump than we have achieved from 1984 until now. But it seems to me that this is a more cyclical business than it was, particularly now that we are reliant solely on our three principal newspapers, and that our company is more vulnerable to a changing economy.

However, on the positive side, you have marvellous strong products, competent and experienced management, a tremendous franchise and a competitor, in my view . . . who will not be keen to cause too much trouble, but will be looking to Australia to help fund his international activities. On John Barber's analysis, your net worth also climbs back quicker than I had earlier envisaged and the bank covenants, although tight, are not now as onerous as they were. If Drexel is seen as 'temporary equity', as John charmingly puts it, then with all the above risks being understood, I think we can proceed.

A couple of other points need, of course, to be considered. Your own future plans and possible short and long-term role in the company; the fact that you must not feel personally responsible for 150 years of history—every dynasty eventually breaks up (if you don't sell, your heirs at some time surely will)—and whether or not a company so loaded with debt can carry out the duties and responsibilities worthy of maintaining the Fairfax lineage.

One final point . . . needs to be said about the sale offer on the table. If the offer is $2.1 B in cash, as against some sort of note, or debt issue, then clearly any rational analysis would say that, looking at the risks, such a bid is enticing. Clearly, if it is to be accepted, it must be done quickly.

Thankfully, I'm not a Fairfax.

Once again Warwick Fairfax resisted the temptation to sell his way out of trouble. The approach from London was rejected, and the refinancing continued on its way to settlement. On 25 January Lady Fairfax held a party at Fairwater for Warwick and his fiancée (the wedding was planned for May, in Chicago), and two days later the refinancing documents were signed in Sydney, Canberra and New York.

Fairfax's total new borrowing of $1.55 billion consisted of $1.1 billion in senior debt and $450 million in debentures. The senior debt, provided equally by Citibank and the ANZ, came in two parts—a $350 million bullet facility, $50 million of which would be conserved for emergency need; and a $750 million zero coupon loan. Both were for seven years, and the interest rates, while nominally floating, were fixed by swap agreements for five years. The zero coupon on the larger facility would provide a five-year interest payment holiday; but as from 1994 John Fairfax Group would have to meet the full annual interest bill in cash—at least until the company refinanced yet again, as was its intention.

The senior bank obligations were secured by the assets of John Fairfax Group and its main subsidiaries. This meant that if events of default occurred the banks could sell all or any part of the group's assets to recoup what was owing to them. The senior facilities agreement contained more than thirty covenants imposing various restrictions intended to ensure as far as possible that events of default did not occur. In future Fairfax would have to meet certain financial tests, including the maintenance of prescribed ratios of current assets to current liabilities, total debt to cash flow, and cash flow to forecast annual interest payment.

Another covenant limited the group's capital expenditure to 50 per cent of excess operating cash plus an annual increment starting at $24 million in 1988–89 and decreasing in subsequent years. Only certain types of investment could be made by group members, and even those were limited to an aggregate annual maximum of $3 million. No dividends or other distributions could be made, except to members of the Fairfax group, and to Lady Fairfax in conformity with her existing agreement. The proprietor himself could not receive dividends. No secured assets could be sold without the banks' consent. Similarly, group members could neither change the nature or scope of their business, nor offer the public any equity interest, without consent from the banks.

Drexel's $450 million consisted of $300 million in senior subordinated debentures, bearing interest of 18 per cent and maturing in January 2000; and $150 million in subordinated debentures at 18.5 per cent, also maturing in January 2000. The debentures were issued by John Fairfax Group (USA) Inc—a subsidiary of the group's financing vehicle, John Fairfax Group Finance Pty Ltd—established in the United States for this and other purposes connected with the private placement, including the filing of quarterly reports with the Securities and Exchange Commission. Interest was payable semi-annually, and under the Payment In Kind provision, JFG (USA) had the option of meeting any five half-yearly instalments by issuing additional subordinated debentures, which would rank after the other debentures. Senior subordinated and subordinated debentures were redeemable at the company's option on or after 15 January 1994, and 20 per cent of the senior subordinated principal had to be repaid on 15 January 1999. In the case of subordinated debentures, 15 per cent had to be repaid on each of 15 January 1999 and 15 January 2000.

Both kinds of debenture included non-detachable Foreign Exchange Appreciation Rights, entitling holders to receive additional payments in the event of adverse change in the United States/ Australian rate of exchange up to aggregate maximums of $A163 million for the senior subordinated debentures and $A67 million for the subordinated debentures. These amounts would be fully payable only if the Australian dollar fell below US59 cents. The best foreign exchange circumstances for Fairfax would have been a weak Australian dollar to start with, followed by a strong one at maturity or redemption. As it happened, however, the Australian dollar was exceptionally strong on the date of issuance, closing at US87.75 cents.

Some of the debentures included Equity Appreciation Rights in John Fairfax Group. These warrants were the 'sweeteners' which Drexel had persuaded Fairfax to issue for the luring of investors. Collectively they represented an ultimate right to receive approximately 40 per cent of the fully diluted common equity value of JFG, either in cash or in shares. Originally the figure was to have been 35 per cent—5 per cent for Drexel, 5 per cent for WSGP, and 25 per cent for investors. Drexel later sought another 5 per cent for investors, and this was agreed to on condition that Drexel refund part of its substantial fee for every additional percentage point used. Drexel's fee for the private placement was $28 million—$18 million for underwriting, plus a success fee of $10 million.

Each 1000 EARs represented the right to receive 1 per cent of the company's equity value on 30 January 1998, or earlier than that if the EARs were repurchased on JFG's call option or the holder's put option. Holders of the EARs could require JFG to repurchase up to 15 per cent of the original number of EARs on each of 30 January, 1995, 1996 and 1997, though JFG was entitled to defer each of these obligations for one year. Similarly JFG had the right to call for the repurchase of up to 25 per cent of the EARs on each of the same dates. In addition JFG had the right to repurchase all the EARs at any time, at a price and upon terms approved by the holders of at least 85 per cent of the warrants outstanding.

JFG could repurchase the EARs either by cash, by issuing shares, or by issuing junior subordinated debentures. If JFG were to merge with another entity, or sell a large part of its property (assuming consent of the senior lenders), each EARs holder would have the right to receive the kind and amount of securities, cash and property which would have been received if the EARs had been repurchased immediately before such an event.

Friday 27 January 1989 was a day of days for the Fairfax proprietorship. In nearly a century and a half the family business had been through several changes of name and form: Kemp and Fairfax, John Fairfax & Sons, John Fairfax & Sons Ltd, John Fairfax & Sons Pty Ltd, John Fairfax Ltd, Tryart Pty Ltd and now John Fairfax Group Pty Ltd. Under one name or another, the business had known many red-letter days: formation of the first partnership between father and son in 1853, the centenary of the *Sydney Morning Herald* in 1931, the move from Hunter Street to Broadway in 1955, incorporation as a public company in 1956, and the *Herald*'s sesquicentenary in 1981. Yet none of these bore comparison with the settlement of John Fairfax Group's refinancing on 27 January 1989. The events of this day were of singular importance to the diminished proprietorial family and the beleaguered management and staff of an enterprise now confined almost entirely to newspapers: the *Herald, Age, Financial Review, Sun-Herald,* BRW Publications, *Newcastle Herald, Illawarra Mercury,* and twenty-one suburban and regional papers. John Fairfax Group did not thereby escape its mortal danger. But it did receive a new lease on life, a stay of execution—and in the circumstances, that was blessing enough.

The day began early for some of the company officers and lawyers who had been finalizing documents in the early hours of the morning. The new company secretary—Stephen Bradshaw, who had succeeded Alan Bailey—returned home at 2 a.m., only to leave again for the office at 5 a.m. Anderson, Cotton, Pride and Bradshaw held preparatory meetings, then at 10.30 a.m. moved to Citibank's office in Margaret Street, where bankers and lawyers were assembling. Others of their kind were at the New York office of O'Melveny & Myers: Peter King and Jerry Austin, Jim Zimmerman and others from Drexel, Bruce Maisey from ANZ, Jim Featherstone from Citibank, and the Los Angeles lawyers, McAniff and Herron. Warwick Fairfax was in Canberra because two of the companies involved in the day's proceedings—John Fairfax Group Finance Pty Ltd and Tailer Investments Pty Ltd—were registered there.

As the morning progressed, certain difficulties arose, requiring conference calls between Sydney, New York and Canberra. In New York, where lawyers had been working with little respite for three days and nights, Drexel's counsel raised a question about references to EARs in JFG's articles of association. This heightened the senior lenders' already growing concern that if the transaction was not completed by 5 p.m. Sydney time they would be financially disadvantaged by the need to reinvest $1.1 billion at the low weekend interest rate.

Van der Merwe asked Fairfax to indemnify Citibank, ANZ, the State Bank of South Australia and the State Bank of New South Wales against that kind of loss. (Citibank had syndicated $250 million of its lending to the two State Banks, but ANZ was going it alone.) A letter of indemnity was drafted, Anderson refused to sign it, but fortunately the EARs difficulty was resolved by means of a conference telephone call to New York. In another conference call, Anderson, Cotton and King approved JFG's entry into thirty-seven different agreements and indentures governing the senior debt and debentures.

Relevant documents were signed, and at about midday Citibank's chairman, Michael Cannon-Brookes, presented Ron Cotton with a king-sized ceremonial cheque. It was made out for $1 363 461 351, a theoretical figure representing the highest debt to which the banks would be exposed, in January 1994. Cotton and Anderson made short speeches, after which Citibank provided champagne and smorgasbord.

The debenture settlement took place at roughly the same time, 11.30 p.m. in New York. In spite of EARs and selling tours, Drexel was still holding a substantial part of the issue, believed to be about $100 million worth, for which buyers had not yet been found. But JFG received the full $450 million ('In the till', as Anderson put it, much to Drexel's distaste), and paid Drexel the fee of $28 million. Placing the remaining debentures would be Drexel's worry, not Fairfax's. With its newly acquired finance from all sources, Fairfax retired $930 million of ANZ's support facility, reducing that bank's exposure to $550 million. Citibank's existing loan was also retired, and replaced with a syndicated exposure equal to that of the ANZ.

In Canberra the proprietor signed a pile of documents almost one metre high. Later in the day he attended a 'meeting of members' of John Fairfax Group Pty Ltd—the members, as the minutes recorded, consisting only of Warwick Fairfax in his personal capacity and Warwick Fairfax representing Kinghaven, Tailer Investments and one of his personal companies, Gilling Pty Ltd. The purpose of this one-man meeting was to amend the articles of association so as to increase the company's authorized capital from $300 million to $302 000 300 by creation of 100 million C Class ordinary shares, 100 million C Class redeemable preference shares, and 30 thousand D Class redeemable preference shares. The new shares all had a nominal value of $0.01 each. C shares were non-voting, like B shares, and were to be available if needed for the repurchase of EARs. The D shares carried voting rights, and most of them were issued on 27 January to Serpentine Pty Ltd, trustee of the Guilford Bell settlement. This diluted Kinghaven's shareholding in JFG from just over 50 per cent to an amount which left JFG having no ultimate holding company.

The upshot of all this was that unless or until non-voting equity was issued to the holders of EARs, JFG would have three shareholders—Kinghaven, Tailer and Serpentine. That meant Warwick Fairfax, with all the issued A and D voting shares, and his mother, with all the issued B non-voting shares.

As Warwick returned to Sydney he had grounds for both

satisfaction and continuing anxiety. If the economy remained healthy, and subject to moderate inflation, Fairfax's prodigious cash flow should continue to grow, enabling the company to meet its fearsome interest payments, at least until some better alternative could be arranged. But would the economy oblige? And would John Fairfax Group, committed to a frugal regimen by bankers' covenants, be able to contend with an increasingly competitive News Ltd? Murdoch had his own debt, of course, and in quantity it dwarfed Fairfax's. But although credit-rating agencies were looking askance at News Corporation's world-wide borrowings of more than $7 billion, the Murdoch empire seemed capable, at least for the time being, of servicing its debt and repaying on time.

With ample resources at its disposal, News Ltd was already applying pressure to Fairfax. Firstly, it was planning a $1 billion press modernization programme between 1989 and 1993. Inspired by the success of Murdoch's Wapping plant in London, News Ltd had ordered MAN offset presses from Germany, capable of great flexibility in the use of full colour on newsprint, to be installed in Adelaide, Brisbane, Melbourne and Sydney. Secondly, News had recently notified Fairfax of its intention to withdraw from their joint publication of the *Sunday Press* in Melbourne, and to launch two separate Sunday papers of its own in that city—an upmarket broadsheet and a popular tabloid. This was a direct threat to David Syme's advertising revenue, and reluctantly the board of John Fairfax Group concluded that Syme would have to respond.

IV

One other event of some relevance to the Fairfax family took place on 27 January 1989. It had nothing to do with senior debt or debentures, or indeed with the present generation of Fairfaxes; and yet, with uncanny timing, it formed an apt connection between the present and the past. At about 10 p.m. a fire began inside the old Congregational church in Jersey Road, Woollahra, a sandstone edifice which had fallen into disuse since its amalgamation with the Uniting Church. Flames rapidly engulfed the organ, pulpit and pews, burnt the green and gold-painted wooden ceiling, and burst up through the purlins, rafters and tiles.

Next morning the church was a charred ruin surmounted by skeletal black beams. Its walls, incorporating a foundation stone laid by John Fairfax, remained intact. So did the side turrets. But all that was left standing on the partly collapsed floor was a stone christening font. Among the embers were some twisted brass plaques, one proclaiming 'A good name is rather to be chosen than great riches', and another 'In loving memory of Lucy Fairfax', widow of Sir James

Reading Fairfax. Of Sir James's memorial window there was no trace. Its angels, like all the other stained glass windows, had either melted or been blown to smithereens by fire hoses.

If there was a moral to be drawn from this, it was perhaps that disaster is not always irrevocable—that when foundations and walls are sound, a roof and windows may be replaced. The Jersey Road church was insured, and was classified by the National Trust. It would not be demolished. Within a few months of the fire, the cause of which had not been determined, the *Sydney Morning Herald* reported that the Uniting Church had retained an architect to recommend suitable future uses for the building. In other words, like the company of heralds and angels, it was to be refinanced and restructured.

21 April 1990

10
Stop Press

I

The rest of this narrative, as it approaches the family's sesquicentenary on 8 February 1991, will be concerned with both optimism and pessimism. In 1989–90 the Fairfax proprietorship was trading well enough for such optimists as Warwick Fairfax and Peter King to remain sanguine even after the economy had disappointed them. Buoyant conditions during the first half of that financial year were followed by a sudden contraction of advertising volumes, starting at the *Age* in February 1990, and the *Sydney Morning Herald* three months later. This drove home the necessity of a second refinancing. But how was it to be accomplished?

The board's pessimists (or realists, as they preferred to think) warned that John Fairfax Group could easily drown in its sea of debt. Only urgent and drastic action—involving elimination of the subordinate debt, injection of new equity and a consequent end to family control—could save the company from receivership or liquidation. As the proprietor and his chief executive did not accept this dire prognosis, two disparate attitudes came more and more into conflict, with resultant delay to a refinancing which all agreed was necessary. The pessimists saw themselves as facing facts, and saw their colleagues as avoiding them. On the other hand the optimists, heartened by the maintenance of gross profit thanks to the earlier buoyant conditions, doubted whether the company's ailment was desperate enough to justify so painful a remedy.

Because of the continuing cash flow and profitability of Fairfax's core assets, the company's EBDIT, having risen from $213.7 million in 1988–89 to $223.1 million in 1989–90, was still well in excess of that required under the senior lenders' financial covenant. In the grim context of Fairfax's debt burden, some comfort could indeed be taken from the daily roar of the presses at Broadway and Spencer Street, Melbourne. Journalists and printers still produced the *Sydney Morning Herald*, the *Australian Financial Review* and the *Age*; advertisers still favoured these papers over their competitors; and readers were still loyal to them.

In the six months ending 31 December 1989 the company's operating revenue was $424 million, compared with $398 million for the same period of the previous year. Most of the additional revenue came from the three core newspapers, but during that half-year the volume of advertising faltered ominously in the *Age* and the *Financial Review*. Only by raising rates was the company able to maintain revenue growth. This unwelcome trend was more noticeable during the next three months. As economic conditions affected advertising more severely, combined volumes for the three newspapers fell by 13 per cent compared with the same period in 1989. Classified advertising fell by 21 per cent in the *Age* and 17 per cent in the *Financial Review*.

II

Before returning to the all-consuming problem of debt, certain developments within the group should be recorded. In July 1989 a weekly investment newspaper, *AFR Investor*, was launched to take some of the editorial and advertising weight out of the *Australian Financial Review*. This was John Fairfax Group's first publishing initiative in Sydney, planned in the style of *Barron's*, but not very well done. It failed to meet circulation targets and on Anderson's initiative, against some board resistance, it was closed in October with a loss of $400 000.

In the same month the *Gold Coast Mail*, a bi-weekly owned jointly by John Fairfax Group and John B. Fairfax's Marinya Media, changed to weekly publication because of continuing losses in its unequal struggle against News Ltd's highly successful *Gold Coast Bulletin*. The *Mail* was a free 88-page paper with fixed circulation of 57 000. Murdoch's *Bulletin* was a 50-cent tabloid with a daily circulation of 32 000, containing up to 400 pages on Saturdays.

Six months later Fairfax sold its 49 per cent holding in Macquarie Publications, the Dubbo firm which had been printing Good Weekend and *BRW*. Together with other associated transactions, this equity sale to the majority shareholder, John Armati, generated approximately $16 million in cash. At the same time Macquarie sold all its commercial printing operations to Hannanprint, a company owned by the John B. Fairfax and Hannan families. This left Macquarie as purely a country newspaper publisher.

Fairfax may have staunched its Sydney and Gold Coast losses, and raised some badly needed cash in Dubbo, but in Melbourne it could not avoid losing heavily in the Sunday newspaper war between Murdoch's Herald and Weekly Times and David Syme. Since August 1989, when Syme responded to the challenge of Murdoch's broadsheet *Sunday Herald* and tabloid *Sunday Sun*, which threatened to take advertising revenue away from the Saturday *Age*, the broadsheet *Sunday Age* had achieved a circulation of 112 000—2000 more than the *Sunday Herald*.

David Syme's paper seemed likely to lose $10 million in its first fiscal year, and the cost to Murdoch would probably be half as much again. This was a contest from which neither side could safely withdraw. The full four-colour offset *Sunday Age* looked better than the colourless *Sunday Herald*, but that advantage would disappear as soon as Murdoch's offset colour plant came into operation at Port Melbourne. Unless Murdoch's own enormous debt problem dictated otherwise, a mutually debilitating war of attrition seemed likely.

During the first audit period of 1990, the *Age*'s daily circulation dropped by 1.1 per cent, to 266 715; the *Financial Review*'s rose by 3 per cent to 76 242; and the *Sydney Morning Herald*'s rose by 1 per cent to 260 660. This was the third consecutive period in which the *Herald*'s sales had increased, and the latest of many such increases since 1980. By general acknowledgement the *Herald* was Australia's best newspaper, but this was not to say that it was infallible. Like any newspaper produced one day for the next, it sometimes contributed to what its onetime editor-in-chief, David Bowman, described as 'the usual dreary chronicle of journalistic crimes, misdemeanours, blunders and ethical misjudgements that in varying degrees afflict all newspapers and encourage their critics'.

In March 1989 the incumbent editor-in-chief, John Alexander, followed the example of several American newspapers by appointing an outside investigator to report on readers' complaints. This was the first experiment of its kind in Australian journalism, and it encountered considerable difficulty. The appointment was accepted by George Masterman, QC, who had recently returned to the Bar after six years as a fiercely independent Ombudsman of New South Wales. As Masterman did not wish to continue using the word 'ombudsman', his service for the *Herald* was to be known as 'Who Is Right?' He declined to accept payment, but one of his former legal colleagues at the Ombudsman's office was employed by Fairfax to assist him with *Herald* inquiries.

Masterman's agreement with the company indemnified him against legal claims, and stated that he should not examine complaints likely to reach the Press Council, the Ethics Committee of the Australian Journalists' Association, or courts of law. The *Herald* would publicize the service, and Masterman would undertake approximately eight cases each year. In the first few months he received more than 100 complaints.

One of these was a complaint from the Minister for Police, E. P. Pickering, about an article written by Mark Coultan, which according to the complainant had wrongly placed him in the Centre Right faction of the Liberal Party. This was an open and shut case, for Coultan freely admitted the complaint was justified. The mistake had occurred at a late stage of production when a sub-editor had deleted a paragraph for reasons of space. Masterman's first report, published in May, explained in detail how that had happened.

A second report, published in November, concluded that the *Herald* had been justified in not publishing a letter to the editor from the president of the New South Wales Bar Association, contesting aspects of an article by Alan Ramsey. Six other reports were completed, but these could not be published because of a ban placed on 'Who Is Right?' by the AJA House Committee.

Reasons advanced for this ban included the following concerns expressed by journalistic staff about the conduct of Masterman's investigations:

> (i) questioning seems to vary from the very casual to a legal cross-examination; (ii) a bias toward complainants and a tendency to presume the worst; (iii) an assumption that journalism consists only of facts rather than (especially in features) impressions or opinion; (iv) the possibility of journalists suing their own paper for defamation; (v) time-consuming procedures; (vi) assumptions that a journalist's observation of facts is not enough.

A meeting between Masterman and representatives of the House Committee failed to resolve the impasse. Surprised that the company was not taking a stronger line in the matter, Masterman wrote to the editor-in-chief in March 1990 demanding publication of a report submitted three months earlier about a complaint from a medical practitioner, Dr Jeremy Bunker, about an article on child abuse in the Agenda section of the *Herald*. Dr Bunker's complaint was that an accompanying photograph had shown a child, identified by name, who was in no way connected with the story. There was a clear implication, he said, that the child's appearance was related to the subject matter, and this had caused the parents to be justifiably angry and embarrassed. Masterman found against the *Herald*, and recommended the establishment of a committee to formulate a code of conduct for obtaining, publishing and captioning photographs.

In his letter, Masterman reminded Alexander that the company was contractually obliged to publish his reports whether it agreed with them or not.

> It certainly was not the intention or the terms of the agreement reached between us that publication of the articles should be subject to the approval of your journalist employees. That of course would have made nonsense of the whole concept. . .The present position is

untenable. I hereby give you and your company notice that in the event that you do not publish the Dr Bunker complaint article within 28 days from the date of this letter I will consider terminating the agreement on account of your company's breach and taking such other action as I consider appropriate.

Twenty-five days later the AJA called a 24-hour stoppage in support of an award claim. That night the *Herald* was produced by non-journalists, and high on its news list was the child abuse report. Appended to it was a reply by the editor-in-chief: 'I do not believe such a committee is necessary. There are established procedures governing the use of photographs which, when followed, prevent any recurrence of [this kind of] case'.

No further reports were published in the next six months. By that time Masterman, who had long since suspended investigations at Broadway, was wondering how best to formally terminate 'Who Is Right?' In retrospect he regretted not having asked in the first place whether the project had staff support. The staff had not been consulted, and in the mood of militancy and insecurity prevailing since the upheavals of 1987 and 1988 it was doubtful whether consultation would have elicited any support.

Since the success of their strike in support of the senior editorial executives' stand against the Dougherty regime, Fairfax journalists had been markedly sensitive about editorial independence and other professional issues. By the same token editorial executives, themselves the recent beneficiaries of industrial action, seemed reluctant to curb that sensitivity. On two issues as well as 'Who Is Right?'—one concerning management of the library, and another the alleged victimization of a senior journalist—staff protests were more effective than might have been expected in former times.

Working under clouds of corporate uncertainty and financial stringency was hardly conducive to harmony or good morale. The *Herald* and the *Financial Review* reported the company's misfortunes with as much assiduity as the Murdoch press, and the House Committee journal made fun of the proprietor, printing a photograph of him under the heading, 'Have you seen this man?' At the *Herald*'s Christmas party in 1989, one of the carols referred to 'our troubled crumbling Fairfax/Where smiles they are few/But Warwick will fix that/With paints grey and blue'. Another was sung to the tune of 'Silent Night'.

Warwick's fight, family fight
Journos quake at the sight
Yankee junk bonds in piles and piles
Circling bankers gloating with smiles
Waiting for their fees
Looking at assets to seize

III

Junk bonds and banks were indeed the consuming preoccupation of the Fairfax board and senior management. Within a few months of the Citibank-ANZ-Drexel signing it had become obvious that another refinancing, the likelihood of which King had discussed with Citibank and Drexel during the negotiations, would need to be effected sooner rather than later. The board now consisted of six directors, three of whom had been appointed recently. The group managing director, Ron Cotton, resigned from the company in March 1989, six weeks after the refinancing. His departure was not explained, but it seemed obvious that in spite of his valiant performance during the desperate weeks of late 1987 and early 1988 he no longer enjoyed the proprietor's support. The proprietor himself was not always able to attend board meetings, for after his marriage in May 1989 he settled in Chicago and began a management training course at the *Chicago Tribune*.

Warwick Fairfax, King and Anderson were joined on the board in July by three non-executive directors: Bryan Nivison Kelman, AO, CBE; Robert Alan Johnston, AC; and William E. Simon, whose many honours included sixteen honorary doctorates, the Distinguished Patriot Award of the Sons of the American Revolution and the Youth Services Award of the Wall Street Division of B'nai B'rith.

They were the kind of directors any board would have been proud to recruit. Bryan Kelman, a 63-year-old former general manager of the building materials, sugar and aluminium group CSR Ltd, was a civil engineer by training. After two years in the RAAF and four years at Sydney University, he worked for Ready Mixed Concrete Ltd until the age of forty, and then joined CSR, which had acquired a half share in that firm. Since his retirement in 1987 he had remained a director of CSR and was also on the boards of Macquarie Bank, Fletcher Challenge and other major enterprises.

As his only previous connection with Fairfax had been through a fishing lodge on the Snowy River, near one used by John B. Fairfax, Kelman was surprised to receive a telephone call from Peter King in May 1989 inviting him to the Union Club for a cup of tea with Warwick Fairfax. Would he join the board? After perusing the balance sheet, Kelman realized that the group was in 'terrible trouble'. He asked Warwick what policy he intended to follow: was his main objective the protection of his own interests, or keeping the group's newspapers together? The proprietor replied that his personal position was secondary to maintenance of the papers. He did not want to sell the *Age* or the *Review*, let alone the *Herald*.

Kelman also inquired whether Lady Fairfax was likely to join the board, and the answer, according to his recollection, was 'No way in the world'. Admitting that he himself did not have sufficient experience for chairmanship, Warwick offered Kelman that post. Kelman asked Macquarie Bank for an urgent analysis of the group's situation, and after receiving its cautious but not discouraging reply he agreed to join the board as chairman.

> In our opinion [reported Macquarie], the achievement of the earnings levels required to service the debt commitments of the Fairfax Group over the next seven years is a difficult but not unachievable task. . .The major assets of Fairfax have unique, quasi-monopoly positions in the markets they serve and this offers strong protection against potential competitive threats as well as the opportunity for the adoption of a more aggressive pricing strategy than has been used by previous management. . .There is now a consistently sharp focus on identifying cost saving and revenue increasing opportunities, which is reflected in above-budget performance in the year to date. . .
>
> The company has in place a management team which is currently performing and has the apparent confidence of Fairfax's major lenders. [In addition to King and Anderson, the management team included Peter Gaunt, general manager Sydney newspapers; Andrew Hogendijk, the former financial director of a New South Wales coal-mining company, who, as Fairfax's new chief financial officer, had assumed some of Cotton's responsibility; Jerry Austin, group chief accountant; Max Pride, group administration manager; and Frank McMahon, general manager group planning and development.]
>
> On the basis of our analysis the major risk for the Group is the possibility of a major economic recession. If a significant recession did occur within the next seven years it would almost certainly result in Fairfax not generating sufficient earnings to meet its debt-related obligations. In these circumstances the Group would have few options and may have to resort to the lenders for support.

As another Australian director was needed, Kelman suggested that he should approach Bob Johnston, who was shortly to retire as governor and chairman of the Reserve Bank. King and the proprietor went to see Johnston on the day before his retirement, and he too, after reading the Macquarie report and making some inquiries of his own, agreed to join the board. The third new director, the American financier and multi-millionaire Simon, was of course no stranger to the Fairfax family and company. He was a friend and, through the projected Australian Simon University, an educational associate of Lady Fairfax; and his merchant bank in Los Angeles, WSGP, had continued to advise Fairfax after the Drexel deal.

At the first meeting attended by Kelman and Johnston in July, Simon tendered his apologies; and at the first meeting which Simon did attend, on 26 September, he tendered his resignation. After having been welcomed by the chairman, Simon announced that he had a problem. His lawyers had advised him, he said, that in view of the corporate crisis then developing from America's horrendous deregulated savings and loan scandal, the sudden collapse of the junk bond market, and his own vulnerability to legal action as a conspicuously wealthy director resident in the United States, he should immediately resign from as many boards as possible. This included a company such as Fairfax, with American debenture holders.

Simon left the meeting to telephone his lawyer, then returned with his resignation. He was permitted to remain for the rest of the meeting as an observer, and at one point during discussion of the accounts he remarked: 'Warwick, you are in deep shit'.

That blunt diagnosis was corroborated by Fairfax's 272-page filing with the Securities and Exchange Commission in September. In spite of a 19 per cent increase in operating revenue for the year to 30 June, the group had made a loss of $54 million. In a section entitled 'Risk Factors', the filing warned debenture buyers as follows:

> JFG's cash flow (income before taxes, interest expenses and depreciation) was A$214 million for fiscal 1989, as compared to estimated debt service payments of A$184 million during the first twelve months after the Refinancing. Cash debt service payments in fiscal 1990 are estimated to be A$206 million. The Fairfax Group's cash flow based on operations for fiscal 1989 are inadequate to meet scheduled debt service on the Bank obligations and the Debentures in fiscal 1991 and thereafter. . .
>
> Based upon current levels of operation and any reasonably anticipated levels of growth, the Fairfax Group does not expect to be able to generate sufficient cash flow to make principal repayments at maturity of the Bank obligations. Consequently it will be necessary to (i) refinance such indebtedness through the issuance of additional debt, (ii) sell equity (whether in JFG or a subsidiary such as David Syme) or assets, and apply the proceeds to those payments, or (iii) engage in a combination of the foregoing. There can be no assurance that such a refinancing could be completed or that such equity or assets could be sold for an amount adequate to enable the Fairfax Group to reduce its indebtedness sufficiently so that principal and interest payments could be made when due.

With considerations such as these in mind, the company established a refinancing committee in January 1990. It consisted of Hogendijk as chairman; Michael Smith, one of the merchant bankers who had acted as an expert witness for Warwick in the Bond Media court case, and had moved from CIBC to Fairfax specifically to take charge of the new refinancing project; Daryl McPherson, an economist recruited by Hogendijk from the Shell group; and Paul Jeffares, a lawyer seconded to Fairfax from the legal firm of Gadens Ridgeway. Macquarie Bank was retained to advise the board on Australian aspects of refinancing.

The proprietor returned from Chicago, settled with his wife in a house leased for them by the company at Chatswood, and late in January he accompanied King, Hogendijk and Smith to New York in search of an American adviser. They spoke to three investment banks—Merrill Lynch, Morgan Stanley and Goldman Sachs—and chose the latter, mainly because of its track record in buying back junk bonds.

The high-risk bond market was now well and truly living up to its name. Values had been declining steadily since the collapse of a big junk-issuer, Campeau Corporation, in September, and certain high-flying angels had fallen heavily to earth. In February 1990 Drexel went bankrupt. This was the largest bankruptcy in the history of Wall Street, and in the case of Michael Milken who admitted guilt on six insider trading charges, the fine of $600 million which he paid in April was by far the heaviest of its kind ever imposed by a United States court. In addition to that financial penalty, Milken was waiting to learn whether the trial judge would sentence him to any of the 28 years imprisonment to which his admitted felonies had rendered him liable.

The collapse of the junk bond market presented John Fairfax Group with a chance of buying back its debentures at deep discount, thereby reducing its total debt by perhaps two or three hundred million dollars. This would probably require bridging finance from the banks, and the company would have to be careful that other facets of a debt restructure, particularly the hoped for injection of new equity, did not give debenture holders too rosy a picture of the Company's real value. But with judicious handling of the debenture holders, the banks and potential equity takers, a buy-back could well be the foundation for a successful restructure of the company's debt, which now amounted to $1.78 billion. In the first half of 1989–90, the debt consisted of the senior facility from ANZ and the Citibank syndicate ($1.1 billion, of which $1.06 billion had been drawn down); debts to trade creditors, leases and Lady Fairfax's annuity ($160 million), and the debentures ($540 million).

Although the two tranches of debentures had a total face value of $450 million (senior subordinated, $300 million; subordinated, $150 million), the actual debt had already increased to $540 million as a consequence of the mechanism protecting holders against currency fluctuation (FEARs).

The main debenture holders were Drexel ($101.8 million), which of course was now bankrupt; one of Drexel's most faithful buyers, Executive Life ($43.5 million), which was close to insolvency; Prudential Insurance ($41.1 million); Security Pacific ($28.5 million); Columbia Savings and Loan ($25 million), one of many S and Ls whose capital Drexel had attracted into the junk market since the deregulation of those federally chartered institutions in 1982; and another S and L, CenTrust ($24.7 million). Columbia was insolvent, and CenTrust was in receivership.

Early advice from Goldman Sachs—after a team led by one of its partners, Mikael Salovaara, had been to Sydney in February—was that it might be possible to buy the debentures back for as little as a blended price of 35 cents in the dollar for the two tranches. This was predicated upon a valuation of assets which was approximately equal to the company's liabilities, meaning that the value of JFG's shares was nil. A successful buy-back tender would require the present shareholders to acknowledge this fact by selling up to 98 per cent of their combined holdings at token prices. Past experience in this field had demonstrated the harsh truth that bondholders would not sell at a deep discount unless they saw that equity holders had been virtually wiped out.

This posed an obvious conflict of interest for the proprietor, who owned 75 per cent of the issued shares (all the A and D class shares, which were the only voting shares), the other 25 per cent (B class, non-voting) all being owned by his mother. (These proportions would be greatly reduced if debenture holders with Equity Appreciation Rights were paid out for their EARs by the issue of new shares which JFG could do if it did not wish to redeem the EARs for cash. EAR holders could receive approximately 40 per cent of the company's equity value in the form of non-voting shares.)

Not surprisingly, Warwick Fairfax refused to become involved in the plan being developed by Salovaara under the code name of Project Arundel unless he obtained independent advice to protect his own interests. Goldman Sachs's brief was at first to plan only a buy-back of bonds, but later the brief was widened to include other options such as the injection of new equity investment and exchange of equity for debt.

As Warwick's financial resources were limited (his personal income was believed to consist mainly of interest from a $1 million loan made to him by John Fairfax Group), he asked the company to meet the cost of independent advice. A majority of the board was concerned about the propriety of meeting expenses for one shareholder and not the other; but after receiving legal advice that it would be in the company's interest to obtain Warwick's co-operation in Project Arundel, the board agreed on 19 March to pay a maximum of $250 000. Warwick was asked to make the independent advice fully available to his mother. He did not undertake to do that, but said he would not use such information to his mother's disadvantage.

The chosen adviser, Lazard Frères & Company in New York, reported that Goldman's proposal was risky and tough, but sensible. On 11 April Warwick wrote to the board, confirming that he would participate in a transaction which in general

> effectively reduces the debt or interest burden of JFG to an extent that affords JFG meaningful relief; potentially dilutes the equity of myself and Lady Fairfax to an extent to be determined, provided that the range of potential dilution bears some reasonable relationship to the extent of the reduction of JFG's debt or interest; and is not unreasonably coercive, either procedurally or substantively, vis-a-vis the holders of the Debentures and EARs.

But his participation would be subject to several conditions, including the obtaining of all governmental approvals and 'reaching a satisfactory accommodation with Lady Fairfax'.

Because Lady Fairfax effectively held the only economic interest in the company's equity (if indeed the equity had any value at all), by virtue of the B shares' entitlement to receive the first $150 million ahead of A shares in the event of winding up, her co-operation was no less important than Warwick's. But obtaining that co-operation was no easy task, for there was a rift between mother and son. Lady Fairfax had been threatening litigation over the basis of the September 1988 settlement which had been essential for JFG's grouping of tax losses.

It is not possible to elucidate the legal intricacies of this falling out, but during the first half of 1990 certain changes occurred in the arcane realm of the Jones Trust (holder of the B class non-voting Fairfax shares, i.e. Lady Fairfax's shares), the Oriolo Trust (holder of Warwick's A class voting shares), Serpentine Pty Ltd (trustee of the Guilford Bell Trust), and Tailer Investments Pty Ltd (trustee of the Jones and Oriolo Trusts).

In early 1990 Warwick Fairfax was removed by Tailer Investments as its authorized representative in relation to the voting shares of John Fairfax Group, and replaced by one of Lady Fairfax's main advisers, Gerald Gleeson, a former secretary of the New South Wales Premier's Department. On 5 April Warwick removed Tailer Investments as the trustee of the Oriolo Trust, and appointed Serpentine instead. Four days later Lady Fairfax removed her son as a director of Tailer Investments. Although the change in trustee of the Oriolo Trust had been effectively confirmed, Tailer refused to transfer all the Fairfax voting shares to Serpentine, maintaining that as trustee of the Jones Trust it was entitled to 50 per cent of them.

How this contretemps was resolved, or whether indeed it was resolved, must remain uncertain. Clearly, however, there were important issues upon which Lady Fairfax disagreed with her son and with the company. Apparently the 'accommodation' mentioned in Warwick's letter to the board concerned a wish on Lady Fairfax's part to sell her B class shares. The company also wanted this to happen, in conjunction with Project Arundel, but the problem was price. Several meetings failed to reach agreement.

On 17 April Kelman and Smith met Gleeson and another of Lady

Fairfax's advisers, Peter Done, to discuss a paper prepared by Smith on parameters of value and conditions for a proposed call option to be given by Lady Fairfax. Under this option, which it was suggested the company should exercise after a buy-back of the debentures, Lady Fairfax would give up all her shares, annuity rights and legal claims. As for price, Kelman said the company had talked about $30 or $35 million. Gleeson replied that he, Done and an American adviser, David Burnham, had talked about $60 million and had agreed they would recommend that figure to Lady Fairfax. 'She won't like it of course', he added.

'Sixty million is out of the question', said Smith. 'There is no possibility we can raise that sort of money or get the banks' consent to pay it out.'

Next day Smith phoned Done to emphasize the role of the banks and the need to bear in mind the interest of incoming equity investors. 'Even if JFG agrees that $35 million is an appropriate figure for Lady Fairfax's entire interest in the company', he said, according to a file note, 'we would need senior banks' consent, and it is imperative we do not endanger any proposed equity raising by putting a substantial liability to Lady Fairfax into the balance sheet'.

> We seem to be just going round in circles', said Done. 'All our meetings [are] a waste of time'.
>
> 'They will continue to be a waste of time', replied Smith, 'as long as Lady Fairfax is allowed to stay in cloud cuckoo land about the state of JFG. Amounts of $60 million are simply ludicrous. Thirty five million is also ludicrous since our banks will never agree to it. The value of the equity is nil. I would be happy to sit down with you and prove it is nil, Lady Fairfax's economic interest in JFG is confined to her annuity. Valued at an appropriate discount rate it is worth around $20 million. The B shares may have some nuisance value.'
>
> 'Maybe the assets would fetch more if sold to Packer or Murdoch.'
>
> 'I doubt it in this climate. But why doesn't Lady Fairfax stay in the company if she thinks it is worth more. She can take her chances with everyone else.'
>
> 'She wants out.'
>
> 'And we would like to buy her out, but her feet must be brought down to the ground.'

The same applied to Warwick Fairfax, at least in the opinion of Kelman, Johnston, Anderson and Smith. After a long talk with the proprietor on 15 May, Anderson reported to Kelman that basically they and Warwick were 'at loggerheads'.

> He said the projections are strong and the company is 'doing well'. He does not feel that the US bondholders would accept the Goldman Sachs position, but he wants that tested independently. My view is that even if a US bank advised, it is still unlikely that WF would

ultimately go ahead. He doesn't believe the company is in a parlous state.

On 27 June the Fairfax board discussed Project Arundel, based upon a bond tender which Goldman Sachs had recently warned would have only a 50/50 chance of success, but now being widened to include other options as well as the buy-back. All directors were present, and others in attendance included Hogendijk, Smith and the head of the corporate services division at Macquarie Bank, Mark Johnson. Addressing the board, Johnson said that the Goldman proposal carried with it extremely grave risks. It should be put into quarantine, he said, while alternative strategies were sought through a United States adviser—either Lazard Frères, a different Goldman partner, a new adviser altogether, or a combined Goldman/Lazard approach.

One alternative strategy which Mark Johnson had in mind was to find investors in the United States interested in buying 20 or 25 per cent of equity, and to structure the equity so that they could have more than the Foreign Investment Review Board's limit—with FIRB approval. Because of the higher EBDIT multiples commonly used in the United States for valuing media companies, he said, it might be possible to raise enough by this means to repurchase the junk bonds. Additional equity could then be sought in Australia, using the United States precedent as a yardstick in order to raise more funds than might otherwise have been expected.

Kelman felt that a 50/50 chance of success was probably unacceptable. Anderson could not accept the logic that a United States media investor (even assuming one existed) would pay American multiples to buy in the Australian market. Nor did he accept that even if such a thing happened it would serve as a yardstick for Australian investors. It sounded to him like 'fanciful nonsense'. Anderson also asked the board to bear in mind 'the parlous state of the company, the low morale of its staff, the falling earnings, negative shareholders' funds, consistent losses and increases anticipated in newsprint prices'.

King said that in the absence of a full explanation of alternatives open to the board he could not support the Goldman proposal. Finally the proprietor said that Lazards, Citibank and ANZ all held the view that a 50 per cent chance of success was optimistic. He believed the board therefore had to consider other alternatives before committing itself to Goldman's course of action. It could well be, he said, that the current shareholders' equity positions would be more diluted under other alternatives, but this might be preferable as it would give the shareholders greater certainty about what the dilution might be.

The meeting decided that Peter King and Mark Johnson should

Financial consultants Nicholas Whitlam and Malcolm Turnbull

Los Angeles merchant banker William E. Simon, a director of John Fairfax Group Pty Ltd from July to October 1989

The fallen angel of Drexel Burnham Lambert, Michael Milken

Gerry van de Merwe, the corporate banking head of Citibank Australia

John McConnell, general manager corporate banking, ANZ

Alan Kohler, editor of the *Australian Financial Review* 1985–88, informing his staff that the proposed sale of their paper to Bell Group has been rescinded

THE AUSTRALIAN

FINANCIAL REVIEW

FRIDAY, OCTOBER 21, 1988

Sydney 282 2833, Editorial 282 2822, Melbourne 829 9999, (Ed.) 670 9811, Perth 481 5888, Canberra 73 1445, Adelaide 212 1212, Brisbane 221 6266 $1

THE AUSTRALIAN FINANCIAL REVIEW

WEDNESDAY, JULY 8, 1964

Major Oil Strikes Near Moonie And In West; Shares Move Up

Budget Plans Based On Slower Growth Rate

From Our Canberra Bureau

AUSTRALIA'S ECONOMIC PROGRESS

25th ANNIVERSARY ISSUE

IT is 25 years today since *The Australian Financial Review* became a daily. Since then it has brought a unique combination of financial, economic and political expertise to reporting and analysing a period of unprecedented national change. These cover pages and a special lift-out record this period as seen in the pages of the *Financial Review*.

THE AUSTRALIAN FINANCIAL REVIEW

THE KERR ELECTION

PM Fraser: 'the team you can trust'

Opposition leader Whitlam: Finds an issue

Jubilation in the marketplace

THE AUSTRALIAN FINANCIAL REVIEW

TUESDAY, OCTOBER 20, 1987

World markets collapse

Shares fall $9bn despite late rise

New York follows London wipe-out

US bombs Iranian oil platforms

On 21 October 1988 the *Financial Review* celebrated the 25th anniversary of its publication as a daily newspaper.

Peter Robinson, editor 1970–74, editor-in-chief 1988–

Gerard Noonan, editor 1988–

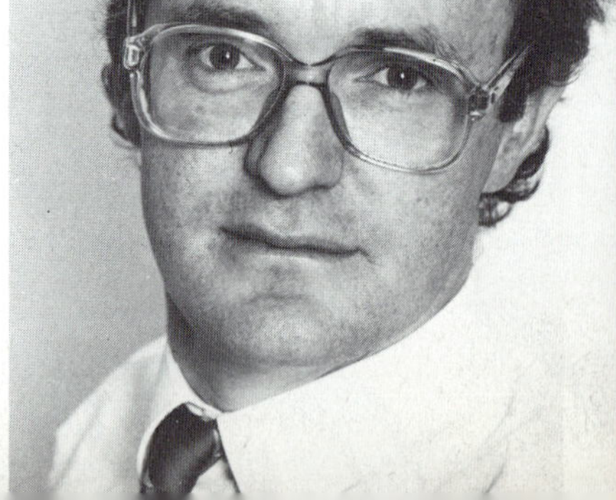

C. J. Anderson, editor of the *Sun-Herald* 1978–80, editor of the *Sydney Morning Herald* 1982–84, editor-in-chief 1984–88, group editorial director and managing director 1988–90, and chief executive of John Fairfax Group Pty Ltd 1990

B. N. Kelman, former chief executive of CSR Ltd, chairman of John Fairfax Group Pty Ltd 1989–90

R. A. Johnston, former governor and chairman of the Reserve Bank, director of John Fairfax Group Pty Ltd 1989–90

Keith Halkerston, chairman of John Fairfax Group Pty Ltd 1990–

Bill Beerworth, director 1990–

In 1875 John Fairfax (below) laid the foundation stone for this Congregational church in Jersey Road, Woollahra. In 1920 a stained-glass window was erected there in memory of his eldest son, Sir James Reading Fairfax. On the night of 27 January 1989, the day when John Fairfax Group Pty Ltd refinanced through Citibank, the ANZ and Drexel Burnham Lambert, the church caught fire and was burnt down to the ruins shown here.

The Fairfax building collapse in Hunter Street, 8 August 1990

develop a plan of action; that King should speak to the managing director of Goldman Sachs, John Weinberg, to see if that firm could work with Lazards to formulate alternative proposals; and that Warwick Fairfax, who was to remain the sole channel of communication with Lazards, should call that firm to ask whether it was prepared to act jointly with Goldman Sachs as adviser to JFG in the light of its role as adviser to himself.

Warwick and his wife flew to the United States, where they were to visit New York after attending a wedding in San Diego; and on 1 July King and Hogendijk also departed for New York. Next day Kelman faxed a strongly worded letter to King, which was waiting for him when he arrived.

> Dear Peter,
>
> I was extremely concerned to learn from a phone call which Warwick made to me yesterday that the purpose of your trip to New York seems to be very different to what you explained to me, and which we agreed was to be the purpose.
>
> You will recall that you suggested you wanted to go to New York for a private meeting with John Weinberg. . .You were to explain to Weinberg that a situation had now arisen whereby the board wanted to reassess the strategy developed with Mikael Salovaara, possibly using a different Goldman Sachs team, with a view to enabling us to improve the chances of our tender succeeding. You also wanted Goldman Sachs to see what alternatives could be suggested particularly in the light of the possibility of better domestic financing being available. . .
>
> I am now deeply concerned to be told that you are taking Hogendijk with you and you are proposing to talk to Lazards as well, even to the extent that you are considering entering into a contract with them to act as the Company's advisers.
>
> I must advise you that I am totally opposed to you pursuing such a course at this time as to do so raises very difficult conflict of interest issues between the Company and each of its shareholders individually since Lazards are already the official advisers to Warwick. Until we know the real views and proposals of the senior banks, I would not support the Company entering into commitments or discussions with any group as an additional adviser and this view applies most particularly to Lazards. Nor has the Board delegated any authority—to you, Warwick or Hogendijk—in respect of these matters. . .I can only conclude by expressing my extreme concern at the changes which appear to have been made to a course of action which we agreed on Friday. I intend to circulate this letter to all other Directors.

Understandably disturbed by this letter, King telephoned Bob Johnston, whose firm advice was to heed the chairman's words. King kept his appointment at Goldman Sachs, and gained the impression there that Weinberg would put a new team on to the buy-back plan in an attempt to improve the 50 per cent chance of success. Then he and Hogendijk returned to Sydney, without seeing Lazards.

This was not the first rough passage in King's tenure of office at Broadway. In spite of his geniality, he had previously incurred the hostility of Lady Fairfax, first by opposing her appointment to the board, next by declining to let the company pay her secretaries' salaries ('The banks would kill me', he said), and finally by insisting that the Rolls-Royce formerly used by Sir Warwick as his company car should be included in a sale of the company's peripheral assets. To keep the car, Lady Fairfax had to match a market price of $215 000.

More detrimentally to King's position, tension was growing between himself at one end of the executive floor and Anderson, the chief editorial director/managing director, at the other. In April, for example, Citibank was claiming to have a cheaper alternative to Goldman's proposal for buying back the debentures, but was reluctant to present it formally because of what it perceived as 'tension in the management' at Broadway. The bank's hesitation was no more specific than that; but, in discussing the matter with King, Anderson said there was 'lack of confidence' in the chief executive officer's handling of his job. According to Anderson's file note, he went on to say that if he himself was the problem the board should ask him to resign, and he would do so discreetly.

King rejected the latter suggestion, saying that he wanted the two of them to 'patch it up'. Anderson said it was wider than that, and could not be patched up. King then told Anderson that Kelman had said Anderson had been critical of his (King's) stewardship. Anderson said that was true, but that such feeling about him and Warwick was widespread in the company. King accused Anderson of disloyalty, but later apologized. Anderson refused to accept the apology until the position was resolved.

According to Anderson's note, King later went to see van der Merwe and Cannon-Brookes at Citibank to inquire about the meaning of 'tension in the management'. 'Citibank refused to be specific with PK', said the note,

> however PK (according to PK) asked was it because of him—was it due to his inexperience? According to PK, Citibank said it was not. However, according to Gerry van der Merwe, Citibank's answer to that question from PK was: 'That is not a question for us—it is not our call'. That is a somewhat different interpretation from PK's understanding. PK said Citibank were concerned about Warwick and thought his involvement would make equity more difficult. Citibank feel resolution of any management problem is for the Board and the Chairman.

Although Citibank did not put forward a buy-back proposal, and some at Fairfax doubted whether it ever intended to, the issue of management tension continued to smoulder at Broadway until it burst into flame. On 3 May Anderson wrote to Kelman saying that he felt in a

> difficult, isolated—and increasingly intolerable—position. This was re-inforced today by calls I had from Peter Gaunt and Greg Taylor [members of JFG's five-man executive committee, the others being King, Anderson and Hogendijk]—basically but politely questioning my impotence. . .While the fabrication and euphemism of 'management tension' is allowed to remain, it puts us all under a cloud. . .You said you intended to act in the next few days and speak to Peter honestly about the position—unless you do I feel it could have grievous repercussions for us all.

Some time later that month King spoke to Kelman. His position was intolerable, he said, and either he or Anderson would have to go. He acknowledged Anderson's media expertise, and offered to go if the company would treat him properly in terms of his contract. The contract provided for a generous cash payout.

King then spoke in similar vein to Warwick, whose response, according to King, was: 'I will not allow this. If need be I will get rid of the board'.

'The reaction to that in the market place would be horrendous', replied King. 'Please do not oppose it. Let me go.'

Kelman and Johnston concluded that King should be asked to resign, and on Friday 13 July Kelman broached the subject with Warwick. Again the proprietor demurred. Kelman told him the other directors felt that the management would not work as presently structured, and asked him to think about it over the weekend. On Monday morning Warwick said he still did not agree, but would not oppose the matter.

A board meeting was called for 19 July, with only one item on the agenda. King and Anderson were notified, but they asked to be excused from attending. After considering the question of senior management, the three attending directors agreed, firstly, that it was no longer appropriate for there to be two separate positions of chief executive officer and group editorial director/managing director; and, secondly, that the two sets of responsibilities should be absorbed into one, to be known as chief executive officer.

The chairman then proposed that in view of the redundancy of the position occupied by King, he be asked to resign with effect from 10 August; and that Anderson be asked to assume the reconstituted position of chief executive officer. When it came to the vote, Warwick remained silent. 'Do I take that as unanimous consent?'

asked the chairman. Warwick nodded his head, and unanimity was recorded in the minutes.

These changes were announced on 9 August, and next day Peter King resigned as a director. His was the fourth resignation from the boards of either John Fairfax Ltd or John Fairfax Group Pty Ltd since the takeover two and a half years earlier. He followed in the path of Martin Dougherty, Laurie Connell and Ron Cotton, thus completing the departure of all the directors who had opened the gates of paradise for Warwick Fairfax.

The list of departures might easily have been longer, for on different occasions during the last few months Anderson and Johnston had each seemed likely to resign from the board. Anderson reached this stage twice (once in connection with his management contract, and later over the failure of Warwick and his mother to settle their differences), but Kelman persuaded him to stay. At a board meeting on 19 March 1990 Johnston announced his intention of resigning, threw his papers on the table and abruptly left the room. Kelman hurried after him, and talked him out of it. Johnston later explained his action by saying that he had found it 'a bit embarrassing to be sitting next to the main shareholder and discussing how we were going to dilute his position'.

Embarrassing though the subject may have been, dilution of the present shareholdings—even to the point of elimination—was freely discussed with the senior lenders by Fairfax directors. It was mentioned, for example, in a briefing paper which Kelman sent to the ANZ for a visit by senior officers of that bank to Broadway on 11 July, shortly before the arrival of Salovaara and two of his colleagues from Goldman Sachs with their eagerly awaited report. According to the briefing paper, JFG hoped to negotiate the departure of Lady Fairfax and the cessation of her annuity for a total cash outlay of about $25 million. Anderson had told Warwick that he should negotiate a 'deal' with his mother regarding the priority agreement of $150 million in Lady Fairfax's favour, and then take 'a realistic (but small) figure' for his own equity, perhaps $5 million.

By the same token, the ANZ group managing director, Reg Nicolson, sent Kelman a list of points which the group chief executive, Will Bailey, and others from the bank intended making to the Fairfax directors. It was a series of warnings to the company, and especially to the proprietor.

> Trading conditions are deteriorating, and the company's performance will shortly reflect this. The domestic economy may not pick up for 12 months or more. On Fairfax's hard-landing projections a breach of at least one and possibly three bank covenants is likely in the next 12 months. Continued delays in finalising a refinancing are unacceptable . . . Mr Fairfax's equity is now worthless. The company

is trading with the Bank's money; it must therefore be accepted that the Bank's wishes cannot be ignored.

The Bank is not prepared to tolerate a situation where Mr Warwick Fairfax uses his position as controlling shareholder to veto plans, delay progress, or impose his own interests on those considered by the Board of JFG to be essential to protect the position of creditors.

We are informed that Mr Kelman accepted the position of Chairman of the Board on a clear understanding that his purpose and brief was to help ensure the financial survival and integrity of the Company as a complete entity.

The Bank is informed that the Company has received legal advice that Mr Warwick Fairfax's role as a director is likely to lead to a conflict of interest with the Company's position in relation to the proposed restructuring and that this may require him not to participate in the refinancing or restructuring discussions, or to stand down from the Board.

If the non-executive directors of JFG, Mr Kelman and Mr Johnston, or the Managing Director of John Fairfax Ltd, Mr Anderson, were forced to or decided to resign from the Board of JFG because their wishes, as expressed in a Board meeting, were over-ruled or obstructed, we would consider that a material adverse change in the affairs of the Company had occurred and we would take such steps as we felt appropriate or necessary to protect our position.

The Bank believes that action to restructure debt is vital in the near future—i.e. a sit and do nothing option or a further delay would not be acceptable to us.

The Bank believes that an attempt to re-purchase the junk bonds is worthy of full consideration. The current Goldman Sachs initiatives appear to be dragging and perhaps unlikely to succeed. The Bank would endeavour to arrange a bridging loan to finance the purchase of the junk bonds subject to being able to arrange a take-out from the subscription of new equity after the [buy-back] has been completed. The Bank would be prepared to assist the Company in attempts to arrange such equity and if the bond tender is successful we imagine the chances of arranging such equity would be enhanced.

This was the first time Bailey had taken part in such a meeting with JFG, and in his opening remarks he said that he was doing so to emphasize the bank's commitment and the gravity with which it regarded Fairfax's situation. The bank's own situation may also have been a factor in Bailey's personal involvement. Like other banks, the ANZ was now feeling the after-effects of lavish lending during the 1980s. Its bad debt charge had doubled in 1988–89, to $528 million; and its profit had declined by 23 per cent in the first half of 1989–90. Much the same applied to Citibank. That bank's global earnings fell by 46 per cent in the first quarter of fiscal 1990, its level of highly leveraged transactions stood at $US7.9 billion, and its rating by Moody's had fallen from Aa2 to A1.

Bailey told the meeting that JFG had to replace its junk bonds with new equity. But until the bonds were 'out of play', he said, no equity was likely to be available. Although the company should not seek equity participants before the bond tender, it should obtain up-front understanding at chairman or chief executive office level that equity could be obtained. The bank could help in this process.

He also said that senior executive staff should become shareholders, because they had held the company together. Warwick Fairfax's position would be dramatically and drastically reduced. The ANZ itself was willing to be an equity participant, perhaps taking a 40 per cent interest with another major institution. The ANZ was ready to take certain risks, but it had to be realistic. It felt aggrieved because it had been 'lied to' during negotiations for the original financing in 1987.

In reply, Warwick Fairfax accepted the tenor of what the ANZ was saying. He wholeheartedly supported a refinancing. He understood that his own position would be reduced. Certainly it had never been his intention to try to cling on to too much in the short term.

Bailey then spoke again, repeating his view that staff should be involved in equity, and saying to Anderson, 'I hope you are committed, Chris?' Anderson said he had spent twenty-five years of his life at Fairfax, which indicated his commitment, but was concerned at the present unsustainable level of leverage. Unless the company refinanced quickly, it would be in the banks' hands by April whether the banks wanted it or not.

Five days later Anderson returned to the subject of commitment in a letter to Bailey. The commitment of senior management, he wrote, depended firstly upon insurance against loss of employment; and secondly upon 'participation in equity ownership, including that equity participation surviving in the event of receivership, liquidation or the looming change of ownership'. In his view an appropriate equity stake for staff would be not less than 20 per cent.

On the same day Kelman and Anderson called at Citibank to see van der Merwe, Featherstone and Reemst. They outlined the ANZ position, and found Citibank broadly in agreement with that. Anderson said he believed the two Fairfax shareholders should be treated realistically because debt holders should not be expected to accept deep discounts if equity holders were allowed more advantageous treatment. Featherstone said that was Citibank's view as well. There was no discussion of new equity, although van der Merwe said he intended raising that subject at a future date.

Some discussion had already taken place between JFG and potential equity investors, both local and foreign. One of the most promising contacts in this regard had been with Dr Anthony O'Reilly, an Irish national who was chairman, president and chief executive of the United States food giant, H. J. Heinz. Among many other business interests, Tony O'Reilly was also the chairman and controlling shareholder of Ireland's largest media organization, Independent Newspapers, and the driving force behind Provincial Newspapers, a Brisbane-based chain of thirty papers which News Ltd had been enjoined to sell by the Trade Practices Commission. Independent Newspapers held 15 per cent of Provincial, and the rest was held by a trust for the benefit of O'Reilly's six children—all of whom, like his wife, were Australians.

Chris Anderson and his Irish wife had become friendly with O'Reilly, and he and Kelman had breakfast with O'Reilly at the Regent Hotel in March 1990. Before returning to the United States, O'Reilly told Anderson that he would be prepared to consider investing in JFG at a level acceptable to Warwick Fairfax and senior management. He was not thinking of control, but rather of being involved in a consortium with Australian banks and institutions. Although an Irish connection seemed feasible at first, foreign investment proved to be more of a problem than expected. In May, O'Reilly's representatives held a long official conversation with the Federal Treasurer and some of his advisers, during which Keating told them that the Maxwell issue (the Treasurer had recently blocked an attempt by Robert Maxwell to buy 49 per cent of the *West Australian*), the role of the Democrats in the Senate, and Labor Party feeling about foreign ownership of the media would all make it difficult to approve any more than 15 per cent for metropolitan papers. They took this to mean that the timing was not right, and advised Anderson that for the time being at any rate O'Reilly was out.

The visitors from Goldman Sachs, who arrived on 18 July, did not bring glad tidings. They brought a drastically revised valuation of JFG's assets, and a set of options from which a course of action could be chosen. The new valuation of assets including mastheads—reflecting the economy's downward turn, the worldwide perception that media properties had been over-valued, and Keating's harder line on foreign investment—was between \$1.2 and \$1.4 billion. This could mean that in the event of liquidation, the current value of the company's assets after liquidation costs and stamp duty might not exceed even the senior debt, which was increasing steadily through capitalization of interest and would be \$1.5 billion by the end of the facility in 1996. Neither shareholders nor bondholders would have any economic interest in the company, and senior lenders' loans would also be at risk.

The prospects for a successful bond tender would presumably be improved by the weakening Australian economy, the world-wide disillusion with media values, and foreign investment limits. All of these would adversely affect the value of JFG assets, and that could be expected to make bondholders more receptive to a low-priced tender. On the other hand, in Goldman Sachs's view, the tender would be adversely affected if the banks insisted on JFG raising equity up-front, and if there was any disruption by third-party counter offers.

One party known to have disruptive intentions was Robert Holmes à Court. In April a *Herald* journalist, Paul McGeough, had reported to Anderson the gist of a conversation with Holmes à Court, who was a long-time friend of his, over a private dinner at Peppermint Grove. 'Fairfax won't ever get those bonds back', Holmes à Court had said. 'Whatever they do, I will over-bid them.' Furthermore he was confident that no international investor, United States newspaper company or institution would take equity in Fairfax. 'I have contacted them', he said, 'and I am certain that [Fairfax] won't be able to raise any finance because I have indicated to them the real position'.

McGeough understood that his host intended these remarks to be passed on to Fairfax. As it happened, however, the threat was in vain, for Holmes à Court had only four more months to live. He died of a heart attack at the age of fifty-three.

In four days of meetings at Broadway with Fairfax directors, the refinancing committee and the banks, the Goldman Sachs advisers presented seven possible courses of action: 'Do Nothing, Sell Enterprise, Sell Assets, Raise Equity Financing, Restructure Bank Debt, Restructure Subordinated Debt, Enter Receivership/Provisional Liquidation'. Although not recommending any particular plan of action, their exposition of the options did point towards conclusions which could be drawn from the new valuation.

On the afternoon of 25 July Anderson had a long talk with Warwick, during which he canvassed four options—three of which were variations of a bond tender, for cash or equity or both; and the fourth, if the tender failed, a managed receivership. Kelman was overseas, but during the afternoon Bob Johnston and Michael Smith joined the conversation in Anderson's office. Smith talked about a revised restructuring proposal which he was preparing, based upon Goldman Sachs's valuation and deliberations at the recent meetings. Johnston and Anderson then urged Warwick to 'make up his mind' about his intended future actions, as continued delays were harming the company's relationship with ANZ and Citibank. 'WF seemed supportive', according to Anderson's file note, 'but indicated he would probably need "more time". He added: "I guess I'll need to think about that"'.

Warwick also undertook to discuss the position with his mother. On the night of 28 July Lady Fairfax made a 90-minute telephone call to Anderson from London. She began by saying that Warwick had told her the directors were 'putting the company into liquidation' next week; he was not sure what to do, she said, and was coming to see her about it. Anderson replied that it was not a case of liquidation (winding up of business and sale of assets to settle liabilities as far as possible); the company had, however, discussed with the banks the prospect that they might place it in receivership (appointing a receiver/manager to help the company trade out of its difficulties) if no other course could be found. Anderson told her the company was in a parlous state and suggested that she wait until Gleeson and Done received the full Goldman Sachs report. Then she would understand. The best action she could take was to see if any of her annuity could be saved. Her equity was worthless. 'We have had this conversation many times before', said Anderson. 'You know I've been telling you for the last two years that the situation is very grim.'

Lady Fairfax agreed, and asked whether there was any role for Warwick, or for herself, on the board. Anderson said that it was not for him to decide, but in his view the banks wanted Warwick out. She asked how she should treat him when he arrived, and Anderson replied: 'As a son—he'll need a lot of help'. Lady Fairfax said she understood, but found it hard to 'forgive Warwick' as she had tried to prevent the original takeover. Anderson said no company could survive the level of debt which Warwick had imposed upon Fairfax, and Lady Fairfax agreed.

Two days later Warwick flew to meet his mother in New York. They returned to Sydney on Thursday 9 August, the day Peter King's resignation was announced. Next day the directors received copies of Michael Smith's proposal, which was now ready for consideration by the directors on 15 August. Warwick showed the proposal to Lady Fairfax, and she was apparently very disturbed by it.

Mother and son must also have been disturbed by the *Herald*'s front page that morning, which reported Peter King's resignation under the headline 'Boardroom coup: Warwick Fairfax's dream dissolves'. The tone was almost valedictory.

> The historic family control of Sydney's John Fairfax newspaper empire will end in as soon as three months, the chairman of John Fairfax Group Pty Ltd, Mr Bryan Kelman, said last night.
>
> The prediction came after a dramatic corporate manoeuvre in which Warwick Fairfax voted for the removal of the man he had brought in to run the company he privatised in 1987, Mr Peter King . . .
>
> Mr Kelman said the end of the Fairfax era would be 'sad for those of us who have grown up with the Fairfax family in Sydney'. . .
>
> It is envisaged that Warwick Fairfax's equity could be reduced to as little as 5-10 per cent following the refinancing . . .

Or even less, according to the refinancing proposal. Starting from the premise that shareholders and bondholders no longer had any economic interest in the company, Smith proceeded to certain logical and painful conclusions. The Fairfax shareholding would be reduced to no more than 5 per cent—probably 3.2 per cent, between Warwick and his mother—and Lady Fairfax's annuity payments would cease. There was no mention of any payment to the two shareholders—only the proffered consolation that if Goldman Sachs was correct in its estimate of JFG's value after the proposed restructuring ($200 million), they would have an economic interest initially worth between $5 and $7 million, compared with the one presently perceived as being worth nil.

There may in fact have been marginally more in the offing, for at a meeting with Gleeson and Done on 27 June Anderson and Smith had mentioned the possibility of $500 000 as an *ex gratia* payment to Lady Fairfax. At another meeting four days later Smith said he realized the figure was very low, and perhaps Lady Fairfax might be able to persuade the banks to agree to a higher one. Presumably this would have been relayed to Lady Fairfax in New York, but it could not have done much to cushion the shock of the restructuring proposal.

The proposal also invited bondholders and banks to accept heavy losses. Bondholders could receive in payment for their junk bonds—which, be it remembered, had a face value of $450 million—either $17 million cash or 8.5 per cent of JFG equity. Subject to the Foreign Investment Review Board, they would also be offered a six-month option to purchase 41.5 per cent of JFG from the senior banks for $83 million. Bondholders with Equity Appreciation Rights could surrender them for a further 1.8 per cent of JFG equity. There would be minimum acceptance levels of 99 per cent for bonds and 85 per cent for EARs.

The banks were asked to give up principal or interest with a present value of $100 million, and thereby acquire 60 per cent of JFG equity. Some of this would be earmarked for senior JFG staff.

Goldman Sachs would underwrite the subscription of $100 million redeemable preference shares in JFG, plus a warrant entitling the preference shareholders to subscribe additional cash for 25 per cent of the company's equity.

Bank debt would be reduced by $100 million from the proceeds of the underwriting, and any additional proceeds from the sale of equity to bondholders would be used to offset the banks' compromise.

If all this went according to plan, Fairfax's total debt (excluding preference shares) would be reduced by $640 million to approximately $1.16 billion, a level which the company should be capable of servicing even in 'a hard landing economic scenario.' The company's fully diluted equity would then be held as follows: Warwick and Lady Fairfax, 3.2 per cent; EAR holders, 1.8 per cent;

bondholders, 8.5 per cent; Goldman Sachs, 25 per cent; senior lenders and JFG staff, 61.5 per cent.

The tone of the proposal was either realistic or callous, depending on one's point of view. In a section entitled 'Practical Approach', it said:

> We expect that bondholders and senior lenders (and possibly equity holders) will all resist crystallisation of their positions and recognition of losses. However, if we argue the logic which Goldman Sachs used in support of their assessment of value, the losses for all levels of investor can be seen to be real and unavoidable.
>
> The current equity holders, being closer to the company than the other parties, are better placed to acknowledge the gravity of JFG's position.
>
> Senior lenders, who are secured, will need to be persuaded of the adverse impact on their position of a failure by JFG to find a solution to its problems, although they appeared to agree with Goldman Sachs's conclusions when they met Goldman Sachs in July.
>
> If senior lenders are so persuaded and agree to acknowledge their position by converting debt to equity, the task of persuading bondholders of their (admittedly much more painful) position becomes more achievable.
>
> We should not delude ourselves into believing that reality will be a prime motivating factor in bondholders' or banks' minds. The ultimate motivating factor will be an awareness that the alternative to a voluntary restructuring will be even less acceptable to all the parties.

Consideration of this restructuring proposal did not go according to plan. It did not even come before the directors on 15 August, for by that time certain developments which had been taking place unknown to any members of the board except Warwick had become apparent. Warwick, it seemed, had made up his mind to part company with the realist-pessimists, avoid a restructuring based upon Goldman Sachs's valuation and advice, and seek a more palatable alternative. Whether or not he retained any economic interest in the company (and another valuation might show that he did), he still indubitably controlled the voting shares and could easily 'get rid of the board' as he had contemplated doing at the height of the King crisis.

The first intimation of this came on Monday 13 August, when Bob Johnston received a telephone call from a corporate adviser of his acquaintance, Bill Beerworth, asking to see him urgently. (Kelman had returned from overseas, but was temporarily away from Sydney.) Johnston went to see Beerworth at the office of Beerworth & Partners, and was informed by him that Warwick had decided to ask for his and Kelman's resignations. They would be replaced by

Beerworth and his partner Keith Halkerston. Beerworth & Partners would be appointed to co-ordinate the refinancing.

Johnston later telephoned this news to Kelman, and so the chairman was forewarned when, on Wednesday, the same news was conveyed to him both by Warwick in writing and Beerworth in person. Kelman also received a solicitors' letter saying that Warwick had convened a general meeting for 28 August to reconstitute the board. Given Warwick's voting power, the outcome of such a meeting would be a foregone conclusion.

> I have been concerned [said Warwick's letter to Kelman] that the Refinancing Committee established about 6 months ago has effectively produced only two plans. Each seems radical in its assumptions and proposals and each is quite different from the other. I believe that the implementation of either of these plans at this stage would destabilise the Group.
>
> Moreover I do not believe that there has been sufficient investigation of the alternative means of refinancing and recapitalising. However, from recent statements attributed to you and Chris Anderson, it seems to have become accepted that only a radical refinancing proposal should be pursued.
>
> You and Bob Johnston have greatly assisted the company in focussing all relevant parties on the need to deal with the refinancing problem. But now that the need has been identified and accepted, I consider it appropriate that the reconstruction phase be handled directly by persons whose experience and skills are primarily financial.
>
> For that reason, I have decided to ask Mr Keith Halkerston to assume the role of Chairman and I should be most grateful if you would agree to resign in his favour.
>
> I would see no embarrassment in your doing so and I believe that this is an entirely appropriate opportunity for you honourably to hand the refinancing baton to him...
>
> I am sure that you will appreciate that I wish Chris Anderson to remain as Chief Executive Officer. There is no intention for Keith Halkerston, Bill Beerworth or anybody else to interfere in management or editorial operations. Because I know you have the interests of the Group at heart, I should be grateful if you would use your good offices to ensure that Chris stays and that he understands my strong desire that he should retain his position and authority...

At 3 p.m. on Wednesday, Kelman, Johnston and Anderson attended a meeting of directors, with Beerworth acting as alternate for Warwick Fairfax, who did not attend. The meeting resolved that a request to Macquarie Bank for a valuation of JFG should be ratified, that Lazard Frères should be invited to advise the company on refinancing, and that Macquarie Bank be asked to explore alternatives in the Australian market for the repurchase of bonds and the raising of fresh equity. These resolutions were not an outcome of Warwick's new orientation. They had been set in train some time earlier as part of a concern by the board to explore alternatives.

While this meeting was in progress, Lady Fairfax departed for New York, which was as much her home nowadays as Sydney or London. She owned two floors of the Pierre Hotel on Fifth Avenue, but stayed at the Metropolitan Club. Soon after arriving there on Friday evening Sydney time, she rang Anderson and resumed some of their earlier discussions. Dismayed though she had been by the restructuring proposal, she did not approve of Warwick's move against Kelman and Johnston, and like her son she wanted Anderson to remain as chief executive, even though angry words had passed between Anderson and herself recently.

On the previous Saturday, the day after Smith's proposal had been circulated, Anderson had telephoned Lady Fairfax at Fairwater to deny that he had been 'talking down the company's value in order to get equity for himself and other members of the staff', as he understood one of her advisers to have been telling journalists. Anderson also spoke to David Burnham, an American management psychologist who had been a trusted adviser to Sir Warwick and Lady Fairfax for several years, and a friend to Warwick since the latter's time at Chase Manhattan.

(The question of staff participation in equity had also been discussed by Kelman at a meeting with Lady Fairfax's advisers on 10 August. He denied that JFG would be 'subjected to a leveraged buyout by its senior management' as a result of refinancing. This denial was reported next morning by the *Herald*, which quoted Kelman as saying that between 10 and 15 per cent of the equity might be made available to staff through the issue of partly paid shares or options.)

At a meeting with Beerworth and Kelman on 16 August Anderson made it clear that if Kelman and Johnston resigned he would also leave the company. Warwick Fairfax then wrote to him expressing disappointment.

> I can understand that you may personally disapprove of my decision, but I frankly fail to see the logical connection between Bryan and Bob leaving the Board and your own position. . .It has been suggested that Bryan and Bob's departure is an event which might demonstrate lack of confidence in you. I do not understand that suggestion. My confidence in you is such that I am writing. . .to request you not to resign.

On 20 August Warwick met the three directors at Beerworth's office. Beerworth asked Anderson to stay, saying that he would 'be in the box seat'; but as there was no relenting about the other two directors, Anderson reaffirmed that he would go with them. Rather than wait for the inevitable result of a one-man general meeting, they tendered their resignations—Johnston on 22 August, Kelman and Anderson the following day. Kelman and Johnston left with nothing more than their directors' fees, but Anderson's contract ensured that he was treated generously.

'Warwick Fairfax's board quits', said the *Herald* on 24 August. Chris Anderson, restricted in his ability to comment by legal agreement with the company, said:

> It is Warwick's undoubted right to pick his board. However, I believe Mr Kelman and Mr Johnston have acted at all times in the best interest of all concerned—the shareholders, the newspapers, the employees and our creditors and bankers. They are honourable and experienced men and restored a level of maturity, judgment and stability to our company. I felt I could not stand by and allow them to go.

Next day Bryan Kelman, who was under no constraint, spoke with great candour about the young proprietor who had invited him to chair the board little more than a year before. Describing the resignations as 'Warwick's latest folly', Kelman said he had found the proprietor 'extremely difficult to deal with' and that it had been 'almost impossible to get him to make logical decisions'. 'I would never again consider entering into any arrangement over which Warwick would have any control whatsoever. I believe up to date he has shown a marked unwillingness to face reality.'

The proprietor said in a press release that the company's most important task was to refinance its capital structure.

> The company has been through an unfortunate period of uncertainty in the last few weeks. Now that the matter of board direction has been settled, I want the company to get on with business as usual. John Fairfax remains the finest newspaper group in the country and I propose that it will stay that way.

The new chairman, 55-year-old Keith Halkerston, was a former merchant banker of high repute. He had been a member of the Campbell Committee, established by the Fraser Government during the early 1980s to advise on deregulation of the financial sector; a director of several large companies, including Cadbury Schweppes and Boral; and, until 1988, senior partner of the Sydney merchant bank Baring Brothers Halkerston. He now lived in an Oxfordshire village called Nettlebed, but was still a director of Boral and continued to advise a select number of Australian clients, including the stockbroking firm, Ord Minnett.

Halkerston may have seemed merely another bright hope in Warwick Fairfax's disillusioning progression from one set of advisers and directors to the next. In turning to him, however, Warwick was in fact coming full circle. It was Baring Brothers Halkerston which had advised him in March 1987 not to make a takeover bid, and that was the best advice anyone had ever given him.

IV

Now comes a third coincidence, no less uncanny in its timing than the opening of the Gates of Paradise during the week of Warwick Fairfax's takeover, or the burning down of John Fairfax's church on the night of the company's refinancing. In the month that Warwick's board resigned, the façade of the property that might once have been transformed into a skyscraper named Fairfax House collapsed in Hunter Street.

The site consisted of a building which had formerly housed Fairfax's downtown office, with rooms used by Angus McLachlan, Rupert Henderson and Sir Warwick Fairfax in their retirement, and several adjoining properties which the company had acquired before the takeover, intending to carry out a major redevelopment there. Then the site was sold, as part of Tryart's asset disposal programme. Virtually all of the property was demolished, and by August 1990 the steel framework for a 21-level office building could be seen rising behind the old façade, a shell of masonry several storeys high which had been preserved by government decree as an architectural reminder of the 1880s.

This precarious remnant of windows, balconies and architraves was supported by scaffolding, but not securely enough. At 12.52 p.m. on Wednesday 8 August it fell down with a noise like thunder, injuring six people, smashing a 'Herald-Sun' neon sign, crushing two cars, and burying part of Hunter Street in rubble. Miraculously no one was killed.

If only metaphors could tell us more! As it is, we have to prise what meaning we can from them, and try not to be misled by their artifice. Had the façade of family ownership finally collapsed, disclosing the reality of ownership by creditors? Would the ANZ keep to its professed intention of regarding resignations by Kelman, Johnston and Anderson as the kind of 'material adverse change' in the affairs of the company which would constitute default and persuade the banks to protect their own position? In the event of default, the banks would be entitled to exercise all or any of several rights: sell the company and its subsidiaries; take possession of the assets; sell the assets, wholly or in part; and appoint a receiver/manager to carry on the business.

Nothing of that kind happened in consequence of the departure of the three directors, and of Michael Smith, who resigned a few days later. The ANZ was deterred from carrying out its threat by the recent legal frustration of another bank's attempt to liquidate Bond

Brewing Holdings. Citibank and ANZ kept their intentions to themselves, and at Broadway there was no industrial action of the kind which had alarmed the banks in 1988. Anderson discouraged any talk of more resignations and persuaded the editor-in-chief of the *Herald* to go ahead with a planned holiday in Greece. Rumour had it that Anderson at some stage would probably be invited back to Broadway by the banks, and there was no suggestion this time that he would go to News Ltd.

Rupert Murdoch, ever considerate of his young competitor, telephoned Warwick to suggest one of his own people—the chief executive of the Adelaide *News*—as successor to Anderson. There was no pressing need for such helpfulness, however, as Warwick himself had taken over the role of chief executive, working in the office formerly occupied by Peter King, and earlier by James Fairfax and Sir Warwick Fairfax. Senior executives and editors who had previously reported to Anderson were now instructed to report directly to the proprietor. This was easier said than done, for matters of refinancing were preoccupying Warwick and it was seldom possible to see him or hear from him. It soon became the established practice for senior executives and editors to run their own bailiwicks as they judged best, so long as they kept within their budgets.

Four weeks after the change of directors, the proprietor, Beerworth and Hogendijk flew to New York, where they were joined by Keith Halkerston. They returned to Sydney on Tuesday 2 October, having seen Lazard Frères and other unspecified parties in connection with restructuring. Beerworth said the trip had been the end of the beginning of what would be a very long process. Beyond that, he was as tight-lipped as the banks.

In this eventful week our narrative must now draw to a close. On the Tuesday of Warwick's return, the directors issued JFG's signed accounts for 1989–90. Despite difficult trading conditions in the second half of the year, the company reported a solid operational performance, based mainly on increased revenue generated as a result of advertising rate and cover price increases. Operation earnings before interest expense rose 3.4 per cent from $189.1 million to $195.6 million. Revenue rose from $803.4 million to $815.7 million, and EBDIT from $213.7 million to $223.1 million. The *Herald* and *Financial Review* had increased their average daily circulations, though the *Age* experienced a small decline. Basically the core newspapers were as sound as ever, despite the calamity of the company and its proprietorship.

The calamity was made all too obvious by the interest costs, which rose 10.6 per cent from $243.3 million to $269.1 million, producing a pre-abnormal items and tax loss of $73.4 million, compared with $54.2 million for the previous year. In their report the directors referred to undrawn credit facilities of approximately $100 million.

If current trading conditions continued, they said, the company was likely to breach certain borrowing covenants in July 1991, or even as early as December 1990. If the banks then withdrew the undrawn credit facilities, and alternative funding was not found, the company might not be able to pay its debts as and when they fell due.

On the following day, Rupert Murdoch announced that his company would close its Sydney and Melbourne afternoon newspapers by merging them with their morning sister publications to form two four-edition, 24-hour tabloids—the *Daily Telegraph Mirror* and the *Herald-Sun*. This was virtually the end of the evening newspaper era in Australia, although the Adelaide *News* and the Brisbane *Sun* were still holding out against television in their smaller markets. The Melbourne *Herald* had fought hard against the inevitable since Murdoch acquired it in 1987; but during that time its circulation had fallen from 217 200 to 170 000, and the paper was now losing more than $20 million per year. In Sydney the *Mirror* had not been able to hold the advantage conferred on it by the closure of Fairfax's *Sun* in 1988. On the contrary, in spite of shock-horror and saucy photography, its circulation had fallen from 396 800 to 360 400, and financially it was barely breaking even. Both papers had in fact outlived their usefulness, and their passing was not widely mourned. For the time being there was no talk of closing the *Sunday Herald* or the *Sunday Sun*.

The 24-hour papers (which could easily become conventional morning papers again if the extra twelve hours proved superfluous) were part of News Corporation's response to a debt problem which, although not so nightmarish as Fairfax's, was certainly a lot to worry about. News had total borrowings of $10.4 billion, and its short-term debt had increased sixfold during the last financial year, from $508 million to $2.95 billion. These figures were global, of course, and were supported by shareholders' funds of $9.5 billion and assets of more than $20 billion. But even so, the market had lost a good deal of confidence in News Corporation, whose 1989–90 net earnings had fallen by 43 per cent (mainly because of losses incurred by Sky Television in the United Kingdom and Europe, and the effect of a long pilots' strike on Ansett) to $282 million. In three weeks the price of News shares had fallen from more than $11 to $6.30.

At his press conference in Melbourne on Wednesday Murdoch disavowed any intention of buying part of the Fairfax group. That was hard to accept, for there seemed no limit to either his appetite for newspapers or the Australian Government's indulgence of this acquisitive American citizen. Murdoch now controlled 70 per cent of Australia's newspaper circulation, for News Corporation owned or sponsored seven of the country's ten surviving capital city dailies, seven of its nine metropolitan Sunday papers, and one of its two national daily newspapers.

Next day the Trade Practices Commission warned Murdoch that it would oppose any attempt by him to gain control of Fairfax-owned papers by means of a consortium such as that formed recently by BHP to bid successfully for one of its competitors, NZ Steel. It was also conceivable (though only barely) that in such an event the Foreign Investment Review Board might at last show some concern about Murdoch's citizenship.

Of the other major bidders in the 1987–88 sale of Fairfax assets, Robert Holmes à Court was dead; John B. Fairfax was, as one commentator put it, 'local and liquid', though apparently not interested in Broadway; and Kerry Packer was also local and liquid, to say the least. By one of the most remarkable deals in Australian corporate history, Packer had recently regained control of the Nine television network. After having sold his Sydney and Melbourne stations to Alan Bond for $1.1 billion in January 1987, he gained control of Bond Media and its television stations in June 1990 for no cash outlay. He simply converted a $225 million debt owing by Bond into a majority shareholding.

The cross-media regulations would not prevent Consolidated Press from owning the national *Australian Financial Review* as well as television stations in Sydney, Melbourne, Brisbane and Perth, for the *Review*'s circulation in each of those regions was too small to incur cross-media restriction. Rumour also had it that Packer might sell his television network to the Melbourne property group, Hudson Conway, leaving him free to bid for all or any part of the Fairfax group. What might well curb Packer's entrepreneurial appetite, however, was the state of his health. He had recently been under treatment for heart trouble, and on Saturday 6 October he suffered a massive heart attack while playing polo.

On the Thursday of this concluding week, it happened that the *Financial Review* was host for the third annual Australia-Japan-Canada Economic Issues Symposium, held in conjunction with the Japanese newspaper company and information network Nikkei, and the Toronto *Globe and Mail*. The opening session received better media coverage than usual because the host speaker was none other than Warwick Fairfax, making one of his rare public appearances—probably his first in Sydney since the court case two years earlier. After gazing impassively at the prying television cameras, he read a brief speech of welcome.

Those who may have been expecting an announcement of some kind, or even a passing reference to debt, were disappointed. Warwick said nothing about his trip to New York, his present position or the company's approaching sesquicentenary.

To any Japanese or Canadians who may have been curious about him, the symposium's *curriculum vitae* offered scant information. 'In August 1987, at the age of 26, he bought out both his family shareholding and publicly held shares in John Fairfax Ltd, privatising the company.' Of course there was much more to be explained than that, but where to begin?

The enormity of Warwick Fairfax's disaster and the composure with which he appeared to be accepting his fate had probably made his name more widely known in the space of three years than his great-great-grandfather's had become in three decades of proprietorship. But Warwick's was a different kind of fame, more akin to myth than to history. His eerie reticence may have had something to do with this, for it gave free rein to the imagination of others. Perhaps one day he would be likened to Adam, driven from the Garden by angels; the Prodigal Son, who gained his inheritance early, only to lose it; or Icarus, the son of Daedalus, who flew so high that the heat of the sun melted the wax of his borrowed wings.

Only Warwick and his mother (and perhaps not even they) knew exactly why he had behaved as he did. But with hindsight and conjecture some sort of answer could be attempted. Like his father before him, Warwick had been brought up in the expectation of a heritage that was rightly his. He and his parents had not always thought that one day he would seek control of the company rather than co-exist, as Sir Warwick had done, with other branches of the family. That ambition was nurtured in the boy after his father had been deposed from the chairmanship, when Warwick was sixteen years old. It was strengthened by his parents' misgivings about the company's management during the 1980s, and by their fears of a hostile takeover. Finally it was primed by Warwick's deepening religious conviction, and by his belief that, in the spirit of the Parable of the Talents, he ought to involve himself wholeheartedly in the company's affairs.

His mounting of the takeover bid, and his persistence with it in the face of worsening odds, were almost certainly influenced by some traits of character at which outsiders could only guess. The guesses included impatience, obstinacy, courage, over-confidence and a degree of naivety. If Warwick had bided his time, he would almost certainly have come into the Kinghaven inheritance sooner rather than later. But he was not prepared to wait. He chose advisers rashly; he took the rest of the Fairfax family for granted, and found he had misjudged them; he decided to keep going in spite of the stock exchange crash, against his mother's plea, and came to regret it; and, perhaps because of his privileged upbringing and later his relatively simple way of life, he seemed to have little sense of the value of money. He borrowed excessively, and agreed to reward his advisers too lavishly.

The privatization of John Fairfax Ltd was not, of course, an unmitigated disaster. Laurie Connell and Alan Bond profited from it, though not nearly enough to alleviate their own business disasters.

Martin Dougherty and other of Warwick's mentors or executives were paid out generously when their time came to an end; and all shareholders in the public company other than Warwick Fairfax and his mother received a good price for their shares. The biggest beneficiaries in the latter regard were James Fairfax, the Fairfax superannuation funds and the John B. Fairfax family.

John B. Fairfax used part of his new capital to buy the Fairfax interests in Rural Press and Eastern Suburbs Newspapers, which became the core assets of his Marinya Media. In the following three years, as Tryart and John Fairfax Group staggered from one crisis to the next, Marinya achieved steady growth, with Rural Press lifting its annual earnings from $7.5 million to $12.6 million in 1989–90. The 51 per cent-owned Rural Press acquired more country newspapers, bringing their number to 75, and Marinya established or invested in several new companies, one of which—IM Publishing—launched a new journal, the *Independent Monthly*, under the editorship of Max Suich.

On the credit side of the ledger it should also be said that Broadway's management achieved some of the rationalization and cost effectiveness usually adduced by new owners as justification for their takeovers. Certainly the cash flow held up remarkably well. But against the closures, cost cutting and other efficiency measures, something less easily measured had to be taken into account.

The order of the day for board and senior management was survival, and the time and effort which they could put into anything other than refinancing and re-refinancing were strictly limited. Middle management, journalists and production workers soldiered on stoically, and to good effect; but it would be wrong to say that the atmosphere of uncertainty in the wake of the takeover did not affect staff morale, or that it might not eventually affect the quality of the products.

Furthermore, the company's capacity to keep pace technologically with competition from News Ltd (even allowing for Murdoch's own financial worries, and for the moderate amount of future capital expenditure built into Fairfax's borrowing) was curtailed by the rigours of repayment. The takeover also raised the prospect that one or more of the core newspapers might have to be sold. Given the shortage of eligible purchasers, there was danger that the *Age* and/or the *Australian Financial Review* (and, in the worst eventuality, the *Sydney Morning Herald* as well) might fall into hands which would degrade them, or at least lessen their present degree of editorial diversity.

Also on the debit side were the financial and psychological effects upon employees made redundant by closures and asset sales; the well deserved embarrassment of the banks at the dangerous pass to which their largess had brought them; and, of course, the sorry plight of those most at risk, Warwick Fairfax and his mother. Before the takeover, Warwick and Lady Fairfax had controlled 15.67 per cent of John Fairfax Ltd. After Warwick's purchase of the Kinghaven 11.3 per cent, the value of their combined 26.97 per cent at the admittedly artificial takeover share price was $688.5 million. Subtract $35 million which Warwick borrowed to buy 1.5 per cent of the company before the takeover bid, and $22.7 million which he borrowed as nominal payment for the Kinghaven parcel, and their personal stake in the takeover may be reckoned at $630 million—$184 million by Lady Fairfax and $446 million by Warwick.

If the Goldman Sachs valuation was correct, and its proposal had gone forward, Warwick and his mother would have been left with only 3.2 per cent of the restructured company's equity. Although those shares would no longer have had the negative value implied by Goldman's valuation, the two Fairfaxes' $630 million would have dwindled to an economic interest of between $6 million and $7 million. No wonder they recoiled from such a solution, or that Warwick began casting about for some less painful alternative!

But whatever the ultimate solution might be—a successful bond tender, debt for equity, foreign or local investment, sale of assets, receivership or liquidation—it would not be painless. And it was hard to see how Warwick Fairfax could possibly retain more than a minority shareholding, let alone regain the control which he had effectively lost to the banks already.

The solution might not be known for months, or it could come quickly. Although this narrative must end here in order to meet its sesquicentennial deadline, it may be worth resorting to the old newspaper expedient of Stop Press, a blank space on the front or back page into which late news could be inserted. The space below these lines may yet serve to announce either 'Adam Expelled' or 'Icarus Survives Hard Landing'.

7 October 1990

During the next few weeks Laurie Connell and Alan Bond were arrested. Connell was charged with breaches of the Companies Code allegedly involving the improper use of Rothwells funds and Bond with allegedly concealing a payment to Bond Corporation. In the United States Michael Milken was sentenced to 10 years imprisonment for insider trading.

As for John Fairfax Group, the banks lost patience with its vain attempts to raise new equity in the United States. On 8 December Beerworth heard from Lazard Frères that the only two angels in sight were unwilling to proceed. And that was the last straw.

The company was then due to roll over $850 million worth of 90-day bank bills, as had been its regular custom since the 1989 refinancing. This time, knowing that Fairfax was likely to be insolvent within a month, the three directors realized they could not certify (as the banks required them to) that there would be no breach of loan agreements during the next three months. They were also in danger of breaching Section 556 of the Companies Code, the section rendering a director personally liable for debts incurred by his company while he had reason to believe it would not be able to repay them when they fell due.

Fairfax therefore asked the banks to issue 14-day bills, which could have been certified in good conscience, and would thus have provided a little more time for the desperate equity search. The banks refused, thereby forcing Fairfax to seek the court appointment of a provisional liquidator for its borrowing subsidiary, Fairfax Finance Pty Ltd. This successful application on 10 December provided the banking syndicate led by ANZ and Citibank with the opportunity to appoint a receiver and manager for all Fairfax companies without challenge from the unsecured creditors, and it did so the same day.

No one could tell what the future might hold for John Fairfax Group of Companies (Receivers and Managers Appointed). The receiver—Des Nicholl, from the accountancy firm Deloitte Ross Tohmatsu—decreed 'business as usual'. He also began cutting costs, and taking expressions of interest from would-be investors and asset buyers. A spokesman for the banking syndicate—none other than Mark Burrows, the merchant banker who had advised Warwick not to make the takeover bid—said that the banks wanted 'to maintain Fairfax as one entity, and to continue all Fairfax's current business operations, with full editorial independence'. Burrows also mentioned, however, that the banks had been advised that their exposure was fully recoverable.

If the company's assets were sold, they would on recent valuation be just sufficient to repay the banks, with little or nothing left over for the junk bond holders (who were threatening legal action unless they received equity in any reconstruction), other unsecured creditors and—last in priority—the two shareholders, whose interests were in theory worthless.

Lady Fairfax would lose her annuity, but she still owned Fairwater, Harrington Park and other substantial properties. Warwick's assets were scant indeed. As he left Broadway on 10 December he refused to answer questions from *Herald* reporters. 'I really don't know how it will all pan out', he said. It was still possible that he might be allowed nominal shareholding in a restructured Fairfax, but probably even less than Goldman Sachs had envisaged earlier in the year. Whatever might happen, Warwick Fairfax's tragic fall now seemed complete. He had been sent forth from the Garden of Eden.

14 December 1990

Notes

2. The Herald and Weekly Times group: HWT held 43.58 per cent of Queensland Press, which in turn held 25.53 per cent of HWT; 35.2 per cent of Advertiser Newspapers, which held 11.13 per cent of HWT; and 49.98 per cent of Davies Brothers (the Hobart *Mercury*), which did not hold a reciprocal interest.
8. Early discussions of a takeover and privatization of John Fairfax Ltd by Sir Warwick and Lady Fairfax: Supreme Court of NSW, *Bond Media Ltd* v. *John Fairfax Group Pty Ltd*, 28405/1988, statement of M. J. Dougherty, p. 6; transcript of evidence by W. G. O. Fairfax, pp. 583-5.
30. The *Leamington Spa Courier*: The *Courier*—then owned by several families, principally Hicks and Clarke—was the subject of a takeover in April 1987, four months before Warwick Fairfax's bid for John Fairfax Ltd. The successful bid, by EMAP Plc, valued the company at £stg 31 million.
44. After distribution of the shares formerly held by the late Sir James Oswald Fairfax, Geoffrey Fairfax and W. G. Conley the company's shares were held from 1930 as follows: W. O. Fairfax, 13 689; J. H. F. Fairfax, 7624; Dr Wilfred Fairfax, 7124; Miss Mary Fairfax, 2256; Lady (J. O.) Fairfax, 7802; Mrs M. E. Fairfax (W. O. Fairfax's wife), 1; John Fitzgerald Fairfax, Wilfred's elder son who joined the *Herald* staff in 1928, 500; Mrs Ruth Fairfax (J. H. F. Fairfax's wife), 1; and Mrs Mary M. Fairfax (Dr Wilfred's wife), 1.
49. 'Australia's Richest Baby is Born', *Truth*, 2 April 1933.
65. The Duchess of Bedford's autobiography: Nicole Russell Bedford, *Nicole Nobody*, W. H. Allen, London, 1974.
85. 'Not the Mafia?' *Sun-Herald*, 10 August 1980.
103. *Seybold Report*, vol. 6, no. 23, 8 August 1977.
115. Inquiry into the Ownership and Control of Newspapers in Victoria: for a detailed account of the Norris Inquiry, see L. Carlyon, *The Paper Chase*, Herald, Melbourne, 1982.
130. Cowley at football match: *Bond Media* v. *Fairfax*, 17 November, p. 580.
131. Press criticism of Fairfax: 'Fairfax fund-raising: the mystery and the drama', Trevor Kennedy, *Bulletin*, 2-9 October 1984; 'Fairfax family fight over prefs', Barrie Dunstan, Melbourne *Herald*, 5 October 1984; 'Fairfax family looks to buy back control', Bryan Frith, *Australian*, 19 October 1984.
134. John B. Fairfax's conversation with Sir Warwick Fairfax: file note by J. B. Fairfax, 16 October 1984.
139. Datamail Pty Ltd: this Melbourne-based company, with a branch in London, was acquired by John Fairfax Ltd in September 1984 as a means of entering the expanding letterbox-drop field.
144. 'Askin: Friend to Organised Crime', *National Times*, 13-19 September 1981.
145. David Hickie, *The Prince and the Premier*, Angus & Robertson, Sydney, 1985.
147. 'It's a jungle out there. And I'm a tiger', *The Eye*, Sydney, July 1987.

147. 'Askin's $55 000 Payment from the Bookies', *National Times*, 27 September-3 October 1981.
149. 'Why Jackson Resigned', *National Times*, 28 October-3 November 1983.
153. Report of Senate Privileges Committee, *Commonwealth Parliamentary Debates*, 23 May 1985, p. 2457.
154. 'Sir Peter Abeles and TNT's Brush with the Mafia', *National Times*, 12-18 December 1982.
160. 'Delays over Costigan's Controversial Recommendations', containing the 'Goanna' case summary, *National Times*, 14-20 September 1984.
161. The suburban newspaper dispute: 'Fairfax, Packer in row over press', *National Times*, 2-8 August 1985; 'Judge gives priority to press dispute', *National Times*, 18-24 October 1985.
164. 'The Death Of Labor', *The Eye*, July 1987.
165. Defamation: Of the total legal costs incurred by the *Sydney Morning Herald* from 1980 to 1987 ($2 188 800), settlements and verdicts accounted for approximately $400 000. This sum, onerous though it seemed at the time, was placed in new perspective by two benchmark verdicts against the *Herald* in 1989. In one action, brought by a restaurateur over an unfavourable review of a meal by the columnist Leo Schofield, the verdict was for $100 000 plus interest. In the other, brought by a solicitor over two columns written by the *Herald*'s legal correspondent, John Slee, the sum awarded was $600 000 plus interest. At the time of writing, both cases were under appeal.
178. Conversation between Warwick Fairfax and Martin Dougherty in December 1986: *Bond Media* v. *Fairfax*, statement of W. G. O. Fairfax, 27 September 1988, p. 3; statement of M. J. Dougherty, pp. 6-7.
179. 'Vincent, James and John have very little business ability': ibid., statement of M. J. Dougherty, p. 7.
180. 'If that is John's attitude': ibid., statement of W. G. O. Fairfax, p. 4.
182. The company's critics: for criticism of Fairfax management from the Packer group, and an account of Tryart's takeover, see T. Sykes, *Operation Dynasty*, Greenhouse Publications, Sydney, 1989.
187. The Albert family of radio 2UW had been part of the consortium which established ATN, and Sir Alexis Albert was an inaugural director.
190. Share capital: in the early 1980s the authorized capital of John Fairfax Ltd was 100 million shares of 50 cents each, of which half ($25 million) had been issued. In 1984-85 two bonus share issues from the asset revaluation reserve increased the issued capital to $35 million. In 1985-86 the authorized capital was increased to 150 million shares ($75 million) and two more bonus issues increased the issued capital to $50 million.
193. Christian and Missionary Alliance: R. Niklaus, J. S. Sawin and S. J. Stoesz, *All For Jesus*, Christian Publications Inc, Camp Hill, Pennsylvania, 1986.
197. Press criticism of the Seven Network sale: *Bulletin*, 4 August 1987; Terry McCrann, Melbourne *Herald*, 24 July 1987; Neal Travis, *Australian*, 1-2 August 1987.
202. 'There, there sonny': *Bond Media* v. *Fairfax*, statement of M. J. Dougherty, p. 10.
202. 'Laurie Connell: King of the Bare-Knuckle Businessmen', Ben Hills, Good Weekend, 4 April 1987.
205. The $100 million fee: *Bond Media* v. *Fairfax*, statement of W. G. O. Fairfax, p. 9; statement of M. J. Dougherty, pp. 20, 22.
206. 'That's an incredible fee': ibid., statement of P. F. S. King, p. 2.
207. The various 'Dynasty' proposals: this account of the main assumptions underlying the share offer derives from two handwritten proposals by Reuter, both dated 'August 1987'. The first, entitled 'Proposal for the acquisition by interest associated with the Dynasty Heir for a controlling interest in the Dynasty Corporation', became identified as B2 during the court case. The other proposal, 'Dynasty Corporation Privatisation Proposal', was identified as B3.
209. 'Bringing the family up to a comfortable feeling about your plans': *Bond Media* v.

Fairfax, statement of M. J. Dougherty, p. 17; 'dawn raid': ibid., second statement of L. R. Connell, p. 13.

211. 'My experience with takeovers': ibid., statement of W. B. Reuter, p. 15.
213. 'I am planning to launch a takeover bid for the company': ibid., statement of W. G. O. Fairfax, p. 19.
214. Debriefing session: ibid., statement of W. G. O. Fairfax, pp. 21-2.
216. 'A game of bluff poker': ibid., first statement of L. R. Connell, p. 11.
224. *Canberra Chronicle*: this equivalent to one of Sydney's larger suburban papers was established on 16 September 1981.
225. 'How do you start a small business?': *Australian Financial Review*, 30 September 1987.
230. Lady Fairfax's letter to her son at the Regent Hotel: *Bond Media* v. *Fairfax*, statement of W. B. Reuter, p. 26.
231. 'The underwriting agreements are firm': ibid., statement of W. G. O. Fairfax, p. 35.
232. 'Dougherty would assert that he had told Warwick about the fee-sharing arrangement': ibid., statement of M. J. Dougherty, p. 48; 'Warwick . . . would maintain that he knew nothing about fee-sharing': ibid., statement of W. G. O. Fairfax, p. 44; Evidence, pp. 648, 656, 664.
236. *Ms* and *Sassy*. The first issue of the new *Ms* appeared in February 1988, under the editorship-in-chief of Anne Summers, and *Sassy* was launched one month later. In April both magazines were put up for sale by Tryart. They were bought for $US14 million by Matilda Publications Inc, a company formed by the two senior executives of the magazines, Yates and Summers. This ambitious enterprise was short-lived. *Sassy* achieved a circulation of 450 000 after only seven issues, but then suffered disastrously from a boycott in protest at the frank sexual material which it was offering its teenage readers. As a result of this boycott, organized by moral and religious fundamentalist groups, *Sassy* lost several of its main advertisers and was delisted by more than 50 retail chains. Matilda's revenue declined so steeply that in February 1989 the board, controlled by the company's principal creditor, Citibank, demanded that a special consultant be brought in to cut costs. Yates left the company, and in October 1989 control of the magazines was sold to a New York publisher, Dale Lang. Lang bought 100 per cent of *Ms*, and 70 per cent of Matilda, which by then owned only *Sassy*.
244. 'Barry, just wait a minute, that's $300 million': *Bond Media* v. *Fairfax*, statement of R. J. Cotton, p. 20.
245. 'What's this about a put option?': ibid., p. 33.
248. 'In a certain sense all life is a falling': 'The Fall: Christian Truth and Literary Symbol', in *Comparative Literature: Matter and Method*, ed. A. Owen-Aldridge, University of Illinois Press, London, 1962. 'Whether the Fall occurs by choice or by act of destiny': T. Otten, *After Innocence: Visions of the Fall in Modern Literature*, University of Pittsburgh Press, 1971.
249. 'Let us pray that Mr Packer . . .': *Canberra Times*, 27 November 1987.
251. 'The hint of desperation in this sale is inescapable': *Australian Financial Review*, 30 November 1987.
252. 'What if he is unable to pay?': *Bond Media* v. *Fairfax*, supplementary statement of W. B. Reuter, p. 3.
257. The most aggressive of all multinational banks: Robert A. Hutchison, *Off the Books*, William Morrow, New York, 1986.
270. Lady Fairfax's telephone calls to R. J. Cotton. *Bond Media* v. *Fairfax*, cross-examination of Cotton, p. 1260.
276. 'No-one is gloating about the demise of the *Sun*': *On Broadway*, Fairfax house committee journal, 2 May 1988.
284. William Simon's LBO tactics: 'William Simon's Pacific Overtures', L. J. Davis, *New York Times* magazine, 27 December 1987.
290. Connie Bruck, *The Predators' Ball*, The American Lawyer/Simon and Schuster, New York, 1988. This excellent account of 'The junk bond raiders and the men

who staked them' was republished as a Penguin paperback in 1989, with some new material.

295. Sale of the Hunter Street property in June 1988: Lady Fairfax did not sell the adjoining Grand Hotel.
295. Decision by Fairfax directors not to pay the Rothwells fee: *Bond Media* v. *Fairfax*, evidence of R. J. Cotton, p. 1129.
298. 'Byzantine perplexity and complexity': T. E. F. Hughes, QC, at preliminary court proceedings, 11 September 1988.
307. Hughes, QC, questions W. G. O. Fairfax about his alleged willingness to 'bring the whole house tumbling down': *Bond Media* v. *Fairfax*, pp. 208-9.
307. 'And just what was that vision?': ibid., pp. 159-60.
309. 'Some of the questions were quite perceptive': ibid., p. 1164.
309. 'He lacked commercial nous': ibid., p. 1287.
312. A bill to amend the Income Tax Assessment Act: Taxation Laws Amendment Act (No 4), assented to 24 November 1988.
319. 'Wocka The Terminator': Russell Miller, *Sunday Times* magazine, 20 November 1988.
331. The *Gold Coast Mail*: in October 1984 John Fairfax Ltd purchased a half share in Longbeach Publications Pty Ltd, the publisher of two weeklies, the *Hinterlander* and the *Tweed Leader*. Under the direction of Peter Allen, a former editor of the *Sun-Herald*, these were amalgamated in August 1988 to form the bi-weekly *Gold Coast Mail*. Fairfax's partners in Longbeach sold their half share to Stereo FM, later known as Pacific Rim Investments Pty Ltd, and taken over by Marinya Media in 1989.
332. 'The usual dreary chronicle of journalistic crimes'. *Australian Society*, April 1989.
333. Concerns expressed by journalistic staff about 'Who Is Right?': the House Committee journal *On Broadway*, 29 Nov 1989.
334. Management of the library: the issue here was an attempt by editorial management to make the Fairfax reference library a 'paperless library' by means of computerization. Many cutting files (including those for all federal elections before 1980) were destroyed, and only protests by library staff and journalists prevented the library's invaluable card index from being culled as well. The cutting file system was resumed, and gaps created by culling were repaired to some extent with photocopies from the *Age* cutting files in Melbourne.
336. Australian Simon University: this offshoot of the University of Rochester, New York State, was planned to be the first private university in New South Wales, offering a 19-month Master of Business Administration course for mid-career students at a cost of $45 000. It was to have opened at Watson's Bay, Sydney, in January 1990. This was postponed, and at the time of writing a first class of 20 students, with faculty from Rochester, was planned to start in January 1991.
359. News Corporation's response to its debt problem: concurrently with closure of its Sydney and Melbourne afternoon newspapers, News Corporation was planning to issue non-voting equity, apparently to raise capital without diluting Rupert Murdoch's holding. The Australian Stock Exchange seemed no happier about this, however, than it had been about Fairfax's PIPs proposal in the 1980s.

Index